Data Science
with Semantic Technologies

Scrivener Publishing
100 Cummings Center, Suite 541J
Beverly, MA 01915-6106

Publishers at Scrivener
Martin Scrivener (martin@scrivenerpublishing.com)
Phillip Carmical (pcarmical@scrivenerpublishing.com)

Data Science with Semantic Technologies

Theory, Practice, and Application

Edited by

Archana Patel

Department of Software Engineering, School of Computing and Information Technology, Eastern International University, Vietnam

Narayan C. Debnath

School of Computing and Department of Computer Science and Engineering, School of Engineering Vietnam

and

Bharat Bhusan

Technology, Sharda University Information Technology, India

Scrivener
Publishing

This edition first published 2022 by John Wiley & Sons, Inc., 111 River Street, Hoboken, NJ 07030, USA and Scrivener Publishing LLC, 100 Cummings Center, Suite 541J, Beverly, MA 01915, USA
© 2022 Scrivener Publishing LLC
For more information about Scrivener publications please visit www.scrivenerpublishing.com.

Wiley Global Headquarters
111 River Street, Hoboken, NJ 07030, USA

For details of our global editorial offices, customer services, and more information about Wiley products visit us at www.wiley.com.

Library of Congress Cataloging-in-Publication Data

ISBN 9781119864981

Cover image: PixaBay.Com
Cover design by Russell Richardson

Set in size of 11pt and Minion Pro by Manila Typesetting Company, Makati, Philippines

Printed in the USA

10 9 8 7 6 5 4 3 2 1

Contents

13 Hybrid Mixed Integer Optimization Method for Document Clustering Based on Semantic Data Matrix 323
Tatiana Avdeenko and Yury Mezentsev

14 Role of Knowledge Data Science During COVID-19 Pandemic 347
Veena Kumari H. M. and D. S. Suresh

Preface

Data Science is an invaluable resource that deals with vast volumes of data using modern tools and techniques to find unseen patterns, derive meaningful information, and make business decisions. To create intelligence in data science, it becomes necessary to utilize the semantic technologies which allow machine-readable representation of data. This intelligence uniquely identifies and connects data with common business terms, and also enables users to communicate with data. Instead of structuring the data, semantic technologies help users to understand the meaning of the data by using the concepts of semantics, ontology, OWL, linked data, and knowledge graphs. These technologies assist organizations in understanding all of the stored data, adding value to it, and enabling insights that were not available before. Organizations are also using semantic technologies to unearth precious nuggets of information from vast volumes of data and to enable more flexible use of data. These technologies can deal with the existing problems of data scientists and help them in making better decisions for any organization. All of these needs are part of a focused shift towards utilization of semantic technologies in data science that provide knowledge along with the ability to understand, reason, plan, and learn with existing and new data sets. These technologies also generate expected, reproducible, user-desired results.

This book aims to provide a roadmap for the deployment of semantic technologies in the field of data science. Moreover, it highlights how data science enables the user to create intelligence through these technologies by exploring the opportunities and eradicating the challenges in current and future time frames. It can serve as an important guide to applications of data science with semantic technologies for the upcoming generation and thus is a unique resource for scholars, researchers, professionals and practitioners in this field. Following is a brief description of the subjects covered in the 15 chapters of the book.

– Chapter 1 provides a brief introduction to data science. It addresses various aspects of data science such as what a data scientist does and why data science is in demand; the history of data science and how it differs from business intelligence; the life cycle of data science and data science components; why data science is important; the challenges of data science; the tools used for data science; and the benefits and applications of data science.

– Chapter 2 provides an overview of the top 10 tools and applications that should be of interest to any data scientist. Its objective includes, but is not limited to, realizing the use of Python in developing solutions to data science tasks; recognizing the use of R language as an open-source data science provider; traveling around the SQL to provide structured models for data science projects; navigating through data analytics and statistics using Excel; and using D3.js scripting tools for data visualization. Also, practical examples/case studies are provided on data visualization, data analytics, regression, forecasting, and outlier detection.

– Chapter 3 presents the use of data modeling for data science, revealing the possibility of a new side of the data. The chapter covers different types of data (unstructured data, semi-structured data, structured data, hybrid (un/semi)-structured data and big data) and data model design.

– Chapter 4 shows data management by considering language based on the novelty view of data. The chapter focuses on data life cycle, data distribution and CAP theorem.

– Chapter 5 presents the role of data science in healthcare. There are several fields in the healthcare sector, such as predictive modeling, genetics, etc., which make use of data science for diagnosis and drug discovery, thereby increasing usability of precision medicine.

– Chapter 6 provides a new balanced binary search tree that generates two kinds of nodes: simple and class nodes. Two advantages make the new structure attractive. First, it subsumes the most popular data structures of AVL and Red-Black trees. Second, it proposes other unknown balanced binary search trees in which we can adjust the maximal height of paths between $1.44 \lg(n)$ and $2 \lg(n)$, where n is the number of nodes in the tree and lg the base-two logarithm.

– Chapter 7 shows the study of machine learning and deep learning algorithms with detailed and analytical comparisons, which help new and inexperienced medical professionals or researchers in the medical field. The proposed machine learning model has an accurate algorithm that works with rich healthcare data, a high-dimensional data handling system, and an intelligent framework that uses different data sources to predict heart disease. This chapter uses an ensemble-based deep learning model with optimal feature selection to improve accuracy.

– Chapter 8 presents an IoT-based automated fire control system in a mining area which will help to protect many valuable lives whenever an accident occurs due to fire. In the experimental application, different types of sensors for temperature, moisture, and gas are used to sense the different environmental data.

– Chapter 9 offers an aspect identification method for sentiment sentences in review documents. The chapter describes two key tasks—one for extracting significant features from the reviews and another for identification of degrees of product reviews.

– Chapter 10 shows the research that paved the way for semantic technology. It then describes each of the semantic pillars with examples and explanations of the business value of each technology.

– Chapter 11 describes the ontology evaluation tools and then focuses on the evaluation of the security ontologies. The existing ontology evaluation tools are classified under two categories; namely, domain-dependent ontology evaluation tools and domain-independent ontology evaluation tools. The evaluation of security ontology assesses the quality of ontology among the available ontologies.

– Chapter 12 discusses the main concepts of health data, data science, health data science, examples of the application of health data science and related challenges. In addition, it also highlights the application of semantic technologies in health data science and the challenges that lie ahead of using these technologies.

– Chapter 13 proposes an original hybrid optimization approach based on two different mixed integer programming statements. The first statement is based on minimizing the sum of pairwise distances between all objects (PDC clustering), while the second statement is based on minimizing the total distance from objects to cluster centers (CC clustering). Computational experiments showed that the hybrid method developed for solving the clustering problem combines the advantages of both approaches—the speed of the k-means method and the accuracy of PDC clustering—which makes it possible to get rid of the main drawback of the k-means, namely, the lack of guaranteed determining of the global optimum.

– Chapter 14 uses a model for the analysis of time series data which highly depend on the novel coronavirus 2019. This model predicts the future trend of confirmed, recovered, active, and death cases based on the available data from January 22, 2020 to May 29, 2021. The present model predicted the spread of COVID-19 for a future period of 30 days. The RMSE, MSE, MAE, and MdAPE metrics are used for the model evaluation.

– Chapter 15 focuses on systems that incorporated real-world data utilized by actual users. It first describes a new methodology for the survey and then covers the various domains where semantic technology can be applied and some of the most impressive systems developed in each domain.

Finally, the editors would like to sincerely thank all the authors and reviewers who contributed their time and expertise for the successful completion of this book. The editors also appreciate the support given by Scrivener Publishing, which allowed us to compile the first edition of this book.

The Editors
Archana Patel
Narayan C. Debnath
Bharat Bhusan
June 2022

1

A Brief Introduction and Importance of Data Science

Karthika N.[1*], Sheela J.[1] and Janet B.[2]

[1]Department of SCOPE, VIT-AP University, Amaravati, Andhra Pradesh, India
[2]Department of Computer Applications, National Institute of Technology, Tiruchirappalli, India

Abstract

Data is very important component of any organization. According to International Data Corporation, by 2025, global data will reach to 175 zettabytes. They need data to help them make careful decisions in business. Data is worthless until it is transformed into valuable data. Data science plays a vital role in processing and interpreting data. It focuses on the analysis and management of data too. It is concerned with obtaining useful information from large datasets. It is frequently applied in a wide range of industries, including healthcare, marketing, banking, finance, policy work, and more. This enables companies to make informed decisions around growth, optimization, and performance. In this brief monograph, we address following questions.

What is data science and what does a data scientist do? Why data science is in demand? History of data science, how data science differs from business intelligence? The lifecycle of data science, data science components, why data science is important? Challenges of data science, tools used for data science, benefits and applications of data science.

Keywords: Data science, history, lifecycle, components, tools

*Corresponding author: bharathikarthika@gmail.com

Archana Patel, Narayan C. Debnath and Bharat Bhusan (eds.) Data Science with Semantic Technologies: Theory, Practice, and Application, (1–30) © 2022 Scrivener Publishing LLC

1.1   What is Data Science? What Does a Data Scientist Do?

Data is very important component of any organization. According to International Data Corporation, by 2025, global data will reach to 175 zettabytes. They need data to help them make careful decisions in business. Data is worthless until it is transformed into valuable data. Data science plays a vital role in processing and interpreting data. It focuses on the analysis and management of data too. It is concerned with obtaining useful information from large datasets. It is frequently applied in a wide range of industries, including healthcare, marketing, banking, finance, policy work, and more. This enables companies to make informed decisions around growth, optimization, and performance. In nutshell, Data science is an integrative strategy for deriving actionable insights from today's organizations' massive and ever-increasing data sets. Preparing data for analysis and processing, performing advanced data analysis, and presenting the findings to expose trends and allow stakeholders to make educated decisions are all part of data science [1, 2]. Data science experts are both well-known, data-driven individuals with advanced technical capabilities who can construct complicated quantitative algorithms to organize and interpret huge amounts of data in order to address questions and drive strategy in their company. This is combined with the communication and leadership skills required to provide tangible results to numerous stakeholders throughout a company or organization.Data scientists must be inquisitive and results-driven, with great industry-specific expertise and communication abilities that enable them to convey highly technical outcomes to non-technical colleagues. To create and analyze algorithms, they have a solid quantitative background in statistics and linear algebra, as well as programming experience with a focus on data warehousing, mining, and modeling [3].

1.2   Why Data Science is in Demand?

Data science is the branch of science concerned with the discovery, analysis, modeling, and extraction of useful information which has become a buzz in a lot of companies. Firms are increasingly aware that they have been sitting on data treasure mines the priority with which this data must be analyzed, and ROI generated is obvious. We look at the most important reasons that data science professions are in high demand [4].

- **Data Organization**
  During the mid-2000s IT boom, the emphasis was on "lifting and shifting" offline business operations into automated computer systems. Digital content generation, transactional data processing, and data log streams have all been consistent throughout the last two decades. This indicates that every company now has a plethora of information that it believes can really be valuable but does not know how to use. This is apparent in Glassdoor's recent analysis, which identifies the 50 greatest jobs in modern era.

- **Scarcity of Trained Manpower**
  According to a McKinsey Global Institute study, by 2018, the United States will be short 190,000 data scientists, 1.5 million managers, including analysts who would properly comprehend and make judgments based on Big Data. The need is particularly great in India, where the tools and techniques are available but there are not enough qualified people. Data scientists, who can perform analytics, and analytics consultants, who can analyze and apply data, are two sorts of talent shortages, according to Srikanth Velamakanni, co-founder and CEO of Fractal Analytics. The supply of talent in these fields, particularly data scientists, is extremely limited, and the demand is enormous."

- **The Pay Is Outstanding**
  A data science position is currently one of the highest paying in the market. The national average income for a data scientist/analyst in the United States, according to Glass Door, is more than $62,000. In India, pay is heavily influenced by experience. Those with the appropriate skillset can earn up to 19 LPA. (source: PayScale.)

- **The "X" Factor**
  A data scientist's major responsibility are exceptional and specific to the position. Because of nature of the profession, they may flourish in their careers by integrating several analytical expertise across diverse areas such as big data, machine learning, and so on. This vast knowledge base gives them an unsurpassed reputation or X-factor.

- **Data Scientists' Democratization**
  Tech behemoths are not the only ones who need data scientists. According to a Harvard Business Report issued many years ago, "Organizations in the top list of their area in the

use of data-driven decision making were, on average, 5% more productive and 6% more profitable than their peers". Even mid-sized and small organizations have been driven to adopt data science because of this. In truth, many small businesses are trying to hire entry-level data scientists for a fair wage. This works well for both. The scientist will be able to further develop his or her skills, and the company will be able to pay less than it would otherwise.

- **Fewer Barriers for Professionals**
  Data science is open to a wide range of experts from varied backgrounds because it is a relatively new discipline. Math/statistics, computer science and engineering, and natural science are all areas of knowledge for today's data scientists. Some perhaps have social science, economics, or business degrees. They have all devised a problem-solving technique and improved their skills through formal or online education.
- **Abundance of Jobs**
  Data science is employed in a wide range of business sectors, from production to healthcare, Information Technology to finance, therefore there are plenty of data science jobs available for individuals who are interested and willing to put in the effort. It is true not only in terms of industries, but also in terms of geography. So, regardless of one's geographical location or current domain, data science and analytics are available to everybody.
- **A Wide Range of Roles**
  Even if data science job is indeed a broad term, there are numerous subroles that fall under its scope. Data scientists, data architects, business intelligence engineers, business analysts, data engineers, database administrators, and data analytics managers are all in considerable demand.

1.3   History of Data Science

The terminology "data science" was just recently coined a new profession interested in trying to make sense of large volumes of data. Making sense of data, on the other hand, has a significant background, and it has been addressed for years by many computer scientists, scientists, librarians, statisticians, and others. The history below shows how the terminology:

data science" evolved over time, as well as attempts to describe it and associated concepts [5].

In 1974, Peter Naur's book gives a broad overview of modern data processing techniques that are employed in a variety of applications. The IFIP Guide to Data Processing Concepts and Terms states that it is organized around the data principle: "Data is a codified representation of ideas or facts that may be communicated and even perhaps changed by certain process." According to the book's preface, a course plan titled "Datalogy, the science of data and data processes, and its position in education" was presented at the 1968 IFIP Congress, and the name "data science" has been widely used since then. Data science, according to Naur, is defined as "the science of working with data after it has been established, but the relationship of the data to what it represents is assigned to other disciplines and sciences."

In 1977, the International Association for Statistical Computing (IASC) was founded as an ISI chapter. "The goal of the IASC is to connect conventional statistical techniques, innovative computer technology, and domain specialists' skills to transform data into knowledge and information," says the organization." 1989 The first Knowledge Discovery in Databases (KDD) workshop is arranged and chaired by Gregory Piatetsky-Shapiro. Figure 1.1 shows the proceeding of IJCAI-Workshop. It was renamed the ACM SIGKDD Conference on Knowledge Discovery and Data Mining (KDD) in 1995. September 1994, an article on "Database Marketing" appears in Business Week: "Enterprises are acquiring vast amounts of data on you, processing it to determine how likely someone really is to purchase a product, after then using that intelligence to design a marketing strategy perfectly tuned to find a way to convince you to do so... A prior spike of anticipation in the 1980s, sparked by the extensive use of checkout scanners, resulted in severe disappointment. Several organizations were overwhelmed with vast amount of data and were unable to do anything valuable with it... Despite this, many corporations recognize that they have no other option except to enter the database marketing arena."

In 1997, the journal Data Mining and Knowledge Discovery is set up, with the reversal of the two terms in the title emphasizing the rise of "data mining" as the standard term for "extracting information from vast datasets." December 1999, "Existing statistical procedures perform effectively with relatively small data sets, Jacob Zahavi says in Knowledge @ Wharton's "Mining Data for Nuggets of Knowledge." Today's databases, on the other hand, can have trillions of rows and columns of data. In data mining, scalability is a major concern. Another technical issue is creating models that would better analyze data, recognize nonlinear relations, and interaction

Figure 1.1 Proceeding of IJCAI-workshop.

among elements. To handle web-site issues, specialized data mining techniques may need to be developed."

2001 "Data Science: An Action Plan for Expanding the Technical Areas of the Field of Statistics," by William S. Cleveland, is published. That is a plan to "expand the key areas of technological endeavor in statistics." The new area will be dubbed "data science" because the notion is ambitious and requires significant change. Cleveland compares and contrasts the proposed new discipline to computer science and current data mining research.2001 "Statistical Modeling: The Two Cultures," by Leo Breiman, is published. When it comes to utilizing statistical modeling to draw conclusions from data, there are two contrasting cultures. A stochastic data model is assumed to have generated the data.

The statistical community has been devoted to using data models nearly exclusively. This emphasis has resulted in useless theory, spurious findings, and the exclusion of statisticians from a wide spectrum of current situations. Algorithmic modeling has advanced significantly in theory and in practice in domains other than statistics that may be used on huge challenging as well as on small datasets as the more useful and consistent alternative to data modeling. If we want to utilize data to resolve problems as a domain, we ought to move away from merely using data models and use a wider range of tools. The International Council for Science's Committee on Data for Science and Technology (CODATA) publishes the journal (ICSU). January in the year 2003 "By data science, people mean practically the whole thing that has to do with data: acquiring, examining, and modeling," according to the launch of the Journal of Data Science. However, the most important feature is its applicability—it may be used in a wide range of situations. The journal is primarily concerned with the application of statistical methods in general. All data scientists will be able to submit their viewpoints and ideas in the Journal of Data Science. The data science venn diagram is depicted by Figure 1.2.

In "A Taxonomy of Data Science," Chris Wiggins and Hilary Mason write in September 2010: One potential taxonomy... of what a data scientist does may be: obtain, scrub, explore, model, and perceive, in approximately chronological order. Data science is evidently a merger of the hacker arts of statistics and machine learning, as well as math and data topic knowledge for the analysis to be understandable. It necessitates creative thinking and a willingness to learn. "To become a properly trained data scientist, one needs comprehend a great deal," writes Drew Conway in "The Data Science

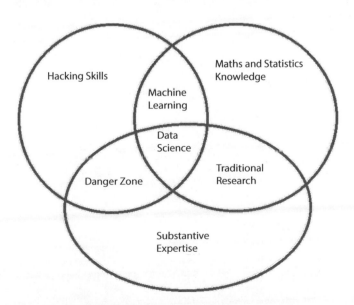

Figure 1.2 Data science Venn diagram.

Venn Diagram" from September 2010. Regrettably, simply citing literature and teachings is insufficient to untangle the tangles.

In the month of May 2011, in his article "Why the phrase 'data science' is wrong but useful," Pete Warden writes: According to P., there is no commonly agreed-upon boundary between what is inside and beyond the purview of data science. Rather than choosing a topic in the beginning and later gathering data to shed light on it, they tend to be more concerned with what the data can disclose and then picking fascinating strands to pursue. Matthew J. Graham presented "The Art of Data Science" at the Astro statistics and Data Mining in Large Astronomical Databases workshop in June 2011. "We need to learn new abilities to succeed in the modern data-intensive world of twenty-first-century science," he says. "We

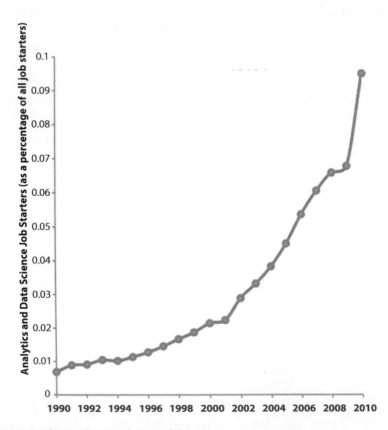

Figure 1.3 Job growth on analytics and data science.

should understand how [data] is perceived and expressed, as well as how it links to physical space and time."

The title of "business analyst" felt too constrictive. The title of "data analyst" was a candidate, but we believed it limited what people could do. After all, many of the members of our teams were highly skilled engineers. The phrase "research scientist" was used by firms, including Sun, Yahoo, HP, IBM, and Xerox as a fitting job title. We assumed, however, that the majority of research scientists worked on future and abstract issues in labs apart from the product development groups. It would take ages for lab research to have an impact on big items. As a replacement, our teams concentrated on developing data applications that can have an instant and significant influence on the firm. Data scientist seems to be the greatest fit: individuals who combine data and research to produce something new [6]. Figure 1.3 shows the job growth on analytics and data science.

1.4 How Does Data Science Differ from Business Intelligence?

Business intelligence (BI) is a method of analyzing descriptive data using technology and knowledge in order to make informed business decisions [7]. The BI toolkit is used to collect, govern, and transform data. It allows internal and external stakeholders to communicate data, making decision-making easier. Business intelligence is the process of extracting useful information from data. Some of the things that BI can help you with are:

- Developing a better grasp of the marketplace
- Identifying new revenue streams
- Enhancing business procedures
- Keeping one step ahead of the competition

Cloud computing has been the most important facilitator of BI in recent years. The cloud has enabled organizations to process more data, from more sources, and more efficiently than they could before cloud technologies were introduced.

Data science vs. business intelligence: Understanding the differences between data science and business intelligence is beneficial. Understanding how they work together is also beneficial. It is not a question of choose one over the other [8]. It all boils down to picking the proper solution to receive the information you need. Most of the time, this means combining data science and business intelligence. The simplest approach to distinguish between the two is to think about data science in terms of the future and business intelligence in terms of the past and present. Data science is concerned with predictive and prescriptive analysis, whereas business

Table 1.1 Comparison of data science and business intelligence.

Factor	Data science	Business intelligence
Concept	It is a discipline that employs mathematics, statistics, and other methods to uncover hidden patterns in data.	It is a collection of technology, applications, and processes that businesses employ to analyze business data.
Focus	It is concentrated on the future.	It concentrated the past and present.
Data	It can handle both structured and unstructured data.	It is mostly concerned with structured data.
Flexibility	Data science is more adaptable since data sources can be added as needed.	It is less flexible because data sources for business intelligence must be planned ahead of time.
Method	It employs the scientific process.	It employs the analytic method.
Complexity	In comparison to business intelligence, it is more sophisticated.	When compared to data science, it is a lot easier.
Expertise	Data scientist is its area of competence.	Its area of specialization is for business users.
Questions	It addresses the questions of what will happen and what might happen.	It is concerned with the question of what occurred.
Tools	SAS, BigML, MATLAB, Excel, and other tools are used.	Insight Squared Sales Analytics, Klipfolio, ThoughtSpot, Cyfe, TIBCO Spotfire, and more solutions are among them.

intelligence is concerned with descriptive analysis. Scope, data integration, and skill set are other differentiating considerations [9]. Table 1.1 shows the comparison between data science and business intelligence.

1.5   Data Science Life Cycle

Data science life cycle contains following steps:

a) **Gathering Data:** The first step of the data science life cycle is to collect the data from the available data sources. The particular packages are available that allow the tools to read the data from the different sources, like Python or R. The alternate option is to use Web APIs for the extraction of the data. The user that uses social media sites (Facebook, Twitter, etc.) access the data via web servers. The most common method for the collection of data is straight from the files. This can be performed via downloading the data from Kaggle, Comma Separated Values (CSV) formats, Tab Separated Values (TSV) formats. These are the flat text files, hence required a parser to read them. The few available databases are MongoDB, Oracle, MySQL, DB2, and PostgreSQL.

b) **Cleaning Data:** The following stage is to clean the information, which entails data scrubbing in addition to filtering. This technique necessitates data conversion to a different layout. It is required for the processing then analysis of data. If the files are web locked, then the lines of these files must also be filtered. Furthermore, cleaning data entails removing and replacing values. The replacement of missing data sets must be done carefully, as they may appear to be non-values. Furthermore, columns are split, combined, and withdrawn.

c) **Exploring Data:** Before the data can be used, it must first be analyzed. It is entirely up to the data scientist in a company context to change the data that is accessible into something that can be used in a corporate setting. As a result, the initial step should be to explore the data. Inspection of the data and its qualities is required. Because different data kinds, such as ordinal data, nominal, numerical data, and categorical data require distinct treatment, this is the case. Following that, descriptive statistics must be computed. It is so that important variables may be evaluated, and features can be retrieved.

Correlation is used to look at the important variables. Even though some of these variables are connected, this does not imply causation. Feature is a term used in machine learning. This aids data scientists in identifying the qualities that represent the data in question. These could include things like a person's "name," "gender," and "age." In addition, data visualization is used to highlight critical data trends and patterns. Simple tools like bar and line charts can help people understand the value of data [10].

d) **Modeling Data:** The modeling phase follows the crucial stages of data cleaning and exploration. It is frequently regarded as the most fascinating aspect of the Data Science Life Cycle. When modeling data, the first step is to reduce the number of dimensions in the data collection. Every value and feature are not required for the results to be predicted. At this point, data scientist must select the critical features that will quickly aid the model's prediction. Modeling entails a variety of tasks. Through logistic regressions, models may be trained to differentiate via classification, such as mails found as "Primary" and "Promotion." The usage of linear regressions can also be used to forecast. It is also possible to group data in order to understand the rationale that behind these parts. E-Commerce consumers, for example, are classified so that their behavior on a certain E-Commerce site can be studied. Hierarchical clustering, as well as K-Means and other clustering techniques, make this possible. For classification and identification, forecasting values, and clustering groups, the most used tools are prediction and regression.

e) **Interpreting Data:** The final and most crucial stage of life cycle is data interpretation. The final phase is to interpret the data and models. The ability to generalize lies at the heart of every prediction model's power. The model's ability to generalize future data, which is ambiguous and unknown, is crucial [11]. Data interpretation refers to the presenting of data to a layperson with no technical knowledge of data. Delivered outcomes provide answers to business queries addressed at the start of the life cycle. It is combined with the actionable insights uncovered via the data science life cycle process [12].

Data science can provide both predictive and prescriptive insights, and actionable insight is an important component of showcasing this. This enables you to reproduce a favorable result while avoiding a negative one. You will be able to comprehend the data science life cycle if you learn data science. Furthermore, these findings must be well visualized. This is accomplished by ensuring that the original corporate matters support them. The most important component of all of this is condensing all the information such that it is truly useful to the company.

1.6   Data Science Components

The primary components or processes of data science are depicted by Figure 1.4:

a) **Data Exploration:** It is the most crucial phase because it takes the most time. Data exploration takes up around 70% of the time. Because data are the most important component of data science, we rarely receive data in a well-formatted format. The data contains a significant amount of noise. The term "noise" refers to a large amount of unnecessary data. So, what are our plans for this step? We verify the observations (rows) and characteristics (columns) and use statistical methods to reduce noise in this process, which includes data sampling and transformation. This stage is also applied to evaluate the relationship between the various characteristics in the data set; by relationship, we indicate whether the features are dependent or independent of one another, as well

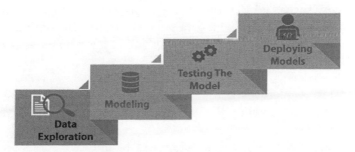

Figure 1.4 Components of data science.

as whether missing values data exist [13]. In a nutshell, the data is transformed and prepared for usage. As a result, this is one of the extremely time-consuming operations.

b) **Modeling:** Our data has been ready and is suitable to use so far then second phase is putting machine learning algorithms to work. The data is really fitted into the model at this point. We choose a model depending on the sort of data and the business need. The model used to recommend an article to a consumer. We fit the data into the model after it has been built.

c) **Testing the Model:** This is the next step, and it is critical to the model's success. The model is tested with test data to ensure that it is accurate and has other desirable properties, and necessary changes are made to the model to achieve the intended result. If the needed accuracy is not achieved, we can return to modeling step, go for a new model, then repeat steps 3 and 4 to find the model that best suits the business needs [14].

d) **Deploying Models:** We complete the model that gives us the best result based on testing findings and deploy it in the production environment whenever we achieve the desired result through rigorous testing in accordance with the business requirements.

1.7   Why Data Science is Important

- Data is important, and the science of deciphering it is as well. Data is being generated in billions of bytes, and its worth has now surpassed that of oil. For firms in a variety of industries, the function of a data scientist is and will continue to be critical.
- Data without science is nothing.
- It is necessary to interpret and analyze data.
- This emphasizes the importance of having high-quality data and knowing how to read it and produce data-driven discoveries.
- Data will aid in the development of improved consumer experiences.
- In the case of commodities and products, data science will use machine learning to help corporations invent and

produce products that people will love. A good recommendation system, for example, can assist an eCommerce company find their consumer personas by examining at their
past purchases.

- Data will be used across verticals.

Data science is not just about consumer items, technology, or healthcare. From banking to transportation to manufacturing, there will be a
huge demand for ds to streamline corporate processes. As a result, everyone interested in becoming a data scientist will have a whole new universe
of possibilities open to them. Data is the way of the future. It is critical to
improve Data science in order to improve marketing. Big data and data
science are critical components of future progress [15]. The data science
process entails analyzing, visualizing, extracting, managing, and storing
data in order to generate significant analytical insights. These data-driven
insights and reports assist businesses in analyzing their marketing strategy,
making more effective data-driven decisions and creating more effective
commercials.

Social media, phone data, e-commerce sites, healthcare surveys, internet searches, and other fields, and platforms are used to collect data. As
the amount of data available grows, a new field of research known as big
data—or exceptionally huge data sets—emerges, which can aid in the
development of better operational tools in a variety of fields. Collaboration
with financial service providers, which employ technology to create and
enhance traditional financial goods and services, allow for easy access to
ever-growing sets and data. The data generated generate more data for
emerging financial technology solutions, like cloud computing and storage, which can be shared easily across all institutions [16]. Companies,
on the other hand, may find that interpreting large amounts of unstructured data for effective decision making is extremely difficult and time-
consuming. Data science has arisen throughout the world to deal with
such annoyances.

1.8   Current Challenges

Incorporating data science into a commercial organization poses extra
hurdles in addition to the analytical ones. We have compiled a list of the
most common issues and difficulty areas that arise throughout a data science project, both organizationally and technically [17].

1.8.1   Coordination, Collaboration, and Communication

Individual, "lone wolf" data scientists are giving way to teams with highly specialized expertise in the field of data science. When addressing data science tasks as a collaborative effort, the main problem for data science projects is coordination. Confusion, inefficiency, and errors occur from poorly coordinated procedures. Furthermore, this absence of effective synchronization occurs within and across data analytics teams. Apart from a lack of direction, there are apparent collaboration challenges, as well as an absence of open statement between the three primary investors: the customer, the analytics group, and the IT sector. The challenge for analytics teams effectively execute to production, cooperate with the IT section, and communicate data science to business associates, for example, is mentioned. It also exposes a lack of business support, in the sense that there is not enough business data and sometimes domain knowledge to provide respectable results. Generally, it appears that the data analytics crew, as well as data scientists, are having difficulty collaborating effectively with the IT department and business agents. Furthermore, scientists emphasize ineffective data analytics management practices and inadequate management, as well as a lack of top management sponsorship. Assert that working in perplexing, chaotic surroundings may be difficult, and that it can reduce team members' drive and capacity to attention on project goals [18].

1.8.2   Building Data Analytics Teams

In other words, it highlights issues with assembling the right team for the job and the scarcity of people with analytical talents. Because of the scarcity of specialist analytical labor, every major institution has started a new analytics, big data, or data science division. In this context, it promotes the necessity for a multidisciplinary group: success in data science projects requires data science, technological, business, and management expertise. For example, due to the lack of a complete team-based strategy and process immaturity, data science crews have a heavy reliance on the senior data scientist. It has extremely uncertain inputs and results, and it is frequently ad hoc, including a lot of back-and-forth among team members, as well as trial-and-error to find the correct analysis appliances and settings. Because projects are experimental in nature, it can be difficult to create appropriate expectations, create realistic project timeframes, and anticipate how long tasks will take to finish. In this regard, emphasis is in the difficulty of determining the project's scope risk exposure, as well as the difficulty of comprehending the business goals. The writers specifically point out the lack of clear business goals, inadequate ROI or business cases, and an inappropriate project choice.

There is a disproportionate focus on technological difficulties, which has hindered firms' capacity to realize the full promise of data analytics. Data scientists must be fascinated with getting state-of-the-art outcomes on benchmarking activities rather than focusing on the business challenge yet striving for a tiny boost in performance can build models too complex to be effective. This approach works well in data science competitions, like Kaggle, but not in the real world [19].

1.8.3   Stakeholders vs Analytics

Analytics vs. Stakeholders, furthermore, the project concept is sometimes unclear, and there is lacking in involvement from the business area, which may only offer data and a smattering of domain expertise, thinking that the data analytics group would perform the rest of the "magic" on its own. The machine learning and deep learning techniques have produced unrealistic expectations, leading to a misunderstanding. Machine learning and deep learning approaches have created excessive expectations, leading to the false belief that these new technologies can do anything a company wants at a fair cost, which is not the case. The lack of involvement on the part of the company might also be due to a shortage of understanding among the two parties: data scientists may not comprehend the data's domain, and the business is typically unfamiliar with data analysis methods.

In fact, having an intermediate who knows, i.e., language of data analytics in addition to the area of application, would be critical to bridging the data science gap between these two parties. The highlighted project management challenges could be the result of a lack of uniform methodologies and processes for approaching the topic of data science, as well as a low level of process maturity. Furthermore, inadequate adoption of processes and techniques may result in the delivery of the "wrong thing," as well as "scope creep." In fact, the lack of efficient processes for engaging with stakeholders raises the risk of teams delivering something that does not meet stakeholder needs. The lack of influence and usage of project outputs by the business or the client is the most visible manifestation of such an issue.

1.8.4   Driving with Data

A data science project's major distinguishing feature is the use of a data-driven strategy. The data is at the heart of the endeavor. It does, however, result in some specific concerns, which are detailed below. We have compiled a list of the most common issues that arise while dealing with data, whether they are linked to tools, technology, or information management. Data scientists frequently complain about the quality of data in actual data science. It is critical for the project's success to know what data is available, how representative it is for the scenario at hand, and what limitations it has. Erroneous results were caused by a lack of synchronized data cleaning or a quality assurance check scan. Data scientists frequently overlook the validation stage in this regard.

It is also crucial to consider the big data perspective. As the volume and velocity of data grow, so do the computing requirements, and the project's reliance on IT resources grows. Furthermore, the scale of data amplifies the technology difficulty, as well as the required architecture then equipment, including the associated expenses. In other words, underscoring the necessity of data security and privacy while underscoring the complexities of legacy systems and data integration concerns.

One of the most common complaints regarding machine learning algorithms' limits is that popular deep learning approaches necessitate a large amount of significant training data, then their robustness is frequently questioned, resulting in high model training and retraining costs. To train machine learning models, data scientists typically employ four times the amount of data required, which requires time and money. Furthermore, data scientists are prone to fixating on the incorrect model's performance measurements without considering general business goals else trade-offs between different goals.

It shows that data science operations lack reproducibility in this respect. In fact, they ask for rapid action and the development of new reproductive tools, claiming that "inconsistent preservation of relevant items" such as packages, data, documentation, then intermediate outputs could "make it harder to build on earlier accomplishments." This could pose a severe threat to the long-term viability of data science programmer. The main output of several practical data science projects would be something intangible like the project process or the created learning along the road, rather than the machine learning technique or the forecast quantity of interest. While reaching project objectives is important, understanding how the project attained those objectives, what path it took, and why it took those steps rather than alternatives are also important in some cases. This newly acquired understanding about a data science project's path is critical for comprehending the outcomes and paving the way for future efforts [20].

As a result, this knowledge must be effectively managed and preserved, and the ability to repeat data science occupations and research is vital Experts recommend that every new machine learning model be documented, and a complete register be made to assist future recruits to quickly replicate work done by their predecessors. Knowledge-sharing across data science teams and across the entire organization is cited as a critical component of project success, as is data and information management. Multiple equivalent but inconsistent data sets were also mentioned by scientists, meaning that different versions of the same data sets could be travelling around the firm with no means of knowing which one is correct.

1.9   Tools Used for Data Science

Extracting, analyzing, preprocessing, and forecasting data is the responsibility of a data scientist. He will need a variety of statistical tools as well as computer languages to do so. We will go through some of the data science tools that data scientists utilize to work with data. The basic features of the instruments, as well as the benefits they give, will be explored [21, 22]. There are two categories of tools arising:

1. Self-service tools (understanding of statistics and computer science as well as programming skills)
2. Tools for business users that automate frequently used analysis.

List of Data Science Tools:

SAS

It is one of those tools that was created solely for statistics purposes. SAS is a proprietary closed-source data analysis tool used by large organizations. SAS is a programming language for performing statistical modeling. Professionals and corporations regularly use this dependable commercial software. As a data scientist, you can utilize SAS's statistical libraries and tools to model and organize your data. SAS is quite dependable and has a lot of firm support, but it is also expensive and only utilized by major companies. SAS is also outclassed by some of the newer open-source alternatives. Figure 1.5 shows the features of SAS.

Apache Spark

It is the most popular data science tool, as well as a sophisticated analytics engine. It was designed from the ground up to handle batch and streaming

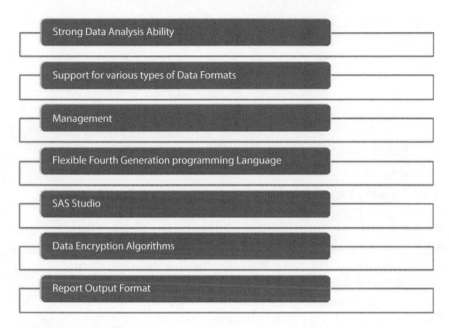

Figure 1.5 Features of SAS.

operations. It offers a number of APIs that enable data scientists to access data on a regular basis for machine learning, SQL storage, and other uses. It outperforms Hadoop by a factor of a hundred and outperforms map reduce by a factor of a hundred. It comes with several machine learning APIs that can assist data scientists in making accurate predictions based on the data they have been given.

In terms of handling streaming data, spark outperforms other Big Data Tools. This means that, unlike other analytical tools that exclusively process historical information in batches, Spark can handle real-time information. Spark provides Java, Python, and R-based APIs. But the most wonderful combination of Spark and Scala is with the JVM-based and cross-platform Scala programming language.

It has a high level of cluster management efficiency, making it far superior to Hadoop, which is mostly used for storage. This cluster management solution enables high-speed application processing. Figure 1.6 shows the features of Apache Spark.

BigML

Another popular data science tool is BigML. It provides a cloud-based, fully interactive GUI for processing machine learning techniques. BigML gives both standard and cloud-based industry-specific tools. Machine learning

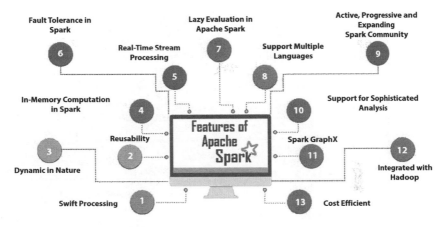

Figure 1.6 Features of Apache Spark.

techniques can be used in a variety of commercial situations. For example, the same platform can be used for risk analytics, sales forecasting, and product creation.

- BigML is a company that focuses on predictive modeling. It uses a various of machine learning algorithms, including clustering, classification, and time-series forecasting, to name a few.
- BigML features a simple web interface that employs rest APIs, and based on your data demands, you may register a free or premium account. It allows you to create interactive data visualizations and export interactive charts to mobile or IoT devices.
- BigML also comes with a set of automation tools that can help you automate hyperparameter model tuning and even reusable script workflows.

D3.js

On the client side, JavaScript is typically used as a scripting language. You may generate interactive visualizations in your web browser with D3.js, a JavaScript library. D3.js (data-driven document) is an open-source platform comprising many pre-defined classes and functions-based JavaScript that can be used to build any type of data visualization. D3.js provides numerous APIs that may be used to build dynamic data display and analysis in

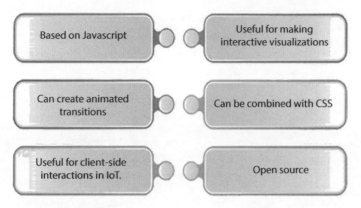

Figure 1.7 Features of D3.js.

your browser. Typically, D3.js is considered as one of the JavaScript libraries. One of the major capabilities of D3.js is the ability to build dynamic data visualizations that enable users to interact with the data visualization, control the data to show and configure more options in the plots such as get further data the mouse cursor hovers or clicks over some places within the visualization, realize lively moving visualizations to discover real time data trends and insights generated form changes over time, and select from a diversity of dissimilar moves among the views. The use of animated transitions is another amazing feature of D3.js. Documents can be made more dynamic by permitting customer updates and browser visual adjustment based on data modifications. Figure 1.7 shows the features of D3.js.

This can be combined with CSS to produce stunning and transient visuals that aid in the creation of unique graphs for web pages. Generally, it can be helpful for IoT-based data scientists requiring client involvement for displaying and processing of data.

MATLAB

MATLAB offers a multiparadigm statistic computing setting for the assessment of mathematical data. This closed-source software accelerates matrix functions, algorithmic execution, and statistical data modeling. A multitude of scientific topics are covered by MATLAB. In the field of Data Science, MATLAB is frequently used to mimic neural networks, as well as fuzzy logic. As a result, data scientists may use it to a variety of problems, starting from data cleansing and analysis to powerful deep learning algorithms [23]. It is also an effective data science tool due to its ease of

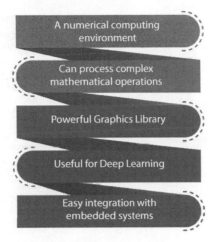

Figure 1.8 Features of MATLAB.

integration into enterprise applications and embedded devices. Figure 1.8 shows the features of MATLAB.

It also aids in the automation of a variety of processes, from data extraction to reuse of scripts for decision making. It does, however, have the drawback of being proprietary closed-source software.

Excel

The data analysis tool most typically used. Microsoft Excel has been designed with calculations in mind, but now it is extensively employed for data processing, viewing and sophisticated calculations. It is a very good analysis aid for data science. Even though Excel is the industry standard for data analysis, it still has a lot of power. Equations, tables, filters, slicers, and other tools are just a few of the features available in Excel. One can also build his/her own functions as well as formulas in Excel. Even if it is not designed to analyze massive volumes of data, it is a superb tool to produce complicated data and tablets visualizations. You can also use SQL to connect, manipulate, and analyze data with Excel. Figure 1.9 shows the features of Excel.

It is right now considerably easier to analyze complex analyses thanks to the release of ToolPak for Microsoft Excel. Excel does, however, pale in comparison to even more complex data science tools like as SAS. Overall, Excel is an excellent data analysis tool for small and non-enterprise businesses.

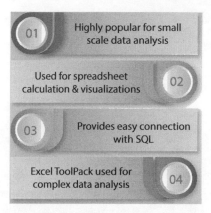

Figure 1.9 Features of excel.

Ggplot2

For the R programming language, ggplot2 is an advanced data visualization software. This program was intended to replace R's native graphics package, and it makes use of strong commands to generate stunning visualizations.

- It is the most popular library for making visuals from examined data among data scientists.
- Ggplot2 is a component of tidy verse, a R package dedicated to data science.
- Aesthetics is one-way ggplot2 outperforms the rest of the data visualizations. Data scientists can use ggplot2 to generate personalized visualizations to participate in more engaging storytelling.

Tableau

Tableau is a data visualization application with a lot of attractive graphics and the ability to make interactive displays. It is intended for businesses involved in the field of business intelligence. Tableau has capacity to interface with spread sheets, databases, OLAP cubes, and other systems. It is its most significant feature. It also offers the capacity to view geographical data and plot longitudes and latitudes on maps, in addition to these characteristics. One may utilize its analytics tool to evaluate data in addition to visualizations. Tableau has a vibrant community, and one may post her/his discoveries on the website. Tableau has a free version named Tableau Public, even though it is commercial software. Figure 1.10 shows the features of tableau.

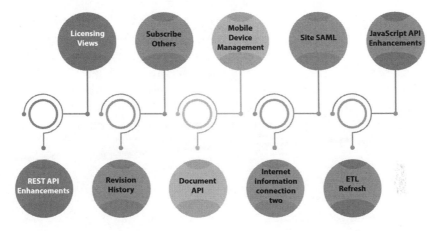

Figure 1.10 Features of tableau.

Jupyter

Project Jupyter is an IPython-based open-source platform that enables developers to create open-source software and interactive computing experiences. It supports a variety of programming languages, including Python, Julia, and R.

- This is a web-based programme designed for writing live code, making visualizations and giving presentations. It is a commonly used programming language designed to fulfill data scientists' needs.
- It is a user-friendly environment in which data scientists can carry out all their duties. It is also a good tool intended for telling stories because it has a lot of presentation features.
- Data cleansing, statistical computing, visualization, then predictive machine learning models may all be done with Jupyter Notebooks.
- It is completely free because it is based on open-source software.
- Collaboratory, an online Jupyter environment that operates on the cloud as well as stores data in Google Drive, is available.

Matplotlib

Matplotlib is a Python-based plotting and visualization package. It is the most often used programmer for making graphs out of data. It is typically used to make complex graphs with only a few lines of code. This can be used to generate histograms, bar plots, scatterplots, and other graphs. There are a lot of significant modules in it. Pyplot is one of the most used modules. It has a MATLAB-style interface. Matplotlib is a favored data visualization tool among data scientists, who prefer it over more modern tools. During the landing of the Phoenix Spacecraft, NASA utilized Matplotlib to display data visualizations. If you are new to Python data visualization, it is also a good place to start.

Natural Language ToolKit

In the discipline of data science, Natural Language Processing has grown to prominence. It is concerned with the creation of statistical models which assist computers in comprehending human language. Machine learning includes statistical models that employ several methodologies to support computers in comprehending natural language. The Natural Language ToolKit (NLTK) suite of libraries was created specifically for this purpose and is included with the Python language. Figure 1.11 shows the features of NLTK.

Tokenization, stemming, tagging, parsing, and machine learning are just a few of the language processing procedures that use NLTK. It includes more than 100 corpora, that are data sets used to train machine learning models. Text to speech, speech recognition, machine translation, parts of speech tagging, word segmentation, and other applications are among them.

Scikit-Learn

Scikit-learn is a Python package that allows you to implement machine learning algorithms. A standard tool for analysis and data science is basic

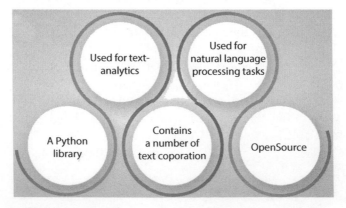

Figure 1.11 Features of NLTK.

and straightforward to use. Scikit-learn makes complicated machine learning methods simple to use. As a result, it is suitable for circumstances that necessitate rapid prototyping, as well as research that necessitates elementary machine learning. This one makes use of various Python basic libraries, including SciPy, NumPy, Matplotlib, and others.

Waikato Environment for Knowledge Analysis

Waikato Environment for Knowledge Analysis (WEKA) is a Java-based machine learning application. It is a collection of various machine learning-based data mining algorithms. It is an open-source graphical user interface (GUI) software which facilitates the deployment of machine learning procedures via an interactive program [24]. Without writing a single line of code, you can learn how machine learning works on data. It is perfect for data scientists who are just getting started with machine learning [25].

TensorFlow

For machine learning, TensorFlow has established itself as a common tool. Advanced machine learning algorithms, such as deep learning, make extensive use of it. Tensors are multidimensional arrays that the developers dubbed tensor flow after. It is an open source, constantly expanding toolkit that is noted for its speed and processing power. TensorFlow is compatible with both CPUs plus GPUs. and is now available on more capable TPU processors. Figure 1.12 shows the features of TensorFlow.

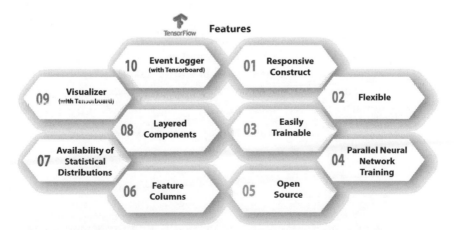

Figure 1.12 Features of TensorFlow.

In terms of advanced machine learning algorithm processing capacity, this gives it an unrivalled advantage. Due to its enormous processing capacity, TensorFlow can be used for a wide range of tasks, Speech recognition, and language synthesis, and other applications are examples. TensorFlow is an essential tool for data scientists who specialize in machine learning.

1.10   Benefits and Applications of Data Science

Benefits of Data Science

- Data science and big data will be critical in helping the organization enhance its operations in the future. For better marketing forecasting, data science is quite useful.
- Data science may assist in the development of a business by reducing the limits of time and money allocation [26].
- Many manual jobs have been selected by data science, which may be preferable than human influences.
- Data science aids in the prevention of debt default, fraud detection, and a variety of other financial applications.
- Data science draws insights from unstructured text data and aids in the prediction of future outcomes, which can assist huge organizations avoid financial losses.

Applications of Data Science

- Personalized healthcare advice
- Detecting and predicting disease
- Real-time optimization of shipping routes
- Getting the most bang for your buck with soccer rosters
- Recruiting the next generation of world-class athletes
- Tax fraud detection
- Digital ad placement automation
- Matchmaking algorithms
- Predicting incarceration rates

1.11   Conclusion

Data science is a multidisciplinary profession that utilize scientific methods, procedures, techniques, and systems to obtain insights and knowledge from raw, structured, as well as unstructured data, and to deploy that knowledge and insight to a variety of application areas. In this chapter, the important parts like what is data science and what does a data scientist do, why data science is in demand, history of data science, how data science differs from business intelligence were penned and also life cycle, as well as components of data science, the importance of data science, challenges and tools used for data science and finally benefits, applications of data science were discussed too for better understanding.

References

1. Provost, F. and Fawcett, T., *Data Science for Business: What You Need to Know about Data Mining and Data-Analytic Thinking*, O'Reilly Media, 2013.
2. Sharma, H., 2021, https://www.edureka.co/blog/what-is-data-science/.
3. Doyle, L., 2020, https://www.northeastern.edu/graduate/blog/what-does-a-data-scientist-do/.
4. Oberoi, T., 2020, https://www.mygreatlearning.com/blog/top-8-reasons-data-science-jobs-demand.
5. Manovich, L., data science and digital art history. *Int. J. Digit. Art Hist.*, 1, 13–34, 2015, https://doi.org/10.11588/dah.2015.1.21631.
6. Pinsky E. Teaching data science by history: Kepler's laws of planetary motion and generalized linear models. *Comput. Sci. Educ. Comput. Sci.*, 16, 1, 72–77, 2020.
7. Chen, Y. and Lin, Z., Business intelligence capabilities and firm performance: A study in China. *Int. J. Inf. Manage.*, 57, 1022325, 2021.
8. Sakshi, 2020, https://www.geeksforgeeks.org/difference-between-data-science-and-business-intelligence/.
9. Ghosh, P., 2018, https://www.dataversity.net/data-science-vs-business-intelligence.10.
10. Ruckstuhl, A. and Stockinger, K., *What we Learned About the Data Science Life Cycle: Best Practices and Open Research Challenges.* Swiss Data Science Conference Proceeding, p. 12, 2021.
11. Hotz, N., 2021, https://www.datascience-pm.com/data-science-life-cycle/.
12. Sivarajah, S., 2020, https://towardsdatascience.com/stoend-to-end-data-science-life-cycle.
13. Pierson, L., *Data science for dummies*, John Wiley & Sons, 2021.
14. Singh, K., 2018, https://dimensionless.in/understanding-different-components-roles-in-data-science/.
15. D'ignazio, C. and Klein, L.F., *Data feminism*, MIT Press, 2020.
16. Janssens, J., *Data Science at the Command Line*, O'Reilly Media, Inc., 2021.
17. de Medeiros, M.M., Hoppen, N., Maçada, A.C.G., Data science for business: Benefits, challenges and opportunities. *Bottom Line*, 1–5, 2020.

18. Meng, X.-L., What is your list of 10 challenges in data science? *Harvard Data Sci. Rev.*, 2, 5–10,2020.
19. Schwab-McCoy, A., Baker, C.M., Gasper, R.E., Data science in 2020: Computing, curricula, and challenges for the next 10 years. *J. Stat. Data Sci. Educ.*, 29.sup1, S40–S50, 2021.
20. Vigilarolo, B., 2020, https://www.techrepublic.com/article/challenges-facing-data-science-in-2020-and-four-ways-to-address-them/.
21. Pathak, P., Iyengar, S.P., Abhyankar, M., *A Survey on Tools for Data Analytics and Data Science*, pp. 28–49, Handbook of Research on Engineering, Business, and Healthcare Applications of Data Science and Analytics. IGI Global, 2021.
22. Baviskar, M.R., Nagargoje, P.N., Deshmukh, P.A., Baviskar, R.R., A survey of data science techniques and available tools. *Int. Res. J. Eng. Technol. (IRJET)*, 08, 2395–0056, 2021.
23. Sardareh, A., Sedigheh, G.T.L., Brown, Denny, P., Comparing four contemporary statistical software tools for introductory data science and statistics in the social sciences. *Teach. Stat.*, 43, S157–S1725, 2021.
24. Ul Haq, H.B. *et al.*, The Popular Tools of Data Sciences: Benefits, Challenges and Applications. *IJCSNS*, 20, 5, 65, 2020.
25. Siegel, E., Predictive analytics: The power to predict who will click, buy, lie, or die. *John Wiley & Sons, Health Inform. Res.,* 19, 1, 63–65, 2013.
26. Peng R.D. and Matsui, E., *The art of data science: A guide for anyone who works with Data.* Skybrude Consulting LLC, p. 28, 2016.

## 2

Exploration of Tools for Data Science

Qasem Abu Al-Haija

Department Computer Science/Cybersecurity, King Hussein School of Computing Sciences, Princess Sumaya University for Technology (PSUT), Amman, Jordan

Abstract

Data science is a multidisciplinary area that concerns managing, manipulating, analyzing, extracting, and interpreting knowledge from a tremendous amount of data (known as a big data field). Data science is a vast body of expertise that uses methods, approaches, algorithms, tools, and concepts belonging to other interrelated areas, such as information science, probability and statistics, mathematics, big data analytics, and computer science and engineering. As such, mechanisms employed in data science include machine/deep learning techniques, data engineering, data visualization techniques, pattern recognition, data mining, probability modeling, signal processing, and computer vision. Data science is being actively adopted by several vital divisions that take advantage of data science, such as organizations, governments, and academia. This chapter will provide an overview of the top 10 tools and applications that must interest any data scientist. Chapter objectives include (but are not limited to): realize the use of Python in developing solutions of data science tasks, recognize the use of R Language can be used as an open-source data science provider, travel around the SQL to provide structured models for data science projects, navigate through data analytics and statistics using Excel, using D3.js scripting tools for data visualization. Also, short emphasis and practical examples/case studies are provided on data visualization, data analytics, regression, forecasting, and outlier detection.

Keywords: Data science (DS), DS tools, DS analytics, DS processing, DS models, DS visualization

Email: q.abualhaija@psut.edu.jo

Archana Patel, Narayan C. Debnath and Bharat Bhusan (eds.) Data Science with Semantic Technologies: Theory, Practice, and Application, (31–70) © 2022 Scrivener Publishing LLC

2.1   Introduction

The term of "data science" has been defined and elaborated recently in different ways. However, all representative definitions of data science will always identify data science as a science of extracting sense, information, and value from the raw unprocessed data records or observations that lead to derive insights and build creative decisions [1]. Simply, data science is an old and new interdisciplinary area of learning and research that employs different raw datasets for diverse sources with different volumes and vicinity to transform raw data into valuable information that can be used to build comprehensive perceptions and develop innovative and convenient solution for a wide range of applications, industries, and multiple areas of studies. Indeed, data science has become a crucial science for invention and development nowadays across various business and industrial fields [2]. Figure 2.1 shows multidisciplinary areas contributed to the emergence of the collective science so-called data science. As can be clearly seen for the figure, diverse fields are collaborating in managing, manipulating, analyzing, extracting, and interpreting knowledge from tremendous amount of data sources, such as statistics, visualization, machine learning, big data, data engineering, and high-performance computing (HPC) [3].

Figure 2.1 Diverse fields of data science.

Big data and data science are tightly coupled fields, and they are significantly correlated and usually used as an integral part to each other. The big data and data science have modernized the life applications. Big data [4] is major part of data science, and it concerns with data exceed processing capacity of conventional database systems. It is characterized by the following:

- Volume: size is too big, starts at Terabyte scales (1012 bytes) and has no upper limit,
- Velocity: latency of data processing relative to growing demand (30 KB/S~30 GB/S)
- Variety: heterogeneous, diversity of sources, formats, quality, and structures.

In its realest arrangement, data science characterizes the enhanced utilization of practices and assets to produce actionable data-driven inferences or decisions that can be employed to comprehend and enhance the diverse applications of real life such as business, economic and finance, medical and health, industrial and manufacturing, and even the social life. With data science, you can go beyond the understanding of your business, you can even bargain data science techniques to envisage and forecast the best undeviating sequence to pass through from your current situation to where you want to be. A noticeable confusion is usually appeared in the use of the two terms of data science and data engineering, which are distinct and different areas of knowledge. Even though data scientists and data engineers often work together, we can merely differentiate between the two fields. To illustrate the distinction between data scientist and data engineer, refer to Figure 2.2, which visualizes the different tools, skills and responsibilities of data scientist and data engineer.

To cope with the various data sources (the three Vs are volume, velocity, and variety), data science commonly works with three variations of data models [6] including structured models where data is warehoused, handled, and deployed using conventional relational database management system (RDBMS), unstructured models where data are normally produced from humanoid actions in which they do not fit within structured models, and semi-structured models where data do not fit into structured models, but is however they are structured using tags that are convenient to generating a form of sequence and ladder in the data/records. Figure 2.3 illustrates the three data variants with examples.

Due to this diversity of data variants, data science became a huge body of knowledge that makes use of methods, approaches, algorithms, tools,

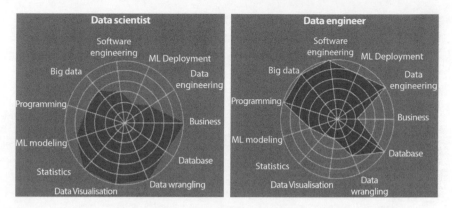

Figure 2.2 Data scientist vs. data engineer [5].

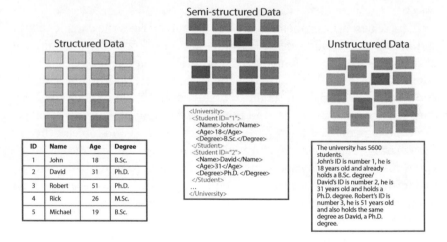

Figure 2.3 Structured data vs. unstructured data vs semistructured data.

and concepts belonging to other interrelated fields such as information science, probability and statistics, mathematics, big data analytics, and computer science and engineering. As such, techniques utilized in data science include machine and deep learning techniques, data visualization techniques, data mining, pattern recognition, probability model, data engineering, signal processing and computer vision. Data science is being actively adopted by several key sectors that benefit from data science such as Corporations, Governments, and Academia. Therefore, the rest of this chapter will provide an overview for the top 10 tools and application that must be of interest of any data scientist. Chapter objectives includes (but not limited to): Python Language for data science, R Language for data science, SQL language for structured data science, data analytics and statistics using Microsoft Excel, using D3.js scripting tools for data visualization. Also, short emphasize and practical examples/case studies are to be provided on data visualization, data analytics, time series modeling, regression, forecasting and outlier detection.

2.2   Top Ten Tools for Data Science

Data science has recently emerged out as one of the most prevalent areas of our new era. The organizations and corporations started to employ data scientists to assist them in gaining visions and more intuitions about the recent states of marketplace and competitors which can greatly help in developing actionable plans and smarter decisions. Indeed, data scientists have become a strategic part of any business since they play a major role in decision making by processing and investigating a huge amount of structured dada, unstructured data, and semistructured data. Therefore, for data scientist to be able to play this important role, data scientist should acquire knowledge and practice in several tools, techniques, applications, and programming languages. There is a wide range of tools and applications that can be used to y of utilize the techniques and models of data science to discourse several real-life concerns and developed adequate solutions that can help in improving the business life cycle and provide improved outcomes and decisions. To sum up, the most common top ten tools for data science are demonstrated in Figure 2.4 and elaborated shortly after the figure. We will also visit some of them in the next sections.

2.3   Python for Data Science

Python is a comprehensive and general-purpose programming platform that can be used to develop programming solutions for web-based applications, artificial intelligence applications including machine and deep

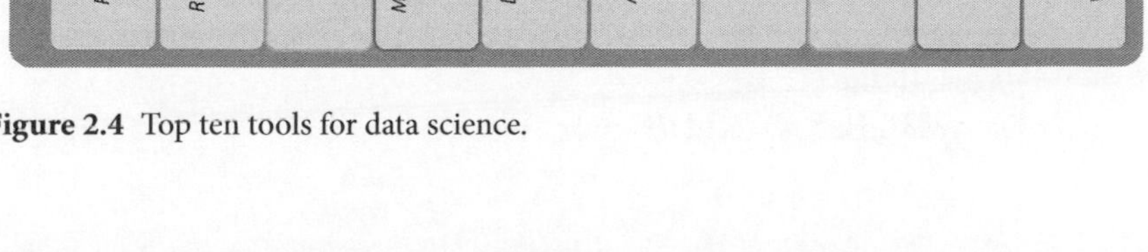

Figure 2.4 Top ten tools for data science.

learning, platform independent desktop applications (can run on windows or Linux operating systems), platform independent mobile applications (can run on Android or IOS operating systems) and many others [7]. Even though conventional languages as C++ and Java can be used to implement platform independent programs, however, the resourcefulness of Python marks it as a superlative language for data computation and analytics and data visualizations. Therefore, Python has attracted most of the programmer, software developer, and data scientists and has grossed a reputation of distinction in as a free publicly available and widely adopted programming language to develop solutions and diverse application for data science arena [8]. Python is an object-oriented programming language, which means that everything in Python is considered an object. We can simply define the object as a datatype that can be declared as a variable and/or assigned numerical or categorical values.

2.3.1   Python Datatypes

Python comprises different datatype forms, the most common datatypes are listed below:

- **Numbers**: this can be integer numbers (signed natural numbers), long numbers (extended integers), float numbers (real number format), and complex numbers (An imaginary number format).
  EXAMPLE: >>> $X = -7$, $Y = 32.3 + e18$, $Z = 3.14j$
- **Strings**: String contains several characters that are written into single or double quotes. and represented by '...' or "...".
  EXAMPLE: >>> $MySTR$ = 'Welcome to my realm'
- **Lists**: a sequence of elements (numbers/strings) represented by [...] or [...,...,...], in which each record in the list is auto-allocated a numeral index, beginning at 0. Another variant of the list is called Tuples that are represented by (...) and they like the lists except that their contents cannot be modified after they are created.
  EXAMPLE: >>> $MyLST$ = [3.1, 0.05, 5.6, −2.9]
- **Dictionaries**: unordered data structures/collections of items where each item of a dictionary is represented as pairs of key and value. Dictionaries are typically boosted to recover values while the key is recognized. They are represented as {'Key': 'Value',...}.
  EXAMPLE: >>> $MyDIC$ = {1: 'apple', 2: 'ball'}

2.3.2   Helpful Rules for Python Programming

Als, there a couple of helpful rules that can be enough to understand the Python code as follows:

- Indentation is important in coding: The coding blocks are designated by indentation.
- Variable datatypes do not require pre-declaration since Python realizes them on its own. Also, for assignment use one equal "= " while for comparison use double equal "== ".
- For number datatype, the basic operations + − * / % are as anticipated with ability to use "+" to concatenate strings and to use % to format strings (such as *printf* in C). Moreover, for logical operations we use the words not symbols, i.e. (*and, or, not*).
- The basic result outputting command is "***print***". Also, any command starts with "#", is ignored as the complier will consider this as "comments".
- Naming convention: Names in Python are case sensitive. They cannot begin with numbers; they can begin with letter or underscore. However, they can comprise letters, numbers, and underscores such as *amr, Amr, _amr, _2_amr_, amr_2, AmR*. Please note that there are some reserved words that cannot be used to name variables or constants such as: {*and, assert, break, class, continue, def, del, elif, else, except, exec, finally, for, from, global, if, import, in, is, lambda, not, or, pass, print, raise, return, try, while*}.
- Assignment: Flexible assignment where multiple names can be assigned simultaneously, for example (>>> x,y = 9,−6). This makes it easy to swap values (>>> $x, y = y, x$). Moreover, Assignments can be chained (>>> $a = b = x = 2$).

2.3.3   Jupyter Notebook for IPython

Jupyter notebook [9] enables you to write and test your code blocks in separate cells. To open Jupyter in your web browser, you need firstly to install Anaconda (https://www.anaconda.com) and then just locate Jupyter Notebook then open it. Anaconda is as free distribution and open-source platform for data science and machine learning development. Figure 2.5 illustrates the Front view of Anaconda platform and Jupyter for IPython.

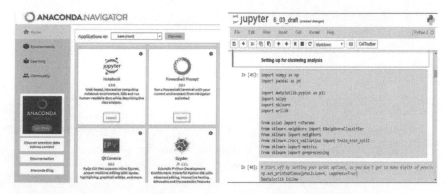

Figure 2.5 Front view of Anaconda platform and Jupyter for IPython.

2.3.4   Your First Python Program

The best way to get along with Python programming, its highly recommended to follow "learn by example" methodology. To do so, we encourage you to open a new project using Jupyter Notebook and start your practice by writing, debugging, and running the following basic program which can be written using several independent cells through Jupyter environment where each cell can be examined and executed individually.

```
x = 34 – 23              # A comment.
y = 'Hello'              # Another one.
z = 3.45
 if z == 3.45 or y == 'Hello ':
       x = x + 1
       y = y + 'World'    # String concatenation
print (x)
print (y)
```

To gain more in-depth programming skills and capabilities, we advise the reader to navigate through Python libraries. Library is collection of pre-developed scripts that are inscribed to perform collections of tasks. To practice specific packages in Python, you need to finish the installation process firstly. Then, you can "import" the installed package to exploit the functions into the package. To import any library such as *numpy* library, you write: *import numpy*. The most common and useful Python libraries that we recommend the reader to practice include:

- *NumPy Library*: concentrates on working with operations related to multi-dimensional arras such as array multiplication, transposing, inversion, decomposition, reshaping, rearranging and others.

- *SciPy Library*: concentrates on working with specific scientific algorithms that extends the capabilities of *NumPy library* such as clustering algorithms, optimization algorithms, signal processing algorithms, and others.
- *Pandas Library*: concentrates on working with specific fast, resilience, and communicative data structures premeditated to enable development with "relational" or "labeled" data both easy and intuitive. For example, to import data records from a comma separated values (CSV) file, one can employ *Pandas library*.
- *Matplot Library*: concentrates on working with creating multifaceted visualizations for dataset to enable further data analytics. Example of visualizations provided by *Matplot library* includes Scatter plot, Bubble plot with Encircling, Scatter plot with line of best fit, jittering with strip plot, Counts Plot, Marginal Histogram, Marginal Boxplot, Correlogram, Pairwise Plot, and many others.

2.4 R Language for Data Science

R is a widespread open source and publicly available statistical programming platform and a cutting-edge tool that has been extensively utilized to develop programming solutions for diverse range of data science applications, such as banking system applications, e-commerce development applications, finance automation applications, manufacturing system applications, healthcare system applications, social media applications and many other sectors [10]. Indeed, R programming language can be found in many useful use cases in the real life. For instance, Figure 2.6 exemplifies several companies that use R language for data analytics. R programming language can be downloaded with its supporting packages from http://cran.r-project.org. Also, you are also able to use R language editor tool provided by Anaconda platform. Moreover, a complete step of download and installation can follow through the link: https://data-flair.training/blogs/how-to-install-r/.

2.4.1 R Datatypes

R comprises different datatype forms [11], the most common datatypes are listed below:

Figure 2.6 Companies that use R language for data analytics.

- **Vector**: A vector is the elementary datatype of R language represented as an ordered list of the same datatype (numerical, logical, and character). To create a vector with several elements, the function c() can be used to combine the elements into a vector.
  EXAMPLE: *apple < − c('red', 'green', "yellow")*.
- **Matrix**: A matrix is simply group of vectors with two-dimensional dataset. To create a matrix, the function *matrix()* can be used to combine the vector inputs into a two-dimensional matrix.
  EXAMPLE: *M = matrix(c('e',' e',' g',' h','d','e'), nrow = 3, ncol = 2, byrow = TRUE)*
- **List**: is a heterogeneous datatype object that allows the combination of several different datatypes of elements such as arrays, vectors, matrices, functions, and nested lists. To create a list, the function *list()*can be used to define the internal elements of the list.
  EXAMPLE: *list1 < − list(c(2,5,3),21.3, sin)*
- **Frame**: also called data frame, it is a tabular datatype objects that might combines different datatype modes in one table (data frame) where every column represents a vector that can be numeric, character or logical. Note that the vectors of single data frame should of equal sizes. To generate a data frame, the function *data.frame()* can be used to define all the tabular elements.
  EXAMPLE: *BMI < − data.frame(gender = c("Male","-Male","Female"), height = c(152, 171.5, 165), weight = c(81,93,78),Age = c(42,38,26))*.

Besides, R language contains a wide range of operators that can be used define the different operations to be performed over different datatypes. These operators can be summarized into four groups including arithmetic operators, logical operators, relational operators, and assignment operators. Figure 2.7 below demonstrate the various operator's groups.

Moreover, the most used operators are further defined in Figure 2.8. These operators are used in most of R programs and the operators also act as functions in R. Unlike Python, note that logical operators in R language are not used as words (e.g., *and, or, not*) but they are used as symbols (e.g., &, |,!).

2.4.2   Your First R Program

Again, the best way to get along with R programming, its highly recommended to follow "learn by example" practice. To do so, we encourage you to open a new project using R notebook editor provided by Anaconda and start your practice by writing, debugging, and running the following basic program. You are advised to run each line of code individually and debug in a step-by-step debugging. The following program will greatly help you exploring objects of R programming language.

```
> GeneticallyEngineeredCorn <- data.frame(list(year=c(2000, 2001,
        2002, 2003, 2004, 2005, 2006, 2007, 2008, 2009, 2010,
        2011, 2012, 2013, 2014),Insect =c(13,
        12,18,23,26,25,24,19,13,  10,  15,  14,  14,   4,   3),
        herbicide=c(3,3,3,4,5,6,12,15,15,15,15,17,18,7,5)))
> GeneticallyEngineeredCorn
      year Insect herbicide
1     2000     13         3
2     2001     12         3
3     2002     18         3
4     2003     23         4
5     2004     26         5
6     2005     25         6
7     2006     24        12
8     2007     19        15
9     2008     13        15
10    2009     10        15
11    2010     15        15
12    2011     14        17
13    2012     14        18
14    2013      4         7
15    2014      3         5
> PredictHerbicide <-
        lm(GeneticallyEngineeredCorn$herbicide ~
        GeneticallyEngineeredCorn$Insect)
> attributes(PredictHerbicide)$names
[1] "coefficients"  "residuals"      "effects"       "rank"
[5] "fitted.values" "assign"         "qr"            "df.residual"
[9] "xlevels"       "call"           "terms"         "model"
> attributes(PredictHerbicide)$class
[1] "lm"
> PredictHerbicide$coef
            (Intercept) GeneticallyEngineeredCorn$Insect
             10.52165581                     -0.06362591
```

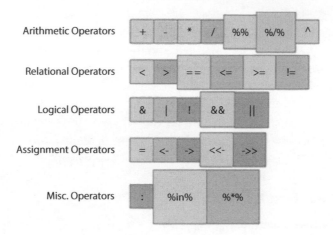

Figure 2.7 Operators of R language.

To gain more in-depth programming skills and capabilities of R language, we advise the reader to navigate through the statistical analysis packages of R Language. Package is collection of pre-developed data and codes that are inscribed to perform collections of tasks. To practice specific packages in R, you must first complete the installation process. You can download R language packages for CRAN site (http://cran.r-project.org/web/packages), which can provide the most recent available packages of R language. Then, you install the required packages according to the directions of downloading and installing packages form the same site. them to use the library's function. The most common and useful R packages that we recommend the reader to practice include:

- *ggplot2 Package*: a collection of data visualization functions that provide capabilities for static or interactive visualizing graphs with one or more variables of categorical and numerical data.
- *data.table Package*: a collection of data processing functions that can handle massive volumes of data during (ranges from 10 GB to 100GB). This package is commonly used with big data applications such as healthcare and medical domains.
- *dplyr Package*: a collection of data manipulation functions by a means of grouping operations such as like *select()*, *arrange()*, *filter()*, *summarise()*, and *mutate()*.
- *tidyr Package*: a collection of data cleansing and preparation functions that helps to fashion tidy datasets.

Operation	Operator
plus	+
minus	–
times	*
divide	/
modulo	%%
power	^
greater than	>
greater than or equal to	>=
less than	<
less than or equal to	<=
equals	==
not equals	!=
not (logical)	!
and (logical)	&
or (logical)		
is assigned; gets	<-
is assigned to	->

Figure 2.8 Most common operators of R language.

- *Shiny Package*: a collection of web application development functions that can be used along with JavaScript and HTML languages to build a high-performance web application with extended features.
- *knitr Package*: a collection of research development functions. This package comprises of tools to reproduce and create research reports and it can be integrated with other types of research development coding such LaTex and LyX.
- *mlr3 Package*: a collection of Machine Learning functions that provides capabilities to address several Machine Learning tasks such as association, clustering, prediction, regression, classification, recognition, and survival analysis.

- *Forecast Package*: a collection of forecasting functions that are commonly used to model univariate time series forecasting system such as ARMA model (Auto Regressive Moving Average), ARIMA model (Auto Regressive Integrated Moving Average) [12], and others

2.5   SQL for Data Science

SQL (Structured Query Language) is a simplest, fastest, customary semantic for creating, updating, and querying relational database (RDB) systems [13]. In RDB, data are stored in a tables & this database contains a schema. Schema is a structural representation to define database elements (tables, columns, relationships). The data is stored in columns (data attributes) and in the rows (data records). For example, the following schema (Figure 2.9) defines a simple relational database of two tables:

- Table A stores product information and Table B stores demographic information.
- The tables are updated (add, delete, read, queried) using SQL statements.
- The tables are queried using a common key (relationship) which connects both tables.
- To define, update and query such RDB and others, one can use *PostgresSQL* software tool which is the most common available open source RDB.
- Example of SQL query to determine gender of customers who purchased a specific product

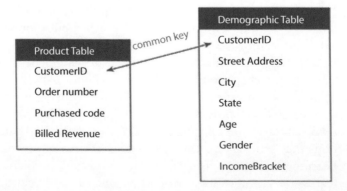

Figure 2.9 Example of schema for RDB of two tables.

Table 2.1 Common SQL commands.

SELECT	Choose records from database
AS	Rename table or column with alias
FROM	Specify table we're pulling from
WHERE	Filter query to match a condition
JOIN	Combine rows from 2 or more tables
AND	Combine conditions in query. All must be met
OR	Combine conditions in query. One must be met
LIKE	Search for patterns in a column
IN	Specify multiple values when using WHERE
IS NULL	Return only rows with a NULL value
LIMIT	Limit the number of rows returned
CASE	Return value on a specified condition
GREATE	Create TABLE, DATABASE, INDEX or VIEW
DROP	Delete TABLE, DATABASE, or INDEX
UPDATE	Update table data
DELETE	Delete rows from a table
ALTER TABLE	Add/Remove columns from table
GROUP BY	Group rows that have same value into summery rows
ORDER BY	Set order of result. Use DECS to reverse order
HAVING	Same as WEHERE but used for aggregate functions
SUM	Return sum of column
AVG	Return average of column
MIN	Return min value of column
MAX	Return max value of column
COUNT	Count number of rows

Table 2.2 Common SQL operations.

Create		Update Table	
CREATE DATABBASE MyDatabase; CREATE INDEX IndexName ON TableName(col1). CREATE TABLE OurTable (id int; name varchar(12));		UPDATE OurTable Set col1 = 56 WHERE col2 = 'something' ;	
		Delete Records	
		DELETE FROM Ourtable WHERE col1 = 'something';	
Delete		**Add/Remove Column**	
DROP DATABASE OurDatabase; DROP TABLE OurTable;		ALTER TABLE OurTable ADD col5 int; ALTER TABLE OurTable DROP COLUMN col5;	

Table 2.3 Common SQL order of execution.

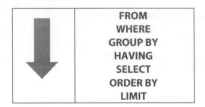

Select CustomerID, State, Gender, Product from
        "demographic table", "product table" where
        Product= XXYY

In this section, we will provide a summary of SQL language commands, operations, order of operations, and several illustrative examples. For instance, the following table (Table 2.1), summarizes the most common SQL commands that are frequently used by data scientists.

Also, the following table (Table 2.2), shows the basic data definition and modification operations for each relational database management system.

Moreover, regarding the order of execution precedence, SQL commands have different execution priorities. The following table (Table 2.3) shows the typical order of execution in SQL starting from top to bottom.

Furthermore, a key SQL operation is used frequently by the data scientist is the Join operation which is used to combine rows from two or more tables. Join operation has four different variants need to be familiarized prior to use, including Inner Join, Left Join, Right Join, and Outer Join. These are summarized and illustrated as follows.

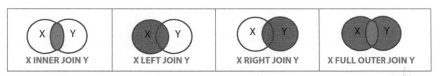

Finally, to gain more insight of the aforesaid commands and operations, we provide a number of examples on SQL statements.

- Select all rows from table with filter applied: SELECT * FROM tbl WHERE col11 > 5;
- Select first 10 rows for 2 columns: SELECT col1, col2 FROM tbl LIMIT 10;
- Select all rows with multiple filters applied: SELECT *FROM tbl WHERE col1 > 5 AND col2 <2;
- Select all rows from col1 and col2 ordering by col1: SELECT col1, col2 FROM tbl ORDER BY 1;
- Return count of rows in table: SELEC COUNT(*) FROM tbl;
- Return sum of col1: SELECT SUM(col1) FROM tbl;
- Return max value from col1: SELECT MAX(col1) FROM tbl;
- Computer summary statistics by grouping col2: SELECT AVG(col1) FROM tbl GROUP BY col2;
- Combine data from two tables using a left join : SELECT * FROM tbl1 AS t1; LEFT JOIN tbl2 AS t2 ON t2. col1 = t1.col1;
- Aggregate and filter results: SELECT Col1, AVG(col2) = AVG(col3) AS total FROM tbl GROUP BY col1 HAVING total > 2
- Implementation of CASE statement: SELECT col1 CASE WHERE col1 > 10 THEN "more than 10", WHERE col1 < 10 THEN "less than 10" ELSE "10" END AS NewColumnName FROM tbl;

2.6   Microsoft Excel for Data Science

Microsoft Excel grasps a distinctive place amid the principal tools of data science. Microsoft Excel was formerly developed to work like an unpretentious spreadsheet with predefined visualization graphs and wide range and diverse formulas. Recently, Microsoft Excel has been extended to provide much more data analytics and visualization tools such as charting, statistical plots, regression, pivot tables, forecasting, outlier boxes, macros and many more [14]. In this section, we will not start from scratch, instead we assume that the reader is familiar with the basic use of Microsoft Excel such as data entry, using common plots (linear charts, bar charts, pie charts, … etc.), using Microsoft formula tool provided by the Microsoft Excel menu bar, saving, printing, selection, sorting, … etc. Here we provide some important tools with examples that are important for every data scientist to learn and use.

2.6.1   Detection of Outliers in Data Sets Using Microsoft Excel

Outliers are abnormal observation records that appear distant from other observation records which they disrupt the technique of producing the ordinary data. Outlier detection has a wide range of applications such as: intrusion detection, telecom fraud detection, customer segmentation, credit card fraud detection and detecting measurement errors [15]. Figure 2.10 illustrates a simplified example for outliers in the data set.

Outliers in dataset can fall in one of three classes: overall outliers, relative outliers, and communal outliers. In overall (global) outliers, the abnormal observations are anomalous regarding nearly all the observations in the dataset feature. In relative (contextual) outliers, the abnormal observations are anomalous regarding a specific context/season. In communal (collective) outliers, the abnormal observations are anomalous regarding their

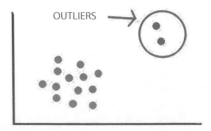

Figure 2.10 Simplified example for outliers in the dataset.

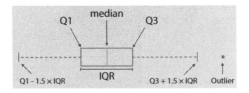

Figure 2.11 Algorithm of outlier detection used in Tukey labeling.

appearance in sequential nearby manner with almost equal values which are anomalous regarding nearly all the observations in the dataset feature. Outliers' detection in dataset can be developed using different statistical models such as Tukey boxplot outlier labeling. Figure 2.11 shows the algorithm used by Tukey to detect the outliers, and can be described as follows:

- How far min and max values are from 25 (*1st quartile: Q1*) & 75 (*3rd quartile: Q3*) percentiles.
- Distance between Q1 & Q3 is called ***inter-quartile range (IQR) and*** defines the extent of data.
- Rule of thumb: Always Calculate A & B where:

$$A = Q1 - 1.5 * IQR \text{ and } B = Q3 + 1.5 * IQR.$$

- Now check, if your smallest value is lower than A, or if your largest value is larger than B ➜ the variable possibly has outliers.

Example (1): Using Boxplot in Microsoft Excel to Detect Outliers
Consider the dataset D = {12, 8, 35, 4, 18, 2, 10, 1, 15, 5, 3}.

- You may start by filling these dataset records into an Excel sheet within the range of cells A1:A11. No need to reorder the data points ascendingly.
- In this example, the median or middle number (8) divides the dataset into two halves: {1, 2, 2, 4, 5} and {10, 12, 15, 18, 35}. The 1st quartile (Q1) is the median of the first half. Q1 = 2. The 3rd quartile (Q3) is the median of the second half. Q3 = 15.
- Now, from Microsoft Excel menus, on the Insert tab, in the Charts group, click the Statistic Chart symbol as shown in the following figure, Figure 2.12 (a) and then Click Box and Whisker.

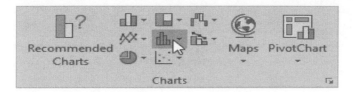

Figure 2.12 Mouse pointer points to statistic chart symbol, and then points box and whisker.

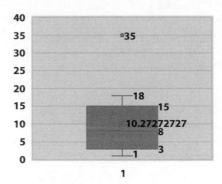

Figure 2.13 Box and whisker with single outlier.

- After selecting the Box and Whisker, this will plot out the Tukey Boxplot as illustrated in Figure 2.13.

According to the figure: the interquartile range (IQR) is identified as the difference between the first quartile (Q1) and the third quartile (Q3) (for instance, in our example IQR = Q3 - Q1 = 15 - 2 = 13). To consider the data point outlier, the value of point should exceed IRQ by 1.5 times either below the first quartile (Q1 - 1.5 * IQR = -17.5) or 1 above the third quartile (Q3 + 1.5 * IQR = 34.5). Thus, in our illustration example, the value (35) is an outlier since its greater than 34.5. Consequently, the upper whisker spreads to the greatest number (18) into this range.

2.6.2 Regression Analysis in Excel Using Microsoft Excel

Regression techniques [16] are mainly used to define the strength of relationship among variables in the target dataset using curve interpolation and then it can be used to predict future values from historical values using curve extrapolation. Two main techniques are commonly used to developed regression models for the datasets: Linear regression and Logistic

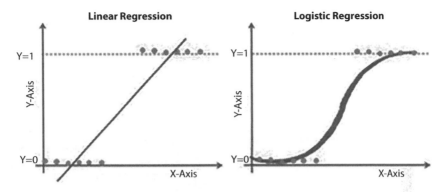

Figure 2.14 Linear regression vs logistic regression.

regression. The idea of both regression techniques is illustrated in Figure 2.14 below.

Example (2): Using Linear regression analysis in Excel

Consider the dataset provided in Table 2.4 below, which represent the amount of worldwide electric energy consumption in (Giga Watt Hour) for the last 40 years from 1981 to 2020 [17]. Please note that (Giga Watt Hour) can be considered as billion kilowatt hours for more familiarity as can be seen in the table where the unit of measurement is used as: Giga Watt Hour = Billion kilowatt hours = KWH * 10^9.

- You may start by filling these dataset records into an Excel sheet within the range of cells A1:A41 (into two columns only, one for year and the other for the energy). After that, select the two columns with your data, including headers. Then, go to the Inset menu, to Charts collection, then select Scatter chart as shown Figure 2.15.
- As a result of previous step, this will enclose a scatter plot in the active excel-sheet, that will look like the plot illustrated in Figure 2.16.

Now, to develop a linear regression for the scatter points in Figure 2.16, we need to produce the line of least square regression by right click on any point and choose to select "Add Trendline" from the perspective menu. This step is shown in Figure 2.17.

On the right panel, select the linear trend line shape and, optionally, check Display Equation on Chart to get your regression formula. As can be seen in Figure 2.18, the linear regression curve has been plotted to fit the

Table 2.4 Worldwide electric energy consumption from 1981 to 2020.

Year	Energy (KWH) * 10^9	Year	Energy (KWH) * 10^9
1981	7,524	2001	13,458
1982	7,825	2002	13,755
1983	8,170	2003	14,052
1984	8,405	2004	14,349
1985	8,658	2005	15,748
1986	8,971	2006	16,045
1987	9,256	2007	16,673
1988	9,540	2008	17,300
1989	9,825	2009	17,928
1990	10,391	2010	18,640
1991	10,513	2011	19,329
1992	10,814	2012	19,719
1993	11,116	2013	20,388
1994	11,418	2014	20,781
1995	11,482	2015	21,227
1996	11,954	2016	21,815
1997	12,249	2017	22,347
1998	12,544	2018	23,000
1999	12,839	2019	23,393
2000	13,277	2020	24,393

maximum number in a linear fashion. Also, within the same right pane, if you go down, you can ask Microsoft Excel to generate the linear equation for the produced regression line/ Trendline as you may ask Microsoft Excel to generate the R2 value for your regression model to express the accuracy of the regression curve in representing the scatter points of your dataset. In this example, we can see that the regression accuracy is almost 97% which

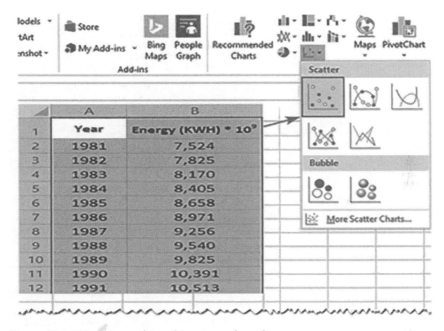

Figure 2.15 Using scatter plot tool in microsoft excel.

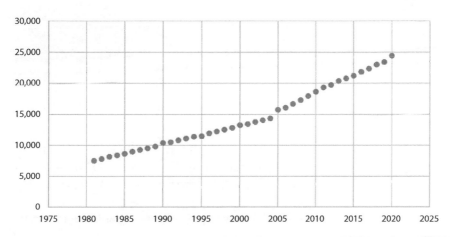

Figure 2.16 The scatter plot for the energy data records provided in Table 2.4.

reveals a conclusion that the identified dataset records are increasing with a linear trend. You may also express the generated curve in terms of the regression equation which can be expressed in this example as follows: $Y = 424.01X - 833696$: Where: Y is the variable used to represent the energy

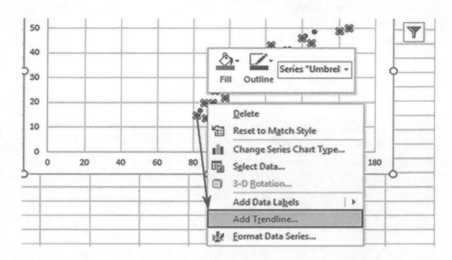

Figure 2.17 "Add Trend line" option for the scatter plot.

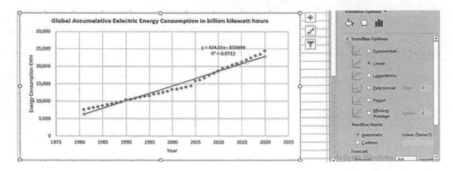

Figure 2.18 Using Linear regression via "Add Trend line" option for the scatter plot.

consumption, and X is the variable used to represent the year. For example, one can check the value of energy consumption at year 2007 by substituting the year value into the equation as follows:

$$Y = 424.01X - 833696 \rightarrow Y = 424.01 * (2007) - 833696 = 17292.07$$

Off course, this is slightly different from the original data point by an error percent of approximately 3.5 %.

Furthermore, one can try other regression techniques and generate the corresponding equation and R^2 score. Note that the accuracy of the used regression method depends on the data distribution and tendency.

Example (3): Using Forecasting Tool Predict Future Values in Microsoft Excel

Consider the previous regression example, one can extend the regression model to forecasting model to predict the future amounts of energy consumption in the next upcoming years [17]. However, in this example,

Table 2.5 Sample dataset: prices of product (X) within 10 consecutive months.

Month	1	2	3	4	5	6	7	8	9	10
Price	22	27	25	30	31	20	28	33	21	26

Figure 2.19 Using forecasting tool in Microsoft Excel.

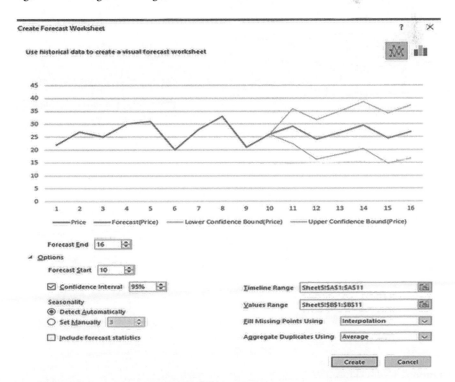

Figure 2.20 Preview of forecasting results.

we will consider different dataset to apply the forecasting tool in Microsoft Excel. Let us consider the data provided in Table 2.5 which express the price changes of product (X) during 10 months' period which can be filled into an Excel sheet into cells A1 to A11.

- You may start by filling these dataset records into an Excel sheet within the range of cells A1:A11. Note no need to sort the dataset points ascendingly, as the forecast tool will do so when visualizing your data and predictions.
- Now select the range of cells A1:A11, and then from the menu bar go to data tab, select Forecast as can be depicted from Figure 2.19.
- After that the following window will show preview of forecasting results. Now, Select Options. Then, change options as you wish such as Start forecast = 10, End forecast = 16. This can be depicted from Figure 2.20.

Month	Price	Forecast(Price)	Lower Confidence Bound(Price)	Upper Confidence Bound(Price)
1	22			
2	27			
3	25			
4	30			
5	31			
6	20			
7	28			
8	33			
9	21			
10	26	26	26.00	26.00
11		29.06597371	22.24	35.89
12		24.04037441	16.40	31.68
13		26.54166546	18.17	34.92
14		29.52746756	20.47	38.58
15		24.50186826	14.81	34.19
16		27.0031593	16.72	37.29

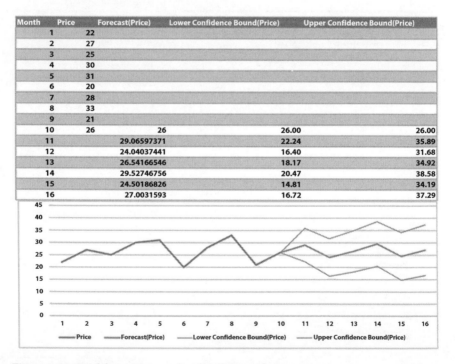

Figure 2.21 Final forecasting results of six future values.

- Now, you may tune up the options according to your application or problem statement. Once finish the configurations, click on create to get the results as shown in Figure 2.21 which shows the forecasting table and plot for six future values. Note that the forecasting tool offers three levels of forecasting confidence, namely, the lower confidence bound, the upper confidence bound and the average confidence bund which is the running forecasting and termed as "Forecast" in Figure 2.21.

2.7   D3.JS for Data Science

D3.js (data-driven document) [18] is an open-source platform comprising many pre-defined classes and functions-based JavaScript that can be used to build any type of data visualization. Typically, D3.js is considered as one of the JavaScript libraries. One of the major capabilities of D3.js is the ability to build dynamic data visualizations that enable users to interact with the data visualization, control the data to show and configure more options in the plots such as: get further data the mouse cursor hovers or clicks over some places within the visualization, realize lively moving visualizations to discover real time data trends and insights generated form changes over time, and select from a diversity of dissimilar moves among the views.

To build up a practical experience of using D3.js, we will develop several examples to comprehend the overall knowledge and skills of D3.js. Also, we advise the reader to refer to (https://www.d3-graph-gallery.com/intro_d3js.html) in order build more complex data visualization graphs and practice the variety of data visualization techniques in an interactive environment. Note that the reader is assumed to be familiar with the following scripting languages and modules as D3.js is built upon those scripting languages, these includes HTML stands for Hypertext Markup Language, CSS stands for Cascading Style Sheet, SVG stands for Scalable Vector Graphic, JavaScript: Technology of World Wide Web (WWW) to enable interactivity in webpages, PhP: Hypertext Preprocessor (sometimes), DOM: Document Object Model. Therefore, in case the reader requires a pre-knowledge on these topics, we recommend the reader to visit the following links for specific and summarized tutorials.

- CSS Tutorial: https://www.d3-graph-gallery.com/intro_d3js.html
- HTML Tutorial: https://www.w3schools.com/css/default.asp/
- JavaScript Tutorial: https://www.w3schools.com/colors/colors_picker.asp
- PHP Tutorial: https://www.w3schools.com/php/default.asp

As for our next examples, make sure to create a folder on the desktop, and inside the folder, create a notepad file to practice the upcoming examples. For every example, make sure to write the D3.js visualization code into the notepad document and then save the document using "save as" option under the extension ".html" inside the same folder of coding. Then, to display the results of your D3.js coding example, double click on the resultant HTML file which will open using your default internet explorer such as google chrome or internet explorer. As for now, let us go ahead with our exploratory examples.

Further configuration can be used in the above example such as:

```
<line x1="0" y1="0" x2="10" y2="10" stroke="black"></line>
<rect x="0" y="0" width="10" height="10"></rect>
<circle cx="5" cy="5" r="5"></circle>
<ellipse cx="10" cy="5" rx="10" ry="5"></ellipse>
<polygon points="0,0 10,5 20,0 20,20 10,15 0,20"></polygon>
<polyline points="0,0 10,5 20,0 20,20 10,15 0,20" stroke="black"></polyline>
<path d="M65,10 a50,25 0 1,0 50,25"></path>
```

2.8   Other Important Tools for Data Science

The other tools of the top ten list for data science are considered as advanced tools, and thus need to be covered in a separate chapter. However, we will familiarize the reader with these tools briefly.

2.8.1   Apache Spark Ecosystem

Apache Spark Ecosystem [19] is a new general framework, developed at AMPLab UC Berkeley and it can leverage the Hadoop ecosystem and solving many of MapReduce shortcomings such as having multiple workflows, having several distributed operations such as: join, union, filter, groupByKey, reduceByKey… etc. Apache Spark supports data analysis, machine learning, graphs, streaming data, etc. It can read/write from a range of data types and allows development in multiple languages. The simplified architecture of Apache Spark Ecosystem is shown in Figure 2.22.

Example (1) Using D3.js to draw basic shapes with title.

D3.js Script

```
<!DOCTYPE html>
<!-- Add a title -->
<h1>Drawing a circle </h1>
<!-- Add a bit of text -->
<p>In this example, we are
going to draw circle and control its colors and dimensions</p>
<!-- Add a svg shape -->
<svg>
   <circle style="fill: #69b3a2" stroke="black" cx=50 cy=50 r=40></circle>
</svg>
```

Output visualization

Drawing a circle
In this example, we are going to draw circle and control its colors and
   dimensions

Example (2) Using D3.js to draw multiple shapes using coordinate system.

D3.js Script

```
<!DOCTYPE html>
<!-- Add a svg area, empty -->
<svg id="dataviz_area" height=200 width=450></svg>
<!-- Load d3.js -->
<script src="https://d3js.org/d3.v4.js"></script>
<script>
var svg = d3.select("#dataviz_area")
svg.append("circle")
   .attr("cx", 2).attr("cy", 2).attr("r", 40).style("fill", "blue");
svg.append("circle")
   .attr("cx", 140).attr("cy", 70).attr("r", 40).style("fill", "red");
svg.append("circle")
   .attr("cx", 300).attr("cy", 100).attr("r", 40).style("fill", "green");
</script>
```

Output visualization

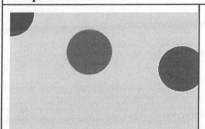

In this example, you may change the
   coordinates of the plot from data to
   pixel (Scales), try the following script.
   Domain ([0, 100]) and .range ([0,
   400]);

2.8.2   MongoDB Data Store System

MongoDB is a source-available cross-platform document-oriented database program [20]. Classified as a NoSQL database program, MongoDB uses JSON-like documents with optional schemas. MongoDB is developed by MongoDB Inc. and licensed under the Server-Side Public License.

Example (3) Using D3.js to perform Data binding to complete a scatterplot.

D3.js Script

```
!DOCTYPE html>
<!-- Add a svg area, empty -->
<div id="scatter_area"></div>
<!-- Load d3.js -->
<script src="https://d3js.org/d3.v4.js"></script>
<script>
// set the dimensions and margins of the graph
var margin = {top: 10, right: 40, bottom: 30, left: 30},
    width = 450 - margin.left - margin.right,
    height = 400 - margin.top - margin.bottom;
// append the svg object to the body of the page
var svG = d3.select("#scatter_area")
  .append("svg")
    .attr("width", width + margin.left + margin.right)
    .attr("height", height + margin.top + margin.bottom)
  .append("g")
    .attr("transform",
          "translate(" + margin.left + "," + margin.top + ")");
// Create data
var data = [ {x:10, y:20}, {x:40, y:90}, {x:80, y:50} ]
// X scale and Axis
var x = d3.scaleLinear()
    .domain([0, 100])          // This is the min and the max of the data: 0 to
100 if percentages
    .range([0, width]);        // This is the corresponding value I want in Pixel
svG
  .append('g')
  .attr("transform", "translate(0," + height + ")")
  .call(d3.axisBottom(x));

// X scale and Axis
var y = d3.scaleLinear()
    .domain([0, 100])          // This is the min and the max of the data: 0 to
100 if percentages
    .range([height, 0]);       // This is the corresponding value I want in
Pixel
svG
  .append('g')
  .call(d3.axisLeft(y));
// Add 3 dots for 0, 50 and 100%
svG
  .selectAll("whatever")
  .data(data)
  .enter()
  .append("circle")
    .attr("cx", function(d){ return x(d.x) })
    .attr("cy", function(d){ return y(d.y) })
    .attr("r", 7)
</script>
```

(Continued)

(*Continued*)

Output visualization

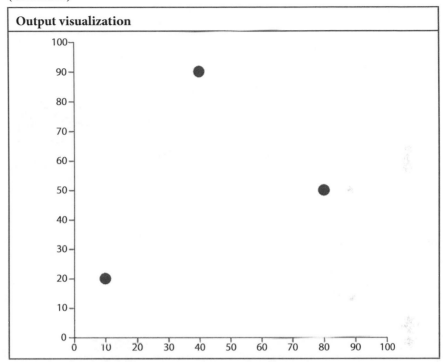

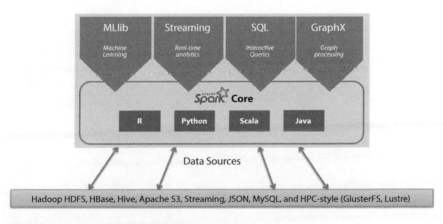

Figure 2.22 Apache spark architecture.

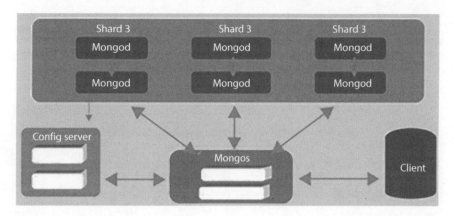

Figure 2.23 MongoDB data store architecture.

The simplified architecture of MongoDB data store system is shown in Figure 2.23.

2.8.3   MATLAB Computing System

MATLAB is a programming and computing platform developed particularly for engineers and scientists for data analytics, algorithms' development, models implementation and creating applications that solve and address several real-life concerns [21]. MATLAB include many toolboxes that are necessary for any data scientist such as deep learning and machine learning, signal processing and communications, image and video processing, test and measurement, computational finance, and computational biology. The simplified architecture of MATLAB Computing System is shown in Figure 2.24.

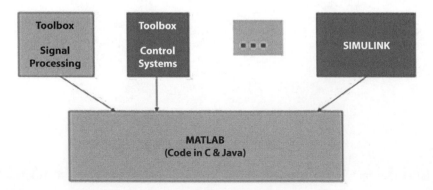

Figure 2.24 MATLAB computing system architecture.

Example (4) Using D3.js to draw a basic histogram.

D3.js Script
Refer to the D3. Js at: https://www.d3-graph-gallery.com/graph/ histogram_basic.html
Output visualization

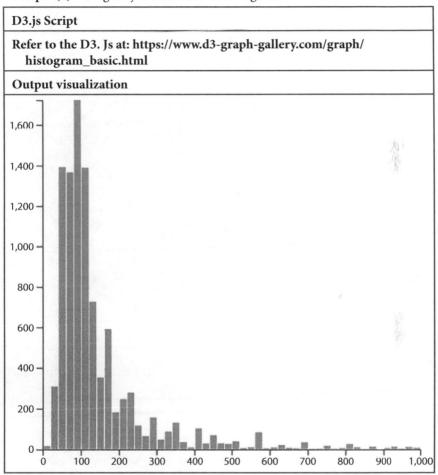

2.8.4   Neo4j for Graphical Database

Neo4j graph database is an Open-source graph database management system developed by Neo4j, Inc. as an ACID (Atomicity, Consistency, Isolation and Durability)-compliant transactional database with native graph storage and processing [22]. The architecture of Neo4j graph database is provided in Figure 2.25. Neo4j is SQL Like easy query language called cypher QL (CQL) that follows property graph data model and contains a user interface (UI) to execute CQL Commands called Neo4j Data Browser. Neo4j It uses Native graph storage that supports exporting of query data to JSON and XLS format and

Example (5)   Using D3.js to draw an Interactive pie chart with input data selector.

D3.js Script	Output visualization
Refer to the D3. Js at: https://www.d3-graph-gallery.com/graph/pie_changeData.html If press data 1 then the plot will show Pie chart related to data 1. If press data 2 then the plot will show Pie chart related to data 2.	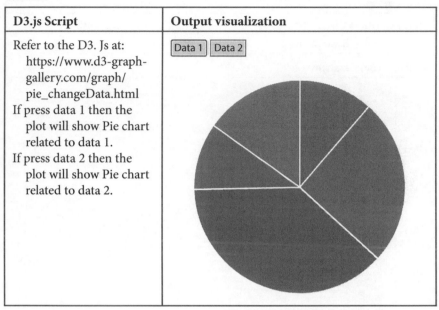

Example (6)   Using D3.js to draw an Interactive Complex Network Graphs.

D3.js Script	Output visualization
Refer to the D3. Js at: https://observablehq.com/@d3/force-directed-graph	

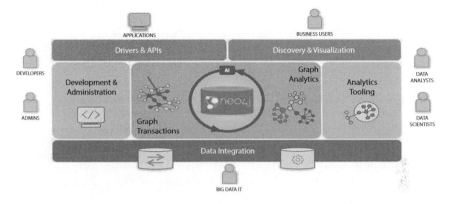

Figure 2.25 Neo4j graph database architecture.

supports two kinds of Java API: Cypher API and Native Java API to develop Java applications.

2.8.5   VMWare Platform for Virtualization

VMWare provides cloud computing and platform virtualization software and services. Its desktop software is a platform independent and can run

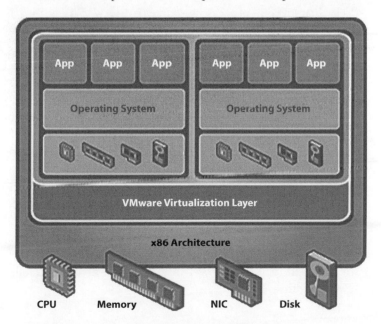

Figure 2.26 VMWare virtualization system architecture.

on Microsoft Windows, Linux, and macOS [23]. It has type 1 hypervisors that run directly on server hardware without requiring an additional underlying operating system. The architecture of VMWare system is provided in Figure 2.26.

2.9 Conclusion

In this chapter, we have addressed several concerns and tools of data science field. A key point to memorize can be summarized as follows:

- Data science is an interdisciplinary area of learning and research that associate the computing techniques, domain expertise, mathematical skills, and knowledge of statistics to excerpt expressive comprehensions from raw data.
- Examples of diverse fields that are employed in data science to drive insights from the tremendous amount of raw data include: statistics, visualization, machine learning, big data, data engineering, and high-performance computing (HPC).
- The Big Data in the data science are commonly characterized the 3Vs: Volume (size is too big, more that Terabytes), Velocity (speed of processing, range from law to high speed), and Variety (heterogeneous, diversity of sources, formats, quality, and structures).
- To cope with the various data sources, data science commonly works with three data varieties including structured data, unstructured data, and semi-structured data.
- The top ten tools for data science include: Python Programming Language, R Programming Language, SQL Programming Language for relational database, Microsoft Excel for statistical modeling, D3.js scripting language for data visualizations, MongoDB data store system, Neo4j for graphical databases, and VMWare platform for virtualization.
- Python is a platform independent general purpose programming language that can be used to implement various types of applications such as web applications, artificial intelligence applications.

- The most common datatypes of Python include numbers, strings, lists, and dictionaries. And the most common libraries of Python include: NumPy, SciPy, Pandas, and Matplotlib.
- R is a platform independent and open source and publicly available statistical programming language that are extensively used in to develop solutions in data science.
- The most common datatypes of R include numbers, strings, lists, and dictionaries. And the most common libraries of R include: ggplot2, data.table, Shiny, knitr and forecast.
- SQL is a simplest, fastest, customary, and publicly available language for creating, updating, and querying relational database (RDB) systems.
- The most common command of SQL includes Select, Limit, Drop, and LIKE. The most common Operations of SQL include Create, Update, Delete, and Add/Remove Column.
- Microsoft Excel has been established to provide modest spreadsheet with predefined visualization graphs and wide range and diverse formulas. It has been recently prolonged for data science to provide much more data analytics and visualization tools such as charting, statistical plots, regression, pivot tables, forecasting, outlier boxes, macros... etc.
- The most common examples of data science applications that can be developed using Microsoft Excel include outlier detection, time series modeling regression and forecasting.
- D3.js is an open-source platform with many pre-defined classes and functions-based JavaScript that can be used to build any type of data visualization.
- Examples of data visualization models that can be developed using D3.js include Distribution visualization (such as Density, Histogram, Boxplot, ... etc.), Correlation visualization (such as Scatter, Heatmap, Correlogram, ... etc.), Ranking visualization (such as Bar plot, Spider/Radar, Word cloud, ... etc.), part of whole visualization (such as Treemap, Doughnut, Pie chart, ... etc.), Evolution visualization (such as Line plot, Area, Stacked area, ... etc.), and many more.
- Other advanced tools for data science can be discussed further in a separate chapter, such as Apache Spark Ecosystem, MongoDB Datastore system, MATLAB Computing System, Neo4j for Graphical Database, and VMWare Platform for Virtualization.

References

1. Grus, J., *Data Science from Scratch: First Principles with Python*, 2nd edition, O'Reilly Media, NY, USA, May 2019.
2. Meitiner, P. and Seneviratne, P., *Beginning Data Science IoT and AI On Single Board Computers: Core Skills and Real-World Application*, Apress, NY, USA, 2020.
3. O'Neil, C. and Schutt, R., *Doing Data Science, Straight Talk from The Frontline*, O'Reilly, NY, USA, 2014.
4. Gessler, N. and Shrivastava, A., *Data Science & Big Data Analytics: Discovering, Analyzing, Visualizing and Presenting Data*, EMC Education Services. John Wiley & Sons, Inc., NY, USA, May 2015.
5. Cao, L., Data science: a comprehensive overview. *ACM Comput. Surv. (CSUR)*, 50, 3, 1–42, 2017.
6. Erraissi, A. and Belangour, A., Data sources and ingestion big data layers: Meta-modeling of key concepts and features. *Int. J. Eng. Technol.*, 7, 4, 3607–3612, 2018.
7. Havill, J., *Discovering Computer Science: Interdisciplinary Problems, Principles, and Python Programming*, CRC Press, FL, USA, 2020.
8. Grus, J., *Data science from scratch: first principles with python*, O'Reilly Media, NY, USA, 2019.
9. Randles, B.M. *et al.*, Using the Jupyter notebook as a tool for open science: An empirical study. *2017 ACM/IEEE Joint Conference on Digital Libraries (JCDL)*, IEEE, 2017.
10. Mount, J. and Zumel, N., *Practical data science with R*, Simon and Schuster, NY, USA, 2019.
11. Baumer, B.S., Kaplan, D.T., Horton, N.J., *Modern data science with R*, CRC Press, NY, USA, 2017.
12. Abu Al-Haija, Q., Mao, Q., Al Nasr, K., Forecasting the number of monthly active facebook and twitter worldwide users using ARMA model. *J. Comput. Sci.*, 15, 4, 499–510, 2019, https://doi.org/10.3844/jcssp.2019.499.510.
13. Krishnarajanagar, G. and Hiriyannaiah, S., Comparative study of different in-memory (no/new) SQL databases, in: *Advances in Computers*, vol. 109, pp. 133–156, Elsevier, Amsterdam, Netherlands, 2018.
14. Greco, C., *Data Science Tools: R• Excel• KNIME• OpenOffice*, Stylus Publishing, LLC, VA, USA, 2020.
15. Wang, H., Bah, M.J., Hammad, M., Progress in outlier detection techniques: A survey. *IEEE Access*, 7, 107964–108000, 2019.
16. Al-Haija, Q.A. and Nasr, K.A., Supervised regression study for electron microscopy data. *2019 IEEE International Conference on Bioinformatics and Biomedicine (BIBM)*, pp. 2661–2668, 2019.
17. Abu Al-Haija, Q.A., Stochastic estimation framework for yearly evolution of worldwide electricity consumption. *Forecasting. MDPI*, 3, 2, 256–266, 2021.

18. Meeks, E., *D3. js in Action: Data visualization with JavaScript*, Simon and Schuster, NY, USA, 2017.
19. Karau, H. and Warren, R., *High performance Spark: best practices for scaling and optimizing Apache Spark*, O'Reilly Media, Inc., NY, USA, 2017.
20. Aluvalu, R. and Jabbar, M.A., Handling data analytics on unstructured data using MongoDB. *IET Conference Proceedings*, pp. 41 (5 pp.)–41 (5 pp.), 2018.
21. Mikhailov, E.E., *Programming with MATLAB for scientists: A beginner's introduction*, CRC Press, FL, USA, 2018.
22. Wiese, L., Data analytics with graph algorithms–A hands-on tutorial with Neo4J. *BTW 2019–Workshopband*, 2019.
23. Chao, L., *Virtualization and Private Cloud with VMware Cloud Suite*, CRC Press, FL, USA, 2017.

Data Modeling as Emerging Problems of Data Science

Mahyuddin K. M. Nasution[1]* and Marischa Elveny[2]

[1]Data Science & Computational Intelligence Research Group, Universitas Sumatera Utara, Jl Universitas, Medan, Sumatera Utara, Indonesia
[2]Data Science & Artificial Intelligence Study Program, Fasilkom-TI, Universitas Sumatera Utara, Jl Universitas, Medan, Sumatera Utara, Indonesia

Abstract

Science considers data differently according to importance and time. So far, data has opened the eyes of many people through data science, and a variety of problems arise, especially with the daily growth of data with large sizes cause processing is not easy. On another side, information comes from processing data, while knowledge that is the backbone of a decision has an information basis. Since the beginning, computers have provided a solution to data processing, but the processing requires data modeling. A data model that structures data into a form that is easy to process. Information technology or computers continue to change and give birth to many advances. Computer networks and the Internet have caused communication traffic between computer users to scatter data in various storage places of the server and everywhere according to their interests. So, it is not easy to collect them back into one unity that describes the current state of the data that talks about something. Moreover, not only has data become so large and diverse, it tends to be generally unstructured. This chapter reveals data modeling as a matter of data science, revealing the possibility of a new side of the data.

Keywords: Data model, big data, database, attribute, relationship, record, table, file

*Corresponding author: mahyuddin@usu.ac.id

Archana Patel, Narayan C. Debnath and Bharat Bhusan (eds.) Data Science with Semantic Technologies: Theory, Practice, and Application, (71–90) © 2022 Scrivener Publishing LLC

3.1   Introduction

From a scientific point of view, data, both small and large, underlies all decision making. However, whether or not a decision is accurate depends on the level of confidence in the data. Data requires organizing that meets the interests of stakeholders to the data, both individually and organizationally, both in terms of theory and technology, or related to the size, diversity, and another dimension of the data itself. From the human side, data, both as information and as knowledge, requires processing and interpretation in such a way that the results lead to policies that guide the direction of the right decision [1].

Data that describes an object and what is in human thought consists of the smallest unities that give meaning. Data has a thought space: metadata/variables. Along with that, data has a meaning: value. Another, in the data, reveals a relationship either linearly or not. Naturally, there are rules that recruit data and its relationships into a data organization formula. Accordingly, data requires design and modeling, which results in data models. Each data model has its own schema that governs the relationships between data and the relationships between objects, but each data model has its own implementation into the storage based on its technology. It is a fact or just an assumption that when technology changes, the data model also changes, and the data model grows according to the capabilities of the technology that adapts it [2]. The presence of Internet technology, then the Web, has formed a different data model, and the result that naturally follows is the accumulation of data into storage and building big data. There are already data sets, but they are meaningless to big data which continues to increase in size [3]. Along with this growth, various problems arise, not only related to data modeling so that the data is easy to manage, but the data is scattered in various storage places like old archives. This paper reveals several alternative solutions and is also accompanied by other problems.

3.2   Data

Data as a noun [4], based on Webster dictionary, is a word that refers to *things known or assumed; facts or figures from which conclusions can be inferred; information.* This concept describes that data is the subject of human thought. In that mind, humans indirectly give the dimension of space. Mathematics provides formality by involving variables as references and values as content. In another status, the variable can be expressed as metadata. Metadata consists of data elements related to the domain and the smallest unit of information at the level of the best granularity representation. As objects, data is characterized by atomicity. In simple terms, data is an expression for the smallest unit that has meaning. Suppose the atoms in the periodic table of elements, each of the atoms has a name, a symbol, and other characteristics. Take, for example, an atom named hydrogen with the symbol H and the atom number or number of protons in the atomic nucleus is 1. An atom as an object has what is called properties, namely na = Hydrogen, sa = H and nm = 1, where na is the variable that refers to the atom name, sa is the variable that refers to the atom's symbol, and nm is the variable that refers to the atom number [5].

As something known, data are things related to any object, which allows the presence of another subject in human thought, namely the relationship between or with anything related to that object. The real world (reality) is an environment of data. For example, any organization is an environment where the activities of designing to developing for carrying out data organizing continue. In this case, each object is characterized by its properties. It represents a relationship between objects and with its characteristics. The relationship serves as a mapping. The set of objects or the characteristics set consists of different elements. Mathematically, a mapping allows the presence of a function, which defines the relationship between objects or the relationship between objects and properties. Thus, Table 3.1 for example, indicates the relationship between an atom and its properties: $sa \leftarrow na$ and $sa \leftarrow nm$. The formulation means that there is an assignment of na and nm to sa. A concept provides a simplified way of modeling data. That is, a way to understand the data as a whole. For it, a schema explains the related things: elements, relationships, and a model [6].

Table 3.1 Atoms and characteristics.

Name	Number	Symbol
Hydrogen	1	H
Helium	2	He
⋮	⋮	⋮
Oganesson	118	Og

3.2.1   Unstructured Data

After prehistoric times, the presence of alphabet letters and paper has caused the encoding of the subject of human thought to be in increasing progress. Data has many forms of recording, including on scattered sheets of paper. Then the sheets are grouped into a folder, and a set of folders is traditionally in a closet or filing cabinet. The grouping of data is guided by a partitions/limiter or later known as a catalog. Organizing data like this raises several problems [7]: (a) data is isolated in separate sheets, causing difficulty for accessing it; (b) there are the same or similar copies, either in partial or complete, in many different places. It is called duplication, which makes customizing difficult; (c) physically, the data has a structure according to the first time it was written on a sheet of paper, causing difficulties in adjusting the data structure. It is called data dependence; (d) the writing format on the sheet of paper is also not uniform. Various arrangements are certainly not harmonious (incompatible).

The presence of technology, such as computer hardware and software, which supports the development of computer science, has turned cabinets into storage memory with limited capacity but adequate ease to collect data. Filing-cabinet has changed to a directory, then there are subdirectories, …, to files containing data or descriptions. However, the computer is still a collection of applications that provide services for end-users that generate report after report and the issues carry over indirectly into the computer file today, where each application declares and manages its data. In general, in this case, the data is declared unstructured, and indirectly, it has shifted the perspective of computer users to data. Unstructured data is considered as data that does not have a specific schema or has no organization in its structure.

3.2.2   Semistructured Data

Semistructured data is considered as data that does not follow a formal structure, but it uses intuitive metadata (tag). A formal structure is a structure with a schema that already has the recognition of its organization as a database, but an atom periodic table of elements is semistructured data, see Figure 3.1. Semistructured presents an internal organization that makes it easy to process according to the side of the interest. Some of the smallest unities, call them as *data items*, have meaning. Placing data items such that where there is a separation between one another but are still in the same file. Separators such as commas or semicolons, for example, are used to signify data unity, such as denoting the following set of integers

Periodic table

Group	1 Hydrogen & alkali metals	2 Alkaline earth metals	3	4	5	6	7	8	9	10	11	12	13	14	15 Pnictogens	16 Chalcogens	17 Halogens	18 Noble gases
Period 1	Hydrogen 1 H 1.008																	Helium 2 He 4.0026
2	Lithium 3 Li 6.94	Beryllium 4 Be 9.0122											Boron 5 B 10.81	Carbon 6 C 12.011	Nitrogen 7 N 14.007	Oxygen 8 O 15.999	Fluorine 9 F 18.998	Neon 10 Ne 20.180
3	Sodium 11 Na 22.990	Magnesium 12 Mg 24.305											Aluminium 13 Al 26.982	Silicon 14 Si 28.085	Phosphorus 15 P 30.974	Sulfur 16 S 32.06	Chlorine 17 Cl 35.45	Argon 18 Ar 39.95
4	Potassium 19 K 39.098	Calcium 20 Ca 40.078	Scandium 21 Sc 44.956	Titanium 22 Ti 47.867	Vanadium 23 V 50.942	Chromium 24 Cr 51.996	Manganese 25 Mn 54.938	Iron 26 Fe 55.845	Cobalt 27 Co 58.933	Nickel 28 Ni 58.693	Copper 29 Cu 63.546	Zinc 30 Zn 65.38	Gallium 31 Ga 69.723	Germanium 32 Ge 72.630	Arsenic 33 As 74.922	Selenium 34 Se 78.971	Bromine 35 Br 79.904	Krypton 36 Kr 83.798
5	Rubidium 37 Rb 85.468	Strontium 38 Sr 87.62	Yttrium 39 Y 88.906	Zirconium 40 Zr 91.224	Niobium 41 Nb 92.906	Molybdenum 42 Mo 95.95	Technetium 43 Tc [97]	Ruthenium 44 Ru 101.07	Rhodium 45 Rh 102.91	Palladium 46 Pd 106.42	Silver 47 Ag 107.87	Cadmium 48 Cd 112.41	Indium 49 In 114.82	Tin 50 Sn 118.71	Antimony 51 Sb 121.76	Tellurium 52 Te 127.60	Iodine 53 I 126.90	Xenon 54 Xe 131.29
6	Caesium 55 Cs 132.91	Barium 56 Ba 137.33	Lutetium 71 Lu 174.97	Hafnium 72 Hf 178.49	Tantalum 73 Ta 180.95	Tungsten 74 W 183.84	Rhenium 75 Re 186.21	Osmium 76 Os 190.23	Iridium 77 Ir 192.22	Platinum 78 Pt 195.08	Gold 79 Au 196.97	Mercury 80 Hg 200.59	Thallium 81 Tl 204.38	Lead 82 Pb 207.2	Bismuth 83 Bi 208.98	Polonium 84 Po [209]	Astatine 85 At [210]	Radon 86 Rn [222]
7	Francium 87 Fr [223]	Radium 88 Ra [226]	Lawrencium 103 Lr [266]	Rutherfordium 104 Rf [267]	Dubnium 105 Db [268]	Seaborgium 106 Sg [269]	Bohrium 107 Bh [270]	Hassium 108 Hs [269]	Meitnerium 109 Mt [278]	Darmstadtium 110 Ds [281]	Roentgenium 111 Rg [282]	Copernicium 112 Cn [285]	Nihonium 113 Nh [286]	Flerovium 114 Fl [289]	Moscovium 115 Mc [290]	Livermorium 116 Lv [293]	Tennessine 117 Ts [294]	Oganesson 118 Og [294]

* Lanthanide	Lanthanum 57 La 138.91	Cerium 58 Ce 140.12	Praseodymium 59 Pr 140.91	Neodymium 60 Nd 144.24	Promethium 61 Pm [145]	Samarium 62 Sm 150.36	Europium 63 Eu 151.96	Gadolinium 64 Gd 157.25	Terbium 65 Tb 158.93	Dysprosium 66 Dy 162.50	Holmium 67 Ho 164.93	Erbium 68 Er 167.26	Thulium 69 Tm 168.93	Ytterbium 70 Yb 173.05
** Actinide	Actinium 89 Ac [227]	Thorium 90 Th 232.04	Protactinium 91 Pa 231.04	Uranium 92 U 238.03	Neptunium 93 Np [237]	Plutonium 94 Pu [244]	Americium 95 Am [243]	Curium 96 Cm [247]	Berkelium 97 Bk [247]	Californium 98 Cf [251]	Einsteinium 99 Es [252]	Fermium 100 Fm [257]	Mendelevium 101 Md [258]	Nobelium 102 No [259]

Figure 3.1 Periodic table of atoms. (Sources: https://en.wikipedia.org/wiki/Periodic_table).

$\{\ldots,-2,-1,0,1,2,\ldots\}$. Thus, semistructured data have different schemas, which place relationships between data in various forms. Classical data types, which follow arithmetic concepts [8], are not fully applicable to traditional data types: strings, arrays, or matrices. The impediment to its implementation is the limit of the technology's ability to represent it, such as integers n less than 2^8, 2^{16}, 2^{32}, or 2^{64}, …. The interpretation of classical data types by computer science is still a problem in many computing activities. It is a result of the weaknesses of hardware and software technology as a legacy of arithmetic. However, more modern data types appear as part of semistructured data such as images, audio, video, or data streams originating from electronic devices.

Often the presence of semistructured data is on request immediately. That is, for revealing something in real time. However, the presence of an adjustment request to a data item or entity will have an effect. An effect to make things better. Not only will the data structure change but it will also change the accessing and processing program. A model for semistructured data that does not cause the access program to change is a model in tabular form. In other respects, it is also called a database as a result of processing the data model. A *database* is an organized collection of data that is generally stored and accessed electronically from a computer system [9].

3.2.3   Structured Data

A table representing structured data, like a worksheet or spreadsheet, is a data model consisting of columns and rows, which is considered a database. The table is a summary of the range of data items and the relationships between them. The arrangement of columns or rows may be like the atomic periodic table of elements or a relational database, but a relational database does not consist of a table alone. The table is a simple description of the database, so the table is the first step to designing a relational database, that is, a database based on the property of the relations. Therefore, a relational database is represented by more than one table [10].

In a database, an entity is an object that is unique and recognizable in a given environment. Each entity has characteristics. A characteristic is a specification that defines the property of an entity. Characteristics that describe an entity are called *attributes*, or according to their position also known as *field* or *data field*. While *record* refers to all data related to an entity or activity. Figure 3.2 shows a schema of attribute, record, field—one row of data is one record. A set of records, as the requirement of an entity, organizes into a file or table. So, the concept of a database is a collection

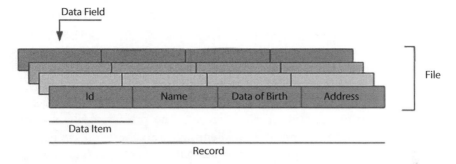

Figure 3.2 Schema of data item, data field, record and file (Sources: https://www. researchgate.net/publication/344074297_Pangkalan_Data_Konsep_dan_Definisi).

of files/tables. However, the modeling data is by organizing files/tables. In order to, it does not into traps of interests that come from any organization. Then, normalization will do to get a relational database. However, there is no official standard relational database, yet one that does not change when dealing with the essence of data in any organization. An issue that continues to carry over into data science. Through concepts of sharing data within an organization was following the level of access allowed.

3.2.4   Hybrid (Un/Semi)-Structured Data

After the presence of computer networks, once again there is a shift in the perspective of data. Initially, the data was protected in the organizational shell or privacy, but by computer networks, there is a shadow shell, namely the organization of computers locally connected to a global network. Logically, data can flow out through the shadow shell. Organizational struggles to protect and defend each other's data unwittingly give rise to cyber wars to maintain or fight over data, including to destroy the enemy's shadow shell. Therefore, following the shift change after a change occurs between determining whether to strengthen data protection or protection against shadow shells, changing the concept of data modeling and data modeling. The reason is that the tendency to shift the concept to practical leads to data sharing. On the other hand, on various occasions, the end-users of computer networks record their data according to the provided *template*. However, some of them try to differ both in the structure and content of the data. It results in a mix of data organization: from unstructured data to structured data, which refer to as hybrid structured data. A data modeling challenge is one of the studies in data science.

Furthermore, in the name of improving human welfare, technology continues to grow and develop. The presence of the internet and web technology has spurred the emergence of virtual organizations that lure people to express information about themselves by increasing human dependence on open applications of these organizations. Virtual organizations are engaged in various interests, such as Facebook as a social media, Grab as an online transportation application, ... The privacy shells of many end-users are gradually fused and integrated into the open application environment. To some extent, organizational shells blend almost imperceptibly into application shells prepared by cyber organizations. End users have unknowingly submitted bits and pieces of information about them into applications. The cyber organizations encode it in various types ranging from numbers, characters or strings, images, audio, video, or other: information streams. The encoding consists of various structures: plaintext, hypertext, tables, online databases, and consists of files. Some of the data is in the system log, but most information is in open files. Although the web provides tags for identifying its content, and thus the web is considered a smart documents. Is the available data ready to provide information following the wishes of end-users for the right decision-making? Various open applications have emerged to try to answer this problem. Each of those open applications has its data model and cannot but be a problem also in data science.

3.2.5   Big Data

In the information age, data flow is recorded into open applications according to their attractiveness, which in accumulation continues to grow. In terms of data models, a lot of tools record data into their storage. Some tools connect to computer networks through the Internet of Things (IoT). By it, IoT is part of the Internet. The information space created by the framework, for which the Internet and the Web have consisted of platforms containing large and more large data, known as Big Data [11]. Big data is a term that refers to massive data sets that have a large, more varied, and complex structure with difficulties to store, analyze and visualize for advanced processes or results. Big data has the following characteristics [12]: (a) Volume-Scale: the size of data in storage; (b) Velocity-Change: data dynamics according to its growth; (c) Variety-Diversity: data differences in all respects; (d) Valence-Relation: data linkage follows the interests of both the source and the destination; (e) Veracity-Heterogeneity: quality and status of grouped elements to derive data; (f) Value-Behavior: the quality of the true level of the data.

Science organizes data in terms of its framework, which makes data modeling dependent on the methodology of that science. Of course, this results in a variety of inharmonious organizations. When big data is present, this disharmony still leaves various problems. Something in hang and set the constraints on the design of the later (big)-database. Of course, not only perspective side keep shifts but also the effects to the scientific framework. Complexity increases as the cause of a tendency for the appearance of data models to be redundant or intersect to come from different interpretations of data modeling. The presence of data science is bridging the different structures of big data, and this requires a new paradigm of (big)-data modeling [13].

3.3   Data Model Design

Every shift from concept, theory, or implementation of data is related to adjustment. More, or less the adjustment is due to a change. While the paradigm refers to and to the change. Therefore, to meet the demands of all these changes, data modeling requires a design. One of the paradigms related to data modeling is data model design. Data modeling is considered to be high-level design and as an abstraction. A concept design is known as schema, which adopts user interests. The design starts from the basic concept. Generally, the basic concepts come from understanding terms and definitions, which form the basis for understanding data and modeling, namely (a) object—something that corresponds to things found in the real world, or something that has a state (data) and behavior (a coding); (b) entity—a single, identifiable, separate object. Something that refers to different individuals, organizations, systems, bits of data, or even system components that are considered significant in and of themselves; (c) characteristic—distinguishing characteristics, qualities, or properties; (d) attribute—a specification that declares the properties of an object, element, or file; (e) data item—something that describes the atomic state of a certain object regarding a certain property at a certain point in time; (f) data field—an area at a fixed or known location in data units such as records, message headers, or computer instructions that have a purpose and are usually fixed in size; (g) data model—an abstraction of the arrangement of data elements and standardizing the relationship with each other and with the properties of real-world entities; (h) database—the process of producing a descriptive diagram of the relationship between the various types of information to be stored in the storage.

Conceptual data modeling is a legal action of developing a conceptual schema from a data model according to user needs. The target of conceptual data modeling is to assess the available content of different information from the structure in which it stores data. Data modeling produces a data model. After the conceptual design as the first stage, the second stage is to reveal data, relationships, and constraints for data modeling. It is to summarize the details, where the result of the data modeling process is a formal representation in the form of a structure or a database. Conceptually, data modeling requires a framework with the purpose is to anticipate possible constraints from storage, adapting to the requirements of the analysis, and providing processing directions [14]. The data model has a classification of representations in storage, namely relational and nonrelational.

1. Relational data model: a database model uses two-dimensional tables, and there is a relationship between each table (schema). Each R table consists of rows L and columns C where the table has a representation in a data file. Tables and relationships between tables involve ranges. A conceptual series is tied to the structured query language (SQL) of the database, in which there is a high-level description of the database structure.

2. Nonrelational data model: A database model does not require a schema and has no relationships for any data or table organization. In this model, the schema concept is tied to an unstructured query language (NoSQL), in which its implementation occurs at the higher level of the structure of the data model.

Thus, conceptual data modeling has the same impact on relational and nonrelational data models. The second stage involves logical design to represent the database in a data model. The third stage involves a physical design to state storage structure, file organization, or indexing techniques. Logical data modeling is a logical schema development process based on conceptual schemas. The logical schema describes the data structure, managing it according to the data model, whether the schema is relational or nonrelational. In other words, all relational or nonrelational databases in the logical design stage are presented as a single file of the data model where the language software (programming) executes after the data model becomes a file or database.

Physical data modeling is a process of developing the physical schema of the database following the previous data modeling. The physical design describes the data structure. A structure has an implementation in software from a relational or nonrelational data model. This modeling is to describe the structure of the storage and effective methods to access them, namely metadata (variables), data types, and data type sizes. For example, if R_1 consists of the attributes a_0, a_1, a_2, R_2 consists of the attributes a_3, a_4, and R_3 consists of the attributes a_5, a_6, then the creation relational tables or databases through a structured query language (SQL). But the simplicity of engaging a structured query language is different from engaging an unstructured query language (NoSQL). NoSQL tends to follow the schema available from nonrelational data models.

3.4   Data Modeling

Through the concept of objects, entities, attributes, ..., data modeling involves the relationship between entities or between attributes. Suppose for the entity set $\{o_i | i = 1, 2, ...\}$, and with the possible attributes set $\{a_j | j = 1, ..., m\}_i$. An entity o_1, for example, has attributes $\{a_1, a_2, a_3, ..., m_1\}$ that support the existence of that entity. Between one attribute with another attribute on any entity has a relationship. The relationship assigns an attribute to another attribute and declares it as ←, i.e. $u_1 \leftarrow a_2$ $a_1 \leftarrow a_3$ or something else. In this example, a_1 is to the left of ←, while a_2 and a_3 are to the right of ←. This concept states that it is possible to have functional dependencies between attributes. *Functional dependency* (FD) is purely one or more attributes that uniquely determine the value of one or more other attributes [15]. All of these attributes support each other to describe an entity. When an attribute becomes a characteristic of an entity, the other attributes one by one compliment them for that entity. Likewise, there are one or more attributes that become the identity of the entity. An attribute a_0 in $a_0 \leftarrow a_1$ is an attribute with a unique data value that refers to that entity. As such, the entity identifier is referred to as *key* and is used to combine two or more relationships based on matching identification.

3.4.1   Records-Based Data Model

A data model is a shared collection of related data that is used to support a particular entity. This data model includes the concept of representing data in a way that is closest to the way the data is received, for example, the entity-relationship model, which involves entities, attributes, and relationships. In general, the model is referred to as a record-based logical data model. This model naturally determines that each attribute that represents data is linearly related to one another, for example $a_0 \leftarrow a_1 \leftarrow a_2 \leftarrow \ldots \leftarrow a_m$ of an entity file o_1, or written $a_0 \leftarrow a_1,\ldots,a_m$. The file has an internal key, for example a_0 for o_1, but it is possible that o_1 has an external key, which links to other files.

A relationship represents an association between entities where the association is determined based on the identity or link key. Suppose there is an entity o_2 with a set of attributes $\{a_5, b_1, b_2\}$. So the a_5 attribute becomes an external key in o_1 to associate with or as an internal key in o_2. Based on that, there is a degree of relationship between associated entities, namely $1 : N$, $N : 1$, or $N : N$. For example, $o_1 \xrightarrow{1:N} o_2$. A manager manages workers, so there is a relationship $1 : N$ between the manager and the worker. A division consists of many departments, so there is a relationship $N : 1$ between departments and divisions. A worker is involved in many projects, or a project involves many workers. A worker has many skills. A skill is possessed by many people. All of which involves degrees of relationship $N : N$. Suppose each object or entity as is a vertex or there is a set of vertices $V = \{o_1, o_2,\ldots,o_n\}$ and the relationship between objects or entities is an edge or there is a set of edges $E = \{e_1,e_2,\ldots,e_m\}$. Based on this association, there are three types of logical data models: *Network model*—represents data as resembling a record type. This model also represents a finite type of one-to-many relationship or is called a set type. Suppose there are six entities: $o_1, o_2, o_3, o_4, o_5, o_6$ or $V = \{o_1, o_2, o_3, o_4, o_5, o_6\}$ with the assignment of relationships between entities: $o_1 \xrightarrow{1:N} o_2$, $o_2 \rightarrow o_3$, $o_3 \rightarrow o_4$, $o_4 \rightarrow o_5$, and $o_6 \rightarrow o_3$ or set of directed edges $E = \{o_1 o_2, o_1 o_2, o_3 o_2, o_4 o_3, o_4 o_5, o_6 o_3\}$. Thus, the entities and the relationships between them form a (directed) network. In this example model, there are parallel edges but with different weights, two directed edges connecting o_1 and o_2. *Hierarchy model*—represents data as a tiered tree structure. Each branch of the ladder represents the corresponding record number. Suppose there are six entities: $o_1, o_2, o_3, o_4, o_5, o_6$ with relationship assignments: $o_1 \rightarrow o_2$, $o_1 \rightarrow o_3$, $o_1 \rightarrow o_4$, $o_4 \rightarrow o_5$, and $o_4 \rightarrow o_6$. The relationships between these entities form a tree, where each entity is a vertex and each relationship is an edge (directed), but none of the edges are parallel or cyclical. *Relational model*—represents data as relations or tables. Each record, in this case, is declared to be an instance of a member of the table. The tables in the relational model show the dependencies of the relationship between its attributes and between tables. Or call it an entity-relationship (ER) model, but require analysis of the possibility of duplication. This analysis involves the normal form design for the database, the steps to normalize the candidate tables as follows.

1. *First Normal Form* (1NF): $R \in 1NF \Leftrightarrow \forall v_a, v_a \in C_a \cap L_a$—a table is in 1NF if and only if all columns contain only atomic values v_a, that is, each column can have only one value for each row in table. Among the attributes will work as:

    - *Superkey*—a set of one or more attributes, which when taken collectively become the unique identity of an entity or table.
    - *Candidate key*—any subset of attributes of a superkey that is also a superkey but does not reduce another superkey.
    - *Primary key*—any identity selected from the candidate key set and used in indexing for that table.

2. *Second Normal Form* (2NF): $R \in 2NF \Leftrightarrow R \in 1NF \wedge a_0 \leftarrow a_1$, $a_2,\ldots, a_m, a_0, a_1, a_2,\ldots, a_m \in R$—a table in 2NF if and only if it is 1NF and every nonkey attribute is fully dependent on the primary key. An attribute is completely dependent on the primary key if there is a right-hand side of the FD for which the left-hand side is the primary key or something that can be derived from the primary key using the transitivity of the dependency function.

3. *Third Normal Form* (3NF): $R \in 2NF \Leftrightarrow x = o_k o_l \cdots \rightarrow y = o_1 o_2 \ldots$—a table in 3NF if and only if for every nontrivial FD $x \rightarrow y$, where x and y are either simple or compsite attributes, one of two condition must hold. Either attribute x is a superkey, or attribute a is a member of a candidate key. If attribute y is a member of a candidate key, y is called a prime attribute.

4. *Boyce-Codd Normal Form* (BCNF): $R \in BCNF \Leftarrow x \rightarrow y$, x is a superkey—a table R is in BCNF if for every nontrivial FD $x \rightarrow y$, x is a superkey. BCNF is a stronger form of normalization than 3NF, where it eliminates the second condition for 3NF, which allowed the right side of the FD to be a prime attribute: Every left side of an FD in a table must be a superkey.

Every table is BCNF is also 3NF, 2NF, and 1NF [16].

The relational data model involves the concept of foreign keys, which are primary keys in one relationship to establish relationships with others for data aggregation to occur. A foreign key is an attribute or a set of attributes in a table of relational data model that provide a link between data in two tables. In general, relationships between data from entities reveal business rules or semantic information: [17]. Assuming the entity o_2 is the explanatory dictionary data file, the relationship $o_1 \rightharpoonup o_2$ states that any attribute in o_1 has meaning in/is interpreted by o_2, or o_1 lookup o_2. For example, when the zip code as o_2 is in the worker entity, then the city entity of o_1 has an area placement following the postal code. A records-based data modeling involves the stages of database design. The modeling depends on conceptual, logical, and physical design, with the target being a conceptual data model, which implies a database such as entity relationships (ER) [18].

3.4.2   Non–Record-Based Data Model

A non–record-based data model is a different data set from a record-based array. The modeling depends on conceptual, logical, and physical design, or it is top down approach. The range of this data model is not limited to *wide column store, key value store, graph database,* and *document store.*

Wide column store [19]. This database has a more complex schema of tables. The table *T* has columns and rows, but not every equal column contains the value in a row. A row key like in a relational database is a unique value. For identifying a specific record, the database applies the key. So in the first column a_0, there is the value v_{0j}, j refers to the row of the key. In the second column there is a timestamp symbolized by *ts* with an integer used to identify the specific version of the data value in the next column, so for $a_1 = \{ts_1, ts_2, ...\}$. The third column, a_2, has the format "Family: Qualifier = Value" a column that consists of two parts: "Family" is the column section named family, and "Qualifier" is the column section named qualifier, while "Value" is the value real of the qualifier column stored in the text. For example for $v_{01} \in a_0$, each row of column a_2 in the format "Family" is descriptions about the product, $f_1, f_2, ...$, while column a_2 is in the format "Qualifier" are descriptions of the quantity, $q_1, q_2, ...$, where the lines $ts_1 = f_1$, $ts_2 = f_2$, ..., and $ts_{i+1} = q_1$, $ts_{i+2} = q_2$, ... Next, $v_{02} \in a_0$, ts... with the next integer, and so on.

Key value store [20]. A database has a schema of the "Key|Value" form. "Key" is a string used to identify a unique value. "Value" is an object that has a value that may be a simple string, a numeric value, a binary large object (BLOB), JSON (JavaScript Object Notation) objects, images, audio, and others, where the JSON object is of the form "Key|value". In this database, operations on values are derived from keys, allowing the user to retrieve, pair, and delete values with a key. A logical data structure can contain any number of key-value pairs. This structure is called a namespace. Thus, the data model involves several namespaces. That is "Products" and "Customers." The key of each is an identity (ID) of the "Products" and the ID of the "Customers." The respective values of them are the details about the product for "Products" and the customer for "Customers."

Graph databases [21]. The *graph data model* is an extension of the network model. A model consists of vertices and edges where each vertex is an entity instance. Each entity instance is equivalent to the relational database model. Edges have a function for expressing the relationship between vertices. However, each vertex and edge contains any number of attributes that store the actual data values. For example, in a graph database, each vertex contains some data, such as nation, city, and local time, while the edge represents the length of the flight between two cities. So the global flight database has ranged as a network between V airports having E paths by various airlines, where there are labels and weights on both vertices and edges. Labels and weights can be structured like tables or relational data models.

Document store [22]. A data model called a document store involves a group of documents with a schema of data related to the same subject, such as workers, products, and others. A document is assigned an ordered key-value pair in the form of a string used to reference a particular value and a value that can be either a string or a document. For example, the document consists of a curriculum for data science, mathematics, statistics, …. Each course subject contains four data fields such as course code, title, credit, and instructor, for example. A collection of documents with content that is more organized and uniform in structure is like a scientific work document: Consisting of a document number or digital object identifier (DOI), header, author, affiliation, abstract, body, references, acknowledgments, attachments, a short Curriculum Vitae of the author, and statements, books/papers/journals/events, ISBN/ISSN and other information. Scientific documents have one or more authors. It results in the possibility of more than one affiliation. Scientific work documents have different content structures, but in general, they consist of an introduction (problems and objectives), methodology (materials and methods), results (evaluation, discussion), and conclusion (conclusions). Likewise, to support scientific work, the bibliography contains several other scientific works.

Other model [23]. In addition to the database model above, there are several database models with different schemas. These databases tend to follow the interests of users, as is the case with the atomic periodic table of elements. Some of them with a formal schema. Other data models are as follows: multimodel databases, object databases, grid and cloud database solutions, XML databases, multivalue databases, event sourcing, time-series databases, scientific and specialized databases, and unresolve databases: A *multimodel database* is a data model consisting of one or more categories of databases. An *object database* is a model that combines object-oriented functions and traditional databases in which there are attributes, relationships, and methods of organizing data. The data in object databases are described in the form of class diagrams. Generally, classes are constructed based on entities. A *grid and cloud database solution* is a category of data models that store the most recent instantaneous access data in random access memory (RAM) and use grid computing to speed up data access times from databases. A *multidimensional database* is a category of storing data in multidimensional arrays. The intention is to analyze the value of each element of the array. An array of dimension 1 is called an array, dimension 2 is called a matrix, and a space of dimension n, which generally has a dimension position pointer (from index) i, ij, ijk, …, to denote dimensions 1, 2, 3, and so on, where $i, j, k, … \in N$, n are integers. A *multivalue database* is a category of storing data: multiple values or a composite attribute into an attribute. An *event sourcing* is an appropriate storage category for past events to track the status of specific events. This kind of data model serves to determine the direction of the next event, such as seminars, conferences, other activities, whether regular or not. A time-series database is a category of databases designed to handle the flow of data over time [24]. A *scientific and specialized database* is a category of databases designed to solve scientific and professional issues.

In particular, there is a weak dependence on a conceptual design of the non–record-based data model, be a strong dependence on the logical design and physical design of the non–record-based data model. However, for databases, the non–record-based data model only has a strong dependence on the physical design. Some of the later models are similar to, or as an extension of, the existing model, either the relational data model or the nonrelational data model. For example, a multivalues database has similarities to the *wide column store* in the schema. Some nonrelational data models are a combination of several different schemas. Database categories are not record-based in some respects as categorized earlier, but in the practice of data modeling, many different schemas emerge, such as databases from Facebook, Twitter, Researchgate, and others. In terms of storage space such as files, the XML (Extensible Markup Language) format is a hybrid database category where the composition of attributes and values depends on the XML schema designed according to the purpose of use [25]. Likewise, it is not wrong to say that the Web is a mixed database that adopts many models with more metadata support as a reference for data items of various types of data or multimedia [26]. Therefore, there is an assigned database that cannot be classified into any schema category as above. The issue of data modeling has become a study issue that continues to develop not only in data science but also in their respective scientific fields as the periodic table of elements has received recognition from the scientific community. Is it a data model? It is possible that each science has a database of objects that are the subject of its framework.

3.5 Polyglot Persistence Environment

Conceptually, the database design follows the importance of using the data itself in an environment for processing data where information is needed [27]. Logically, data modeling produces a data model that organizes data units, attributes, involves relationships between those attributes following dependency reasoning, and forms a schema between data organizations. It produces the concept of a (big)-data model [28]. Logical data models naturally adhere to rules in the environment. It is directly attached to each object and its characteristics. Thus, some studies already produce various data models as relational and nonrelational data models, but other data models are also possible. Physically, data will store in the storage technology, the database, whether in the form of tables or files. It is an environment that has its constraints along with its limitations. Thus, there is physically an assignment of software technology to database creation, accessing data, processing data. Then, implement the model using the query language that is not structured (NoSQL) such as the query embedding to any search engine. This implementation is by presenting it according to an implemented scheme against hardware limitations and by software capabilities, a (big)-database [29].

The *polyglot persistence environment* (PPE) is an environment that conceptually has many interests even though it is from the side of one organization. Perhaps every large organization that deals with many people will accumulate data into big data. For example, a hospital consists of human entities: doctors, nurses, workers, and patients, supported by assets: tables, chairs, other equipment, and facilities together with a living room, operating room, consultation room, doctor's room, patient inpatient room, and others. Every doctor has the expertise that is not only supported by diplomas but other documents such as scientific papers. Hospitals also have a drug supply or pharmacy shop. Each drug has its properties, prohibitions, cautions, composition, and instructions for use [30]. Thus, a concept of a PPE is an attempt to interpret the organization's interest in organizing data as a whole so that the organization operates well. Logically, this means that there are multiple connected data models, i.e. the main schema of data models consisting of multiple-data model schemas. Physically, schemas and sub-schemas are implemented in a database environment involving several different hardware and software technologies. Of course, from design, conceptual-logical-physical data modeling, to database operations, either needs administrative logging or not, also need a collection of documents with each character, all of those in a PPE. Therefore, (big)-data modeling is not only a study of data science but administratively concerns the dissemination problem of data modeling, which is summarized in this paper as teaching material in data science study programs.

References

1. Coussement, K. and Benoit, D.F., Interpretable data science for decision making. decision support systems. *Decis. Support Syst.*, 150, 2021.
2. Shi, H. and Deng, H., Teaching and experimental schema of data mining technology combined with the cloud computing. *J. Internet Technol.*, 22, 1, 157–163, 2021.
3. Nasution, M.K.M., A method for constructing a dataset to reveal the industrial behaviour of big data. *IOP Conf. Ser. Mater. Sci. Eng.*, 1003, 1, 2020.
4. Nasution, M.K.M., Aulia, I., Elveny, M., Data. *J. Phys. Conf. Ser.*, 1235, 1, 2019.
5. Kaiser, S.K., CHen, Z., Faust, Akl, D., Mitchell, S., Pérez-Ramiírez, J., Single-atom catalysts across the periodic table. *Chem. Rev.*, 120, 21, 11703–11809, 2020.
6. Yesin, V., Karpinski, M., Yesina, M., Vilihura, V., Warwas, K., Ensuring data integrity in databases with the universal basis of relations. *Appl. Sci. (Switzerland)*, 11, 18, 637–646, 2021.
7. Rao, R., From unstructured data to actionable intelligence. *IT Prof.*, 5, 6, 29–35, 2003.
8. Mansmann, S., Ur Rehman, N., Weiler, A., Scholl, M.H., Discovering olap dimensions in semi-structured data. *Inf. Syst.*, 44, 120–133, 2014.
9. Lee, S.Y., Lee, M.L., Ling, T.W., Kalinichenko, L.A., Designing good semi-structured databases, in: *Lecture Notes in Computer Science (including subseries Lecture Notes in Artificial Intelligence and Lecture Notes in Bioinformatics)*, vol. 1728 KNCS, pp. 131–145, 1999.

10. Whitney, V.K.M. and Doll, D.R., A database system for the management and design of telecommunication networks. *Data Networks: Analysis and Design—3rd Data Communications Symposium, DATACOMM 1973*, pp. 141–147, 1973.

11. Frankel, F. and Reid, R., Big data: Distilling meaning from data. *Nature*, 455, 7209, 30, 2008.

12. Nasution, M.K.M., Sitompul, O.S., Elveny, M., Syah, R., Data science: A review towards the big data problems. *J. Phys. Conf. Ser.*, 1898, 1, 2021.

13. Alias, N., Al-Rahmi, W.M., Yahaya, N., Al-Maatouk, Q., Big data, modeling, simulation, computational platform and holistic approaches for the fourth industrial revolution. *Int. J. Eng. Technol. (UAE)*, 7, 4, 3722–3725, 2018.

14. Albdaiwi, B., Noack, R., Thalheim, B., Pattern-based conceptual data modelling. *Front. Artif. Intell. Appl.*, 272, 1–20, 2014.

15. Demetrovics, J., Katona, G.O.H., Miklos, D., Seleznjev, O., Thalheim, B., Asymptotic properties of keys and functional dependencies in random databases. *Theor. Comput. Sci.*, 190, 2, 151–166, 1998.

16. Zhang, Y. and Orlowska, M.E., A new polynomial time algorithm for bcnf relational database design. *Inf. Syst.*, 17, 2, 185–193, 1992.

17. Schmid, H.A. and Swenson, J.R., On the semantics of the relational data model. *Proceedings of the ACM SIGMOD International Conference on Management of Data*, pp. 211–223, 1975.

18. Andon, P. I., Reznichenko, V.A., Chistyakova, I.S., Mapping of description logic to the relational data model. *Cybern. Syst. Anal.*, 53, 6, 963–977, 2017.

19. Mozaffari, M., Nazemi, E., Eftekhari-Moghadam, A.M., Feedback control loop design for workload change detection in self-tuning nosql wide column stores. *Expert Syst. Appl.*, 142, 2020.

20. Huang, C., Hu, H., Qi, X., Zhou, X., Zhou, A., Rs-store: Rdma-enabled skiplist-based key-value store for efficient range query. *Front. Comput. Sci.*, 15, 6, 2021.

21. Su, Y.F. and Wong, K.F., Conceptual graphs as schemas for semi-structured databases. *Proceedings—7th International Conference on Database Systems for Advanced Applications, DASFAA 2001*, pp. 150–151, 2001.

22. Shah, M., Kothari, A., Patel, S., Influence of schema design in nosql document stores, in: *Lecture Notes on Data Engineering and Communications Technologies*, vol. 68, pp. 435–452, 1997.

23. Cansler, C.A., Hood, S.M., van Mantgem, P.J., Varner, J.M., A large database supports the use of simple models of post-fire tree mortality for thick-barked conifers, with less support for other species. *Fire Ecol.*, 16, 1, 25, 2020.

24. Calatrava, C.G., Fontal, Y.B., Cucchietti, F.M., Cuesta, C.D., Nagaredb: A resource-efficient document-oriented time-series database. *Data*, 6, 8, 91, 2021.

25. Engelfriet, J., Hoogeboom, H.J., Samwel, B., Xml navigation and transformation by tree-walking automata and transducers with visible and invisible pebbles. *Theor. Comput. Sci.*, 2021, 40–97, 2021.

26. Castro-Medina, F., Rodríguez-Mazahua, L., López-Chau, A., Cervantes, J., Alor-Hernández, G., Machorro-Cano, I., Application of dynamic fragmentation methods in multimedia databases: A review. *Entropy*, 22, 12, 1–25, 2020.
27. Prasad, S. and Avinash, S.B., Application of polyglot persistence to enhance performance of the energy data management systems. *2014 International Conference on Advances in Electronics, Computers and Communications, ICAECC 2014*, 2014.
28.. Khine, P.P. and Wang, Z., A review of polyglot persistence in the big data world. *Information (Switzerland)*, 10, 4, 141, 2019.
29. Kaur, K., Sharma, S., Kahlon, K.S., A middleware for polyglot persistence and data portability of big data paas cloud applications. *Comput. Mater. Con.*, 65, 2, 1625–1647, 2020.
30. Nasution, M.K.M., Noah, S.A.M., Harahap, U., Overview of the pharmacy management system in a hospital. *Syst. Rev. Pharm.*, 11, 1, 650–655, 2020.

## 4

Data Management as Emerging Problems of Data Science

Mahyuddin K. M. Nasution[1,2]* and Rahmad Syah[3]

¹Data Science & Computational Intelligence Research Group, Universitas Sumatera Utara, Jl Universitas, Medan, Sumatera Utara, Indonesia
²Bagosso Innovation House, Jl Ekasurya, Gedung Johor, Medan, Sumatera Utara, Indonesia
³Data Science & Computational Intelligence Research Group, Universitas Medan Area, Jl Kolam, Gedung PBSI, Medan, Sumatera Utara, Indonesia

Abstract

Technology has caused a shift in the way the sapiens view data. The data organization considers data items and their dependencies on each of them in a structure, like the tables reduce redundancy into a database technology. The database is an implementation of data modeling. The purpose of data modeling is to facilitate data management. Data modeling adapts the availability of technology so that data management is easy. A system for organizing data, such as in a database management system, consists of the inter-reaction components for building the system, where a data item is a component. Meanwhile, a system with different technologies does not guarantee that dependencies are always appropriate and not consistent from one server to another. It invites not only talk about the data distribution but also data consistency and transaction models. By analyzing the characteristics and requirements of the data, it is possible to obtain a general approach to data management. The procedures do operations both in structured query language (SQL) and nonstructured query language (NoSQL). Technology developments present problems from a data science point of view regarding data management. The chapter will reveal data management by considering language based on the novelty view of data.

Corresponding author: mahyuddin@usu.ac.id

Archana Patel, Narayan C. Debnath and Bharat Bhusan (eds.) Data Science with Semantic Technologies: Theory, Practice, and Application, (91–104) © 2022 Scrivener Publishing LLC

Keywords: Data model, big data, database, data management life cycle, ACID, CAP

4.1   Introduction

Data modeling aims to facilitate data management by confirming the relationship between data into a data organization and then ties the data organizations with relationships in one schema. Modeling, thus, produces different models according to the demands of interest, which result in conceptual, logical, and physical designs. It implements technology, such as database management systems (DBMSs), by not only influencing other technologies, such as programming language translators, but also changing the way technology views data by updating it. In principle, data modeling follows its design to produce a data model that satisfies all interested parties. One of the models is the relational model, which consists of tables organized according to the schema. A relational database is a model that follows the principle of structured data, but some data modeling only reaches semistructured data, or some are even unstructured data. Indirectly, it affects data management. It does the database management system physically organize storage so that accessing data quickly naturally. It also causes query languages to have different rules. Indeed, according to the data management life cycle, the database holds the principles of atomicity, consistency, isolation, and durability when data changes and transactions occur [1]. However, semistructured and unstructured data need to take other considerations or not.

Each data model relates to its management, however, the data model exists because of its context and design perspective. The benefits to be taken make it possible to exert a strong influence on each data model, reducing bias interests by involving the technological context and organizational context in data management to determine decisions in the context of design, storage, processes, and people who benefit. Therefore, data management involves the output of data modeling, namely the data model. Also, what relates after the modeling, what is carried out, like data orientation, decision making, and transaction processing.

4.2   Perspective and Context

The background of the study on data management refers to data modeling and design because is data has a life cycle. Thus, data is not only related to the process of input into a storage area with the nature of its accumulation. Based on side of the data itself, some benefits inspire sapiens to deal with data, and this requires management. In particular, data residing in repositories requires responsible access through the management of all data-related resources.

4.2.1   Life Cycle

From a data perspective, the context of data lifecycle management (DML) [2] includes collection, access, usage, storage, transfer, and destroy/deletion.

The DML starts from information gathering, collection, by following the subject of sapiens thinking. This initial phase allows for the creation of value that does not yet exist but is urgently needed by interested parties, especially organizations. Information gathering is the transformation of its source in a certain way and generates data, involving extraction, exploration, and other implementations of data mining. About the involvement of electronic devices and sensors, whether integrated with IoT or not, information gathering is referred to as data acquisition. For example, the object of the discussion is a sustainable living environment. Automatically, it is about a physical phenomenon, an environment that involves data collection tools. Tools for getting temperature, wind speed, vibration, light intensity, gas pressure, fluid flow, air heat, rain-(fall), or force. Or about other objects that can capture by sensors or other electronic equipment. Of course, to cover the entire environment on earth, some points of location that represent randomly from the oceans and land are the sample of gathering data. It is generally expressed as a type of physical property to be measured, i.e., the physical signal [3]. A sensor, which is a type of transducer, is a device that converts a physical property into a corresponding electrical signal. A signal is represented by an irregularity on a graphical drawing or also called a strain gauge. The picture requires refining by building an approximate graphic called a conditional signal [4]. All of the information still in analog form (continuous) and requires conversion into digital form (discretization) so that the resulting data is recognized by the computer in binary form. The binary arrangement is converted into certain values, these values flow indirectly from all electronic devices into storage on the computer, or data stream occurs. Every signal generated by a physical system involving electronic devices requires discretization and to be further managed into a data model and used according to its interests. Meanwhile, traditionally information collection is done by entering it into storage. It involves a certain entry pattern by the operator, and as a consequence, each data unit requires validation so that no errors occur. In contrast to the use of entry, but similar to the application of sensors, each computer network user enters information from wherever the computer is connected to the computer network. The problem is that the data that enters the network varies according to the user's knowledge and behavior.

The next data management life cycle is data access. The existence of data follows the nature of the (information) source and destination (model data). Data from survey results or data recorded through the input interface follows the boring arrangement that has been prepared, but data from electronic equipment activities follow the attached template. Therefore, access to automatically recorded information is the activity of reading machine encoding based on the template. Much of the data is not recorded digitally and is only visualized on a monitor screen or analog storage. In general, every electronic machine has a template that holds information as a cause for accessing the environment in which it works. On the other side, modern electronic machines have an interface. Because of it, the computer can access the template and place the information into a file. In this case, even though the content of the file is digital, but is an unstructured string or is an array of one or more dimensions. This collection requires a recognition process to determine the smallest data unities that have meaning. Thus the issue about access is to align what is generated from the collection and what is ensured that the cleanliness of the data is maintained. It is for processing of business processes of the data run effectively.

The next phase of the data management life cycle is the usage, where data have details based on the application of information gathering and processed by involving administrative records [5]. The goal is for the usefulness of managed data and demonstrate the importance of that data and provide benefits not only for the data organization but for the organization that owns it. The use of data is a challenging problem from the point of view of data science. In addition, data requires protection, data also requires usability, and it involves data legality, i.e., permitted use of data. To obtain the legality of data in specific cases sometimes involves a committee, for example, clearance ethic [6]. One of its duties is data curation [7], namely organizing and integrating data through extracting data-information-knowledge from various sources.

The storage is something that is set up in advance but is in the fifth position of the data management life cycle, on the grounds that the data is stored without further processing. Archiving data according to a data model is the act of copying data to the environment in which it is stored and to the active production environment. Active production environment, an environment where operations take place to reveal what meaning behind the data, while the storage environment is usually declared as master data. On the other hand, deletion of data can be done from the active production environment if it is not required, but the data is still maintained and managed in the storage as something historically related.

Transformation, the next phase of the data management life cycle. This phase involves reasoning to generate meaning or increase the value of data or other value additions. The reasoning process can be inductive in nature, where the transformation provides input for investment decisions, while the reasoning process is deductive in nature, there are advantages in the business environment. In an active production environment, reports contain data from governance results. Reports are a form of publication. Publication generally provides reliable and correct information that is supported by facts, namely data and descriptions of reasons as an explanation. However, the published data is not always in accordance with the reality, the possibilities in the implementation of making publications are exposed to choice from data science assignments, extracting information from sources, through a systematic review or data curation [8]. A decision comes from the process of reasoning, as a transformation.

Destroying or deleting data is the end of the data processing cycle [9]. Abandoned data in its storage possible/sometimes interfere with operations or is seen as useless. Under certain conditions, it may be a clue to a decision where useless data must be deleted by who is responsible. The deletion process must be considered and carried out to ensure data management runs purely. But the destruction of data must go through careful consideration where when the organization still exists the data is also there [10].

4.2.2   Use

Data deals with the description of any object in which there are various details associated with it. The details are characteristics, properties, features, components, entities, and the relationships between them [11]. Each of these details naturally has a description and requires a different operation. Descriptions also are an explanation of the details and also an explanation of the object. In general, the type of data and the storage capacity assigned to it (called the data width) takes up storage space in a structured manner and recognizes it through metadata. Temporarily consider metadata as a variable that represents the smallest unit of data that has meaning. Thus, metadata, data types, and data width are descriptions to manage how things work and perform strategies that will be carried out in their operations based on the nature of quantitative or qualitative data. Following the data model, each query language, whether structured or unstructured (SQL or NoSQL), has a role-based in managing the data lifecycle.

The operation that follows the access activity is an attempt to acknowledge the organizing of data for the data model protects the data from the beginning again. Data management and its implementation into the database is nothing but to determine related data collections, identifying data as facts that can be recorded and have meaning, representing aspects of the world, creating objectives, and achieving the targets of the organization. Thus, the basic operations of insert, delete or update (modify) only change the state of the relationship in the database.

Inaccuracies between the data model and operations as a result of the demands for changing data meaning may require adaptation but do not change the data model [12]. It is declared as reconciling. For example, when an object is characteristic so diversely, it will allow the presence of more than one criteria (multi-criteria) that becomes choices in decision making. The multi-criteria data structure may not be the same as the data structure based on the data model [13]. Multicriteria are composed in data structures such as tables, relational databases also consist of tables, but they are not in the same schema. Thus, there are constraints involving inheritance properties (derived from the origin of data), especially the relationship between them in databases, explicit schemas of multi-criteria, for example, and applications that implement them [14]. Therefore, the reconcile strategy is based on a data retrieval operation, where to complete data related to an object, it is possible explored from different databases or other information spaces. This adjustment step is to provide a reconciled solution to the problem. Likewise, nowadays any operation to get benefit from the data will be dealing with a large composition of data with unusual details. Therefore, challenges come not only from operational access but also from its management based on the data science framework. Information space: internet, and web, which contains many criteria about any object, and to add completeness of information in multi-criteria, for example, the task of extracting data from information space provide answers based on data science. The strategy for that is a problem that exists for data science [15].

Disclosure of the benefits of data requires several strategies. Modeling is always inter-followed by simulation [16], so data modeling is directly related to simulating access and possible operations [17]. However, simulation specifically to reveal other possible benefits of data is a step to deliver prospects for the data model and the data itself from the management side [18]. In this case, the simulation will show the advantages and disadvantages of the data model when dealing with other forms of analysis such as forecasting or predictions and optimization [19]. For example, for any object that has various criteria, of course, there is the multi-criteria as the decisions, but it allows for the presence of multi-objective as decisions [20]. It requires management to make choices and also requires management to determine different objective choices as the target of analysis so that a solution that is beneficial to the parties is considered contradictory, a form of multi-objectives as producing a decision. By preparing multi-criteria and multi-objective to conduct research and development (R&D) based on big data, there is a benefit to optimization, it calls as the Multi-criteria Objective and Decision Analysis (MODA), a task of data management for formulating a decision analysis based on multi-criteria, multi-..., and until multi-objective [21]. Considered choice, compliance with environmental requirements, or luxury requirements for humans from any object based on data, becomes the task of data science [22]. With data, it is possible to predict the future of human life, as well as the future of the environment.

As a description of objects, data consists of text: words, sentences, or a collection of documents, which express meaning, or semantically have another meaning behind it [23]. Traditional text analysis is legendary since sapiens recognize and involve symbols in their language as a cultural force. Literacy activity in culture reveals meaning after meaning of the life of sapiens about the object of their thought. Traditional text analysis is legendary since sapiens recognize and involve symbols in their language as a cultural force. Literacy activity in culture reveals meaning after meaning of the life of sapiens about the object of their thought. From poetry to the contents of the scriptures explain the behavior of sapiens towards any object. As a cultural product, the web is a technology that shifts the tradition of information flow from one direction to another and multiplies the flow of information describing any object. For example, there are n computers that connect to a computer network/internet that involves n users, and as a consequence, the complexity of the information flow as the descriptions are $n(n-1)$ units, a multiplier of the average information collected in big data [15].

Furthermore, when special data is needed to support a process, as a learning dataset [24], for example, that data requires delivery to where need it. However, when processing data in its environments, delivery only needs to involve a dashboard to manage the information as needed and send it to the destination. Delivery is the task of every system seen in data science, both static in *e*-system (*electronic*) and dynamic in *m*-system (*mobile*). It is based on considerations of data distribution.

4.3   Data Distribution

The data management environment is a consequence of the appearance of technology - from computer networks, the internet to the web undergoing changes, involving new requirements and its presence in an organization based on various requests for resources [25]. The changes relate to running the database from a group of servers to provide the capability order in handling large amounts of data, the ability to process larger read or write traffic, or to address data presence/availability in case of network throttling due to crashes. For example, if a database management system (DBMS) is a transaction processing system by involving the usage of the structured query language (SQL), then it applies that all data to be present on different systems from the first system (called atomicity), completion when there is a transaction (sending) data to a system (called consistency), no two the unity of data that is mixed during operation (called isolation), and the facility meets the overall demand (called durability). Atomicity, consistency, isolation, durability, or abbreviated as ACID, are properties of database distribution activities that guarantee data validity. Thus, the implementation of the database path in different machines in parallel (scale-out) is an activity option from the management based on the impact on the database operation, not a series arrangement option (scale-up).

By using a query language assessment to the appropriate data model, the distributing data can be done by copying the data to several machines. Let it as a system or a computer device as a node. This replication action causes the data bits to be in several places. Units of data can also be placed on different nodes separately. Database partitioning, for example, is the process of having data split into databases to distribute large amounts of data into smaller, distributable segments between two or more servers. So each shard called a fragment can be a table or a different physical database maintained on a separate instance of the database server. The activities of distributing data, sharding, across multi-nodes, where each node acts as a single source for a subset of data. Sharding consists of:

1. The vertical fraction is a method of storing data from different columns into separate fragments.

2. The horizontal fraction is an arrangement made under the condition that the rows of the database table are interrelated in different ways. Likewise, data management must meet data models, where sharding follows a conceptual, logical, and physical design, in order to be concerned with customizing domains related to data models. While logical sharing occurs in application data, but storage is performed in a different place. At the application level generally apply this type of division [26].

In accordance with the needs and convenience available in data management, and to meet the availability of data in the application. Some of the data in the database persist in all vertical sharding, but some appear only in horizontal sharding. The scheme of this division involves key concepts and data ranges, namely key-based sharding or range based sharding. However, other strategies are still being developed. Data that is accessed together for example stays in the same node, so queries on physical sharding are single and efficient. Likewise, if access is based on physical location, data is placed close to where it is accessed. Another factor to maintain data balance, even distribution, is to arrange the aggregates for the data units are evenly distributed so that each node receives the same amount of load. Regarding the exact time and duration of access, some databases at the beginning of development were intended to carry out sharding. Development starts from a single node, and after establishing it to be thing distributed, and performs sharding. However, late implementation of sharding may cause problems. Especially if done in a production environment, where the database becomes unavailable during data transfer to the new sharding. Of course, these problem-solving studies become left for the work in data science.

However, data distribution and related matters, such as sharding, refer to a database configuration in which multiple copies of the same dataset are placed on separate nodes. Again, this is expressed as replication, in order to present redundancy. Based on the side of management, the many advantages of using replication include fast recovery in the event of a single hosting node failure. For easy, replication, a master node is defined as the data source, then several nodes are set up as slaves. The master node replicates data to slave nodes, where all services from the master are doing the writes, although reads can come from either the master or the slave. Regarding read-write operations, it requires management to address issues related to the possible failure of the master node and the possibility of a slave node becoming a master node. Replication that satisfies consistency requirements is operations that resolve the scalability of the relevant reads along with the scalability of writes. In other words, the resistance to slave node failure does not come from the master node.

Although replication with master nodes and slave nodes corresponds to read write data sets implemented via a query language. Balancing the capabilities of master nodes and slave nodes needs to be considered in order to achieve peer-to-peer replication, where the two nodes are on an equal footing [27]. Thus, data consistency becomes the biggest complication of activities of data management, when inconsistencies occur, namely at the time of writing different nodes. By involving queries, for example, two clients try to write/update the same data at the same time, causing write-write conflicts.

4.4   CAP Theorem

The property theorem - Consistency, Availability, and Partition Tolerance (CAP) - is a fundamental postulate in distributed systems that states that any distributed system can only enforce two of the three properties [28].

The proof of this system is stated as follows. Suppose the system is composed of two server nodes, s_1 and s_2. These two nodes keep track of the same two variables v which have the initial value v_0. s_1 and s_2 can communicate with each other and also communicate with external c client nodes. Simply, this concept is represented by $s_1 s_2$, $s_1 c$, and $s_2 c$.

Consistency is expressed through any read operation that starts after the writer operation completes the return of that value or the result of the last write operation, otherwise, it doesn't do. This can be described as follows. Suppose the $\hookrightarrow$ sign represents writing to, while $\hookleftarrow$ indicates reading from, $c \xrightarrow{v_1} s_1$ means that the client node c writes the value of v_1 into s_1 (for replace the value of v_0 in s_1), in the same way $s_1 \xrightarrow{v_1} s_2$ means that s_1 writes v_1 into s_2 (to replace the value of v_0 in s_2), and $c \xleftarrow{v_1} s_2$ means the client c reads the content of s_2 and gets the value v_1. In short, an operation is said to be consistent if

$$c \xrightarrow{v_1} s_1, c \xrightarrow{v_1} s_2 = c \xleftarrow{v_1} s_2 \tag{4.1}$$

otherwise

$$c \xrightarrow{v_1} s_1 \neq c \xleftarrow{v_0} s_2 \tag{4.2}$$

Any request received by a nonfailing node in the system must result in a response. In a given system, if the client sends a request to the server and the server does not crash, then the server must eventually respond to the client. Servers are not allowed to ignore client requests. This means that availability provides two options for consistency,

$$cs_2 = c \xleftarrow{v_1} s_2 \tag{4.3}$$

for Eq. (4.1), or

$$cs_2 = c \xleftarrow{v_0} s_2 \tag{4.4}$$

for Eq. (4.2). That is $cs_1 = c \xrightarrow{v_1} s_1$ and $s_1 s_2 = s_1 \xrightarrow{v_1} s_2$ or $s_1 s_2 = s_1 / \hookrightarrow s_2$, then the above equation applies.

In general, the network will be allowed to lose a lot of messages sent from one node to another. This property is expressed as partition tolerance, which states that any messages s_1 and s_2 send to each other can be dropped, and when all messages are discarded, the system shows $cs_1 = c \xrightarrow{v_1} s_1$ and $cs_2 = c \xleftarrow{v_1} s_2$, otherwise $cs_2 = c \xleftrightarrow{v_1} s_2$ and $cs_1 = c \xleftarrow{v_0} s_1$. The write read condition of the data against the two servers is the second option of Eq. (4.3).

The three data flow concepts above prove that of the three principles only two apply at once. It will affect data lifecycle management activities. This problem that weighs on all the activities of data science.

4.5 Polyglot Persistence

Data management runs on a wider and larger environment, is the management that involves big data [15], not only causes data clustering to introduce complexity [29], but also polyglot persistence as something complex. A polyglot includes all the data models of an organization, running on both structured and unstructured query languages. However, the variety of data based on the dimensions of importance will require changes in the design conceptually, logically, and physically [30]. It will result in the presence of various problems related to data modeling, which will result in data modeling. However perfect the data model and implementation may be, certain data units require more extensive and additional descriptions. The description requires space and storage space based on a suitable model, perhaps a new model, and this is related to maintaining the implementation of the properties of the CAP over the data management life cycle, but also requires ensuring a better and more reliable description. For example, if the additional description or explanation comes from search engine searches, the consistency between the search engines and the clients using them requires a study. Perhaps, stronger consistency semantics can be achieved with fractions. It is as the novelty view of data. Thus, problem after issue related to data management that requires answers from data science.

References

1. Huh, T., Park, G., Ahn, S., Hwang, S., Jung, H., Design criteria of korean lter data platform model for full life-cycle data management. *Int. J. Appl. Eng. Res.*, 12, 3, 336–342, 2017.
2. Demestichas, K. and Daskalakis, E., Data lifecycle management in precision agriculture supported by information and communication technology. *Agronomy*, 10, 11, 1648, 2020. doi 10.3390/agronomy10111648.
3. McConnell, E., Reading/recording devices: Data acquisition systems, in: *Electrical Measurement, Signal Processing, and Displays*, pp. 36–10–36–22, 2003, doi 10.1201/9780203009406.
4. Imaino, W., Munce, C., Yerry, M., Mcdonald, N., Tran, N., Data acquisition and signal processing using a laptop personal computer. *Rev. Sci. Instrum.*, 62, 2, 516–521, 1991. doi 10.1063/1.1142096.
5. Hawn Nelson, A.L. and Zanti, S., A framework for centering racial equity throughout the administrative data life cycle. *Int. J. Popul. Data Sci.*, 5, 3, 2020. doi 10.23889/IJPDS.V5I3.1367.
6. Hawk, S.R., Dabney, D.A., Teasdale, B., Reconsidering homicide clearance research: The utility of multifaceted data collection approaches. *Homicide Stud.*, 25, 3, 195–219, 2021. doi 10.1177/1088767920939617.
7. Fan, Z., Context-based roles and competencies of data curators in supporting research data lifecycle management: Multi-case study in china. *Libri*, 69, 2, 127–137, 2019. doi 10.1515/libri-2018-0065.
8. Choi, J., Kaghazchi, A., Sun, B., Woodward, A., Forrester, J.D., Systematic review and meta-analysis of hardware failure in surgical stabilization of rib fractures: Who, what, when, where, and why? *J. Surg. Res.*, 268, 190–198, 2021. doi 10.1016/j.jss.2021.06.054.
9. Halstead, B., Koh, Y.S., Riddle, P., Pears, R., Pechenizkiy, M., Bifet, A., Recurring concept memory management in data streams: exploiting data stream concept evolution to improve performance and transparency. *Data Min. Knowl. Discov.*, 35, 3, 796–836, 2021. doi 10.1007/s10618-021-00736-w.
10. Harvey, M., Research data centres-a regulator's perspective. *J. Priv. Confid.*, 11, 2, 2021. doi 10.29012/jpc.769.

11. Wasik, Z., Modeling the epistemological multipolarity of semiotic objects, in: *Studies in Computational Intelligence*, p. 314, 2010, doi 10.1007/978-3-642-15223-8_31.

12. Li, X. and Hodgson, M.E., Vector field data model and operations. *GI Sci. Remote Sens.*, 41, 1, 1–24, 2004. doi 10.2747/1548-1603.41.1.1.

13. Nasution, M.K.M., Multi-criteria as decisions. *IOP Conf. Ser. Mater. Sci. Eng.*, 1003, 1, 2020a. doi 10.1088/1757-899X/1003/1/012118.

14. Sahin, O., Akay, B., Karaboga, D., Archive-based multi-criteria artificial bee colony algorithm for whole test suite generation. *Eng. Sci. Technol. Int. J.*, 24, 3, 806–817, 2021, doi: 10.1016/j.jestch.2020.12.011.

15. Nasution, M.K.M., Sitompul, O.S., Elveny, M., Syah, R., Data science: A review towards the big data problems. *J. Phys. Conf. Ser.*, 1898, 1, 2021. doi 10.1088/1742-6596/1898/1/012006.

16. Nasution, M.K.M., Syah, R., Ramdan, D., Afshari, H., Amirabadi, H., Selim, M.M., Khan, A., Lutfor Rahman, M., Sani Sarjadi, M., Su, C.H., Modeling and computational simulation for supersonic flutter prediction of polymer/ gnp/fiber laminated composite joined conical-conical shells. *Arab. J. Chem.*, 15, 1, 2022c. doi 10.1016/j.arabjc.2021.10346.

17. Nasution, M.K.M., Elveny, M., Syah, R., Behroyan, I., Babanezhad, M., Numerical investigation of water forced convection inside a copper metal foam tube: Genetic algorithm (GA) based fuzzy inference system (GAFIS) contribution with CFD modeling. *Int. J. Heat Mass Transf.*, 182, 2022a. doi 10.1016/j.ijheatmasstransfer.2021.122016.

18. Yang, P.L., Xu, H., Shen, W.Q., Simulation data lifecycle management based on engineering flight simulation platform. *Appl. Mech. Mater.*, 654, 385–390, 2022. doi 10.4028/www.scientific.net/AMM.654.385.

19. Syah, R., Faghri, S., Nasution, M.K.M., Davarpanah, A., Jaszczur, M., Modeling and optimization of wind turbines in wind farms for solving multi-objective reactive power dispatch using a new hybrid scheme. *Energies*, 14, 18, 2021. doi 10.3390/en14185919.

20. Nasution, M.K.M., Syah, R., Elveny, M., Multiple-objective as decisions in computing. *AIP Conf. Proc.*, 2022.

21. Allanic, M., Hervé, P.Y., Pham, C.C., Lekkal, M., Durupt, A., Brial, T., Grioche, A., Matta, N., Boutinaud, P., Eynard, B., Joliot, M., BIOMIST: A platform for biomedical data lifecycle management of neuroimaging cohorts. *Front. ICT*, 3, JAN 2022. doi 10.3389/fict.2016.00035.

22. Nasution, M.K.M., Sitompul, O.S., Nababan, E.B., Nababan, E.S.M., Sinulingga, E.P., Data science around the indexed literature perspective, in: *Advances in Intelligent Systems and Computing*, vol. 1294, pp. 1051–1065, 2020, doi 10.1007/978-3-030-63322-6_91

23. Nasution, M.K.M., Syah, R., Elveny, M., Studies on behaviour of information to extract the meaning behind the behaviour. *J. Phys. Conf. Ser.*, 801, 1, 2017. doi 10.1088/1742-6596/801/1/012022.

24. Nasution, M.K.M., A method for constructing a dataset to reveal the industrial behaviour of big data. *IOP Conf. Ser. Mater. Sci. Eng.*, 1003, 1, 2020. doi 10.1088/1757-899X/1003/1/012156.

25. Lee, J.S., Zeigler, B.P., Venkatesan, S.M., Design and development of data distribution management environment. *Simulation*, 77, 1-2, 39–52, 2001. doi 10.1177/003754970107700103.

26. Kwak, J.Y., Yim, J., Ko, N.S., Kim, S.M., The design of hierarchical consensus mechanism based on service-zone sharding. *IEEE Trans. Eng. Manage.*, 67, 4, 1387–1403, 2020. doi 10.1109/TEM.2020.2993413.

27. Majed, A., Raji, F., Miri, A., Replication management in peer-to-peer cloud storage systems. *Cluster Comput.*, 25, 1, 401–416, 2022. doi 10.1007/s10586-021-03395-0.

28. Polyanskii, A., A cap covering theorem. *Combinatorica*, 41, 695–702, 2021. doi 10.1007/s00493-021-4554-1.

29. Shao, M., Qi, D., Xue, H., Big data outlier detection model based on improved density peak algorithm. *J. Intell. Fuzzy Syst.*, 40, 4, 6185–6194, 2021. doi 10.3233/JIFS-189456.

30. Nasution, M.K.M., Aulia, I., Elveny, M., Data. *J. Phys. Conf. Ser.*, 1235, 1, 2019. doi 10.1088/1742-6596/1235/1/012110.

## 5

Role of Data Science in Healthcare

Anidha Arulanandham[1]*, A. Suresh[2] and Senthil Kumar R.[1]

[1]*Department of Computer Science & Engineering, New Horizon College of Engineering, Bangalore, India*
[2]*International School of Engineering, Bangalore, India*

Abstract

Data Science technologies have widened the usage of digital health data thereby enhancing the ways of diagnosing diseases and precision medicine. Knowledge extraction plays a vital role in finding patterns with respect to molecular sequences. Data analytics based preventive medicine reduces the cost for healthcare. Whereas unstructured healthcare data complicates the standard of serving patients which increases medical cost and life risk due to the complexity in medical decision-making.

Disease diagnosis and drug discovery will be enhanced over a period of time with the help of Data Science methodologies. Machine Learning methods are used in computing probability of different diseases according to environmental conditions and various food habits across world. Advancements in drug discovery enhances personalized medicine techniques thereby reducing the risk of severe medical conditions and even death. Emerging Data Science technologies are constantly expanding the ways to extract patterns in molecular sequences, as a result, mutations are being discovered. These mutant patterns are mainly helpful in predicting, preventing, treating and curing diseases well in advance. This advancement in technology, reduces gap between medical research and medical care to mankind.

The role of data science technologies is crucial in precision medicine, which is one of the major future scopes in the healthcare industry. The advent of Data Science technologies gives us accurate diagnostic measures thereby increasing accuracy in disease diagnosis and drug design. Therefore, the above-mentioned knowledge acquired is helpful in decision making toward medical research against the personalized drug design and medical practices. This chapter provides an

---

Corresponding author: arul.anidha@gmail.com

Archana Patel, Narayan C. Debnath and Bharat Bhusan (eds.) Data Science with Semantic Technologies: Theory, Practice, and Application, (105–138) © 2022 Scrivener Publishing LLC

overview of demand and scope of using Data Science technologies especially in healthcare sector. There are several fields in healthcare sector, such as predictive modeling, genetics, etc., which make use of data science for diagnosis and drug discovery, thereby increasing usability of precision medicine.

Keywords: Data science, disease diagnosis, drug discovery, mutations, precision medicine, healthcare industry

5.1 Predictive Modeling—Disease Diagnosis and Prognosis

Predictive modeling is considered as a subset of data analytics, which is used for predicting uncommon and unknown events to be occurred as a consequence of current state of the events. Predictive models analyze historical data and determine likelihood of possible future outcomes. Also, it plays a dominant role in significant clinical and medical decision making. The role of decision making in the healthcare industry is crucial that includes type of treatment and type of medication. A predictive model is helpful for medical decision making for medical practitioners and biologists. Predictive modeling makes use of machine learning and deep learning, which are subfield of artificial intelligence for diagnosis and prognosis of diseases [1].

By using these models, efficiency of medical data can be improved, and it leads to reduction in treatment cost by making right decision at right time, which helps to determine kind of treatment and medicine. These are frequently used for investigating diagnostic reports, and the analyses are much better than the other methods [2]. Death rates due to chronic diseases, such as cancer, can be very much reduced by early detection, perfect treatment and proper medicine [3]. Hence, almost all biologist and medical scientists are fascinated toward the innovative, advanced techniques of predictive modeling in disease diagnosis and prognosis [4].

These new advancements in healthcare have widened the usability of electronic medical data and opened new ways to effective decision support and overall clinical practices [5]. The evolvement high-dimensional big data in medicinal and clinical service networks makes use of accurate medical data analysis that could improve patient healthcare [6]. On the contrary, poor quality of medical data analysis results in poor decision making, which increases patient risk and death rates. With the help of data science tools and techniques, it is possible to find accurate data patterns, which can enrich the domain expert's knowledge in healthcare that results in empowered clinical care, such as precision medicine and personalized treatments.

The future of predictive data analytics in healthcare widespread its hands everywhere in all fields of medicine, and its impact increases exponentially. Improved outcomes toward critical clinical decision support, considerable cost reduction and reduced patient life risk make predictive modeling a worthy preference in healthcare operational environments. Finally, predictive modeling helps in effective and accurate decision support. In particular, scenarios, such as similar cases with similar medical evidences and also accurate diagnostic symptom knowledge, are not available. The following categories are common predictive models:

1. Supervised machine learning models
   a. Classification models
   b. Forecast/regression models
2. Unsupervised machine learning models
   a. Clustering models
   b. Associative models
   c. Outlier models
3. Time series models

5.1.1 Supervised Machine Learning Models

Classification models in disease diagnosis and drug discovery can be developed same as predictive modeling but these models predict the results in a categorical result, such as yes or no, sequence pattern in category, etc. Classification models must be trained and tested before validating on the new gene data. Classification models are supervised approach in which the model must be trained with known label of disease discovery. The most popular classification models of machine learning techniques in disease diagnosis and drug prediction are discussed.

1. **Bayesian Model:** The Bayesian model approach is a probability-based prediction model, which predict a numerical probability value from 0 to 1 as a result in gene expressions or gene variants or the gene sequence interpretations etc. The numerical values can be interpreted to the categorical results, such as the new drug helps in identifying the disease as yes or no category. The probability value can be extended to multiple categorical values such as diagnosis result is Good, Average, Bad. The naïve

Bayes model applies conditional probability on the selected gene data with the assumption that all the attributes of the gene dataset are conditionally independent. The probability of each feature calculated from the available gene dataset and multiplied is mentioned the given formula.

$$P(h|D) = P(D|h)P(h)/P(D) \qquad (5.1)$$

where D is the gene dataset and 'h' is the hypothesis on disease prediction. The improved naïve Bayes model with the conditional assumption finds the probability as

$$V_{NB} = \operatorname{argmax}(V_i \prod_i P(a_i|v_i)) \qquad (5.2)$$

where V_{NB} is the target value output by the naive Bayes classifier.

2. **Regression Model:** The regression-based prediction model can be used to predict a numerical value. Predicting the position of gene sequence numerically or interpreting the sequence numerically, the performance of the regression models is comparatively better. Simple linear regression can be used to predict using a single feature, and multiple features can be used with multiple linear regression. The coefficient values of each input features indicate the strength of association and contributes with the predictor variable. The regression technique identifies a linear relationship among the input features of disease dataset and predicts the future value. A linear relation may exist among the disease dataset in a higher-order polynomial degree. A higher-order polynomial degree can be applied to identify the hidden gene sequence, gene pattern, or drug predictions. The following equations are showing the simple, multiple, and polynomial regression equations (3%), (4%), and (5%)

$$y = \beta_0 + \beta_1 X \qquad (5.3)$$

$$y = \beta_0 + \beta_1 X_1 + \beta_2 X_{2+...+} \beta_n X_n \qquad (5.4)$$

$$y = \beta_0 + \beta_1 X_1 + \beta_2 X^2_{+...+} + \beta_n X^n \qquad (5.5)$$

3. **Artificial Neural Network Models:** Artificial neural network (ANN) model approaches are very efficient to fit linear regressions in disease predictions and gene expressions, if the number of samples in the data set is very large. ANN model supports classification and predictions with

different loss functions. An ANN contains three layers, such as input, hidden, and output layers. A heuristic approach will be performed to decide the number of units in each layer. The number of input features of the gene database can be given in the input layer. All the units in the first layer will be connected to all the units of hidden layer and from hidden layer to output layer. The number of output units and its type will be decided based the expected outcome of the identifying the gene expression model or disease prediction model or drug discovery model. Each unit of the all the layers is assigned with a small random initial weight value and bias value.

The ANN model can be trained based on the gene features, such as gene description, gene accession number position, frequency etc. The output layer classes can be designed as Yes or No types or multiple classes, which will be set based on the problem models such as disease prediction, drug prediction or gene sequence predictions. The model accuracy depends on the quality of the training data and test data. Gradient decent algorithm is mostly used to improve the accuracy in ANN model. The final model will be selected based on the highest accuracy and least error. The model error reduced by adjusting the weights and bias of each ANN unit in all the layer. ANN model can be used for both classification and regression in disease prediction, drug prediction or gene sequence classifications, pattern classifications etc.

4. **Decision Tree Model:** Prediction in regression models' performance is good, if the disease datasets features are linear. If the features of nonlinear decision tree-based model can be used for prediction. Decision tree model can be used in classification and prediction in disease datasets. The model selects the best attribute selected using the measurements such as information gain or gain ratio or Gini index based on the numeric dataset features or categorical features. An entropy measure is used to find the homogeneity of the dataset. The uncertainty or the randomness of the data set calculated by using entropy. Information gain of the attributes calculated using entropy to select the best attribute form the input dataset.

$$Entropy = \sum_{i=0}^{c} \text{Pi} \log_2(Pi) \tag{5.6}$$

The tree will be constructed by creating the best attribute as root node. The tree grows by splitting the dataset based the values of the attribute. For each possibility of the values in values are further split into sub tree. The approach is recursively called after removing the selected best attribute. Best attribute will be identified from the remaining attributes and tree grows till all the training rows covered. Pruning process reduce the size of the classification tree by assigning the label to the leaf node by using voting mechanism. The limitations of decision tree is the model may have overfitting issues and the linearity among the features may not be identified.

5.1.2   Clustering Models

5.1.2.1   Centroid-Based Clustering Models

The centroid based clustering algorithms are partitioning the disease or drug prediction training features into clusters. The cluster centers are represented by using mean or median values. The number of clusters are chosen randomly from the disease or drug prediction features for the initial value. A similarity measure is used to identify each instance, which are similar to the clusters. The centroid values are updated continuously along with the new added values. Clustering technique is repeated until there is no change in the centroid values. The clustering on features performed using mean or medoids to discover the new predictions.

5.1.2.2   Expectation Maximization (EM) Algorithm

The K means algorithms clusters the disease or drug prediction features dataset in circular form. If disease data set is noncircular shape, then the k-mean assigns the new instances near to mean values. The cluster instance tends to assigned to another cluster in case of considering only mean value because the mean value is considered as centroid, which works better for circular cluster. If the cluster shape is not in circular Gaussian mixture model (GMM) provides flexibility with the assumption that instances are following normal distribution. The assumption of normal distribution provides less restriction on circular shape clusters. The initial random values are assumed from normal distribution data and computes the probability of the instance belongs to the type of clusters. The Gaussian distribution takes mean and standard deviation to compute the probability of an instance belong to the group. EM algorithm maximizes the probability of the instance by repeatedly performing the maximization technique until convergence.

5.1.2.3 DBSCAN

The DBSCAN performs clustering on non-spherical shape clusters which considers two parameters such as epsilon (ε) and minimum number of points which forms a dense region. The epsilon uses a minimum value as radius and selects the minimum number of points within the radius. This method performs well if the disease dataset contains outlier and the prediction performed on nonspherical shape clusters. The parameter value for epsilon and minimum number of points is a heuristic approach to improve the accuracy.

5.1.3 Feature Engineering

This is popularly known as feature engineering, which focuses on preparing data for increasing the efficiency of predictive models. These techniques are significant preprocessing steps, increases the rate of accuracy of predictive models.

5.2 Preventive Medicine—Genetics/Molecular Sequencing

When the genomic data are stored in compatible formats, we may not lose any subtle genetic signals. These genetic signals provide significant information to understand likelihood of developing a particular disease. It is also important to recognize the pattern with which an individual responds to particular therapies are understood by the medical practitioners.

Sequencing is the process of determining the order of the chemical building blocks. This sequence reveals the secrets about the molecular/genetic properties and functionalities of a cell, which is base to understand the root causes of diseases under various circumstances. Also, this information is useful to determine which part of DNA contain genes, which part carries regulatory instructions to turn genes ON or OFF. These regulatory instructions are very complex and useful mechanism with which the time for a gene to be expressed to make RNA and protein, amount of protein to be made and time to stop this process are determined. Predominantly sequence data can pinpoint changes in a molecular structure which may cause diseases.

Molecular sequencing has the potential to capture the changes and causes in molecular structure and can suggest effective treatments especially red-flag treatments which causes adverse reactions. It is strongly proved that certain gene variations confer high risk of developing Breast,

Ovarian, Bowel and Colon cancers. In such cases accurate level of surveillance with medical interventions helps to detect early or prevent cancer.

Changes in the DNA sequences are analyzed by the Genetic Testing which is linked to certain diseases [7]. It is found that there are 7000 disorders linked with Mendelian genetics and over 700 tests are available currently. Mendelian genetics deals with the disorders as a result of a mutation in a single genetic locus. It will operate in either dominant or recessive mode.

Genetic disorders, Cancer, Neurological diseases, Cardiovascular disease, Blood disorders, Endocrine disorders are curable and researches are going on with this powerful combination of cutting-edge technological advents in biotechnology and rapidly advancing Data Science techniques which are predominantly useful to extract patterns to take significant decisions. Also, this leads to the evolution and growth of quantitative biology which will have bright future in next 20 years. Many basic fundamental secrets are unraveled in Genomics regarding molecular structure and cellular function of Genomics, molecular interactions within cells and organs. Interactions between molecules are happened due to attractive or repulsive forces between molecules and non-bonded atoms. Analyzing these patterns with the help of Data Science tools are helpful to reveal the secrets of biological processes of proteins of unknown or unexpected molecular functions [8].

Quantitative Biology is enriched with high-dimensional molecular data especially in the fields of genomics, molecular biology, computational neuroscience, neuronal dynamics of cognition and neuronal imaging. These fields had grown tremendously from recent technological advancements to sensor technology to probe into the internal structure and functionalities of cells with greater resolution. There are many neuroscience databases available, which provide significant information regarding gene transcription, translation, neuron structure, brain structure to identify neurological disorders. Some will provide quantitative and descriptive data and some will provide imaging data.

These high-dimensional molecular data will be used to analyze and identify the genetic patterns, which are used as signature biomarkers for diseases and medical decisions can be taken that leads to appropriate treatments before any symptoms can be seen. The following are termed as innovative genomics applications used to unravel disease patterns in molecular levels.

(1) Next Generation Sequencing (NGS—both WGS and WES)
(2) Single Cell DNA/RNA Sequencing

(3) Whole transcriptome sequencing (captures gene expression changes)
(4) Pharmacogenomics
(5) Cell-free gene expression system testing

Genomics technological breakthroughs rapidly moving toward personalized treatments and precision medicine which impacts healthcare industry crucially [9]. Advancement in nucleic acid sequencing technologies have created a pathway to translational medicine which broadens our understanding of chronic, metabolic and genetic disorders. Genomic technologies are used to understand and analyze genes and gene expression patterns. High-dimensional DNA sequencing and bioinformatics are used to assemble and analyze the function and structure of entire genome. Sequencing and analysis of genomes play vital role in disease diagnosis and prognosis. Molecular diagnostics deal with tools and techniques to learn and analyze biological markers in the genome and proteome. These have widened the scope of precision medicine and are catalyst for healthcare revolution. The impact of these technologies is uncountable which positively affect the healthcare from prevention to diagnosis to therapy.

The advancements in Data Science tools and technologies lead to the phase of integrating these technologies into healthcare centers to guide medical decisions based on the understanding and analysis of individual's molecular/genetic information, which leads to the most effective prevention of disease and targeted therapies. Also, advancements in genomics and molecular genetics with the help of Data Science widespread the pathway to P4 medicine which in turn broadened individualized early disease diagnosis and specialized treatment strategies [9].

5.2.1 Technologies for Sequencing

Sanger method is an early version of classical DNA sequencing method which uses fluorescent ddNTPs (dideoxynucleosides) to prevent inclusion of additional nucleotide.

Long-read sequencing includes pacBIO SMRT sequencing and Oxford nanopore sequencing are able to examine billions of DNA and RNA profiles and detect variable methylations.

The advantage of Long-read methods over short-read methods is that long-read methods are able to detect more subtle variations which cannot be observed with short-read methods. The history of DNA sequencing is illustrated in Figure 5.1.

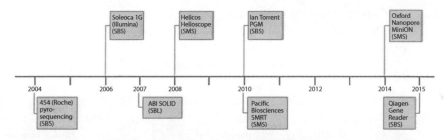

Figure 5.1 The history of DNA sequencing technologies (Source: https://www.
cd-genomics.com/blog/dna-sequencing-definition-methods-and-applications/) [10].

5.2.2   Sequence Data Analysis with BioPython

In data science perspective, DNA sequencing is the collection of high-dimensional datasets which comprises of millions of read sequences which is popularly known as high-throughput sequencing (HTS) and HTS experiments require substantial data analysis capabilities. There are good number of dedicated computational, statistical tools, and standard analysis workflows available for HTS data types [11].

5.2.2.1   Sequence Data Formats

1. Plain sequence format
A plain sequence format consists of IUPAC characters and numbers (IUPAC stands for International Union of Pure and Applied Chemistry).
   (e.g)
   A plain sequence data file will consist of only one sequence where as other sequence data files may contain more than one sequences.

An example sequence in plain format is:

```
ACAAGATGCCATTGTCCCCCGGCCTCCTGCTGCTGCT
GCTCTCCGGGGCCACGGCCACCGCTGCCCTGCCCCT
GGAGGGTGGCCCCACCGGCCGAGACAGCGAGCATAT
GCAGGAAGCGGCAGGAATAAGGAAAAGCAGCCTCCT
GACTTTCCTCGCTTGGTGGTTTGAGTGGACCTCCCAG
GCCAGTGCCGGGCCCCTCATAGGAGAGGAAGCTCGG
GAGGTGGCCAGGCGGCAGGAAGGCGCACCCCCCAG
CAATCCGCGCGCCGGGACAGAATGCCCTGCAG
GAACTTCTTCTGGAAGACCTTCTCCTCCTGCAAATA
AAACCTCACCCATGA
```

2. FASTQ format

A FASTQ sequence file will consists of many sequences and it's a text based format which will have values in form of {nucleotide: quality scores} pairs. A FASTQ file have 4 lines per sequence

1. It starts with @ symbol which is followed by a sequence identifier and description which is optional
2. Next line consists of Sequence letters
3. Third line consists of a + symbol
4. Last line contains quality values for the sequence characters in Line 2 Quality values or scores are numeric values in the range 2-40 represented as ASCII characters

An example sequence in FASTQ format is:
@SEQUENCE_ID

AGTGTTGAAGGTTCTTAGGGCATGGCAGAGGTCCAGAA TTGAAC
+
FFAFFADEDGGDBBGEGGBCGGHHE>EBBA@@=

3. EMBL (European Molecular Biology Laboratory) format

This file will also contain several sequences. Each sequence entry will have separate identifier line and annotation line. Sequence line starts with "SQ" and end of the sequence is marked by two front slashes("//"). Description line starts with "DE". XX denotes no data or comments

4. FASTA format

It will also contain many sequences. Each sequence will start with single line description with > symbol(greater-than)

An example sequence in FASTA format is:

>AB000263 |acc=AB000263|descr=Homo sapiens mRNA for prepro cortistatin like peptide, complete cds.|len=368
ACAAGATGCCATTGTCCCCCGGCCTCCTGCTGCTGCTGCTC
TCCGGGGCCACGGCCACCGCTGCCCTGCCCCTGGAGGG
TGGCCCCACCGGCCGAGACAGCGAGCATATGCAGG
AGCGGCAGGAATAAGGAAAAGCAGCCTCCTGACTT

TCCTCGCTTGGTGGTTTGAGTGGACCTCCCAGGCCAGTGCC
GGGCCCCTCATAGGAGAGGAAGCTCGGGAGGTGGCCAG
GCGGCAGGAAGGCGCACCCCCCCAGCAATCCGCGC
GCCGGGACAGAATGCC
   CTGCAGGAACTTCTTCTGGAAGACCTTCTCCTCCTGCAAAT
AAAACCTCACCCATGAATGCTCACGCAAGTTTAATTACAGA
CCTGAA

5. GCG format

This sequence file will consist of only one sequence and it starts with annotation lines.

End of the annotation is indicated by two dots(..). This line contains identifier, length of the sequence and a checksum.

6. GCG-RSF (Rich sequence format)

This file format will contain several sequences in a single file. The format is similar to GCG format.

7. GenBank format

This file can contain several sequences and it begins with the word "LOCUS" and a number of annotation lines. Start of the sequence is denoted by a word, "ORIGIN", and end of the sequence is denoted by two slashes (//). It is a collection of nucleotide sequences and their protein translations

There are several ways to search and retrieve sequence data from GenBank

1. By using Entrez Nucleotide
2. BLAST (Basic Local Alignment Search Tool) can be used
3. NCBI-e utilities can also be used

8. IG format

This format contains several sequences. Each sequence may consist of one or more comment lines which begins with ;(semicolon). Sequences will contain only the characters without blank spaces. 1 will be used as a terminating character and 2 is used to denote circular sequence.

An example sequence in IG format is:

AB000263
ACAAGATGCCATTGTCCCCCGGCCTCCTGCTGCTGCTGCTCT
CCGGGGCCACGGCCACCGCTGCCCTGCCCCTGGAG

GGTGGCCCCACCGGCCGAGACAGCGAGCATATGCAGG
AAGCGGCAGGAATAAGGAAAAGCAGCCTCCTGACTT
TCCTCGCTTGGTGGTTTGAGTGCGACCTCCCAGGCCAGT
GCCGGGCCCCTCATAGGAGAGGAAGCTCGGGAGGT
GGCCAGGCGGCAGGAAGGCGCACCCCCCCAGCAATC
CGCGCGCCGGGACAGAATGCCCTGCAAGGAACT
TCTTCTGGAAGACCTTCTCCTCCTGCAAATAAAACC
TCACCCATGAATGCTCACGCAAGTTTAATTACAGAC
CTGAA

G028uaah 240 bases
G028uaah
CATAAGCTCCTTTTAACTTGTTAAAGTCTTGCTTGAATTAAAG
ACTTGTT
TAAACACAAAATTTAGACTTTTACTCAACAAAAGTGATT
GATTGATTGAT

5.2.2.2 BioPython

Biopython is an open-source tool contains rich set of libraries for computational biology and Bioinformatics written in Python. To install Biopython in Jupyter Notebook, the following command should be used [12].

pip3 install Biopython

To install Biopython in Google Colab, the following command should be used.

!pip install Biopython

Some of its usages are listed below

1. **Working effectively with sequences**—Bio.Seq package and its modules are used to work with sequences. The Seq object is used for this purpose. If additional details such as identifier (or) name, description or annotation are required, SeqRecord object can be used. SeqIO module is used for writing and reading sequence files.

from Bio.Seq import Seq
myseq1 = Seq("AGGGCCTTGAAT")
print(myseq1)
Seq('AGGGCCTTGAAT ')

Complement of the sequence can be obtained with the following
print(myseq1.complement())
Seq(' TCCCGGAACTTA')
We can get the reverse complement as follows. It complements the sequence and then reverses from left to right.
print(myseq1.reverse_complement())
Seq(' ATTCAAGGCCCT')
Find method is be used to find the start position of a sub sequence in the given sequence. It returns -1 if the sub sequence is not present in the sequence. print(myseq1.find("CAA") output: 3 print(myseq1.find("CGT") output: -1
Count method is used to count number of characters in a sequence print(myseq1.count("AA")) output: 1
Transcribe method is used to transcribe(convert) DNA sequence into RNA sequence. print(myseq1.transcribe()) output: AGGGCCUUGAAU
Translate method is used to translate RNA into sequence of Amino Acids. This is the process of translating the mRNA sequence into sequence of Amino Acids during protein synthesis. print(myseq1.translate()) output: RALN - this is an amino acid sequence

It is very Interesting to know that the **Bio.Data.IUPACData** module provides a variable called **ambiguous_dna_complement** which is used to perform the complement operations very easily. CodonTable package of Biopython is used to access list of translation tables available in NCBI's genetic code page.

It is also used for the following operations effectively

    A. Sequence operations
    B. BLAST is an algorithm available online at NCBI website which is used to understand and analyse similarity between

sequences and it computes statistical significance. It is a critical tool in ongoing genomic research projects. This sequence similarity can be used to infer structural and functional evolutionary relationships of newly cloned genes and also whole genome. To deal with NCBI BLAST operations, Biopython provides Bio.Blast module.

```
from Bio.Blast import NCBIWWW
```

qblast function of NCBIWWW module supports to query the BLAST online https://blast.ncbi.nlm.nih.gov/Blast.cgi and it supports all the parameters of online version.
To understand the features of this module, following help command can be used.

```
help(NCBIWWW.qblast)
```

C. Entrez is an online search system of NCBI which integrates most of the popular molecular databases which includes DNA and Protein sequence, gene expression, genetic variations and genome with global query support.

Essential and basic Biopython codes are listed below:

```
from Bio import Entrez
# To link our email
Entrez.email='<user mail-id>'
# To set Entrez tool parameter which denotes the Name of application that
    makes the E-utility call. Values must be string without blankspaces
Entrez.tool= 'Demoscript'
# To know about last update and available links etc.,
Info=Entrez.einfo( )
Data=Info.read( )
print(Data)
```

D. Protein Data Bank (PDB) provides access to annotated information about the 3-D structures of macromolecules such as nucleic acids, proteins and small molecules such as drugs, inhibitors which is helpful to understand about the structure and interactions of biological molecules such as protein-protein, protein-DNA, protein-RNA whose impacts are crucial in many fields such as Translation medicine, Computational neuroscience, Biotechnology, Genetics and Biomedicine.

```
from Bio.PDB import *
# To download an example database
 Pl=PDBList( )
 Pl.retrieve_pdb_file('2FAT',pdir=' . ', file_format='mmCif'))
# To load cif file, the following command is used
 Parc=MMCIFParser(QUIET=True)
 Data=parser.get_structure("2FAT"," 2FAT.cif")
```

http://www.molsoft.com/bio/how-to-search.html is an online resource to search and download PDB databases. The PDBx/mmCIF is the file format for wwPDB data repository which supports all experimental methods. Crystallographic Information File (CIF) is a standard text file format represents crystallographic information [13].

(Arrangement of atoms in crystalline solids structure) given by International Union of Crystallography (IUCr). The mmCIF is the extended Crystallographic Information File format which include macromolecular crystallographic experiments along with small molecular experiments.

E. BioSQL is a generic relational database model primarily used to store sequences, features, annotations and ontologies. It is possible to get data from all popular bioinformatics databases such as GenBank, Swissport etc., BioSQL supports all Bio* projects (BioPerl, Biopython, BioJava and BioRuby) with a specific schema. Currently BioSQL supports MySQL, PostgreSQL, Oracle and SQLite. Biopython provides BioSQL module to do the following functionalities:

A. BioSQL database creation/Deletion

B. Connect to existing BioSQL database

C. Load sequence data from databases, like GenBank, BLAST result, Entrez results into BioSQL database and parse those data.

D. Retrieve taxonomy data from NCBI BLAST and store it in BIOSQL.

E. Access BioSQL database with SQL query

The following are the steps to create BioSQL database based on SQLite since it is very easy to follow.

```
Download and install SQLite engine.
Download BioSQL project from GitHub -https://github.com/biosql/biosql
Open console and create a directory
    >mkdir mysqlite
    >cd mysqlite
The following command is used to create a new SQLite database
>sqlite3.exe mybiosql.db
Copy the biosqldb-sqlite.sql file from BioSQL and store it in the current
    directory.
Use the following command to create all the tables
sqlite> .read biosqldb-sqlite.sql
To load all the tables
sqlite> SELECT name FROM sqlite_master WHERE type='table';
use the following to establish connection and the sequence data can be parsed
from Bio import SeqIO
from BioSQL import BioSeqDatabase
import os
server=BioSeqDatabase.open_database(driver='sqlite3', db="orchid.db")
db = server.new_database("orchid")
count=db.load(SeqIO.parse("orchid.gbk", "gb"), True) server.commit( )
server.close( )hid")
```

5.3   Personalized Medicine

The key idea behind personalized, precision or P4 medicine which is seen as an advanced medical approach is based on two factors. Initially, the first or external factor takes into consideration about individual patient's disease subtype, disease diagnosis and prognosis, treatment response using specialized tests and drugs. The second or internal factor includes molecular and behavioral biomarkers. The considered factors are specific to the individual patient, which is used to take medical decisions rather than taking medical decisions based on population averages. It is proved that personalized medicine is deeply and tightly connected with data science, especially machine learning as a predictive modeling techniques. It is clear that biological/molecular factors have higher impact in precision medicine, which is closely connected with genomics. The results of transcriptomics, epigenomics, proteomics, metabolomics is carefully captured through clinical processing and are stored as high through data with Data

Science tools and techniques. Not only these data but also bioimages, such as MRT and CT scan data and electronic medical records (EMRs).

Identifying signature biomarkers are of two types. Single-analyte bio-marker stratification is helpful in few special cases only. An alternative to this, multianalyte signature biomarkers, which are stored as high-dimensional and high throughput data are very useful in personalized medicine. Identifying signature biomarkers requires state-of-the-art Data Science techniques especially multivariate stratification algorithms whose role is crucial. In Cancer, personalized medicine is effectively used to make diagnosis, prognosis related medical decisions. One such example is targeted therapies or tumor marking testing to treat specific cancer cells such as HER2-Malignant cancer cells for an individual's cancer diagnosis and prognosis. To detect coronary artery disease, radiologists and car-diologists are in need of high-dimensional image processing algorithms for the images from CT scans. Similarly, radiologists and pulmonologists are using Artificial intelligence based data science tools and techniques to identify signature biomarkers of lungs from chest CT scan images. The following are some of the emerging trends in healthcare industry,

(i) Molecular diagnostics (MDx): MDx technologies are evolv-ing rapidly which applies molecular biology to medical test-ing and treatments which analyzes how cells express genes to proteins and are being deployed in the clinics from diag-nosis to therapy in a personalized fashion (e.g., breast cancer testing). This is a combination of molecular data extraction (e.g-nucleic acid extraction), real-time PCR, and result anal-ysis with the advent of data science tools.

(ii) The direct-to-consumer (DTC) diagnostic: the DTC genet-ic-testing industry gives awareness about the genetic disor-ders. Even though these give 99% accurate results than other methods, it does not provide conclusive and decisive results. Data science tools and techniques are very helpful to do pre-dictive analysis, and rate of decisive results is increased.

5.4   Signature Biomarkers Discovery from High Throughput Data

Microarray Gene Expression Datasets are widely used to identify signature biomarkers with the help of Feature Selection Techniques.

5.4.1   Methodology I — Novel Feature Selection Method with Improved Mutual Information and Fisher Score

Input S is a matrix of gene expression data, defined as

$$S = [X_{m \times n}]$$

where m is number of samples and n is number of genes , whose expression values are represented as

$$X = \begin{bmatrix} x_{11} & x_{12} & \cdots x_{1n} \\ x_{21} & x_{22} & \cdots x_{2n} \\ \vdots & \vdots & \vdots \\ x_{m1} & x_{m2} & \cdots x_{mn} \end{bmatrix}$$

where x_{ij} represents expression value of a gene x.

The expression matrix S is discretised to three major levels as base level, overexpression level which can further split into two based on a threshold value in the overexpression level and underexpression level which is also split into 2 levels based on the threshold value in the underexpression level.

$$D = [d_{m \times n}]$$

which is a discretised matrix.

Mutual information (MI) is computed as follows

$$MI(X, Y) = H(X) + H(Y) - H(X, Y)$$

where $H(X) = -\sum_i p_i \log_2 p_i$ is the entropy of the probability of gene (X_i) expression value x_{ij} and the entropy of the conditional probability between genes X_i, X_j is defined as

$$H(X, Y) = \sum_{y \in Y} \sum_{x \in X} p(x, y) \log \left(\frac{p(x, y)}{p(x)p(y)} \right)$$

MI is a matrix consisting of information content emitted by each gene based on its other genes. The mean value for each gene is computed which is considered as information gain of each gene. Genes are ranked according to information gain, and top ranked genes are selected as an input to F-Score.

$$MI = \begin{bmatrix} mi_{11} & mi_{12} & \cdots mi_{1n} \\ mi_{21} & mi_{22} & mi_{2n} \\ \vdots & \vdots & \vdots \\ mi_{m1} & mi_{m2} & \cdots mi_{mn} \end{bmatrix}$$

$$IG_i = \frac{1}{n}\Sigma_{j=1}^{n} m_{ij} \tag{5.4.1}$$

Feature subset, which is selected using improved information gain, is given as input to the F-score.

$$F(y_i) = \frac{(\mu_{i0} - \mu_i) - (\mu_{i0} - \mu_{i1} - \mu_i)}{\sigma_{i0} + \sigma_{i1}} \tag{5.4.2}$$

All the genes are ranked with F score values, and top ranked genes are selected as a final subset of discriminative feature subset, which is given as input to the classifier.

5.4.1.1   Algorithm for the Novel Feature Selection Method with Improved Mutual Information and Fisher Score

1. Microarray Gene Expression Samples $S_{i., i=1...N}$, the Inputs.
2. For Each Gene G in sample S_i Compute
   2.1 All the Expression profiles are discretized to many levels according to improved MI technique
   2.2 Probability of genes in each state in accordance with its neighbor is computed
   2.3 Initial entropy is computed based on the formula given
   2.4 Conditional entropy is computed
   2.5 Information of that gene with respect to its neighbor is computed with mutual information formula
3. Genes are ranked based on MI values in descending order
4. F-score values for the selected genes are computed.
5. All the genes are ranked in descending order based on F score values.

6. The top ranked genes are highly informative and are given as input to the classification algorithm.

Figure 5.2 is the block diagram which depicts the algorithm, Improved Mutual Information and Fisher Score pictorially.

5.4.1.2   Computing F-Score Values for the Features

Gene expression dataset is a continuous dataset it contains expression levels genes for samples/conditions. Let $g = \{g1, g2, ..., gN\}$ with targeted classes $h = \{h1, h2, ..., hK\}$. For continuous variable, the F-statistic between the genes and the classification variable h is chosen as maximum relevance between the genes and class variable.

The formula for the F-statistic is

$$F = \frac{between - class\ variability}{withih - class\ variability}$$

5.4.1.3   Block Diagram for the Method-1

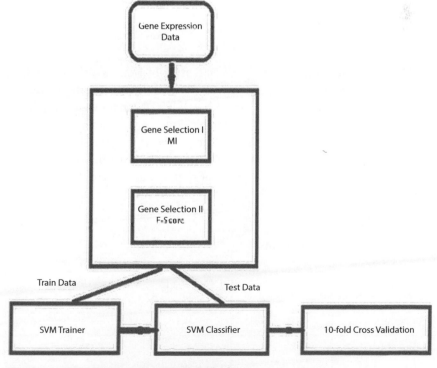

Figure 5.2 Block diagram of proposed method I.

The between-class variability is defined as

$$bc = \frac{\sum_{i=1}^{K} n_i (\overline{gi} - \overline{g})^2}{K - 1}$$

where $\overline{gi}$ denotes the sample mean in the ith class, n_i is the number of genes in the ith group, $\overline{g}$ denotes the overall mean of the genes and K denotes the number of classes.

The within-class variability is defined as

$$wc = \frac{\sum_{i=1}^{K} \sum_{j=1}^{n_i} (gij - \overline{gi})^2}{N - K}$$

where gij is the jth dimension in the ith gene expression out of K groups and N is the overall gene size. The F-statistics is shown in equation (5.1)

$$F(h, gi) = \frac{bc}{wc} \qquad (5.4.3)$$

5.4.1.4   Data Set

The data sets shown in Table 5.1 are taken from Kent Ridge Biomedical Data Repository. Below are the descriptions of the Data sets used. DLBCL has two classes DLBCL (Diffuse large B cell lymphomas) and FL (follicular lymphoma) with 77 total samples among which 58 belong to DLBCL and 19 belong to FL. DLBCL is a cancer of B cells, a type of white blood cell which is an aggressive tumor which can arise in virtually any part of the body. It is the most common type of non-Hodgkin lymphoma among adults.

Table 5.1 Data sets [14].

Data set name	Number of genes	Class	Total samples
DLBCL Harvard	7129	DLBCL, FL	77(58/19)
AML-ALL	7129	AML, ALL	72(47/25)
Lung Harvard2	12533	ADCA, Mesothelioma	181(150/31)

Lung cancer data set has 181 samples with ADCA and mesothelioma classes. ADCA (adenocarcinoma) is one of the histological subtypes of lung cancer.

5.4.1.5   Identification of Biomarkers Using the Feature Selection Technique-I

Table 5.2 shows the identified biomarkers related to AML-ALL data set. zyxin, ZYX is adhesion plaque protein, which is essential to know about signaling pathways of molecular processes. It is shown that cystatin C CST3 is responsible for subtype (AML-ALL) classification of leukemia. cyclin D3, CCND3 are prognostic factors in various cancers including leukemia.

Table 5.3 shows the genes identified in lung cancer data set.

Table 5.2 Genes selected—AML/ALL data set [14].

Gene no	Gene ID	Gene description	F-score
4847	X95735_at	zyxin, ZYX	1.31
1882	M27891_at	cystatin C (amyloid angiopathy and cerebral hemorrhage), CST3	1.14
2354	M92287_at	cyclin D3, CCND3	1.12
2642	U05259_rna1_at	MB-1 gene	1.11
4328	X59417_at	PROTEASOME IOTA CHAIN	1.1
1685	M11722_at	Deoxynucleotidyltransferase, terminal, DNTT	1.07
4196	X17042_at	PRG1 Proteoglycan 1, secretory granule	1.06
1745	M16038_at	LYN V-yes-1 Yamaguchi sarcoma viral related oncogene homolog	1

Table 5.3 Genes selected - Lung Harvard2 data set [14].

Gene no	Gene ID	F-score
5301	PIN1P1	1.39
7249	TSC2 tuberous sclerosis 2	1.32

(*Continued*)

Table 5.3 Genes selected - Lung Harvard2 data set [14]. (*Continued*)

Gene no	Gene ID	F-score
3764	KCNJ8 potassium voltage-gated channel subfamily J member 8	1.27
9824	ARHGAP11A Rho GTPase activating protein 11A	1.26
7046	TGFBR1 transforming growth factor beta receptor 1	1.2
3508	IGHMBP2 immunoglobulin mu binding protein 2	1.06

5.4.2   Feature Selection Methodology-II — Entropy Based Mean Score with mRMR

Input S is a matrix of microarray mRNA expression data, defined as

$$D= [X_{m \times n}]$$

where m is number of samples and n is number of genes, whose expression values are represented as

$$X = \begin{bmatrix} x_{11} & x_{12} & \cdots x_{1n} \\ x_{21} & x_{22} & \cdots x_{2n} \\ \vdots & \vdots & \vdots \\ x_{m1} & x_{m2} & \cdots x_{mn} \end{bmatrix}$$

where x_{ij} represents expression value of a gene x.

The data set D is Normalized with z-score Normalization.

$$Z = [R_{M \times N}]$$

$$R_{ij} = \frac{r_{ij} - \mu_i}{\sigma_i}$$

$$Z = \begin{bmatrix} r_{11} & r_{12} & \cdots r_{1N} \\ r_{21} & r_{22} & \cdots r_{2N} \\ \vdots & \vdots & \vdots \\ r_{M1} & r_{M2} & \cdots r_{MN} \end{bmatrix} \qquad (5.4.4)$$

F-statistics values are computed as follows

$$F(g_i) = \frac{[\sum_k n_k (\bar{g}_k - \bar{g})/(K-1)]}{\sigma}$$

where g is the mean value of g_i in all tissue samples, g_k is the mean value of g_i within the kth class. It represents the maximum relevance of the chosen features. This ensures the dissimilarity between the features.

Linear correlation coefficient (lcc) is computed as follows

$$lcc(g_i) = \frac{\sum(x - x_{mean})\sum(y - y_{mean})}{(\sigma_x + \sigma_y)}$$

where x and y represents expression values, x_{mean}, y_{mean} are mean values and σ_x, σ_y are standard deviations of feature i belongs to class 0 and class 1.

It is a measurement of the strength of the relationship between dependent variables and independent variables.

The mRMR is computed by combining F test with correlation using the difference.

$$mRMR_i = F(g_i) - lcc(g_i) \qquad (5.4.5)$$

Mean score is computed as follows. The normalized gene expression data Z is converted as matrix S

$$
S = \begin{bmatrix}
S_{11} & S_{12} & S_{13} & S_{14} \\
S_{21} & S_{22} & S_{23} & S_{24} \\
\cdots & \cdots & \cdots & \cdots \\
S_{M1} & S_{M2} & S_{M3} & S_{M4}
\end{bmatrix}
$$

The entropy values of S are computed using the formula given below:

$$
H_{ij} = \frac{1}{n_i}\left(S_{ij} log_2 \left(\frac{S_{ij}}{n_i} \right) \right) \tag{5.4.6}
$$

The Relevant Information Gain (*RIG*) is computed using the equation (5.4.7) to measure the relevance between features and the redundancy among the relevant features.

$$
RIG_i = -1 \times \left((H_{i1} + H_{i4})(H_{i2} + H_{i3}) \right) \tag{5.4.7}
$$

To maximize the relevance and minimize the redundancy the above Information Gain Score is added with the mRMR

$$
ImRMR_i = mRMR_i + RIG_i \tag{5.4.8}
$$

5.4.2.1 Algorithm for the Feature Selection Methodology-II

a) Let D denote a microarray gene expression data matrix. Let $G = \{1, 2,...,n\}$ be the indexed set representing the features.

b) F-statistic values are computed according to the eq given, which represents the maximum relevance of the chosen features. This ensures that the dissimilarity between the features and the level of independence and correlation are minimized.

c) Pearson correlation coefficient is computed according to the equation given below, which is the simplest way of computing the correlation between the features with the help of Linear correlation coefficient. This is useful to minimize the redundancy.

d) Mean score value is computed as follows
   a=Number of below the mean of class 1
   b=Number of above the mean of class 1
   c=Number of below the mean of class 2
   d=Number of above the mean of class 2
e) Entropy values are computed according to eq. given below which is useful to measure the information with the feature. So the relevant features will have high information gain. The Information Gain score is computed according to eq given below which is a good measure of indicating how a feature discriminates between two classes.
f) The *F* test is combined with correlation using difference
g) To maximize the relevance and minimize the redundancy the above information gain score is added with the Step 6.

The proposed methodology-II, Entropy Based Mean Score with mRMR is pictorially represented as a block diagram in Figure 5.3.

The improved minimum redundancy and maximum relevance technique gives better performance by selecting relevant and highly informative features to the classification algorithm, and it has the following benefits (1) Efficiency—true independent and representative features of the entire feature space (2) The generalization ability of the feature set is increased.

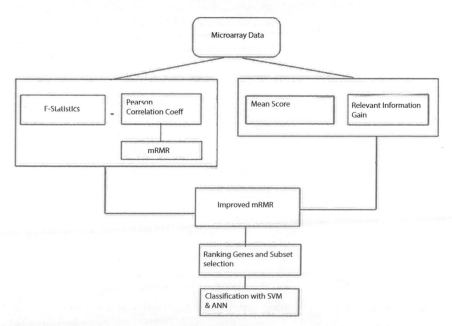

Figure 5.3 Block diagram of proposed method II [14].

5.4.2.2   Introduction to mRMR Feature Selection

The proposed feature selection is based on minimum redundancy maximum relevance (mRMR). In order to combine two effective features which are highly correlated then the issue of redundancy may arise. The issue of redundancy will lead to inefficient set of features selected for classification since the feature set will be consisting of fewer independent or representative features. Second, the features selected are not maximally representative of the original space covered by the entire dataset and they will represent narrow regions of the relevant space. It is strongly recommended to manipulate the dissimilarity between features by maximizing their mutual Euclidean distances, or minimizing their pairwise correlations.

To specify minimum redundancy, the Pearson correlation coefficient is used.

$$\min W_c \, , W_c = \frac{1}{|S|^2} \sum_{i,j} |c(g_i, g_j)| \tag{5.4.9}$$

Both positive and negative correlations are considered as redundancy, so absolute value of Pearson correlation coefficient (pcc) is taken. To calculate pcc, linear correlation coefficient (lcc) is computed, which is a measurement of the strength of the relationship between dependent variables and independent variables (class variables and features) as follows.

$$lcc = \sum (x - x_{mean}) \sum (y - y_{mean}) / (\sigma_x + \sigma_y) \tag{5.4.10}$$

Now, the simplest mRMR optimization criterion function involving above conditions is given as follows.

FCD: combine F-test with correlation using the difference.

$$\underset{i \in \Omega s}{\max} \{F(i,h) - \frac{1}{|S|} \sum_{j \in S} |c(i,j)|] \tag{5.4.11}$$

5.4.2.3   Data Sets

The data sets used in this study are downloaded from The Cancer Genome Atlas (TCGA) (http://cancergenome.nih.gov). It is a good source of benchmark cancer data sets. This work considers level 3 (normalized, segmented, and interpreted expression calls) of gene expression data of ovarian cancer. The gene expression data set is from AgilentG4502A, which is consisting of 46 samples and 17,814 features. The gene expression data set was consisting of 64 null values, which are replaced with a mean value of the expression values of corresponding feature. The dataset is having the samples with the following categories: normal, ovarian triplet, stage I, Prior malignancy, prior malignancy of breast cancer, subject positive for neoadjuvant therapy.

5.4.2.4   Identification of Biomarkers Using Rank Product

The function of RankProd-, a Bioconductor package, is used for the analysis of microarray data, especially to identify differentially expressed features. Fold changes (FC) of the genes are captured which are then used to rank the genes to identify up-regulated and down-regulated features under one condition against another condition (e.g., tumor vs normal samples) or differentially expressed features under a specific condition (e.g., stage I samples). To find the probability of a specific item among the top r of n items in a list is p = r/n. Multiplying these probabilities leads to the definition of the rank product RP =∏i ri/ni , where ri is the rank of the item in the ith sample and ni is the number of items in the ith sample. The High RP value denotes that the probability of occurring an item at the top is high. The rank product represents the calculation of geometric mean rank. The rank can be replaced by the sum, which leads to a statistic that is sensitive to noise and outliers.

5.4.2.5   Fold Change Values

The fold change (FC) is a ratio of mean of normal and test sample values and is a measure of denoting the quantity changes from control to test sample values, which is used to select the differentially expressed and discriminative genes in a microarray dataset with two biological conditions. For log2-fold change, its formula is log2FC=Log2(B)-Log2(A). For calculating Fold change from log2, the following formula must be used : Power(2, log2_Value).

From Table 5.4, it is observed that SCGB2A1 is highly expressed in prior malignancy of breast cancer, stage I, ovarian triplet and is less expressed in fallopian normals. Matrilysin (MMP7) is overexpressed in all stages of ovarian cancer including epithelial ovarian cancer (EOC) invasion and metastasis. Table 5.4 shows that MMP7 is highly expressed Gene next to

Table 5.4 Signature genes related with various conditions for data set II (Ovarian Cancer) [15].

Various states of ovarian cancer	Signature genes			
	Up-regulated genes with fold-change values		Down-regulated with fold-change values	
Stage I	SCGB2A1	293.5831	TTR	0.0159
	MMP7	213.3754	C3orf57	0.0152
	EMX2	185.6868	DKK1	0.0143
	FCGR3A	140.6954	AHSG	0.0125
	DAPL1	127.0298	TYR	0.0117
	CD163	128.7888	FGB	0.011
	RGS1	116.4501	RPS4Y1	0.01
	EHF	115.9796	FABP1	0.0095
Positive to neoadjuvant therapy	FLJ22655	287.0818	C10orf81	0.0369
	OGN	96.93	LAMP3	0.0336
	MMRN1	73.3262	CCNA1	0.0369
	LRRC17	65.1782	C1orf172	0.0332
	HS3ST2	50.6136	VTCN1	0.0256
	ANGPTL5	56.018	TMPRSS4	0.0222
Prior malignancy	CD163	265.9249	IGFBP1	0.0064
	FCGR3A	200.0633	FGL1	0.0098
	RGS1	192.9723	FGB	0.0099
	SCGB2A1	180.1783	DKK1	0.0104
	EMX2	146.7661	RPS4Y1	0.011
	ZBED2	145.6009	TYR	0.0113
	MMP7	100.4355	FABP1	0.0119
	DAPL1	101.3929	DSCR8	0.0125

(Continued)

Table 5.4 Signature genes related with various conditions for data set II (Ovarian Cancer) [15]. (*Continued*)

Various states of ovarian cancer	Signature genes			
	Up-regulated genes with fold-change values		Down-regulated with fold-change values	
Fallopian normal	SCGB2A1	154.1038	BUB1	0.0324
	FAM81B	124.7401	HBG1	0.0299
	ARMC3	125.7912	DSCR8	0.0305
	MMP7	124.5705	C3orf57	0.0273
	DAPL1	105.9425	PAH	0.0275
	CRISP3	93.6339	IGFBP1	0.025
	FLJ44379	94.9876	AHSG	0.0253
	TTC29	90.3322	RPS4Y1	0.0239
			FABP1	0.0198
			DKK1	0.0167
Ovarian triplet	SCGB2A1	172.319	IGFBP1	0.0056
	MMP7	170.883	FGL1	0.0094
	RGS1	134.9849	RPS4Y1	0.0119
	SPON1	129.3304	FABP1	0.0169
	EMX2	118.7361	FGB	0.0141
	FCGR3A	104.0767	AHSG	0.0143
	CD163	91.6076	TYR	0.0147
	EIIF	76.3206	UTS2	0.0183
			DKK1	0.0219
			TTR	0.0183

(*Continued*)

Table 5.4 Signature genes related with various conditions for data set II (Ovarian Cancer) [15]. (*Continued*)

Various states of ovarian cancer	Signature genes			
	Up-regulated genes with fold-change values		Down-regulated with fold-change values	
Prior malignancy of breast cancer	SCGB2A1	379.2888	HBG1	0.0155
	MMP7	303.5474	TTR	0.0152
	EMX2	198.0159	DKK1	0.013
	FCGR3A	167.7239	TYR	0.011
	DAPL1	160.7336	AHSG	0.011
	RGS1	159.9741	FGB	0.0112
	CD163	157.5652	FABP1	0.0092
	EHF	141.8555	RPS4Y1	0.0081

the SCGB2A1, MMP7, EMX2, FCGR3A, DAPL1, RGS1, CD163, EHF are highly expressed, upregulated and commonly present in stage I, ovarian triplet and prior malignancy of breast cancer cases. The SPON1 is upregulated, highly expressed gene present in ovarian triplet patients.

Conclusion

It is a clear evident that the unstructured healthcare data complicates the standard of serving patients, which increases medical cost and life risk due to the complexity in medical decision-making. Advancements in drug discovery enhance personalized medicine techniques, thereby reducing the risk of severe medical conditions and even death. The advent of data science technologies gives us accurate diagnostic measures thereby increasing accuracy in disease diagnosis and drug design.

References

1. Battineni, G. *et al.*, Applications of machine learning predictive models in the chronic disease diagnosis. *J. Pers. Med.*, 10, 2, 21, 31 Mar. 2020.

2. Napolitano, G., Marshall, A., Hamilton, P., Gavin, A.T., Machine learning classification of surgical pathology reports and chunk recognition for information extraction noise reduction. *Artif. Intell. Med.*, 70, 77–83, 2016, [CrossRef].

3. Polat, H., Mehr, H.D., Cetin, A., Diagnosis of chronic kidney disease based on support vector machine by feature selection methods. *J. Med. Syst.*, 41, 55, 2017, [CrossRef] [PubMed].

4. Eslamizadeh, G. and Barati, R., Heart murmur detection based on wavelet transformation and a synergy between artificial neural network and modified neighbor annealing methods. *Artif. Intell. Med.*, 78, 23–40, 2017, [CrossRef].

5. Martinez, D., Pitson, G., Mackinlay, A., Cavedon, L., Cross-hospital portability of information extraction of cancer staging information. *Artif. Intell. Med.*, 62, 11–21, 2014, [CrossRef] [PubMed].

6. Chen, M., Hao, Y., Hwang, K., Wang, L., Wang, L., Disease prediction by machine learning over big data from healthcare communities. *IEEE Access*, 5, 8869–8879, 2017, [CrossRef].

7. Committee on Bioethics Ethical issues with genetic testing in pediatrics. *Pediatrics*, 107, 6, 1451–1455, Jul 2001, [PubMed] [Google Scholar].

8. Sandler, S., Alfino, L., Saleem, M., The importance of preventative medicine in conjunction with modern day genetic studies. *Genes Dis.*, 5, 2, 107–111, 2018, Published 2018 Apr 12.

9. Nader, I., AL-Dewik, M., Qoronfleh, W., Genomics and precision medicine: Molecular diagnostics innovations shaping the future of healthcare in Qatar. *Adv. Public Health*, 2019, Article ID 3807032, 11 pages, 2019, https://doi.org/10.1155/2019/3807032.

10. https://www.cd-genomics.com/blog/dna-sequencing-definition-methods-and-applications/

11. https://www.genomatix.de/online_help/help/sequence_formats.html

12. https://github.com/biopython/biopython/blob/master/README.rst

13. http://biopython.org/DIST/docs/tutorial/Tutorial.html#sec7

14. Anidha, M. and Premalatha, K., A hybrid gene selection technique using improved mutual information and fisher score for cancer classification using microarrays, World Academy of Science, Engineering and Technology. *Int. J. Comput. Inf. Syst. Control Eng.*, 10, 3, 554–557, 2016, [SJR: 0.12].

15. Anidha, M. and Premalatha, K., An mRMR with mean score feature selection for ovarian cancer classification using joint analysis. *Int. J. Pharma Bio Sci.*, 8, 2, 495–504, 2017, [SJR: 0.274].

## 6

Partitioned Binary Search Trees (P(h)-BST): A Data Structure for Computer RAM

Pr. D.E Zegour

ESI: Ecole Supérieure d'Informatique, BP 68M, Oued Smar,
Alger, Algérie

Abstract

We present a new balanced binary search tree that generates two kinds of nodes: simple and class nodes. The latter form a partition on the tree with classes of heights h-1 or h-2. Furthermore, every class holds an AVL tree. Two advantages make the new structure attractive. First, it subsumes the most popular data structures AVL and Red-Black trees. Indeed, for h=2, the new structure is identical to a Red black tree with completely different algorithms, whereas for h=∞, it produces an AVL tree perfectly. Second, it proposes other unknown balanced binary search trees in which we can adjust the maximal height of paths between 1.44 lg(n) and 2 lg(n) where n is the number of nodes in the tree and lg the base-two logarithm. The P(h)-BST structure is similar to a standard binary search tree, with the exception that each node has an extra byte of storage for both the kind and the height. Simulation results reveal that the performance of the new structure is comparable to the one of the AVL and Red-Black trees when inserting items, whereas the performance of the new structure outperforms the one of the AVL and Red-Black trees when deleting items.

Keywords: Data structures, algorithms, balanced binary search trees, AVL-trees, Red-Black trees, partitioning

Email: d_zegour@esi.dz

Archana Patel, Narayan C. Debnath and Bharat Bhusan (eds.) Data Science with Semantic Technologies: Theory, Practice, and Application, (139–178) © 2022 Scrivener Publishing LLC

6.1   Introduction

Binary trees are hierarchical data structures to represent collections of items. They are now employed in a variety of computer science fields: memory management, compilers, mathematics, etc.

Among the advanced data structures on binary trees, we can cite binary search trees, tries and balanced trees. These structures are more complex and permit to represent large sets.

Binary search trees are hierarchical and dynamic data structures. They denote sets in which the members are arranged in a linear order. All values stored in the left subtree of any node x are fewer than the one stored at x, and all values stored in the right subtree of x are higher than the one stored at x, and that is an important property of a binary search tree. This is true for each node in a binary search tree (binary search tree property).

Most books about data structures and algorithms contain an important part on binary search trees. The most referenced books are certainly the ones of Knuth and Aho & co. [1, 2]. Many other books have more practical aspects. We can retain as examples: [3] offer various examples of binary tree operations using Pascal language [4]; explore binary search tree implementations in ML and Prolog, among other languages [5]; outlines binary search trees' basic structure and operations [6–8]; contain more programming of binary search trees in C and C++.

A delicate part of algorithms on binary search trees consists in maintaining them balanced or balancing them from time to time to keep good performance of operations. Recall that balancing the tree makes the cost of finding any key in lg (n).

There are many variations of balanced binary search trees. Among the most classic and widely used balanced binary trees we can cite AVL trees [9], Red-Black trees [10] and AA trees [11]. Among recent balanced binary trees, we can cite weak AVL trees [12] and zip trees [13]. In all of these methods, tree rebalancing is performed during each update operation.

We want through this work to present a new balanced binary search tree allowing to partition nodes of a binary search tree in classes with height h-1 or h-2, h being the parameter of the data structure. Each class holds an AVL tree. As a consequence, two kinds of nodes are generated: simple and class nodes. We have thus a double balance: globally the tree is perfectly balanced considering only class nodes and locally, i.e., inside a class, tree balance is provided by the AVL tree technique.

One additional byte at the level of any node suffices to represent both its kind and its height. The latter controls balance of the tree inside classes.

One of major advantages of the new structure is that it includes Red-Black trees and AVL trees. Indeed, when h is equal to 2, the new structure generates a binary search tree equivalent to a Red-Black tree. When h reaches a certain value h', i.e. when one class is created, it is about an AVL tree. For each value of h between 2 and h', the new structure generates a new balanced binary search tree unknown until now.

Note that two doctoral thesis works focused on the proposed structure. The first [14] proposes a unique representation for AVL and Red-Black tree. The second [15] proposes a generalization of the Red-Black tree structure.

We shall show through simulation that the insert algorithm of the proposed data structure is comparable to the one of AVL and Red-Black trees. On the other hand, the delete algorithm is much faster.

Section 6.2 presents the P(h)-BST structure with two examples. Section 6.3 describes maintenance algorithms. Section 6.4 gives the insert and delete algorithms with examples sketching the mechanisms. Section 6.5 shows that the new structure includes Red-Black trees and AVL trees. It also shows that a family of data structures can be generated by the proposed structure. Some simulation results are presented in Section 6.6. Finally, Section 6.7 concludes our contribution and gives some perspectives.

6.2 P(h)-BST Structure

Mathematically, a P(h)-BST defines a partition on the tree. Each class of the partition holds an AVL tree of depth h-1 or h-2. h being the parameter of the data structure. It is self-evident that the intersection of any two classes is empty, and that the union of all classes yields all of the tree's elements.

A P(h)-BST node can be of two different kinds: simple node or class node. It also contains a height holding the length of the path from it to the deepest leaf of the class. A node has an extra byte in addition to the data field. The first bit denotes its kind and the seven other bits control the balance of classes.

Formally, a P(h)-BST can be defined as follows:

- Every node must be either a simple node or a class node.
- The root class has a depth between 0 and h-1.
- Every class that is not the root class must have a depth equal to h-1 or h-2.
- There must be the same number of class nodes on every direct path from any node to a leaf.

Let us consider two examples of P(h)-BST in Figures 6.1 and 6.2. In order to simplify the presentation, class nodes are represented inside squares and the classes are surrounded. Simple nodes are inside circles. Values under nodes denote their heights.

Figure 6.1 shows a P(2)-BST. Every class contains an AVL tree of depth 0 or 1. From bottom to the root and from left to the right, we have the following classes {2, 15}, {34}, {39}, {51, 43, 54}, {94}, {31}, {40, 71}, {35}. Figure 6.2 shows a P(3)-BST. Here, every class contains an AVL tree of depth 1 or 2.

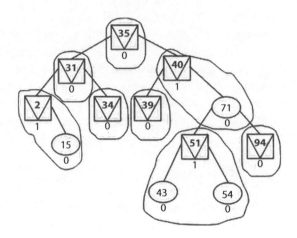

Figure 6.1 P(2)-BST.

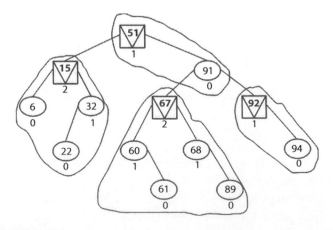

Figure 6.2 P(3)-BST.

6.2.1 Preliminary Analysis

When a class (a subtree) reaches depth h after an insert operation, a partitioning operation (defined below) is completed in order to transform it into two classes. In this way, the maximal height of a class is (h-1). After a delete operation, a class height can become equal to (h-3) and thus the class becomes under loaded. A Departitioning operation (defined below) is completed in order to transform two classes into one class. In this way, the minimal height of a class is (h-2).

6.2.2 Terminology and Conventions

Let us introduce some terms with examples. In Figure 6.2:

Class {51, 91} is the mother class of classes {15, 6, 32, 22}, {67, 60, 61, 68, 89} and {92, 94}.

Class {51, 91} is the root class.

{15, 6, 32, 22}, {67, 60, 61, 68, 89} and {92, 94} are leaf classes.

{15, 6, 32, 22} and {67, 60, 61, 68, 89} are two direct sister classes. Thus, they have the same parent node.

{15, 6, 32, 22} and {92, 94} are simply two sister classes. They have not the same parent node.

A class can be designated by its class node. We can then write class 15 instead {15, 6, 32, 22}.

Class 15 has a height equal to 2. Class 92 has a height equal to 1.

Node 67 has a balance equal to 0. It is the difference between heights of its two children.

In the figures below, we adopt the following conventions:

- A class surrounded by a continuous line designates a valid class.
- A class surrounded by a discontinuous line designates an underflow class.
- A class surrounded by a double continuous line designates an overflow class.

6.3 Maintenance Operations

Maintenance operations can be divided into two groups: those performed within a class and those performed outside of class. The first category includes operations like Restructuring, AVL tree insert, and AVL tree delete. Partitioning, departitioning, restructuring-partitioning, and transforming are the operations in the second group.

Before we present them, let us begin by introducing the abstract data types on the new data structure and some useful basic operations.

Abstract data types

Left_Child(P): Node P's left child

Right_Child(P): Node P's right child

Make_Right_Child(P, R) : Make R a right child of node P

Make_Left_Child(P, R): Make R a left child of node P

Kind(P) : Kind of node P

Make_Kind(P, A_Kind): Make A_kind the new kind of node P

Simple_Height(P) : Height of left or right child node P inside the class it belongs

Height(P) : Height of node P

Make_Height(P, H) : Make H the new height of node P

Basic operations

We will use the following operations :

- Rotation(P, Dir) is a function that rotates node P to the left if Dir=1 and to the right if Dir=0. It returns the node that will take the place of P.

```
Case Dir Of
    0 :    { F := Right_Child ( P ) ; Make_Right_
Child( P , Left_child ( F ) ) ; Make_Left_Child ( F ,
P ) }
    1:     { F := Left_child( P ) ; Make_Left_Child (
P , Right_Child ( F ) ) ; Make_Right_Child ( F , P )  }
    Endcase
    Rotation := F
```

- The procedure KindSwap (P, F) swaps the types of nodes P and F.

```
    Save_kind := Kind ( P ) ; Make_kind ( P , Kind(F)
) ;  Make_kind ( F , Save_kind )
```

- KindFlip(P, F, Dir) is a procedure that transforms new children of F into class nodes and assigns the initial kind of P to F.

```
    Save_kind := Kind ( P )
    Case Dir of
    0: { Make_kind ( Right_Child (F), Class) ; Make_
kind ( P , Class ); If h >2 Make_kind (Left_child(P) , Simple )   }
    1: { Make_kind ( Left_child ( F ) , Class ) ;  Make_kind
( P , Class ); If h >2  Make_kind (Right_Child(P) ,Simple) }
    Endcase
    Make_kind ( F , Save_kind )
```

6.3.1   Operations Inside a Class

In terms of the operations mentioned above, we will describe the many basic maintenance procedures needed to run insert and delete algorithms on the new structure.

Restructuring

After an AVL tree property violation, the restructuring operation simply involves rebalancing the tree. It employs the restructure operation, which implies a rotation and then updates their heights. In the Restructure operation, the KindSwap operation is also possible. A Reverse balance operation, which reverses a node's balance, can also be used before the latter. Let us recall that rotating a node is the only way to reverse its balance. All these operations are mentioned below.

Restructuring (P, Dir) → Pointer to the new node

```
      Case Dir
      0 : {
              If Simple_Height(Right_Child(Right_Child(P)))
- Simple_Height( Left_child(Right_Child(P))) = -1
      Make_Right_Child ( P, Reverse_Balance ( Right_
Child ( P ) , 1 ) )
      Restructuring := Restructure ( P , 0 )
              }


      1 : {
              If Simple_Height(Right_Child(Left_child(P)))
- Simple_Height(Left_child(Left_child(P))) = + 1
      Make_Left_Child ( P, Reverse_Balance ( Left_
child ( P ) , 0 ))
      Restructuring := Restructure ( P , 1 )
      }
      Endcase
```

Restructure (P, Dir) → Pointer to the new node

```
      F:= Rotation(P, Dir)
      If (h= 2) or (Kind(P)=Class) KindSwap(P, F)
      Make_Height(P, Max(Simple_Height(Left_child(P),
Simple_Height(Right_Child(P)) + 1)
      // Max denotes the largest.
```

```
     Make_Height(F,  Max(Simple_Height(Left_child(F),
Simple_Height(Right_Child(F)) + 1)
     Restructure := F
```

Reverse_Balance (P, Dir) → Pointer to the new node

```
     F:= Rotation(P, Dir)
     Make_Height(P,  Max(Simple_Height(Left_child(P),
Simple_Height(Right_Child(P)) + 1)
     Make_Height(F,  Max(Simple_Height(Left_child(F),
Simple_Height(Right_Child(F)) + 1)
     Reverse_Balance := F
```

AVL tree insert

The restructuring operation is used by the AVL tree insert method to rebalance the tree anytime it becomes imbalanced in the sense of AVL trees. The algorithm is described in terms of height rather than balance for our needs.

When a new item is added to the tree, the algorithm below is used. The path covered by the search process from the tree root Root to the parent P of the newly inserted node is stored in stack Branch. To update their height fields, nodes are popped. The tree is reorganized and if a node's balance exceeds 1 (in absolute value), the process is terminated. The algorithm returns a pointer to the new root and it is depicted in Screenshot 6-01 as expressed in [14].

```
Avl_Insert := Root
Continue:= True
Repeat
    {
        Pop(Branch, P)
        Kind_P := Kind_(P)
        Update P's height
        If ABS ( Simple_Height ( Left_child ( P ) - Simple_Height ( Right_child( P ))) > 1
            {
                If Simple_Height ( Left_child ( P )) > Simple_Height ( Right_child ( P ))
                    Q := Restructuring(P, 1)
                Else Q := Restructuring(P, 0)
                If Kind_P = Simple
                    {
                        Pop(Branch, Parent)
                        Modify node Parent to point now Q
                    }
                Else Avl_Insert := Q
                Continue:= False
            }
        Else Continue := (Kind_P= Class)
    }
Until ( Not Continue)
```

Screenshot 6-01 AVL tree insert algorithm.

AVL tree delete

The restructuring operation is also used by the AVL tree deletion technique. The algorithm below is performed when an element is removed from a leaf class rooted at Root. The stack branch stores the path traversed by the search process from the tree root Root to the parent P of the deleted node. To update their height fields, nodes are popped.

The tree is reorganized if the balance of a node exceeds 1 (in absolute value). If the height of the node that replaces the removed node is different of the one of the removed node, the process continues in cascade (Condition Save_height − Height(P) = 0).

The algorithm returns a pointer to the new root and, likewise, it is shown in Screenshot 6-02 as expressed in [14].

```
Avl_Delete := Root
Continue:= True
Repeat
    {
        Pop(Branch, P)
        Kind_P := Kind(P)
        Save_height := Height(P)
        Update P's height
        If ABS( Simple_Height ( Left_child ( P ) - Simple_Height ( Right_child )) > 1
            {
                If Simple_Height ( Left_child ( P ) ) > Simple_Height ( Right_child ( P ) )
                    Q := Restructuring(P, 1)
                Else Q := Restructuring(P, 0)
                If Kind_P = Simple
                    {
                        Parent := Top(Branch)
                        Modify node Parent to point now Q
                    }
                Else Avl_Delete := Q
                P:= Q
            }
    }
Until   (Save_height − Height( P ) = 0 ) Or (Kind_P= Class)
```
Screenshot 6-02 AVL tree insert algorithm.

6.3.2   Operations Between Classes (Outside a Class)

An item is always added into a leaf class first throughout the insert procedure. The latter has the potential to overflow, with a height of h. After that, a partitioning procedure is carried out. Whenever an item is deleted, it is always removed from a leaf class first. The latter can overflow, resulting in a height of h-3. Several scenarios can be reported:

- There is no direct sister class for the underflow (or its sibling node is a simple node). It is necessary to carry out a transformation operation.
- The underflow class has a direct sister class with height h-2 (or a sibling node that is a class node). It is necessary to undertake a departitioning operation.
- The underflow class has a direct sister class with height h-1 (or a sibling node that is a class node). There is a restructuring-partitioning operation.

All of the operations mentioned will be described here.

Partitioning

It entails dividing one class into two. After an insert operation, class Z's height reaches h in Figure 6.3(a1). Class Z is surrounded by a double continuous line that designates then a not valid class since it overflows. It is thus partitioned. Figure 6.3(a2) shows how node Z becomes a simple node, and its two descendants, X and Y, become class nodes. As a consequence, node Z joins the mother class as a new leaf.

This operation relates to a simple change in the kinds of three nodes. Partitioning corresponds then to a splitting operation. This process can lead to Partitioning operations in cascade if the mother class reaches again

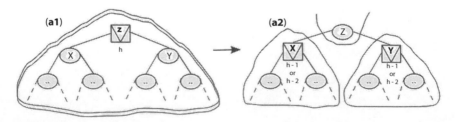

Figure 6.3 Partitioning.

height h. Partitioning operation does not require a restructuring of the tree and works in O (1).

Partitioning ensures that newly generated classes have a height of h-1 or h-2. In fact, the balance of the partitioned class's root justifies this. When this root balance equals 0, both of the newly formed classes have a height of h-1. Otherwise, if the root balance is +1 or −1, the two newly generated classes are of heights h-1 and h-2, or h-2 and h-1, respectively.

The code of partitioning (P) is the following:

```
Make_kind(P, Simple)
Make_Height(P, 0)
Make_kind(Left_child(P), Class)
Make_kind(Right_Child(P), Class)
```

Departitioning

It consists in transforming two classes into one class. In Figure 6.4(a1), class Y has a height of h-3 after a delete operation, but its direct sibling class X has a height of h-2. A Departitioning operation is still in progress. The mother class's Node Z is removed. The kinds of three nodes will be changed: the parent (Z) and its two children (X and Y). The parent node is renamed to a class node, while the children are renamed to simple nodes.

Departitioning corresponds then to a merging operation. This process can lead to departitioning in cascade. As partitioning, departitioning operation does not require a restructuring of the tree and works in O(1).

When the parameter h is equal to 2, h-3 takes value -1, what it means that we are an underflow situation. In this case, departitioning considers only one class as depicted in Figure 6.5.

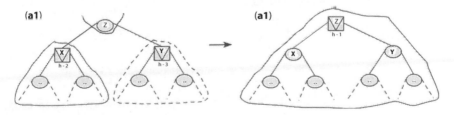

Figure 6.4 Departitioning.

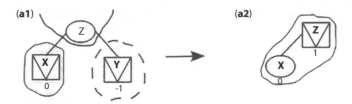

Figure 6.5 Departitioning (special case).

The code of Departitioning (P) is the following:

```
Make_kind(P, Class)
If h= 2 // Special case
        Case Dir of
                0 : Make_kind(Right_Child(P), Simple)
                1 : Make_kind(Left_child(P), Simple)
        Endcase
Else // Ordinary case
        {
        Make_kind(Left_child(P), Simple)
        Make_kind(Right_Child(P), Simple)
        Make_Height(P, Max(Simple_Height(Left_child(P),
Simple_Height(Right_Child(P)) + 1  )
        }
```

Restructuring-Partitioning

When a class underflows and a direct sibling class with height h-1 exists, a restructuring-partitioning is done. Figures 6.6 (a1), 6.6 (b1), and 6.6 (c1) show such cases in which the underflow class Y is to the right of node P. Node P is depicted inside a triangle since it might be either a simple or a class node. Consider the left child of node P, X, and its two children, C and D.

The conflict can be resolved quickly by using the Reverse Balance function on the sister class (a simple rotation). Then there is the restructuring-partitioning operation. The latter rotates the node, executes a KindFlip operation, and updates their heights.

In Figure 6.6(a1), the difference between heights of nodes C and D is null. A right rotation of node P is sufficient to restore balance. Indeed, heights of C and D are both equal to h-2. Therefore, after the rotation, the two subtrees of node X will have h-2 as height for C and h-1 for node P.

In Figure 6.6(b1), the difference between heights of nodes C and D is −1. A right rotation of node P is also sufficient. Indeed, heights of nodes C and D are h-2 and h-3, respectively. Therefore, after the rotation, the two subtrees of node X will have h-2 as height. As results, Figures 6.6(a2) and 6.6(b2) are new situations of Figures 6.6(a1) and 6.6(b1).

In Figure 6.6(c1), the difference between heights of nodes C and D is +1, i.e., a subtree of height h-2 to the right of X and a subtree of height h-3 to the left of X (because node X is of height h-1). A right rotation of node P does not solve the conflict because the node C converted into a class node will have a class height equal to h-3. In this case, the balance of node X is first reversed before a right rotation of node D is performed. Recall that Reversing balance consists simply to do a rotation of a class node in the direction of node with a weaker height. Figure 6.6(c2) depicts the new situation of Figure 6.6(c1).

Nodes C, D, and P become class nodes in all three cases, whereas Y remains a simple node. After the rotation, the kind of node X is the same as it was before the rotation.

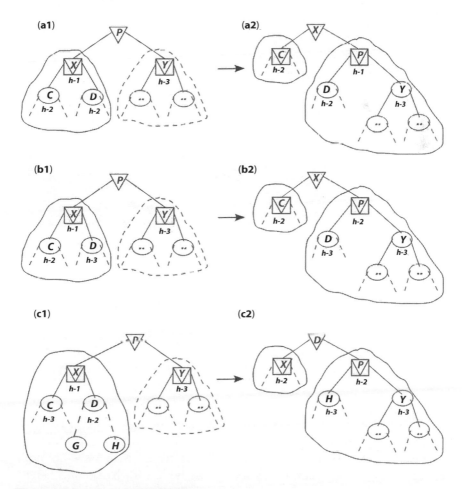

Figure 6.6 Restructuring-partitioning.

The code of restructuring-partitioning (P) works in O(1) and is the following:

Restructuring_Partitioning (P , Dir) → pointer to a new node

```
Case Dir of
0:
        {
        //Reverse balance
        if Simple_Height(Right_Child(Right_Child(P)))-
Simple_Height(Left_child(Right_Child(P))) = - 1
                Make_Right_Child(    P,        Reverse_
Balance ( Right_Child ( P ) , 1 ) )
                Restructuring_Partitioning            :=
Restructure_Partition ( P , 0 )
        }
    1:
        {
        // Reverse balance
            if    Simple_Height(Right_Child(Left_
child(P))) - Simple_Height( Left_child(Left_child(P)))
= + 1
            Make_Left_Child ( P, Reverse_Balance
( Left_child ( P ) , 0 ) )
                Restructuring_Partitioning        :=
Restructure_Partition ( P , 1 )
        }
    Endcase
```

Restructure_Partition (P, Dir) → pointer to the new node

```
    F := Rotation (P, Dir)
    KindFlip(P, F, Dir)
    Make_Height(P,  Max(Simple_Height(Left_child(P),
Simple_Height(Right_Child(P)) + 1)
    Make_Height(F,  Max(Simple_Height(Left_child(F),
Simple_Height(Right_Child(F)) + 1
    Restructure_Partition := F
```

Transforming

Remember that when a class overflows without having a direct sister class, it is first transformed. The underflow class in Figure 6.7 (a1) is Y, which has no direct sister class. Their parent node is P. If node A is to the left of node P, then node A's right child must be a class node with h-1 or h-2 height.

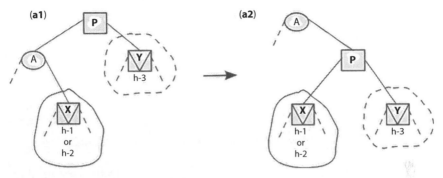

Figure 6.7 Transforming.

To locate a direct sibling class of the underflow class, a single right rotation of node P is performed. The transformation technique yielded Figure 6.7(a2). The process either proceeds with departitioning or restructuring-partitioning operation now that the underflow class has a direct sister class.

The code of Transforming(P) works in O(1) and is the following:

Transforming (P, Dir) → pointer to the new node

```
    F := Rotation(P, Dir)
    If (h = 2) or (Kind(P)=Class) KindSwap(P, F)
    Make_Height(P,        Max(     Simple_Height(Left_
child(P)), Simple_Height(Right_Child(P))) + 1)
    Make_Height(F,        Max(     Simple_Height(Left_
child(F)), Simple_Height(Right_Child(F))) + 1)
    Transforming := F
```

6.4   Insert and Delete Algorithms

We may now provide the insert and delete algorithms on the new structure after the maintenance operations have already been presented.

6.4.1   Inserting a New Element

The search operation is similar to the one of the ordinary binary search tree.

The insert operation proceeds by two steps:

> Step 1: similar to an ordinary binary search tree. The key is always inserted as a leaf in a leaf class.
> Step 2: go back in the tree from the node inserted toward the root of the P (h)-BST by making eventually the following tasks:

- Balance the leaf class according to the AVL method.
- Eventually partitioning the leaf class

Partitioning can be in cascade.

An element is always added to a leaf class during the insert procedure. After that, if the height of this class becomes equal to h, the pseudo-algorithm described below is used. It employs a stack (Branch) that contains all nodes visited from the root (PBST) to the parent of the newly inserted node.

It uses a stack containing all the nodes traversed from the root until the parent of the node newly inserted. We have organized this stack as a set of elements where each one holds three items:

- A class node
- Its parent
- The simple nodes traversed inside the class.

The parent is used when a restructuring is performed and the simple nodes are used to update the height of the class.

Thus, each Pop operation gives the element [C, Parent, Simples] where C is a class node, Parent its parent and Simples the path traversed inside the class C. Branch designates this stack.

The algorithm uses either Restructuring or Partitioning operation to go up the tree from the inserted node to the root of the entire tree. The procedure comes to an end once the restructuring is completed. Cascade Partitioning, on the other hand, is possible.

In the following algorithm we use the function AVL_*insert(C)* which adjusts the balance in the subtree rooted at C after an insert operation and returns the root of the class.

PBST designates the root of the entire tree.

```
Repeat
    {
        Partitioning(C);
        If Parent <> Null
        {
            Pop (Branch, C, Parent, Simples)
            C':= AVL_insert(C)
            If C' <> C
                {
                If Parent <> Null
```

```
                    Adjust the Parent link to point to C'
                    Else   PBST := C'
              C := C'
              }

          }

    }
Until (Parent = Null) Or (Height(C) < h)
```

Comment

Using the AVL-insert technique, the element is first entered into a class. At most one restructuring can be done. If the height of the class does not reach height h, the insert process is stopped. A Partitioning procedure is conducted if this is not the case making the root of the partitioned class a leaf in the mother class. The process continues in cascade if the mother class overflows, i.e. its height reaches h again.

Scenario example

Figure 6.8 illustrates the construction method step by step using an example with h=3.

Insert (49) - - > (a): a class is made up of only one element.

(a) Insert (88) - - > (b): 88 is inserted into class 49.

(b) Insert (89) - - > (c): 89 is put into class 49, causing node 49 to rotate to the left. 88 becomes the class's root.

(c) Insert (50, 16) - - > (d): 50 and 16 are inserted into class 88.

(d) Insert (44) - - > (e): 44 is put to the right of node 16 and causes node 88 to rotate to the right.Until now, only one class exists with a height equal to 2.

(e) Insert 63 - - > (f): the addition of 63 increases the height of class 49, which is balanced in terms of the AVL tree. Since this class reaches its limit, it is partitioned into two new classes: 16 and 88. 49 remains a class with an element because it was the root class.

(f) Insert (29) - - > (g): class 16 is restructured with a right rotation of node 44 followed by a left rotation of node 16.

(g) Insert (73) - - > (h): 73 is put to the left of node 63, and node 50 is rotated to the left.

(h) Insert (81) - - > (i): Class 88 is reorganized by a left rotation of node 63 followed by a right rotation of node 88 always according to the AVL technique. 73 becomes the new root of this class.

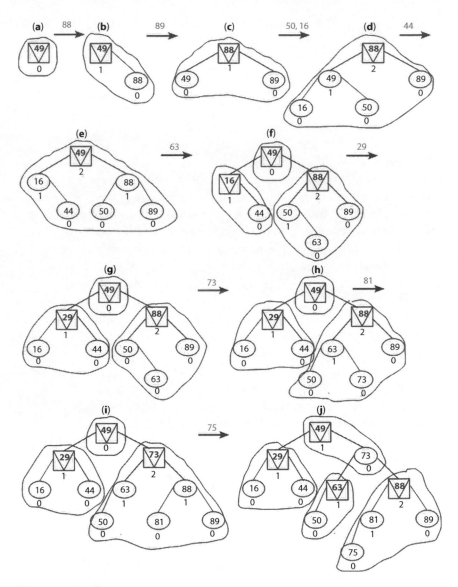

Figure 6.8 Step-by-step insert process.

(i) Insert (75) - - > (j): 75 is inserted into class 73 that overflows. Partitioning is completed to split the class into two
classes: 63 and 88. Node 73 belongs now to the mother
class 49.

6.4.2   Deleting an Existing Element

The delete operation proceeds by two steps:

> Step 1: similar to an ordinary binary search tree.
> Step 2: go back in the tree from the node deleted toward the root of the P(h)-BST by making eventually the following tasks:

- – Balance the leaf class according to the AVL method.
- – Eventually, restructure or departition the leaf class as described hereafter.

We have the following cases:

> Case 1: After a delete operation, a class underflows (h-3) and its direct sister class exists that has h-2 as height. A Departitioning operation holds.
> Case 2: After a delete operation, a class can underflow (h-3) and its direct sister class exists that has h-1 as height. A restructuring-partitioning operation holds.
> Case 3: After a delete operation, a class can underflow (h-3) and has not a direct sister class. A Transforming operation holds. The process continues then according to case 1 or case 2.

Notice that departitioning can be in cascade.

In the delete process an element is first removed from a leaf class. If the height of this class becomes smaller than h-2 and this class has a parent node, the algorithm described below is applied. It uses a stack containing all the nodes traversed from the root until the parent of the node removed. We have organized this stack as a set of elements where each one holds four items:

- – A class node
- – Its parent
- – Its grandparent
- – The simple nodes traversed inside the class.

The parent and the grandparent are used when a transforming or a restructuring is performed and the simple nodes are used to update the height of the class.

Thus, each Pop operation gives the element [C, Parent, Grandparent, Simples] where C is a class node, Parent its parent, Grandparent its grandparent and Simples the path traversed inside the class C. Branch designates this stack.

In the following algorithm we use the function AVL_*delete(C)* which adjusts the balance in the subtree C after a delete operation and returns the root of the class.

PBST designates the root of the entire tree and Sibling(C) provides the brother of node C.

```
Repeat
   {
   C':= Sibling(C)
   If Kind (C') ='Simple'
       {
           C" :=Transforming (C')
           If Grandparent <> Null
                Adjust the Grandparent link to point
to C'
           Else  PBST := C'
           Grandparent := C'  ;   C':=C"
       }
   If ABS( Height(C) - Height (C') ) > 1
       {
           Q:=Restructuring-Partitioning (Parent)
           If Grandparent <> Null
                Adjust the Grandparent link to point to Q
     Else PBST := Q
           Exit
       }
   Else
       {
       Departitioning (Parent)
       Pop (Branch,  C,  Parent,  Grandparent,
Simples)
       C' := AVL_Delete(C)
       If C' <> C
           {
           If Parent <> Null
                Adjust the Parent link to point
to C'
           Else  PBST := C'
           C := C'
           }
       }
   }
Until (Parent=Null) Or (Height(C) > h-3)
```

Comment and analysis

When a class underflows, i.e., its height becomes equal to h-3, then if this class has not a direct sister class we must find it one by a transforming operation. If the difference in height between the underflow class and the sister class is greater than one (in absolute value) then a restructuring operation is performed and the delete process is stopped. Otherwise, a departitioning operation holds and the delete process can continue in cascade.

Scenario example

Figure 6.9 illustrates the deletion mechanism step by step using an example with h=3.

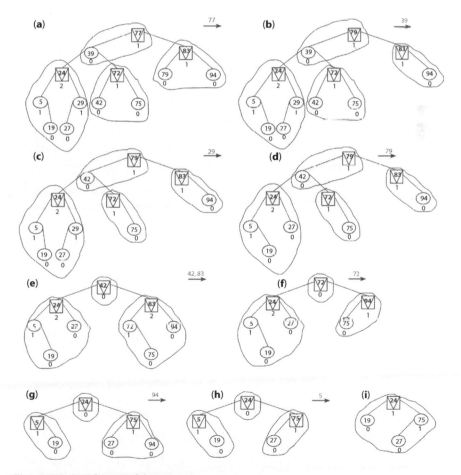

Figure 6.9 Step-by-step delete process.

(a) Delete (77) - - > (b): 77 is replaced by its inorder successor 79, which is then deleted from class 83.

(b) Delete (39) - - > (c): again, 39 is removed from class 72 and replaced with 42 (its inorder successor).

(c) Delete (29) - - > (d): 29 is removed from class 24.

(d) Delete (79) - - > (e): 79 is replaced with 83 (its inorder successor). As 83 is a class node, 94 becomes the new root. This class underflows (height equal to 0) and its direct sister class does not exist. A right rotation of node 83 completes a transformation. Node 83 now has classes 72 and 94 on its left and right sides, respectively. After that, node 83 is departitioned.

(e) Delete (42, 83) - - > (f): 42 is replaced with 72 (its inorder successor) and 83 is removed from class 83. The new root becomes 94.

(f) Delete (72) - - > (g): 72 is replaced with 75 (its inorder successor). Class 94 underflows and its direct sister class is of height 2. A right rotation of node 75 completes the Restructuring process.

(g) Delete (94) - - > (h): 94 is removed from class 75.

(h) Delete (5) - - > (i): a Departitioning of node 24 is performed.

Now, only one class exists and the future deletions are accomplished inside the unique class.

6.5   P(h)-BST as a Generator of Balanced Binary Search Trees

We show in this section that the P(h)-BST structure includes Red-Black trees, AVL trees and other unknown data structures more balanced than Red-Black trees and less balanced than AVL trees.

It is straightforward to observe that P(h)-BST becomes exactly an AVL tree when only one class is created. This case occurs from a certain value that depends on the number of items to be inserted. In the rest of the chapter, h' designates this value. More precisely, for any value h greater than h' (h=∞ with exaggeration) the structure behaves just like an AVL tree. Thus, P(h')-BST or P(∞)-BST denotes the structure equivalent to an AVL tree.

P(h)-BST becomes a structure equivalent to a Red-Black tree for h=2. Indeed, the definition of P(2)-BST is the following:

- Every node must be either a simple node or a class node.
- Every class must have a depth equal to 0 or 1

- There must be the same number of class nodes on every direct path from a node to a leaf.

We get a data structure that looks like a Red-Black tree by replacing simple nodes with red ones and class nodes with black ones. The second condition stipulates that we cannot have more than two consecutive simple nodes since the maximal height of a class is equal to 1. In terms of Red-Black trees we have never two consecutive red nodes. Regarding only class nodes, the tree is perfectly balanced. It is also the case for black nodes in Red-Black trees. Figure 6.10 (a2) gives the Red-Black tree corresponding to the P(2)-BST depicted in Figure 6.10 (a1).

Although a P(2)-BST is identical to a Red-Blacks are simpler and easier to understand. Furthermore, we shall show in simulation that delete algorithm is faster than the one on Red-Black trees. This is certainly due to the fact that the new algorithm works with both the height and the kind of nodes.

The new structure can be seen as a generator of partially balanced binary search trees.

- For h=3, the classes have 1 or 2 as height. This means that we can accept on each path of the tree one or two consecutive simple nodes between class nodes.
- For h=4, the classes have as 2 or 3 height. This means that we can accept on each path of the tree two or three consecutive simple nodes between class nodes.
- And so on...
- The P(h)-BST structure could be defined in terms of Red-Black trees as follows:
- Every node must be either a red node or a black node.
- Every path from the root to the next black node can contain 0 to h-1 red nodes.
- There must be h-1 or h-2 successive red nodes on every direct path from any node (excluding the root) to a leaf.
- There must be the equal number of black nodes on every direct path from any node to a leaf.

Figure 6.10(b2) gives a new balanced data structure expressed with colors corresponding to the P(3)-BST depicted in 10(b1).

In this way, a P(3)-BST could be called a Red^2-Black tree and a P(4)-BST a Red^3-Black tree. And generally, a P(h)-BST could be called a Red^{h-1}-Black tree. As a good exercise, it would be interesting, to redefine—in each structure—maintenance operations, as well as the insert and delete algorithms using only colors as this is done in Red-Black tree algorithms.

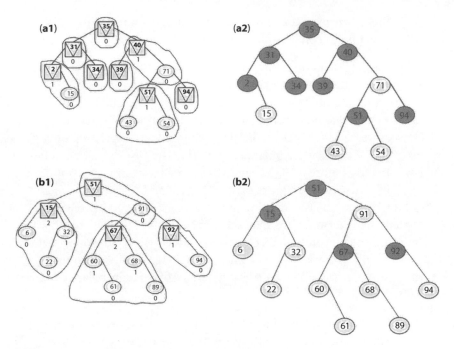

Figure 6.10 P(2)-BST and P(3)-BST versus corresponding Red-Black trees.

Let us observe that more h is larger, more the balance is better. In this way, according to application needs, we can regulate the balance. Contrarily to the standard Red-Black tree, more there are red nodes, more the balance is better.

6.6   Simulation Results

To conduct the performance comparison, the search, insert and delete algorithms on the new structure, AVL trees and Red-Black trees were implemented in Lazarus. We focused our simulation mainly on the number of rotations and execution time. All the algorithms were exposed to the same scenario that consists first in inserting random numbers in the range [0 .. 999 999 999]. Then all the values that were used to construct trees are deleted. A particular simulation study is done for sequential (ascending and descending) insertions because these are often the sequences that yield worst-case height behavior in many data structures.

We first observed the behavior of the P(h)-BST structure through insert and delete algorithms when varying h from 2 to h'. The latter depends on the number of items to be inserted. We considered two scenarios: random and ascending cases. The AVL and Red-Black trees generated by our proposed data structure are then compared to the usual AVL and Red-Black data structures.

In order to keep the tree balanced, each data structure makes rotations. It is then judicious to compare methods through the number of rotations performed. Moreover, In order to compare the balance of the trees generated it is interesting to observe the maximal height of trees and the ratio Max/Min. Max is the length of the longest path and Min is the length of the shortest path. Naturally, the execution time is an important issue to compare data structures.

To achieve this, we planned the following steps:

A. Generate files of random numbers with sizes: 100,000, 200,000, 500,000 and 1000,000.

- For each file, insert all the numbers by varying h from value 2 to h'. We observe the number of rotations performed and the execution time. Once the P(h)-BST is built, we compute the ratio Max/Min.
- For each binary search tree previously built (by varying h from value 2 to h'), delete all the items. We observe the number of rotations and the execution time.

B. Generate files of ascending numbers with sizes: 100 000, 200 000, 500 000 and 1000 000.

– For each file, insert all the numbers by varying h from value 2 to h'. We observe Min (length of the shortest path), Max (length of the longest path), the ratio Max/Min, the number of rotations, the execution time, the number of class nodes and the number of simple nodes.

C. Generate files of random numbers with sizes: 100 000, 200 000, 500 000 and 1000 000.

– For each file, insert all the numbers using P(2)-BST, P(∞)-BST, Red-Black tree and AVLtree. We observe the execution time.

– For each binary search previously built (by varying h from 2 to h'), delete all the items. We observe the execution time.

Before presenting simulation results, let us begin by giving how we have defined data structures.

6.6.1   Data Structures and Abstract Data Types

We give hereafter the Pascal Lazarus code of data structures and abstract data types used in simulation programs.

Every node in the new structure has an extra byte. If the node is a class node, bit 1 is set to 1. This bit is set to 0 otherwise. Bits 2 to 8 are used to store node height. Simple_Height (Code) becomes Code Mod 128 in this way. Furthermore, it is a class node if Code ≥ 128. Otherwise, it's a simple node.

Every node in the Red-black tree has a color field and every node in the AVL tree has a balance field.

We have taken the same implementations of the nodes of PBST, AVL and Red-Black trees described in [14]. Screenshots 6-03, 6-04 and 6-05 show these implementations.

6.6.2   Analyzing the Insert and Delete Process in Random Case

Insert process
Tables 6.1 and 6.2 show the numbers of rotations, the ratios Max/Min and the execution times performed by the P(h)-BST structure insert algorithm—by varying parameter h from 2 to h'—for the different random files of shown sizes. Due to space reason, only the first and the last lines of tables are shown.

First, let us note that for a file of size 100 000 nodes, P(20)-BST is a structure equivalent to an AVL tree. For a file of size 200 000 nodes, P(21)-BST represents an AVL tree. For files of 500 000 and 1000 000 nodes the new structure is similar to an AVL tree for h=23 and h=24 respectively.

For all the sizes, P(2)-BST is a structure equivalent to a Red-Black tree.

Figures 6.11 and 6.12 give a better vision on the behavior of the numbers of rotations and execution times. Indeed, the curve depicted in Figure 6.11 shows clearly that the number of rotations is smaller for h=2, then increases quickly for the first values of h. Finally, it is stabilized from h=5. Likewise, the curve depicted in Figure 6.12 shows also clearly that the execution time is higher for h=2, then it decreases slowly.

```
Type Typenode = (Simple, Class)              Function Height (A: Ptr_node): integer;
Type Ptr_node = * T_node;                    Begin
T_node = record                               If A = nil
Begin                                         Then Height := -1
 Data: Anykind ;                              Else Height := A.Code Mod 128
 Code: Byte ;                                End ;
 Left_Child, Right_Child: Ptr_node           Procedure Make_Height (P: Ptr_node; H:
End ;                                         integer);
Function Kind (A: Ptr_node): Typenode        Begin
Begin                                         If P.Code < 128
 If A.Code >= 128                             Then P.Code := H
 Then Kind := Class                           Else P.Code := 128 + H
 Else Kind := Simple                         End
End ;                                         Function Simple_Height(A: Ptr_node):
Procedure    Make_kind    (A:Ptr_node,        integer;
A_kind: Typenode)                            Begin
Begin                                         If A=nil
 If A_kind = Simple                           Then Simple_Height := -1
 Then A.Code:= A.Code Mod 128                 Else
 Else A.Code := 128 + A.Code Mod 128           If A.Code >= 128 // Class node
End ;                                          Then Simple_Height := -1
                                              Else Simple_Height := A.Code Mod 128
                                             End :
```

Screenshot 6-03 PBST node implementation.

```
Type TypeColor=(Red, Black);
// Node type
Type Ptr_Node = ^T_Node;
   T_Node = Record
   Data   : Anytype;
   Color : TypeColor;
   Left_Child, Right_Child: Ptr_node


End;

Function Color ( P:Ptr_Node ) : TypeColor ;
   Begin
      If P = NIL
      Then    Color := Black
      Else    Color := P^.Color
   End;

Procedure Ass_Color (P:ptr_Node; A_Color:typeColor);
   Begin
      P.Color := A_Color
   End;
```

Screenshot 6-04 Red-Black tree node implementation.

```
//Node type
Type Ptr_node = ^t_Node;
  T_Node = Record
  Data : Anytype;
  Balance : Short;
  Left_Child, Right_Child: Ptr_node
End;

Function Balance ( P : Ptr_Node) : Short;
  Begin
    Balance := P^.Balance
  End;

Procedure Ass_Balance (P: Ptr_Node; A_Balance: Short);
  Begin
    P.Balance := A_Balance
  End;
```

Screenshot 6-05 AVL tree node implementation.

Table 6.1 Rotations, Ratios Max/Min, Execution times–Insert algorithm–Random case—Sizes 100,000 and 200,000.

h		100000			200000	
	Rotations	Max/min	Times	Rotations	Max/min	Times
2	58214	1.46	281	116423	1.5	765
3	64406	1.58	264	129390	1.54	702
4	67360	1.46	265	135547	1.43	640
5	68731	1.58	250	137577	1.43	609
...	...	...	...	...	...	...
18	69830	1.46	219	139455	1.43	594
19	69830	1.46	203	139455	1.43	610
20	69830	1.46	219	139455	1.43	578
21				139455	1.43	625

Table 6.2 Rotations, Ratios Max/Min, Execution times–Insert algorithm–Random case—Sizes 500,000 and 1000,000.

h		500000			1000000	
	Rotations	Max/min	Times	Rotations	Max/min	Times
2	291330	1.47	1968	582602	1.6	4421
3	323225	1.57	1891	646285	1.6	4078
4	338579	1.47	1843	675567	1.53	3920
5	344522	1.47	1780	686707	1.53	3828
...	...	...	...	...	...	...
21	349548	1.47	1608	697527	1.44	3468
22	349548	1.47	1605	697527	1.44	3422
23	349548	1.47	1546	697527	1.44	3406
24				697527	1.44	3422

It remains almost stable for files of sizes 100 000 and 200 000. On the other hand, for files of sizes 500 000 and 1000 000, execution times decrease slightly when h increases.

The ratios Max/Min shown in Tables 6.1 and 6.2 mean that all the binary search trees built are well balanced. We observe also that the ratios are higher for the first values of h. This also means that more h is higher, more the tree is balanced.

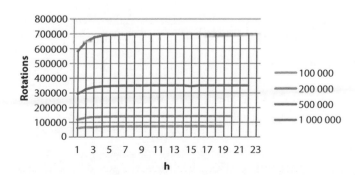

Figure 6.11 Numbers of rotations–Insert algorithm–Random case.

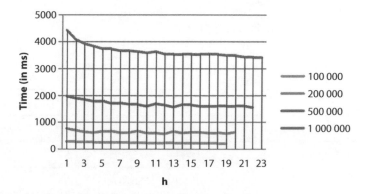

Figure 6.12 Execution times–Insert algorithm–Random case.

Delete process

Table 6.3 shows the numbers of rotations and the execution times performed when deleting all the elements from the trees built in the previous section. Here also, only the first and the last lines of tables are shown.

Simulation results show clearly that the number of rotations is higher for h=2, then it is quickly stabilized from h greater to 2 despite the file size. Execution time is higher for the first value of h.

These results confirm well the performances of standard AVL and Red-Black trees. For h=h', the structure equivalent to an AVL tree performs less rotations and consumes less in execution time.

Between values 2 and h', the numbers of rotations and the execution times decrease slightly until they reach the performance of the structure equivalent to an AVL tree.

Figures 6.13 and 6.14 give more information on the behavior of these parameters.

6.6.3   Analyzing the Insert Process in Ascending (Descending) Case

Table 6.4 shows some important parameters when inserting 1000 000 items in ascending case using the P(h)-BST structure (by varying h from 2 to h'). The same results are obtained in descending case. Similar results are observed for the other sizes.

We can make the following observations:

- The number of rotations is almost the same for all values of h (Column "Rotation").

Table 6.3 Number of rotations, execution times–Delete algorithm–Random case.

h	100000		200000		500000		1000000	
	Rotations	Times	Rotations	Times	Rotations	Times	Rotations	Times
2	42385	156	85234	344	210239	1047	422393	2358
3	40638	155	80600	359	201036	1047	403600	2358
4	40398	156	80872	358	201646	1063	403319	2374
5	40268	141	80501	343	200385	1047	400815	2562
...	...	...	...	...	...	...	...	...
19	40138	125	80270	328	199791	1016	399684	2281
20	40138	125	80270	327	199799	1016	399686	2266
21			80270	328	199799	1015	399684	2265
22					199799	1000	399684	2233
23					199799	1000	399684	2265
24							399684	2218

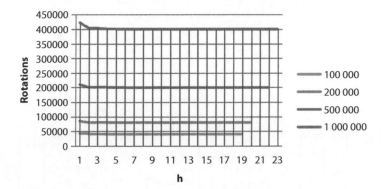

Figure 6.13 Number of rotations–Delete algorithm–Random case.

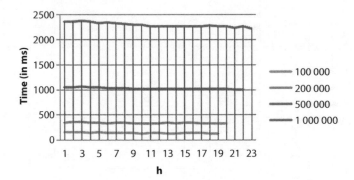

Figure 6.14 Execution times–Delete algorithm–Random case.

- The length of the shortest path is the same for all values of h (Column "Min").
- The length of the longest path decreases when h increases (Column "Max"). Figure 6.15 shows how the maximal height of paths decreases according to h. indeed, from h=11, it is stabilized with value 20. For h=20, i.e. the structure equivalent to an AVL tree, the maximal height is the lowest.
- The ratio Max/Min gives an idea on the tree balance (Column "Max/Min"). The structure equivalent to a Red-Black tree (P(2)-BST) is the least balanced tree with a ratio close to 1.89. The structure equivalent to an AVL tree P(20)-BST is almost perfect since the ratio Max/Min is close to 1. Between these two data structures the binary search trees

Table 6.4 Insert algorithm—Ascending case.

H	Rotations	Min	Max	Max/min	Times	Classes	Simples
2	999963	19	36	1,89	1828	9999976	24
3	999971	19	28	1,47	2984	333325	666675
4	999974	19	25	1,32	3000	142853	857147
5	999976	19	23	1,21	2906	66666	933334
6	999977	19	22	1,16	2844	32257	967743
7	999977	19	22	1,16	2766	15873	984127
8	999978	19	21	1,11	2717	7874	992126
9	999978	19	21	1,11	2640	3922	996078
10	999978	19	21	1,11	2547	1957	998043
11	999979	19	20	1,05	2483	977	999023
12	999979	19	20	1,05	2468	489	999511
13	999979	19	20	1,05	2467	245	999755
14	999979	19	20	1,05	2452	123	999877
15	999979	19	20	1,05	2453	62	999938
16	999979	19	20	1,05	2437	31	999969
17	999979	19	20	1,05	2422	16	999984
18	999979	19	20	1,05	2374	8	999992
19	999979	19	20	1,05	2313	4	999996
20	999980	19	19	1	2233	1	999999

generated are very suitable and approach the results of the AVL trees. Figure 6.16 shows clearly this.

- The best execution time is obtained for h=2, i.e. the structure equivalent to a Red-Black tree (Column "Times"). For all the other values of h, the best execution time is the one of the structure equivalent to an AVL tree (h=20). Let us notice that execution time increases first for h=3 and h=4. Then, it decreases progressively until it reaches the second better

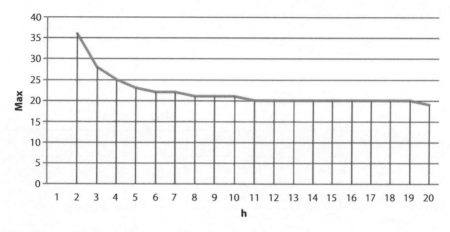

Figure 6.15 Maximal height of path–Insert algorithm–Ascending case.

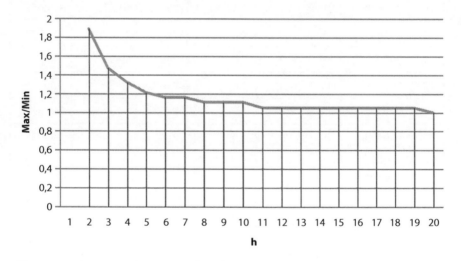

Figure 6.16 Ratio Max/Min–Insert algorithm–Ascending case.

execution time, i.e. the one of the structure equivalent to an
AVL tree. Figure 6.17 shows this.
- The number of class nodes is very significant for the first
  values of h (Column "Classes").

Almost all of the nodes in the structure analogous to a Red-Black tree
(P(2)-BST) are class nodes. There is one class node that is the root of the
tree in the structure corresponding to an AVL tree (P(∞)-BST).

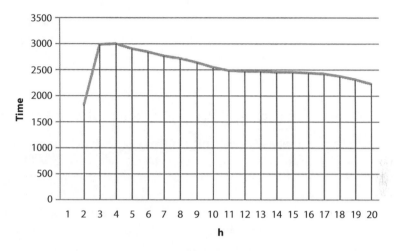

Figure 6.17 Execution time–Insert algorithm–Ascending case.

- The number of simple nodes is insignificant for the structure equivalent to a Red-Black (P(2)-BST). There is only 24 nodes on a total of 1000 000 nodes. For h=3, this number attains 666675. The number expands first quickly and then slightly. For the structure equivalent to an AVL tree (P(∞)-BST) all the nodes are simple nodes except the root of the tree. Figure 6.18 shows the distribution of class and simple nodes when h takes values between 2 and h'. The symmetry of curves is due to the fact that the sum of the numbers of class and simple nodes is constant (equal to 1000 000). The number of class nodes decreases very quickly. Between two

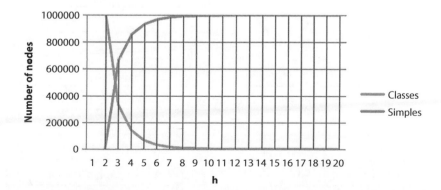

Figure 6.18 Distribution of class and simple nodes–Insert algorithm–Ascending case.

consecutive values of h, it is almost divided by 2. The number of simple nodes reaches very quickly the number of simple nodes inside the structure equivalent to an AVL tree.

6.6.4   Comparing P(2)-BST/P(∞)-BST to Red-Black/AVL Trees

We showed before that P(2)-BST and P(∞)-BST are structures equivalent to a Red-Black tree and an AVL tree, respectively. Table 6.5 shows the execution times made by each data structure when inserting the considered files in random case. Results reveal that execution times are all comparable.

Table 6.6 shows the execution times made by each data structure when deleting all nodes from trees built in Table 6.5. Unlikely, the execution times obtained by the new structure are here faster than those performed by standard Red-Black and AVL trees. Indeed, this is explained by the fact that the delete algorithm on the new structure significantly reduces the number of tests. This is due to the fact that the delete algorithm works on heights instead of node types.

The performance of the AVL tree obtained by the new structure (row P(∞)-BST) is unexpected, since it outperforms AVL trees (Row AVL tree).

Table 6.5 Execution time–Insert algorithm–Random case.

	100000	200000	500000	1000000
AVL tree	250	546	1546	3354
Red-Black tree	251	540	1520	3359
P(∞)-BST	213	484	1473	3369
P(2)-BST	235	514	1525	3463

Table 6.6 Execution time–Delete algorithm–Random case.

	100,000	200,000	500,000	1,000,000
AVL tree	765	1677	4624	9963
Red-Black tree	765	1650	4535	9723
P(∞)-BST	140	328	984	2208
P(2)-BST	145	354	1047	2334

This could be explained by the fact that the new structure employs node heights, whereas the standard AVL uses balance (0, +1, or -1) and so avoids multiple balance tests.

It's worth noting that the performance of the Red-Black tree obtained by the new structure (P(2)-BST) is similar to the AVL tree produced by the new structure (P(∞)-BST).

6.7   Conclusion

We exposed a new balanced binary search tree that is partitioned in classes at the price of only one additional byte: one bit to differentiate between simple and class nodes, and seven bits to control both partitioning and tree balance. Each class is in fact a subtree of height H equal to h-1 or h-2 able to contain until 2^H nodes. A class can then attain 2^{128} nodes! Tree balance is guaranteed by two ways: globally by the Partitioning operation and locally by the AVL technique.

We presented in details all the algorithms. Maintenance operations are exclusive to the new structure and are shortly expressed. At our opinion, the algorithms are simpler and easier to understand since they are, for the most part, expressed in terms of heights.

We showed that the new structure includes Red-Black trees when parameter h is equal to 2 and AVL trees when the parameter h is equal to h' (or greater than h'). So, the same code is used for both AVL and Red-Black tree algorithms. Furthermore, parameter h allows regulating the maximal height of paths (Max) and the ratio Max/Min. Indeed, when h=2, the maximal height is the highest (2 lg (n) in a Red-Black tree) and for h=h' it is the lowest (1.44 lg (n) in an AVL tree). Thus, we can claim the new structure allows generating balanced binary search trees with maximal heights between 1.44 lg (n) and 2 lg (n).

Simulation results showed that the P(h)-BST structure can generate very competitive balanced binary search trees including AVL and Red-Black trees.

The performance of the new structure's insert algorithm is also similar to that of the AVL and Red-Black tree insert algorithms, according to simulation results. On the other hand, the delete algorithm of the new structure is particularly fast. For h=2 and for h=h' the execution time is four to five times faster compared to the standard AVL and Red-Black trees. This is particularly due to the fact that the delete algorithm of the new structure reduces significantly the number of tests.

Thanks to the new structure, it is now possible to use a unique code and to adapt it—by choosing h—for update-intensive applications as well as for lookup-intensive applications.

As a perspective to this work, it would be necessary to do more simulations with other benchmark data sets. A deeper mathematical analysis of the proposed balanced binary search tree is also required.

Acknowledgments

A major expression of thanks must go to my dear colleague Pr W.K Hidouci by his reflection and his constructive suggestions. A particular expression of thanks must also go to students R. Akrour, M.E.A Chouiha, M. Mehaddi & S. Abbar for their contribution in the elaboration of the P(h)-BST structure.

References

1. Knuth, D.E., *The art of computer programming. Vol III: Sorting and Searching*, Addison Wesley, Reading, Mass, 1973.
2. Aho Alfred, V. *et al.*, *Data structures and algorithms*, Addison-Wesley, USA, 1983.
3. Schneider, G.M., Weingart, S.W., Perlman, D.M., *An Introduction to Programming and Problem Solving with Pascal*, 2nd ed., pp. 374–80, John Wiley & Sons, Inc., Hoboken, New Jersey, U.S., 1982.
4. Sethi, R., *Programming languages concepts and constructs*, Pearson Publishing Co., Hudson, New York, U.S., 1996.
5. Stubbs, D.F. and Webre, N.W., *Data structures with abstract data types and Ada*, Brooks/Cole Publishing Co., Pacific Grove, Ca, U.S., 1993.
6. Horowitz, E., Sahni, S., Anderson-Freed, S., *Fundamentals of data structures*, vol. 20, Computer Science Press, Potomac, MD, 1976.
7. Brass, P., *Advanced data structures*, vol. 193, Cambridge University Press, Cambridge, 2008.
8. Drozdek, A., *Data Structures and Algorithms in C++*, Brooks/Cole, Pacific Grove, Ca, U.S., 2001.
9. Adel'son-Velskii, G.M. and Landis, Y.M., An algorithm for the organization of information. *Dokl. Akad. Nauk SSSR*, 146, 263–266, 1962, *English translation in Soviet Math. Dokl. 3*, pp. 1259-1262.
10. Guibas, L.J. and Sedgewick, R., A Diochromatic framework for balanced trees. *Proceedings of the 19th Annual Symposium on Foundations of Computer Science*, 1978.

11. Anderson, A., Balanced Search trees made simple. *Workshop on algorithms and data structures*, Springer Verlag, pp. 60–71, 1993.
12. Tarjan, R.E., Levy, C.C., Timmel, S., Zip Trees. *WADS*, pp. 566–577, 2019.
13. Haeupler, B., Sen, S., Tarjan, R.E., Rank-balanced trees. *ACM Trans. Algorithms (TALG)*, *11*, 4, 1–26, 2015.
14. Bounif, L. and Zegour, D.E., Toward a unique representation for AVL and red-black trees. *Comput. y Sist.*, *23*, 2, 435–450, 2019.
15. Zouana, S. and Zegour, D.E., Partitioned binary search trees: A generalization of Red Black Trees. *Comput. y Sist.*, *23*, 4, 1375–1391, 2019.

## 7

Security Ontologies: An Investigation of Pitfall Rate

Archana Patel* and Narayan C. Debnath

Department of Software Engineering, School of Computing and Information Technology, Eastern International University, Binh Duong, Vietnam

Abstract

This chapter shows the pitfall rate of the security ontologies by utilizing the integrated framework of ontology evaluation (InFra_Ont) along with few questions related to the work of security ontologies. The InFra_Ont uses four well-known approaches for evaluation of ontology. These approaches are as follows: (a) five roles of knowledge representation, (b) evaluation of the effectiveness of the coding standard (a software engineering approach), (c) OOPS! tool for anomalies detection, and (d) a layer-based approach. This chapter helps analysts and researchers in finding a road map to what exists in terms of security ontologies. Our main objective is to review, analyze, select, and classify security ontologies, as a scope study, with an interest in the field of semantic web.

Keywords: Security ontology, ontology evaluation tools, semantic web, OWL, pitfall rate

7.1 Introduction

An ontology is a knowledge representation scheme that represents real-world entities in a machine understandable manner. Earlier than ontologies, semantic network and semantic frame emerged, but they were lacking in formal semantics despite the fact that they had semantic in the name [1]. Ontologies offer the richest machine-interpretable (rather than just machine-processable) and explicit semantics and are being used today

---

Corresponding author: archana.patel@eiu.edu.vn

Archana Patel, Narayan C. Debnath and Bharat Bhusan (eds.) Data Science with Semantic Technologies: Theory, Practice, and Application, (179–198) © 2022 Scrivener Publishing LLC

extensively for semantic interoperability and integration. The first step of ontology development is to determine the scope of an ontology. In ontological engineering, ontology scope shows the specification and design aspects for the representation of the knowledge [2]. The scope of an ontology can be classified into three aspects: domain scope (determines that the scope of the ontology is relevant to the task for which ontology is designed), conceptual scope (determines that ontology well represent the hierarchical and taxonomical concepts), technical scope (shows that the specifications and requirements for ontologies are integrated smoothly and correctly in terms of ontology integration and application in practice). Mainly, four types of ontologies are available, namely upper ontology, domain ontology, task ontology, and application ontology. The upper ontology occupies general concepts or terms like matter, time, and space. The aim of the upper ontologies is to support broad semantic interoperability among domain ontologies by providing a common platform for the formulation of the definitions. The domain ontology is developed to capture and relate the content of specific domains (e.g., medical, electronic, digital domain) or part of the world. Domain ontologies use the services of upper ontologies. The task ontology contains fundamental concepts according to a general activity or task. It is a specification of element relationships of tasks to explain how tasks can exist and be used in a specific environment. Task ontology serves as a foundation for using tasks in certain fields, like in the field of management, and it defines what element it has and what type of relationships can be established with other tasks. The application ontology is a specialized ontology focused on a specific application. It has a very narrow context and limited reusability because it depends on the particular scope and requirements of a specific application. Application ontologies are typically developed ad hoc by the application designers.

Ontology does not only provide sharable and reusable knowledge but also provides a common understanding of the knowledge; as a result, the interoperability and interconnectedness of the model make it priceless for addressing the issues of querying data. Ontology work with concepts and relations that are very close to the working of the human brain. It also provides a way to represent any data format like unstructured, semistructured, structured, and enables data fetching with semantics. The key requirement of ontology is the development of suitable languages for the representation and extraction of information. Varieties of ontology languages have been developed, and the currently used language is web ontology language (OWL) [3]. The OWL is the most powerful knowledge representation language in the semantic web. Figure 7.1 shows the hierarchy of knowledge representation languages and their relations. KL-one is s a groundbreaking

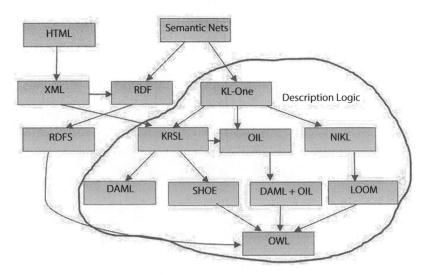

Figure 7.1 Languages leading to OWL.

language, however, it cannot be applied to real problems due to its slow performance. New Implementation of KL-One (NIKL) was an attempt to design description logic (DL) language with similar power as KL-One but with better performance so that it can be applied to real-world problems. The Loom was a very powerful language (good performance and portability) based on DL and was implemented in LISP. SHOE was one of the first languages to add DL semantics to HTML pages directly. The Ontology Interchange Language (OIL) defines DL semantics on top of HTML, whereas The DARPA Agent Markup Language (DAML) adds DL semantics to RDF. The goals of DAML and OIL were the same; that is why DAML+OIL was developed, which was one of the most significant influences on the web ontology language (OWL).

Ontology query language plays a very important role in extracting and processing the information. SPARQL is one of the most widely used ontology query languages [4]. By using these semantic technologies (ontology, SPARQL, OWL), users and systems can interact and share information with each other in an intelligent manner. For this reason, ontologies are widely used in security context. The available security ontologies can hold the different characteristics of the security. These ontologies play a vital role in securing the information on the semantic web.

The vision of the semantic web is the extension of the World Wide Web and offers the software program with metadata that allows the semantical interpretation of data and information. The semantic web transforms

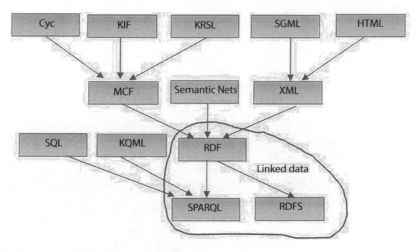

Figure 7.2 From HTML to linked data.

the Internet into a semantic graph rather than a graph of hypertext links. Figure 7.2 shows the standards that provide the foundation for the semantic web known as linked data [5].

- Cyc is an AI project that aims to provide a comprehensive ontology and knowledge base about common sense and encyclopaedic. This project has created its own inference engine, frame-based language, and tools to pass the information into ontologies.
- Knowledge interchange format (KIF) enables the system to exchange knowledge among different knowledge representation systems like Loom. KIF is similar to the frame language; however, it focuses on the transmitting of knowledge among the systems instead of providing a framework for the expression or use of knowledge.
- The knowledge representation standard language (KRSL) aims to support the community for the specification of the knowledge representation language. It did not lead to implementation and was subsumed by LOOM for practical applications.
- Knowledge query manipulation language (KQML) is a protocol that enables agents to query (delete/modify/update) ontologies and knowledge bases. The KQML was influenced by the design of the SPARQL, and many analysts worked with both KQML and SPARQL.

- XML is the first technology in the history of the Internet that addresses semantics. It is a powerful meta-language that defines domain-specific tags and structures for documents. XML is the first and still one of the most widely used languages to go beyond simple hypertext and to add basic semantics to HTML pages.
- Standardized general markup language (SGML) is designed for document sharing within large organizations like governments. XML is designed to be simpler than SGML.
- Meta-content framework (MCF) is the next step of XML. It is a specification of a content format for structuring metadata. It describes objects with attributes and relations to other objects.
- A semantic network provides a way to model human memory. It is an undirected graph of concepts (nodes) and connections (links) and has hierarchy because they are modeled concepts starting from very general to more specific.
- RDF is the foundation for the Semantic Web, and it has two primary datatypes, namely, resources (a resource has a unique identifier, that is, an Internationalized Resource Identifier (IRI)) and literals (a literal is a simple datatype, such as a string, integer, or date). The fundamental representation scheme in RDF is triple (subject, predicate, and object). The subject and predicate must be resources (IRIs). The object can be either a resource or a literal.
- RDFS builds on top of RDF. RDF provides a model for describing graphs in terms of triples. RDFS provides the basic concepts to provide meaning to these graphs. RDFS is itself an RDF resource with an IRI: http://www.w3.org/2000/01/rdf-schema. All files that leverage RDFS will begin with a prefix that maps this IRI to the preface "rdfs."

The graph structure of RDF/RDFS requires a query language to traverse, retrieve, and modify information in the graph. This language is SPARQL. SPARQL is to RDF as SQL is to relational databases. SPARQL has built-in capabilities to link to and request data from any resource on the Internet. Queries can match and retrieve data from many different distributed sources like DBpedia. All the layers of semantic web architectures add some security features that ensure the overall security of information on the web. However, the current architecture is lacking in providing the complete security aspects. To achieve the vision of the semantic web, various languages (like DAML, RDF, RDFS, OWL, etc.) have been developed to encode the ontology. OWL-S language is developed for the security aspects, and many security ontologies utilize these constructs.

In this chapter, we evaluate the domain security ontologies based on the InFra_Ont framework to know their pitfall rate. The organization of this chapter is as follows: Section 7.2 shows the secure data management in the semantic web. Section 7.3 analyses all the available articles and ontologies related to security. Section 7.4 shows the evaluation of the security ontologies via Infra_Ont framework. Finally, the last section concludes this paper.

7.2   Secure Data Management in the Semantic Web

According to the definition of the Data Management Association (DAMA), data management comprises all the steps related to data processing (initial creation of data, its storage, and usages). DAMA defines a data management framework that contains 10 components to implement these steps, and each component covers the different aspects of data management. One of these components is data security management that aims to implement the security requirements, namely confidentiality, integrity, data availability, data provenance, and access control mechanisms. There are three different policy languages: access control, flow control, and usage control used to regulate information processing.

- **Access Control Languages:** It helps the configuration of access control systems that aim to provide access to digital resources. There are two types of access control languages proposed, (a) languages that allow access of information in an open environment (b) language that allow access of the information in a close environment. The Access control languages, namely Access Management Ontology (AMO) [6], WebAccessControl, and CommonPolicy [7] are designed to regulate the information in an open environment, whereas Enterprise Privacy Authorization language (EPAL) and eXtensible Access Control Markup Language (XACML) [8] are designed for the close environment.

  The AMO is built-in RDFS format and defines the rule for the access control. Few rules like prohibitions are not allowed. The design of AMO is simple, and to ease the creation of access rules and their integration, it allows to model only permitted actions. All the actions that AMO does not support are considered to be forbidden. WebAcessControl is a lightweight ontology that is written in RDFS format and describes the access control rule for the decentralized systems where web resources and users are managed by different parties. The users are uniquely identified with the help of a WebID identifier, and a WebID authentication protocol is used to check the authentication of the users. Similar to AMO, a WebAccessControl allows modeling only permitted actions. CommonPolicy is an XML-based language that describes access rules for personal data. It is a lightweight model and allows only permitted actions. It is used in combination with application-level protocols, like FTP, HTTP. These protocols aim to check the authentication of the user request and the requested data.

Two languages, namely Enterprise Privacy Authorization Language (EPAL) and eXtensible Access Control Markup Language (XACML), allow much more expressive policies than AMO, WebAccessControl, and Common Policy. The EPAL and XACML are XML-based access control languages and designed for closed network environments. EPAL focuses only on access to personal data, whereas XACML can regulate access to arbitrary data as it does not have any predefined use cases. Hence, XACML is more expressive than EPAL and can replace EPAL in various applications [9].

- **Usage Control Languages:** There are different types of usage control languages used to regulate the information [10]. The usage control policies for the digital objects are defined by right expression languages (REL). The REL defines an abstract policy model, which has a basic syntax and is shared by all policies. To describe the Creative Commons license, ccREL ontology is designed in RDFS format. The usage policies for the digital images are defined by PLUS License Data Format that offers lightweight RDFS ontology. These policies cannot be imposed by a technical system because these are specially designed for human recipients. The usage control licenses for linked data resources are defined by linked data rights ontology (LDR) which has a lightweight ontology written in OWL [11]. This ontology can be extended in a particular use case by adding terms. A model based on metadata encoding and transmission standard (METS) is defined [12]. METS has a basic XML language structure that can be extended with the help of vocabulary to annotate the digital resource. METSRight is a vocabulary that defines basic REL and allows parties to perform actions on a digital resource. However, it does not support defined prohibitions.

Two languages, namely MPEG-21 REL [13] and Open digital rights Language (ODRL) [14], are more complex usage control languages. MPEG-21 REL is a part of MPEG-21 (similar to the METS and used to annotate the digital resources) and the successor of XrML [15]. Both MPEG-21 REL and ODRL can be utilized in the same use case and permit arbitrary control policies. MPEG-21 REL is based on the XML, whereas ODRL provides an abstract model, which is expressed in OWL, XML, and JSON encoding. In summary, RELs usually do not offer a human-readable explanation of their policies. For this reason, different interpretations of the same policy may be considered valid. REL describes which user has the right to perform which actions on which digital resources.

- **Flow Control Languages:** These languages are designed to control the flow of communication within the closed network environment and help in the configuration of the network. These languages imposed high-level security policies on different network systems like switches and routers. Various languages describe the flow control regulations like XML-based firewall meta-model [16], UML-based DEN-ng [17], and the OWL-based policy Translator (OPoT) [18]. Both XML-based firewall meta-model and UML-based DEN-ng do not directly cover communication endpoints and only focus on the low-level router. The OPoT supports different nodes of the communication path along with end systems. XML-based firewall meta-model only supports those rules that are permitted, and it does not define prohibited communication flows. All communications, which are not endorsed, are considered to be forbidden. OPoT has a set of 12 predefined basic policies, which can be viewed as a template to implement the organizations' specific security policies, and every policy covers a particular use case. To implement the specific security policy, a corresponding basic policy of OPoT has to be selected and then mapped with the current network with the help of IP addresses.

7.3   Security Ontologies in a Nutshell

As of now, many articles about security ontologies are available in the different repositories. We have queried several well-reputed repositories to retrieve these articles for the literature review. This review collects the articles from the journal papers, conference proceedings, books, and magazines published in the last decade (from 2010 to September 2021). The online repositories have been queried using a search string "security ontologies." We have used four well-reputed repositories, namely Science Direct, ACM Digital Library, IEEEXplore, and Google scholar. The total number of obtained articles from period 2010 to September 2021 from these repositories—Science Direct has 11,504 articles; ACM Digital Library has 132,986 articles; IEEEXplore has 1,764 articles, and Google scholar has 4,148 articles. Figures 7.3 (a), (b) (c), and (d) show the number of articles retrieved during the period of 2010 to September 2021 from four repositories, namely Science Direct, ACM Digital Library IEEEXplore, and Google scholar, respectively.

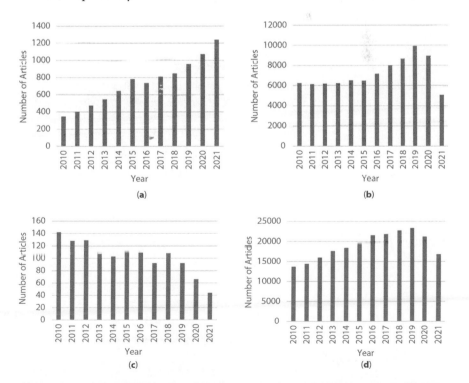

Figure 7.3 Obtained articles per year (from 2010 to July 2021) (a) Science direct (b) ACM Digital Library (c) IEEEXplore (d) Google Scholar.

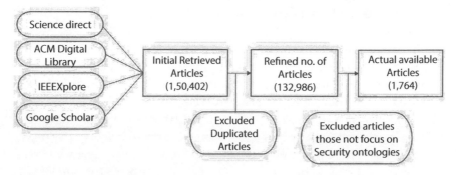

Figure 7.4 Screening of the articles.

Figure 7.4 shows the screening of the articles that has been done manually, and we have taken 2 months to complete this screening. Initially, we have got a total of 1,50,402 articles from the four repositories described above. The refined number of articles is 132,986 because 17,416 articles are found duplicates (out of 1,50,402) that have been excluded from the review. After reading the abstract of the obtained articles, we have seen only 1,764 articles where security ontology is the main topic.

Classification Framework for Security Ontologies: We have defined an abstract framework based on the articles selected for the literature review. The classification framework is depicted in Figure 7.5. This framework classified the obtained articles into four categories: security ontologies (general), security ontologies (applied in a specific domain, i.e., domain-oriented ontologies like software security ontologies, cloud security ontologies, information security ontologies, and many), Theoretical works (authors only defined the

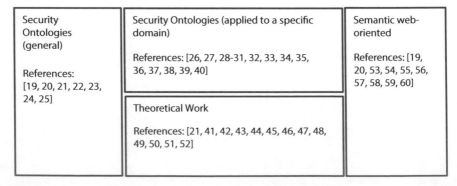

Figure 7.5 Classification framework for security ontologies analysis.

security ontologies theoretically), semantic web oriented (security ontologies that have been developed especially for semantic web).

Our focus is to cover all the security ontologies that have been developed in the context of the semantic web. To the best of our knowledge, 11 ontologies have been developed for the security aspect of the semantic web that support confidentiality, integrity, data availability, data provenance, and access control mechanisms. These ontologies are [61] agent security ontology, credential ontology, OWL-S (profile ontology, process ontology, grounding ontology), information object ontology, main security ontology, security ontology, security view ontology, service ontology, and service security ontology. These ontologies are summarized below.

7.4   InFra_OE Framework

The InFra_OE framework consists of three phases, namely input phase, processing phase, and output phase, whereas the processing phase contains four modules: (a) evaluation based on role of knowledge representation, (b) OOPS!, (c) ontology code effectiveness, (d) layer-based evaluation. The InFra_OE framework is depicted by Figure 7.6. The human interaction is

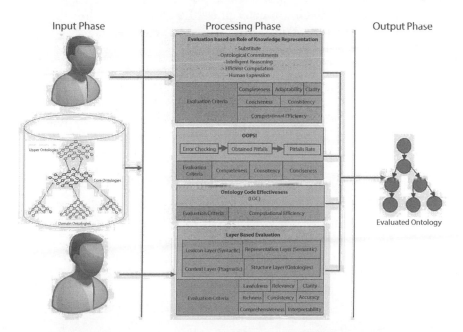

Figure 7.6 Evaluation of security ontology via OOPS! tool of InFra_OE framework.

required in two modules, namely evaluation based on the role of knowledge representation and layer-based evaluation. All the modules of the processing phase are executed parallelly, and the final result is calculated by taking the mean value of obtained results from all four modules. For the evaluation of security ontologies, we use second and third module of InFra_OE. The second module focuses on the investigation of pitfall rate whereas the third module shows the size of the ontology.

OOPS! is a web-based tool that shows the pitfalls or anomalies of an ontology. OOPS! shows the 41 types of pitfalls starting from P01 to P41. Basically, OOPS! groups the pitfalls under three categories, namely minor pitfalls (these pitfalls are not serious and no need to remove them), important pitfalls (not very serious pitfalls but need to remove), critical pitfalls (these pitfalls hamper the quality of an ontology and need to remove them before using ontology). These pitfalls are also classified by dimension and evaluation criteria.

- Dimension: OOPS! tool has three types of dimension pitfalls, namely Structural dimension, Functional dimension, and Usability-Profiling dimension. The structural dimension determines those pitfalls related to modeling decisions, wrong inference, no inference, and ontology language. The functional dimension determines the pitfalls related to the real-world modeling (common sense), requirement completeness, and application context. The usability-profiling dimension shows the pitfalls related to ontology clarity, ontology understanding, and ontology metadata.

- Evaluation Criteria: OOPS! determines the pitfalls under the three ontology evaluation criteria, namely consistency, completeness, and conciseness. It checks the consistency of an ontology by examining wrong inverse relationships, cycles of the class hierarchy, merging of the concepts in the same class, checking multiple domains or ranges of a property, and by recursive definitions. The completeness is measured by checking unconnected ontology elements, missing disjointness, domains and ranges, explicit equivalent property, and inverse relationships. The conciseness of an ontology is checked by measuring three pitfalls, namely making synonyms as a class, using a miscellaneous class, making "is" relationship instead of using "rdf:type" and "rdfs:subClassOf."

After running the OOPS! tool, we have found that only five ontologies, namely main security, grounding, profile, and service ontology, and process ontology have critical pitfalls that need to be removed before using them in any application. The description of obtained pitfalls is listed below:

Important Pitfalls:
P10—This pitfall explains the number of disjoint axioms between classes or properties that exists in an ontology.
P11—It determines the number of properties that do not have domain and range.
P12—It shows that equivalent property is not explicitly declared.
P24—It indicates the number of recursive definitions of the elements.
P25—It indicates the number of relationships that defines inverse to itself.
P26—It shows that how many symmetric object properties are defined as the inverse of another object properties.
P30—It indicates that equivalent classes are not explicitly declared.
P34—It indicates the number of untyped class.
P41—It shows that ontology has no license.

Minor Pitfalls:
P02—It shows the information about creating synonyms as classes.
P04—It shows how many elements are unconnected.
P08—It shows how many elements do not have annotation properties.
P13—It shows that inverse relationship is not explicitly declared.
P20—It shows that how many annotations of an ontology are misused.
P22—It shows different naming conventions in the ontology.

Critical Pitfalls:
P31—It shows how many classes have been wrongly defined as equivalent classes.

The pitfall describes the number of features that could create problems during reasoning. We have calculated the pitfall rate by using the following formula [61]

$$\frac{\Sigma_{i=1}^{n} P_i}{N}$$

Pi represents the total number of pitfall cases according to the pitfall type Pi, and N is the total number of tuples (ontology size). The high value of the pitfall rate implies a more significant number of anomalies and vice-versa. Figure 7.7 shows the pitfalls rate of the available security ontologies. Four ontologies have pitfalls rate higher than 1.

Ontology code effectiveness evaluates the size and complexity of the ontology's code. Basically, it shows the conciseness of the developed ontology by identifying the similarity in an ontology code and identification of the duplicate in a code (known as clones). In software engineering, the quality of the code is determined by various techniques, like line of code (LOC), function point, etc. We calculate the ontology size by LOC, which shows the number of tuples stored in the ontology. The size of the ontology does not depend on the annotation properties as they serve metadata information about the entities. We have ignored nine annotation properties, namely backwardCompatibleWith, comments, deprecated, incompatibleWith, isDefinedBy, label, priorVersion, seeAlso, and versionInfo.

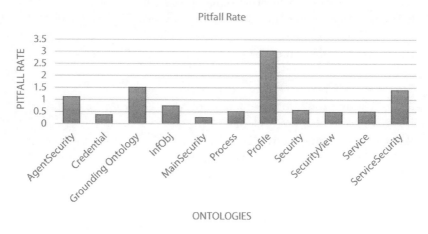

Figure 7.7 Pitfall rate of security ontologies.

Table 7.1 Size of security ontologies.

Ontologies	Agent security	Credential	Grounding ontology	InfObj	Main security	Process	Profile	Security	Security view	Service	Service security
Size	9	146	144	31	1953	322	70	148	55	55	10

These properties are supported by the protégé tool. The size of all security ontologies is depicted by Table 7.1.

7.5   Conclusion

This chapter has presented an abstract framework for classification of the security ontologies and evaluated the security ontologies via InFra_ont framework. The proposed abstract framework classified the security ontologies in four categories, namely general security ontology, theoretical security ontology, semantic web-oriented security ontology, and domain specific security ontology. The extensive literature has shown the available number of articles of security ontologies from 2010 to September 2021 based on four well-known repositories. We have used two modules (OOPS! tool and ontology code effectiveness) of InFra_ont framework for the evaluation of security ontologies. The OOPS! tool has calculated pitfall rate for the investigation of anomalies, whereas ontology code effectiveness has shown the size of the ontology. This chapter also described information about ontology language and linked data.

References

1. Rashid, P.Q., *Semantic network and frame knowledge representation formalisms in artificial intelligence*, Doctoral dissertation, Eastern Mediterranean University (EMU)-Doğu Akdeniz Universitesi (DAÜ), Gazimağusa, North Cyprus, 2015.
2. Devedzić, V., Understanding ontological engineering. *Commun. ACM*, 45, 4, 136–144, 2002.
3. Kalibatiene, D. and Vasilecas, O., Survey on ontology languages, in: *International Conference on Business Informatics Research*, 2011, October, Springer, Berlin, Heidelberg, pp. 124–141.
4. Patel, A. and Debnath, N.C., Development of the InBan_CIDO ontology by reusing the concepts along with detecting overlapping information, in: *Inventive Computation and Information Technologies*, pp. 349–359, Springer, Singapore, 2022.
5. Debellis, M. and Neches, R., Knowledge representation and the semantic web: An historical overview of influences on emerging tools. *Recent Adv. Comput. Sci. Commun.*, 2022. https://www.academia.edu/s/901df31a00
6. Buffa, M. and Faron-Zucker, C., Ontology-based access rights management, in: *Advances in Knowledge Discovery and Management*, pp. 49–61, Springer, Berlin, Heidelberg, 2012.

7. Schulzrinne, H., Tschofenig, H., Morris, J.B., Cuellar, J.R., Polk, J.M., Rosenberg, J.D., Common policy: A document format for expressing privacy preferences. *RFC, 4745*, pp. 1–32, 2007.

8. Anderson, A., Nadalin, A., Parducci, B., Engovatov, D., Lockhart, H., Kudo, M., Moses, T., extensible access control markup language (xacml) version 1.0. *OASIS.* 2003. https://docs.oasis-open.org/xacml/3.0/xacml-3.0-core-spec-os-en.html

9. Anderson, A.H., A comparison of two privacy policy languages: EPAL and XACML, in: *Proceedings of the 3rd ACM Workshop on Secure Web Services*, 2006, November, pp. 53–60.

10. Sandhu, R. and Park, J., Usage control: A vision for next generation access control, in: *International Workshop on Mathematical Methods, Models, and Architectures for Computer Network Security*, 2003, September, Springer, Berlin, Heidelberg, pp. 17–31.

11. Rodrıguez-Doncel, V., Suárez-Figueroa, M.C., Gómez-Pérez, A., Poveda, M., License linked data resources pattern, in: *Proc. of the 4th Int. Workshop on Ontology Patterns (to appear)*, 2013.

12. Cantara, L., METS: The metadata encoding and transmission standard. *Cat. Classif. Q., 40*, 3-4, 237–253, 2005.

13. Wang, X., MPEG-21 rights expression language: Enabling interoperable digital rights management. *IEEE MultiMedia, 11*, 4, 84–87, 2004.

14. Steyskal, S. and Polleres, A., Towards formal semantics for ODRL policies, in: *International Symposium on Rules and Rule Markup Languages for the Semantic Web*, 2015, August, Springer, Cham, pp. 360–375.

15. Wang, X., Lao, G., DeMartini, T., Reddy, H., Nguyen, M., Valenzuela, E., XrML–eXtensible rights markup language, in: *Proceedings of the 2002 ACM Workshop on XML Security*, 2002, November, pp. 71–79.

16. Cuppens, F., Cuppens-Boulahia, N., Sans, T., Miège, A., A formal approach to specify and deploy a network security policy, in: *IFIP World Computer Congress, TC 1*, 2004, August, Springer, Boston, MA, pp. 203–218.

17. Strassner, J., De Souza, J.N., Van der Meer, S., Davy, S., Barrett, K., Raymer, D., Samudrala, S., The design of a new policy model to support ontology-driven reasoning for autonomic networking. *J. Netw. Syst. Manage., 17*, 1-2, 5–32, 2009.

18. Dividino, R.Q., Managing and using provenance in the semantic web, 2017. https://www.semanticscholar.org/paper/Managing-and-using-provenance-in-the-semantic-web-Dividino/60bf98e8bd6c7e113c99e823157d7de93916bde2

19. Denker, G., Kagal, L., Finin, T., Security in the semantic web using OWL. *Inf. Secur. Tech. Rep., 10*, 1, 51–58, 2005.

20. Brown, C., Semantic web technologies for data curation and provenance, in: *19th International Congress of Metrology (CIM2019)*, EDP Sciences, p. 26002, 2019.

21. Kim, A., Luo, J., Kang, M., Security ontology for annotating resources, in: *OTM Confederated International Conferences" On the Move to Meaningful Internet Systems"*, 2005, October, Springer, Berlin, Heidelberg, pp. 1483–1499.
22. Karyda, M., Balopoulos, T., Dritsas, S., Gymnopoulos, L., Kokolakis, S., Lambrinoudakis, C., Gritzalis, S., An ontology for secure e-government applications, in: *First International Conference on Availability, Reliability and Security (ARES'06)*, 2006, April, IEEE, p. 5.
23. Lee, S.W., Gandhi, R., Muthurajan, D., Yavagal, D., Ahn, G.J., Building problem domain ontology from security requirements in regulatory documents, in: *Proceedings of the 2006 International Workshop on Software Engineering for Secure Systems*, 2006, May, pp. 43–50.
24. Tsoumas, B. and Gritzalis, D., Towards an ontology-based security management, in: *20th International Conference on Advanced Information Networking and Applications-Volume 1 (AINA'06)*, 2006, April, vol. 1, IEEE, pp. 985–992.
25. Zhou, J., Niemela, E., Savolainen, P., An integrated QoS-aware service development and management framework, in: *2007 Working IEEE/IFIP Conference on Software Architecture (WICSA'07)*, 2007, January, IEEE, pp. 13–13.
26. Do Amaral, F.N., Bazílio, C., Da Silva, G.M.H., Rademaker, A., Haeusler, E.H., An ontology-based approach to the formalization of information security policies, in: *2006 10th IEEE International Enterprise Distributed Object Computing Conference Workshops (EDOCW'06)*, 2006, October, IEEE, pp. 1–1.
27. Dobson, G. and Sawyer, P., Revisiting ontology-based requirements engineering in the age of the semantic web, in: *Proceedings of the International Seminar on Dependable Requirements Engineering of Computerised Systems at NPPs*, 2006, November, pp. 27–29.
28. Fenz, S. and Weippl, E., Ontology based IT-security planning, in: *2006 12th Pacific Rim International Symposium on Dependable Computing (PRDC'06)*, 2006, December, IEEE, pp. 389–390.
29. Firesmith, D.G., Engineering safety-related requirements for software-intensive systems, in: *Proceedings. 27th International Conference on Software Engineering, 2005. ICSE 2005*, 2005, May, IEEE, pp. 720–721.
30. Geneiatakis, D. and Lambrinoudakis, C., An ontology description for SIP security flaws. *Comput. Commun.*, *30*, 6, 1367–1374, 2007.
31. Giorgini, P., Mouratidis, H., Zannone, N., Modelling security and trust with secure tropos, in: *Integrating Security and Software Engineering: Advances and Future Visions*, pp. 160–189, IGI Global, Pennsylvania, USA, 2007.
32. Mouratidis, H., Giorgini, P., Manson, G., An ontology for modelling security: The tropos approach, in: *International Conference on Knowledge-Based and Intelligent Information and Engineering Systems*, 2003, September, Springer, Berlin, Heidelberg, pp. 1387–1394.
33. Undercoffer, J., Joshi, A., Pinkston, J., Modeling computer attacks: An ontology for intrusion detection, in: *International Workshop on Recent Advances*

in Intrusion Detection, 2003, September, Springer, Berlin, Heidelberg, pp. 113–135.

34. Yu, E., Liu, L., Mylopoulous, J., A social ontology for integrating security and software engineering, in: *Integrating Security and Software Engineering: Advances and Future Visions*, pp. 70–106, IGI Global, Hershey, Pennsylvania, USA, 2007.

35. Zhou, J., Niemelä, E., Evesti, A., Ontology-based software reliability modelling. *Proc. SSVM*, pp. 17–31, 2007.

36. Charpentier, R. and Debbabi, M., Security hardening of open source software. *Open Source Business Resource*, June 2008.

37. Schwittek, W., Schmidt, H., Beckers, K., Eicker, S., Faßbender, S., Heisel, M., A common body of knowledge for engineering secure software and services, in: *2012 Seventh International Conference on Availability, Reliability and Security*, 2012, August, IEEE, pp. 499–506.

38. Syed, R. and Zhong, H., Cybersecurity vulnerability management: An ontology-based conceptual model, in: *24th Americas Conference on Information Systems, AMCIS 2018*, New Orleans, LA, USA, August 16-18, 2018. Association for Information Systems, 2018.

39. Maroc, S. and Zhang, J., Comparative analysis of cloud security classifications, taxonomies, and ontologies, in: *Proceedings of the 2019 International Conference on Artificial Intelligence and Computer Science*, 2019, New Orleans, LA, USA, July, pp. 666–672.

40. Arruda, M.F. and Bulcão-Neto, R.F., Toward a lightweight ontology for privacy protection in IoT, in: *Proceedings of the 34th ACM/SIGAPP Symposium on Applied Computing*, 2019, April, pp. 880–888.

41. Mouratidis, H. and Giorgini, P. (Eds.), *Integrating Security and Software Engineering: Advances and Future Visions: Advances and Future Visions*, Igi Global, Hershey, Pennsylvania, USA, 2006.

42. Donner, M., Toward a security ontology. *IEEE Comput. Archit. Lett.*, 1, 03, 6–7, 2003.

43. Blanco, C., Lasheras, J., Valencia-García, R., Fernández-Medina, E., Toval, A., Piattini, M., A systematic review and comparison of security ontologies, in: *2008 Third International Conference on Availability, Reliability and Security*, 2008, March, IEEE, pp. 813–820.

44. Rosa, F.D.F., Bonacin, R., Jino, M., The security assessment domain: a survey of taxonomies and ontologies. *arXiv preprint arXiv:1706.09772.*, 2017.

45. Souag, A., Salinesi, C., Comyn-Wattiau, I., Ontologies for security requirements: A literature survey and classification, in: *International Conference on Advanced Information Systems Engineering*, 2012, June, Springer, Berlin, Heidelberg, pp. 61–69.

46. Kasten, A., *Secure semantic web data management: confidentiality, integrity, and compliant availability in open and distributed networks*, Doctoral dissertation, Universität Koblenz-Landau, 2016. https://kola.opus.hbz-nrw.de/frontdoor/index/index/docId/1393

47. de Franco Rosa, F., Jino, M., Bonacin, R., Towards an ontology of security assessment: A core model proposal, in: *Information Technology-New Generations*, pp. 75–80, Springer, Cham, 2018.

48. Gonzalez-Gil, P., Skarmeta, A.F., Martinez, J.A., Towards an ontology for iot context-based security evaluation, in: *2019 Global IoT Summit (GIoTS)*, 2019, June, IEEE, pp. 1–6.

49. Mozzaquatro, B.A., Melo, R., Agostinho, C., Jardim-Goncalves, R., An ontology-based security framework for decision-making in industrial systems, in: *2016 4th International Conference on Model-Driven Engineering and Software Development (MODELSWARD)*, 2016, February, IEEE, pp. 779–788.

50. Herzog, A., Shahmehri, N., Duma, C., An ontology of information security. *Int. J. Inf. Secur. Priv. (IJISP)*, 1, 4, 1–23, 2007.

51. Fenz, S. and Ekelhart, A., Formalizing information security knowledge, in: *Proceedings of the 4th International Symposium on Information, Computer, and Communications Security*, 2009, March, pp. 183–194.

52. Denker, G. and Kagal, L., Security Annotation for DAML web services, in: *Proc. 2nd International Semantic Web Conference (ISWC2003)*, Sanibel Island, Florida, USA, 2003, October.

53. Kagal, L. and Finin, T., Modeling conversation policies using permissions and obligations. *Auton. Agent. Multi-Agent Syst.*, 14, 2, 187–206, 2007.

54. Kwon, J. and Moon, C.J., Visual modeling and formal specification of constraints of RBAC using semantic web technology. *Knowledge-Based Syst.*, 20, 4, 350–356, 2007.

55. Maamar, Z., Narendra, N.C., Sattanathan, S., Towards an ontology-based approach for specifying and securing Web services. *Inf. Software Technol.*, 48, 7, 441–455, 2006.

56. McGibney, J., Schmidt, N., Patel, A., A service-centric model for intrusion detection in next-generation networks. *Comput. Stand. Interfaces*, 27, 5, 513–520, 2005.

57. Tan, J.J. and Poslad, S., Dynamic security reconfiguration for the semantic web. *Eng. Appl. Artif. Intell.*, 17, 7, 783–797, 2004.

58. Thuraisingham, B., Security standards for the semantic web. *Comput. Stand. Interfaces*, 27, 3, 257–268, 2005.

59. Vorobiev, A. and Han, J.H.J., Security attack ontology for web services, in: *2006 Semantics, Knowledge and Grid, Second International Conference on*, 2006, November, IEEE, pp. 42–42.

60. Vorobiev, A. and Bekmamedova, N., An ontology-driven approach applied to information security. *J. Res. Pract. Inf. Technol.*, 42, 1, 61–76, 2010.

61. Patel, A., Debnath, N.C., Shukla, P., Kumar, SecureOnt: A Security Ontology for establishing data provenance in semantic web. *J. Web Eng.*, 21, 1347–1370, 2022. River Publisher.

IoT-Based Fully-Automated Fire Control System

Lalit Mohan Satapathy

Department of EEE, SOA Deemed to be University, Bhubaneswar, India

Abstract

Mining is treated as the primary source of the economy for each and every economically growing country. Mined materials are especially used in construction, automobiles and the generation of electricity. Moreover, this leads to the provision of other goods and services as required by consumers from time to time. By providing the raw materials essential to every production sector, mining helps create jobs and stimulate economic growth. But the major factor in mining is its safety precautions. To improve the safety of the workers, effective risk management is required in the mining industry. Furthermore, on a regular basis, a risk assessment process must be followed to decide the control measures. Apart from that, coal fires are a serious challenge to the environment, health, and safety. This not only damages the environment but threatens the health of people living nearby. It also burns away the nonrenewable coal, which results in serious economic losses. In this paper, we have considered fire as a determining factor in accidents in mining, and it causes losses of life as well as mining material. This paper presents an Internet of Things (IoT)-based automated fire control system in a mining area, which will help to protect many valuable lives whenever an accident occurs due to fire. In this experimental application, different types of sensors for temperature, moisture, and gas are used to sense the different environmental data. These data are collected using a data mining system and shared with a remote server using the IoT and the cloud. A local processor is used to share the data with the server through a communication module. Based on the information from the sensors and the feedback from the local processor, decisions are taken and implemented. But the major decisions can be taken at a remote place, and the rescue team can take the necessary preventive measures. Based on the variation of temperature and humidity, the sprinkler system works, which reduces unnecessary water loss and

Email: lalitmohan.satapathy@gmail.com

Archana Patel, Narayan C. Debnath and Bharat Bhusan (eds.) Data Science with Semantic Technologies: Theory, Practice, and Application, (199–224) © 2022 Scrivener Publishing LLC

can protect the coal mines from unnecessary loss due to fire. It also reduces the manpower needed for this type of risky work.

Keywords: IoT, arduino, safety, automated control, sensor

8.1   Introduction

The mining sector is well known as a complex work environment and a hazardous sector where millions of skilled and unskilled laborers are directly or indirectly involved in the exploitation of natural resources like coal, petroleum, water, etc. After China, India is the world's largest coal producer. As per records, India produced 716 million metric tons of coal in the year 2017, which is equivalent to 294 million tons of oil. Coal is considered the primary energy source and plays a vital role in meeting global energy needs. As per industries' concern, coal is used for 38% of the world's electricity production and 71% of the world's steel production [1]. But more than a year's worth of coal fires occur extensively in different parts of Asian and African countries due to climate change, massive but weakly mined coal deposits, and uncontrolled exploitation, which not only affects the country's economy but also affects the world's economy. Therefore, it is necessary to think about the coal fire to ensure the national energy requirements, which will help the ecological environment and health of the inhabitants in the fire zone.

The government is creating policies for the safety and sustainability of workers employed in different sectors. To ensure the safety of working environments, every industry must take steps to develop a well-defined safety rule [2]. A separate establishment is required to ensure the internal safety of unskilled workers deployed in hazardous places. Even after taking so many precautions, accidents in these sectors are still a major problem, and it is due to the failure to take safety measures in the field and the carelessness of some people. This incident is occurring more frequently all around the world. As a result, approximately 2.3 million workers die each year as a result of occupational hazards [3] accidents are taking place in coal mining due to coal fires. This poses severe health, environmental, and safety risks in every part of the world. According to a study, it was reported that in the last two decades, accidents due to coal fires have increased in different countries in South Asian and African countries [4]. This is not only a threat to the environment but also to the health condition of the people engaged in this sector.

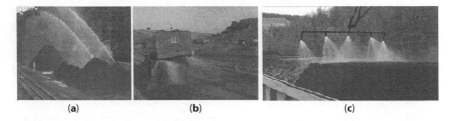

(a)   **(b)**   **(c)**

Figure 8.1 Water used in coal mining.

According to coal India records as of April 1, 2015, India has a total of 430 coal mines. These mines are divided into three categories, such as open cast (175 mines), underground (227 mines) and mixed (28 mines). During the summer, it was observed that coal was automatically fired at an atmospheric temperature in coal mining and thermal power plant areas. As a preventive measure, water is sprinkled in coal reservoirs throughout the day and night. This process is a wastage of a large amount of drinking water, as shown in Figure 8.1 (a-c). Adding to this, it is time-consuming and expensive too, because it adds up the cost of labor and machinery.

Fires occur in certain areas of coal mining where unattended coal is dumped. It can start either from a nearby fire, or due to spontaneous combustion of certain minerals in coal, such as sulphides and pyrites. Unfortunately, coal is a bad conductor of heat, and as a result, the heat formed is not easily dissipated. Coal in its natural state absorbs oxygen, which helps an increase in oxidation, resulting in heat up to ignition temperature. At this stage, if precaution is initiated, it will be possible to control the fire breakout. But it is not possible by human monitoring systems. Automation can help us monitor the heat from a remote at every instant of time, and precaution measures can be carried out to avoid a dangerous situation.

8.2   Related Works

The Internet of Things (IoT) is a network of objects and systems that are integrated with sensors, software, and other technologies in order to connect and exchange data with other devices and systems through the internet. One can easily understand the Internet of Things (**IoT**) as a network without human intervention. An internet-connected system is able to transfer data both ways over a wireless network [5–7]. IoT has a wide range of applications, including health monitoring, transportation system tracking, home automation [8] building surveillance, smart energy, and many others. In this innovation, data from different sensors and actuators is used for gathering information and storing this data in the cloud using IoT. The cloud is not only used for storing data but also for data analysis. Nowadays, IoT is used in the agriculture field for smart irrigation purposes [9, 10]. The prime and most advantageous characteristics of the cloud are its user-friendly and versatile applications.

Kumarsagar *et al.* [5] have proposed a design for coal mine safety based on MSP430. Here they have considered various parameters like temperature, humidity and smoke for monitoring. They have used a Zigbee transceiver as a communicating module, which controls a motor.

Li-min *et al.* [6] implemented a wireless sensor network-based system, where they used sensor nodes for measuring different weather conditions in the coal mine, and based on the information collected by the ARM processor, the prevention measure was initiated. Zigbee is used for communication, just like the previous method. They have implemented an SMS alert system to ensure the safety of their employees. Jiang *et al.* [7] described a wireless sensor network controlled by an ARM controller. They have used an IR sensor in certain high-risk areas to check the physical condition of mining.

Later on in the year of 2017 Deokar *et al.* [11] has suggested coalmine safety monitoring and Alerting system. The basic purpose of their research is to monitor the dangerous gases that cause accidents. To provide safety to the workers, a local alarm system was introduced, and it works based on the feedback of measured values. A switch is installed with the transceiver system for an emergency system. Before that, in the year 2014, Arathi and Elango [12] developed an atmospheric condition monitoring system using an ARM9 processor. Using the processor and Wi-Fi module, the database is updated regularly.

In the year 2018, Ankit Singh *et al.* [13] have also proposed a precaution model which monitors the supporting system of underground mining using IoT. They have used the cloud for storing the measured parameters and controlling the system using a smart phone.

In this direction, J. Cheng *et al.* [14] have proposed a model using ZigBee and GPRS. They have used ZigBee for transmitting the local information to the remote server and GPRS for tracking the affected area. A short message service was added along with the feature to send information to the smart phone. This gives added advantages in communicating genuine accidents and early treatment.

8.3   Proposed Architecture

Monitoring of different parameters and control is a useful measurement employed in real-time for people's safety, security, and comfort. With the developments in Internet technology and Wireless Sensor Networks (WSN), it is quite easy to establish a close monitoring system [8, 15]. The IoT most commonly uses a microcontroller as its brain. A microcontroller works as a small computer with the help of a microprocessor, internal or external memory, and input/output ports. It handles all the local data for necessary manipulation as well as for decision-making. The memory includes Read-Only Memory and Random Access Memory, from which ROM stores the software program.

The proposed IoT-based monitoring system has two parts. One part collects the data using sensor nodes and the other one makes the decision. For decision-making two processors are used named as local processor and a remote processor. The local processor, generates an alarm for a local alert before the mining material reaches its ignition temperature and the hazard gases reaches its threshold value. The remote processor controls the local processor from a remote location with the help of the Internet to determine the present environmental conditions based on temperature, humidity, and moisture. When an alarming circumstance occurs, the local safety team will get an alarm message from remote processor indicating what corrective action should be taken.

Figure 8.2 demonstrates a block diagram representation of the proposed coal mining fire control model. This is an IoT-based application system that uses the Arduino UNO as a local processor. This total system is battery-operated with solar backup. In open cast mining, methane (CH_4), hydrogen sulphide (H_2S), carbon monoxide (CO), carbon dioxide (CO_2), and other toxic gases like sulphur dioxide (SO_2) and nitrogen dioxide (NO_2) are found. This is the cause of any fire-related accident. So in mining, the temperature, humidity, and gases like oxygen, carbon dioxide, nitrogen, and methane are measured using different sensor nodes. This information is important and it requires display using an LCD display.

The Wi-Fi module, which uses Internet Protocol (IP) to communicate between endpoint devices and the local area network, is the next most important component. A wireless router is linked to the network, which allows the devices to access the internet. In the present approach, the WiFi module is used as both a transmitter and a receiver device. The detailed information gathered by the data acquisition system is always updated in

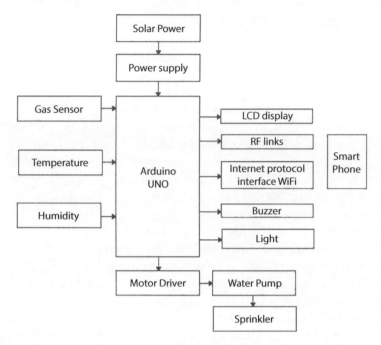

Figure 8.2 Interfacing block representation of proposed architecture.

the spread sheet and stored in the cloud. The threshold for every piece of data is fixed at a value under which it is safe for operation. At any time, a change in threshold value may be recorded as an accident.

Step by step operation:

(i) Initially, when the device is switched on, the sensors start measuring the environmental factors. The measured data is updated in the cloud. The information is also displayed on the local LCD display.

(ii) The measured values are compared with the threshold value with the help of the Arduino UNO. This process was repeated at regular intervals of time.

(iii) A value deviation causes the system to take preventive measures. A local alarm was initiated by giving a buzzer sound, which will alert the people working nearby. The security system will also be alerted by hearing the buzzer. The special provision of the light system facility was given for low-light areas. The lights are automatically controlled by the processor based on the natural light density.

(iv) With the help of the communication module, the local information is shared with the remote server. A special provision is incorporated for accessing the cloud data or monitoring the parameters with the help of a smart phone at any place with prior authorization.

(v) Based on the threshold value, the motor driver IC drives the water pump and sprinkles water to reduce the temperature and humidity of the affected area. As a result, the percentage of accidents due to fire may decrease. It also reduces unnecessary water wastage.

Based on the measured data, the central safety team may decide to delay the deployment of workers in particular zones. Also, it can create a record database which will carry information about the local zone at different seasons. This may give information to the managing authority to take a decision before time.

8.4   Major Components

The proposed system accumulates several subsystems that help to carry out the process smoothly and efficiently. The components and modules required for the operation are mentioned below along with their functionalities.

8.4.1   Arduino UNO

Arduino UNO is one of the widely used Atmega328P-based microcontroller for real-time embedded application (Figure 8.3(a)). This board has the good feature that it can easily interface with other Arduino boards or Raspberry Pi boards. Its popularity is increasing because it is a low-cost processor as compared to its similar type and low power consumption. The basic advantage is its open-source electronics platform with easy-to-use hardware and software. It has six analog pins and 14 digital pins (Figure 8.3(b)). The digital pins can be used as input pins and output pins as per requirement. A 16-MHz ceramic resonator decides the speed of operation. The operating voltage of UNO is 5 volts. This board contains a USB port for interface with Integrated Development Environment (IDE) software to program the board. A single unit comes with 1 KB EEPROM, 2 KB SRAM, and 32 KB of flash memory.

(a)

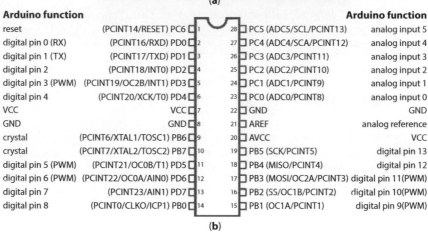

Arduino function				Arduino function
reset	(PCINT14/RESET) PC6	1 · 28	PC5 (ADC5/SCL/PCINT13)	analog input 5
digital pin 0 (RX)	(PCINT16/RXD) PD0	2 · 27	PC4 (ADC4/SCA/PCINT12)	analog input 4
digital pin 1 (TX)	(PCINT17/TXD) PD1	3 · 26	PC3 (ADC3/PCINT11)	analog input 3
digital pin 2	(PCINT18/INT0) PD2	4 · 25	PC2 (ADC2/PCINT10)	analog input 2
digital pin 3 (PWM)	(PCINT19/OC2B/INT1) PD3	5 · 24	PC1 (ADC1/PCINT9)	analog input 1
digital pin 4	(PCINT20/XCK/T0) PD4	6 · 23	PC0 (ADC0/PCINT8)	analog input 0
VCC	VCC	7 · 22	GND	GND
GND	GND	8 · 21	AREF	analog reference
crystal	(PCINT6/XTAL1/TOSC1) PB6	9 · 20	AVCC	VCC
crystal	(PCINT7/XTAL2/TOSC2) PB7	10 · 19	PB5 (SCK/PCINT5)	digital pin 13
digital pin 5 (PWM)	(PCINT21/OC0B/T1) PD5	11 · 18	PB4 (MISO/PCINT4)	digital pin 12
digital pin 6 (PWM)	(PCINT22/OC0A/AIN0) PD6	12 · 17	PB3 (MOSI/OC2A/PCINT3)	digital pin 11(PWM)
digital pin 7	(PCINT23/AIN1) PD7	13 · 16	PB2 (SS/OC1B/PCINT2)	digital pin 10(PWM)
digital pin 8	(PCINT0/CLKO/ICP1) PB0	14 · 15	PB1 (OC1A/PCINT1)	digital pin 9(PWM)

(b)

Figure 8.3 (a) Arduino Uno (b)Arduino Uno Atmega328p pin mapping.

The components and specifications Arduino UNO board (Figure 8.3(b)):

ATmega328	:	brain of the board	Power LED	:	lights up when the board is connected
Ground Pin	:	several ground pins	Micro SD Card	:	allows the board to store more information

Pulse Width Modulation	:	6 PWM pins	SPI	:	Four Pins 10(SS), 11(MOSI), 12(MISO), 13(SCK) are used for this communication.
Digital I/O Pins	:	14 pins	TX/RX	:	Transmit and receive serial data.
Analog Pins	:	6 pins	Power supply	:	5 V
AREF	:	set an external reference voltage	Reset Button	:	reset the code loaded

The Arduino Uno has a versatile application area, basically used in prototype projects. It is a code-based control structure used for the development of automation systems. One can directly load the programmes into the device without the help of an external hardware programmer. The ATMEGA microcontroller processes the data and facilitates the proper functioning of the IoT system.

8.4.2   Temperature Sensor

The LM35 (Figure 8.4) is a widely used temperature sensor operating at 60 µA and 5 V. It was observed that during application, it has very low self-heating, which is measured as less than 0.1°C at room temperature. This device is popularly used because of its high temperature range and linear property. The same can be represented with a linear transfer function as represented below.

$$V_{OUT} = 10 \text{ mv/°C} \times T \tag{8.1}$$

where V_{OUT} indicates that the output voltage of LM35, and T is the temperature. The temperature is represented in °C. The low output impedance, linear output, and precise inherent calibration make the system compatible with other devices. It has three external connecting pins as power supply, ground, and output line sequentially. It requires a 5-V power supply for operation.

Figure 8.4 LM 35 temperature sensor.

8.4.3   LCD Display (16X2)

The LCD is used in an automatic fire control system for local display of real-time values. LCD modules are very commonly used in most Arduino-based projects because of their low price, availability, and user-friendly features. The name **16×2 LCD** indicates that it has 16 columns and 2 rows as shown in Figure 8.5. LCD (liquid crystal display) consumes less power than LED (light-emitting diode).

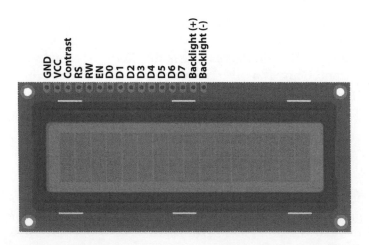

Figure 8.5   16X2 LCD display module.

8.4.4 Temperature Humidity Sensor (DHT11)

Humidity sensors operate on three different principles: capacitive, resistive, and thermal. For the measurement of low-range temperatures and humidity, the low-cost digital sensor DHT11 is popularly used (Figure 8.6). It has an operating voltage range of 3.5 V to 5.5 V with 60 μA to 0.3 mA.

The humidity range is 20% to 90% with an accuracy of ±1%. Each DHT11 is treated as extremely accurate in humidity calibration because each element is strictly calibrated in the laboratory. The DHT11 calculates relative humidity by measuring the electrical resistance between two electrodes. It provides high reliability, long-term stability with a high degree of accuracy and can be interfaced with any microcontroller. It consists of a humidity-sensing component and a thermistor. The humidity sensor consists of a moisture-holding substrate between two electrodes. The conductivity of the substrate changes with respect to humidity changes. The change in resistance is measured and represented. Furthermore, for measuring temperature, a negative temperature coefficient (NTC) temperature sensor or a thermistor is used (Figure 8.7). A thermistor is a variable resistor that changes its resistance with temperature variations.

(a)   (b)

Figure 8.6 (a) DHT11 temperature-humidity sensor. (b) DHT11 connection with processor.

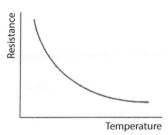

Figure 8.7 Negative temperature coefficient of resistance.

Specifications of DHT 11

Operating voltage	:	3.5 V to 5.5 V				
Operating current	:	0.3mA				
Output	:	Serial data				
Temperature				**Humidity**		
Measuring range	:	0°C ~ 50°C	Measuring Range	:	20%RH ~ 90%RH (25°C)	
Resolution	:	1°C	Resolution	:	1%RH	
Accuracy	:	±2°C	Accuracy	:	±5%RH (0~50°C)	

8.4.5   Moisture Sensor

The soil moisture sensor uses either the resistive property or the capacitive property of material to measure the water content of the soil. The resistive moisture sensor sends an electric current from one node to another and measures the resistance of soil. With the high water content of soil, a lower resistance reading is obtained, indicating the high moisture level. With low water containment, resistance is reversed. In the case of a capacitive moisture sensor, a change in capacitance indicates the moisture level. It has positive and negative plates separated by a dielectric. In capacitive moisture sensors, soil acts as a dielectric and its capacitance is directly proportional to moisture content. Apart from a resistive or capacitive sensor, the moisture sensor module consists of a potentiometer and a comparator (LM393 IC) (Figure 8.8).

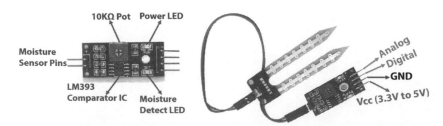

Figure 8.8 Moisture sensor module.

8.4.6   CO$_2$ Sensor

The MQ series gas sensors are the most popularly used low-cost devices specifically used for air quality measurement. Specifically, the MQ-135 gas sensor is used in our study because of its suitability for measuring NH$_3$, NOx, alcohol, benzene, smoke, and CO$_2$. The sensor module comes in a digital package with digital and analog outputs, which can detect a particular gas in a stand-alone mode. It can also operate without the help of a microcontroller and can provide a stable output with a long life (Figure 8.9). Furthermore, it requires +5 V for operation and takes 20 seconds for preheat duration. It has a simple working principle because it uses SnO$_2$, whose resistance decreases with the increase in pollution.

The fresh air resistance value is R$_0$. Initially, it was calibrated to R$_0$ in fresh air. Then, for calculating the resistance of the sensor (Rs) value, the following formula is used.

$$Rs= (Vcc / V_{RL}-1) \: X \: R_L \qquad\qquad (8.2)$$

where Vcc is 5 V, V$_{RL}$ is the sensor value, and R$_L$ is the load resistance (10 KΩ to 47 KΩ).

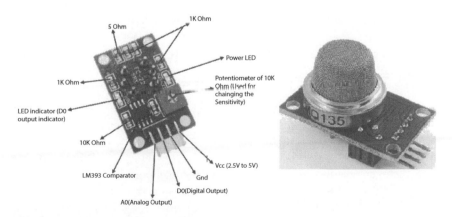

Figure 8.9 MQ 135 gas sensor module.

Technical Specifications of MQ135 Gas Sensor

Operating Voltage	:	2.5 V to 5.0 V
Power consumption	:	150 mA
Detect/measure	:	NH3, Nox, CO_2, alcohol, benzene, smoke
Typical operating voltage	:	5 V
Digital output	:	0 V to 5 V (TTL Logic)
Analog output	:	0–5 V

8.4.7   Nitric Oxide Sensor

Nitrogen oxides are a family of poisonous, highly reactive gases. This is a nonflammable oxidizing gas having the odors of sweet and sharp. It is produced by making nitric acid, welding, and using explosives. The MQ-135 gas sensor is used for detecting nitric oxide. Even if a person is removed from exposure to NO, they can still face serious lung injury if they have breathed it in. This gas has three shapes based on temperature and is heavier than air.

8.4.8   CO Sensor (MQ-9)

Every year, carbon monoxide kills nearly a thousand people (CO). It is a danger to every home. The proposed model can detect CO with the help of MQ-9 and generate an alarm if a threat is detected. The MQ-9 gas sensor works on the same fundamental principle as the MQ-135: where the density of gas changes the conductivity of the circuit. As a result, the output signal changes.

8.4.9   Global Positioning System (GPS)

GPS is used here for tracking the accident area and time with a satellite-based navigation system through the 30+ satellites in orbit around the earth. The GPS receiver requires at least four satellite data points for accuracy. The GPS does not require any data from the user and operates independently based on the IoT. The NEO-6 module is a stand-alone GPS receiver having high-performance u-blox 6 positioning with higher timing accuracy mode. The GPS module has four pins, such as VCC, GND, R_x, and T_x. These modules communicate with a simple serial RS232. The GPS receiver module gives output serially on the T_x pin, which gives information about location and time with a default 9600 Baud rate. The Rx receives serially when it is required to configure the GPS module.

8.4.10   GSM Modem

A Global System for Mobile Communication (GSM) is an international standard for mobile telephones that can be used as a modem to communicate over a network. This modem uses time division multiple access (TDMA) for communication. It is also possible to attach the data transmission to the internet to access it. In addition to the GSM shield, a SIM card is the basic requirement. The GSM module uses different frequency bands such as 850 MHz, 900 MHz, 1800 MHz, etc. for voice and data transmission. The SIM900 GSM Module used in different Arduino projects carries data at a rate of 64 kbps to 120 Mbps (Figure 8.10).

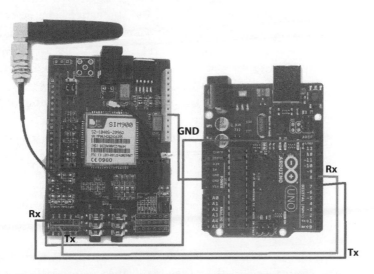

Figure 8.10 SIM900 GSM GPRS Module connection with Arduino Uno.

8.4.11   Photovoltaic System

A solar panel is a combination of a number of photovoltaic cells connected electrically in series and/or parallel to produce higher voltages, currents, and power levels. The light from the sun, which has packets of energy called photons, falls onto the solar panel. With the photovoltaic effect, an electric current is generated from the PV cell. The amount of energy generated is relatively small. PV cells are organized into modules and arrays to produce higher amounts of energy. The electricity generated from the solar array is direct current. This can be utilized in some electronic gadgets. But the maximum devices used in grid utilities require alternate current. Therefore, solar power must first be converted from DC to AC using an inverter before it can be used. The performance of PV modules is rated according to their maximum power output under standard test conditions. The operating conditions include a temperature of 25°C, a solar irradiance level of 1000 W/m2, and air mass, among other things. Batteries are often used in PV systems to provide a stable voltage and surge current to the DC load and inverter. This also stores energy during the daytime and supplies it to electrical loads during the night and periods of cloudy weather.

Solar charge controller

The most important part of the solar system is a charge controller used for voltage and current regulation. The charge controller delivers optimal power output to run electrical loads. But the battery charge controller regulates the flow of electricity to the battery to prevent overcharging and discharging of the battery (Figure 8.11). Solar panels are producing maximum energy at the middle of the day, and the excess electricity is stored in the battery bank. When the battery charge is nearly empty, the charge controller directs power to the battery and charges it quickly. But at night, the charge controller protects the flow of current to the solar panel. Additionally, charge controllers automatically disconnect noncritical loads from the battery bank when the voltage falls below a certain threshold.

There are two main types of charge controllers:

- Maximum power point tracking (MPPT) charge controller
- Pulse width modulation (PWM) charge controller.

The MPPT charge controller is 30% more efficient compared to the PWM charge controller. On the other hand, the cost of MPPT controllers is higher than that of PWM controllers. Still, in small power systems,

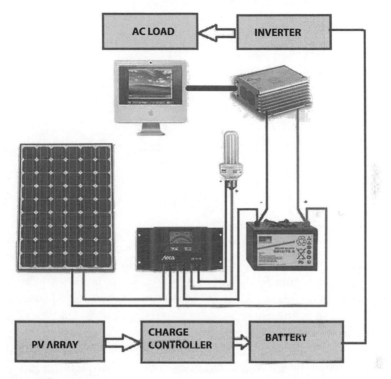

Figure 8.11 Solar PV system.

PWM charge controllers are used to minimize the overall installation cost. The charge controllers are decided based on the size of the solar energy system.

Solar Inverter

The maximum electrical loads used in day-to-day life require a stable alternate current, whereas the generated voltage from a solar system is direct current. Therefore, a conversion is required, which can be accomplished by a solar inverter. A set of Insulated Gate Bipolar Transistors (IGBTs) are used in the inverter, which are connected in the form of an H-Bridge. The inverter not only gives analytical information by tracking the maximum power point but also fixes the system issues by protecting against anti-islanding. In all types of solar inverters, different types of algorithms are executed and use a pre-programmed microcontroller. This controller increases the output power with the help of the Maximum Power Point Tracking (MPPT) algorithm.

Types of solar inverters

- ✓ Battery-based inverters
- ✓ Central inverters
- ✓ Hybrid inverters
- ✓ Micro inverters
- ✓ String inverters

Photovoltaic modules are extremely safe and reliable, with service lifetimes of 20 to 30 years.

8.5   Hardware Interfacing

The detailed interfacing of the LM 35 temperature sensor with the Arduino is presented in Figure 8.2. The 16X2 LCD display is used to display the temperature in degrees Celsius. The middle pin of LM 35 generates an output voltage that is linearly proportional to temperature. The alternate temperature sensor, DHT 11, generates the calibrated digital output. This can also measure the humidity of the environment. DHT11 has four pins, out of which three pins are connected to the microcontroller and produce an instant result (Figure 8.12).

Due to the fact that DHT 11 can measure both the quantities in the range of humidity (20–90%RH) and temperature (050°C), it can replace LM 35. But LM 35 is used here because it can measure temperatures up to 150°C (Figure 8.13).

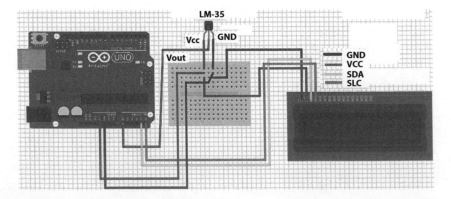

Figure 8.12 LM-35 interfaces with Arduino.

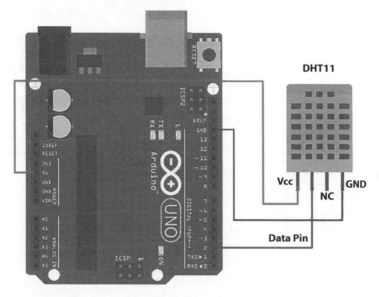

Figure 8.13 DHT11 interface with Arduino.

The MQ-X sensor interface with Arduino is shown in Figure 8.14. The sensor is capable of giving both analog and digital output.

The analog voltage range is 0 V to 5 V based on gas intensity and air quality. Initially, it is calibrated in fresh air, and then it measures the gas in

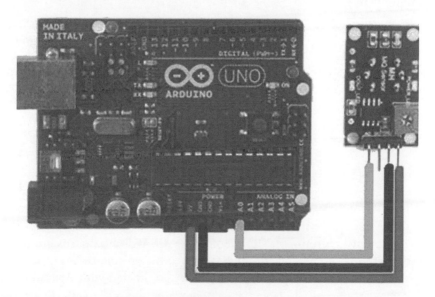

Figure 8.14 MQ-X module interface with Arduino.

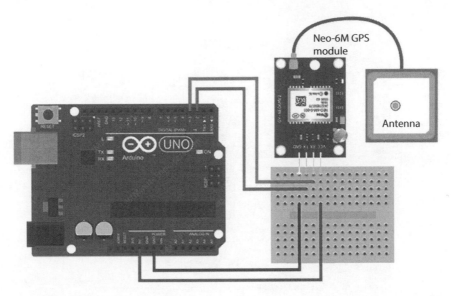

Figure 8.15 NEO 6M GPS module interface with Arduino.

comparison of sensor resistance. Initial calibration increases the accuracy of the system. The MQ-135 requires a preheat duration of 20 seconds. The SIM 900 GSM is an all-in-one Arduino compatible module. It has so many features, such as location-tracking, data storage ability, voice, text, and data communication.

AT commands are used in GSM/GPRS connectivity with the NMEA protocol. The GSM module-based project can be controlled with a computer, and it has the flexibility to be controlled by an Arduino Board (Figure 8.15). The best alternate system for GPS is NEO 6M, and the detail interface is shown in Figure 8.15. But in our work, we have considered SIM 900.

8.6   Software Implementation

Software Description

Arduino is an open-source, easy-to-use hardware and software system compatible with Windows, MacOS, and Linux. It consists of a microcontroller circuit board that can be programmed easily using Integrated Development Environment (IDE) software. All Arduino boards are capable of reading both analog and digital inputs. As a result, different sensors with different operating principles are easily connected with Arduino and are able to drive different devices such as motors, LED, LCD displays, etc. The programming part uses a simplified version of C and C++.

Nowadays, the Arduino processor simplifies its process of working with other microcontrollers. The following advantages are enlisted for Arduino:

- ✓ Inexpensive
- ✓ Cross-platform
- ✓ Simple, clear programming environment
- ✓ Open source and extensible software
- ✓ Open source and extensible hardware

Because Arduino processors are inexpensive and can run on Windows, Linux, and Mac OSX, they are used in thousands of projects. As IDE software is an open source software and quite easy to use for writing codes it helps execute experimental projects. Here, different sensors used for data collection are connected with the Arduino Uno. Every sensor is first identified by the processor, which then performs the desired operation. The details of the sensors connected to the processor and their programming are described as follows:

LM35 interfacing and loop programming

Before measuring the temperature, the output pin, Vcc, and GND of the LM35 must be connected to pin A1, +5 V out pin, and GND of the Arduino. Then, it is required to configure pin A1 of the Arduino as an input pin, as shown below.

```
void setup()
{
pinMode (sensor, INPUT);
Serial.begin (9600);
}
```

The setup function initialises the processor and sets the initial values. After setup, the loop function is created to allow the programme to change and respond.

```
void loop()
{
vout=analogRead(sensor);
vout=(vout*500)/1023;
```

```
tempc=vout;  // Storing the values
tempf=(vout*1.8)+32; // Converting to Fahrenheit
Serial.print(tempc);
delay(1000);
}
```

The ATmega328P processor of the Arduino has a 10-bit resolution (1024 steps) and the maximum input voltage is 5 V. This means 0 V is represented as 0 and 5 V as 1023. The equation used for the conversion of the ADC reading to voltage is

$$\text{Voltage} = \text{Vout} * 5 / 1023 \qquad (8.3)$$

As the LM35 scale factor is 10 mV/°C = 0.01 V/°C, the actual temperature can be obtained by multiplying 100 to eq. 8.3. So the mathematical formula used for temperature calculation is

$$\text{Temp} = \text{Voltage X } 100 = \text{Vout} * 500 / 1023 \qquad (8.4)$$

A delay is a blocking function where the Arduino stops for a specific period of time. In the above programme, a delay of 1 second is added to display the result.

DHT11 interfacing and loop programming

Different types of humidity temperature sensors, such as DHT11, 21, 22, 33, and 44, are available. A single function, dht.read() is used to read data from any kind of DHT sensor. These kinds of sensors use the following formula for relative humidity calculation:

$$\text{RH} = \quad (\text{W/S}) \, 100\% \qquad (8.5)$$

Where RH denotes relative humidity, w denotes water vapour density, and s denotes water vapour saturation density. The following programme is used on the Arduino for reading temperature and humidity using DTH11.

```
void loop()
  {
    float hum = dht.readHumidity();
    float temp = dht.readTemperature();
```

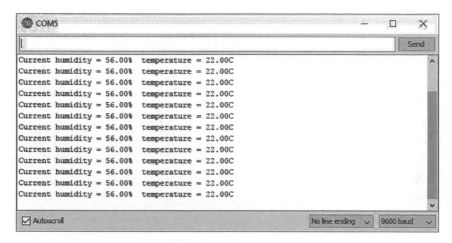

Figure 8.16 DTH11 module pc display result.

```
Serial.print("humidity in % = ");
Serial.print(hum);
Serial.print("temperature in °C = ");
Serial.print(temp),
delay (1000);
}
```

After execution the result is demonstrated in Figure 8.16.

MQ-X Interfacing and Loop Programming

The MQ-135 gas sensor is used in air quality monitoring equipment. This is suitable for detecting NH3, NO_x, alcohol, Benzene, smoke, CO2, etc. During the interfacing, A_0, D_0, GND, and VCC pins of the gas sensor are connected with A0, D0, GND, and 5 V pins of the Arduino. To interface MQ-X with Arduino, the following instruction is used:

```
void loop()
{
        sensorValue = analogRead(0); // read analog input pin 0
        digitalValue = digitalRead(2); // read digital input pin 1
                if(sensorValue>400)
                        {
                                digitalWrite(13, HIGH);
                        }
```

```
            else
                          digitalWrite(13, LOW);
      Serial.println(sensorValue, DEC);
      Serial.println(digitalValue, DEC);
      delay(1000); // next reading after 1 sec


}
```

The result returns for normal air is appx.100-150 and lighter gas 750.

Moisture Sensor Interfacing and Loop Programming

To use the sensor in analog mode, the analog output of the moisture sensor module is connected to the Arduino. As a result, the range of analog output is monitored from 0 to 1023. Moisture is always represented in the form of a percentage. So the final value is mapped between 0 and 100 and the result is shown using a serial monitor. The connection of the soil moisture sensor FC-28 to the Arduino is a pin-to-pin connection, where VCC, GND, and A0 of the sensor are connected to 5 V, GND, and A0 of the Arduino. The following programme is used to show the moisture level.

```
void loop()
    {
              output_value= analogRead(sensor_pin);
               output_value = map(output_value,550,10,0,100);
               Serial.print("Mositure : ");
              Serial.print(output_value);
              Serial.println("%");
              delay(1000);
    }
```

The above programme uses a resistive moisture sensor with 550 as dry soil and 10 as wet soil. The value of moisture is mapped to a range of 0 to 100.

8.7   Conclusion

Here, we are concentrating on different processes like collecting data, processing it, and then taking necessary action. The way we are controlling this module is referred to as automation. This is basically a concern about its efficiency. We have used DHT11 as it provides accurate values. This module is easy to use and easy to install. As it is wireless, it reduces the wiring cost. As it is based on a Wi-Fi connection, people within the range can easily achieve the values.

People with simple knowledge of coding can change the threshold value of the module. This module will help to save water as it will stop water supply by sensing its moisture level using a moisture sensor. This module works flawlessly in any android setup and on any server. People with less money can easily avail of it. Farmers may use it to sprinkle water on their crop fields, which will reduce water wastage. In the future, we can increase its WIFI range, which will enable more people to avail the sensor's values. This module does not consume much electricity, which will reduce its installation cost.

References

1. *Statistics of mines in India*, vol. I (coal), pp. 53–57, Directorate General of Mine Safety, 2015, https://www.dgms.net/Coal_2015.pdf.
2. *Safety in Coal Mines - Annual Report*, Ministry of Coal, New Delhi, 2017–18.
3. Shao, Z., Wang, D., Wang, Y. *et al.*, Controlling coal fires using the three-phase foam and water mist techniques in the Anjialing Open Pit Mine, China. *Nat. Hazards*, 75, 1833–1852, 2015.
4. Stracher, G.B., Prakash, A., Schroeder, P., McCormack, J., Zhang, X., Dijk, P.V., Blake, D., New mineral occurrences and mineralization processes: Wuda coal-fire gas vents of Inner Mongolia. *Am. Mineral.*, 90, 11-12, 1729–1739, 2005, doi: https://org/10.2138/am.2005.1671.
5. Dange, K.M. and Patil, R.T., Design of monitoring system for Coal mine safety based on MSP430. *Int. J. Eng. Sci. Invent.(IJESI)*, 2, 7, 14–19, July 2013.
6. Li-min, Y., Anqi, L., Zheng, S., Hui, L., Design of monitoring system for coal mine safety based on wireless sensor network. *2008 IEEE/ASME International Conference on Mechtronic and Embedded Systems and Applications*, Beijing, pp. 409–414, 2008.
7. Tiantian, J. and Zhanyong, Y., Research on mine safety monitoring system Based on WSN. *Proc. Eng.*, 26, 2146–2151, 2011.
8. Satapathy, L.M., Bastia, S.K., Mohanty, N., Arduino based home automation using internet of things (IoT). *Int. J. Pure Appl. Math.*, 17, 118, 769–778, 2018.
9. Satapathy, L.M., Arduino based automatic agricultural support system. *Test Eng. Manage.*, 83, 7445–7449, 2020.
10. Xu, L.D., He, W., Li, S., Internet of things in industries: A survey. *IEEE Trans. Ind. Inf.*, 10, 4, 2233–2243, Nov 2014.

11. Deokar, S.R. and Wakode, J.S., Coalmine safety monitoring and alerting system. *Int. Res. J. Eng. Technol. (IRJET)*, 4, 3, 2146–2149, March 2017.
12. Aarthi., K. and Elango, S., Coal mine safety monitoring system using ARM9. *Int. J. Sci. Res. (IJSR)*, 3, 11, 943–945, November 2014.
13. Singh, A., Singh, U.K., Kumar, D., IoT in mining for sensing, monitoring and prediction of underground mines roof support. *2018 4th International Conference on Recent Advances in Information Technology (RAIT)*, Dhanbad, pp. 1–5, 2018.
14. Cheng, J., Gao, D.W., Wang, J.F., Wen, D.G., Coal mine safety monitoring system based on ZigBee and GPRS. *Appl. Mech. Mater.*, 422, 215–220, 2013.
15. Zhu, Y., Zeng, W., Xie, L., Design of monitoring system for coal mine safety based on MSP430 and nRF905. *2011 International Conference on Intelligence Science and Information Engineering*, Wuhan, pp. 98–101, 2011.

9

Phrase Level-Based Sentiment Analysis Using Paired Inverted Index and Fuzzy Rule

Sheela J.[1*], Karthika N.[1] and Janet B.[2]

[1]Department of SCOPE, VIT-AP University, Amaravati, Andhra Pradesh, India
[2]Department of Computer Applications, National Institute of Technology, Tiruchirappalli, India

Abstract

Customer textual comments (i.e., reviews) scraped from various social media sites are used to automatically uncover the exact emotive concepts about a product (or service, social event, etc.). Phrase level-based sentiment analysis, in which we need to calculate sentiment ratings and important degrees of product elements, has recently seen a rise in demand. We present an aspect identification method for sentiment sentences in review documents in this research. In this paper, we proposed two key tasks, one is extracting significant features from the reviews and another one identification of degrees of product reviews. Initially, we construct an pair inverted index system to extract significant information from the massive value of an review document. The artificial neuro-fuzzy inference system (ANFIS) model was then built to categorize review patterns in order to capture the degree of product present in review, and the fuzzy rule was evaluated using the member function. The following are some of the highlights of our paper: 1) syntactic rules are used to extract features from reviews, 2) identifying the degree of an opinion based on the intensity of their sentiments.

Keywords: Sentiment, phrase based, pair inverted index, fuzzy system

Corresponding author: sheela.nitt@gmail.com

Archana Patel, Narayan C. Debnath and Bharat Bhusan (eds.) Data Science with Semantic Technologies: Theory, Practice, and Application, (225–246) © 2022 Scrivener Publishing LLC

9.1   Introduction

As e-commerce grows in popularity, customers are increasingly encouraged to post online product reviews on e-commerce sites and community media platforms. Consumers can stake their online product reviews on sites like Amazon, Taobao, and automobile home online product reviews have been proven to have a considerable impact on consumers' buying decisions in some studies [1–3]. That is, before making a purchase decision, customers can research similar sites and read online reviews on other products. For example, a customer wishes to choose a nice iPhone from a variety of options. The consumer can browse internet evaluations of alternative iPhones to gain a better understanding of the alternative iPhones. However, there are a number of research issues that need to be addressed before successful social analytics systems can be designed.

Sentiment analysis, on the other hand, is a recent research area in which industrialists can learn about people's attitudes about their products by evaluating text expressed in the form of reviews, blogs, survey responses, and other forms of text. Sentiment Analysis is commonly used as the voice of the customer in marketing and customer service applications. It extracts and studies affective and subjective information using NLP tools and methodologies. The sentiment lexicon, which is an archieve of lexical structures that are classified according to their semantic orientation, is used in most sentiment analysis methodologies (positive or negative). In an e-commerce area, both the buyer and the seller are assisted by the recommendation system. The relevant products and a personalized recommending system based on the behavior and interest of the user from a huge range of products is necessary. Recommendation systems are required. Collaborative and content-based recommended systems approaches are commonly used. The customer just had a more relevant and more interesting demographic reference and context-based recommendation methods.

However, the design of effective social analytical tools presents several research challenges. First, because these comments are unstructured and free in writing, Products and their features in online consumer comments are very difficult to correctly identify. Second, traditional methods of sentiment analysis are frequently performed outside the context. The emotions inherent in consumer comment depend, however, often on the context. For example, while the token "small" in the expression "hospitality" implies a negative meaning (polarity), in an other comment, "that's so convenient to sauté." In "novels" like "unpredictable plot" the same symbol is however positively addressed. In fact, the token "unpredictable" in famous sentiment lexicons, such as OpinionFinderand SentiWordNet was defined as a powerful negative feeling. It may, therefore, not be sufficiently effective to use lexicons of sentiment to carry out sentimental analysis and to extract social intelligence incorporated into consumer comments. Current studies suggest various methods to measurements and represent the results of online assessments. These approaches make decision study based on online reviews easier to develop. However, the results of feeling analysis usually have low rates of accuracy. Generally, in the case of two classes (positive and negative) of the sentimental analyses, the accuracy rates are between 60% and 90%, whereas in the case of the sentimental classification of multiple classes, the accuracy is below. These rates affect the precision of decision analysis and should be considered when reflecting the findings of the sentimental analysis of structural online examinations

The e-learning recommendation system is being developed to propose courses based on individual learning interests. The customer views are the customer's views and may be positive or negative. The identification of data is referred to as an analysis of opinion or feelings. The analysis of feelings is generally carried out on three levels: document, phrase and aspect level. There are three levels in the analysis. Sentiment classification techniques are generally referred to as lexical and machine learning. Profound methods of study are used to identify unstructured data sensations. Fuzzy Logic helps in improving the predictive accuracy of the recommendation list with the online shopping recommendation system and provides customers with highly personalized and interested products. Recently, in government sectors, fuzzy recommendation systems are being applied in applications like tax payment, giving some confidence in raising public awareness of tax payment. In order to enhance decision-making accuracy in decision-making, the fuzzy method is utilized and thus most apps use furious logic to decide on the best vendor in a range of vendors.

Fuzzy logic is a logic expansion where the truth is between 0 and 1. A problem of black and white becomes a problem of grayness. The simplest way of describing human knowledge in the artificial intelligence sector is to convert it in IF-THEN rules in natural language expressions. These rules are based on natural representations and models based on fugitive sets and misconduct. The goal of this research is to systematize the available knowledge about the many uses of fuzzy logic in opinion mining through a literature review. The main focus of this research is on the wide range of activities in the area of feeling analysis and further applications that obviously rest on the tasks of sentiment analysis to achieve their objectives. The key method used to accomplish an essential mining opinion task, phase or application should be fuzzy logic in all these cases in order to see the requirement of this assessment. Other strategies, on the other hand, could be used as part of the overall method or application.

The rest of the document is organized accordingly. The existing study effort is discussed in Section 9.2. Section 9.3 explains the recommended methodology. Finally, in Section 9.4, we emphasize the potential future applications of the work presented.

9.2   Literature Survey

Techniques have recently been used in applications, such as mining ideas from consumer product reviews [3], categorizing buyers' product as positive and negative product evaluations [4], tracking sentiment patterns in online discussion boards, locating Internet hot spots, and tracking political events. The bulk of SA applications, according to a thorough assessment of the literature. The product reviews, film reviews, policy orientation extraction and predictions in stock markets are grouped into four categoriesIn addition, Google Maps' data was used to analyze customers' feelings about hotels, department stores and restaurants. The method developed was able to summarize emotion about many features of the service offered, such as value for money and ambience, by using polarity values (positive/negative). Consumer emotions on major aspects of digital cameras, such as image quality and resolution, were extracted using online text reviews. It employed probabilistic Latent Sentiment Analysis (PLSA) to find out what people were thinking about.

Despite scholarly interest in sentiment analysis of internet texts, research into product rating based on online reviews is still in its early phases. There are only a few papers that directly or indirectly address this issue. The product ranking system based on the Internet review. They offer a dynamic programming technique for the identification in online product reviews of subjective and qualified sentences, where a subjective sentence refers to a consumer's subjective product position and a comparative sentence to a comparative relationship between two products. The sentiment analysis method is then applied to determine whether each subjective and comparative sentence has a positive or negative sentiment orientation. Furthermore, the number of dissimilar types of utterances (positive subjective sentences, negative subjective sentences, positive comparative phrases, and negative comparative sentences) was based on the emotional orientations collected. Finally, a product ranking is constructed using an improved page rank algorithm created on the directed and weighted product graph.

For recommendation, the health sector had used the reference system to group patients based on influencing factors in order to recommend the appropriate clinic. By analyzing unknown preferences, this approach divides patients into multiple groups. In taking certain decisions to buy, sentiments stated in the review play a significant role. There are a variety of methods for identifying the viewpoints represented in tweets. The analyses of tweet feelings help the products to rank more efficiently. A multimodality attentive recommendation model to provide predictive references on microvideos is being proposed by Yang *et al.* [10]. In order to express their opinions, users now use images and microvideos. The accuracy of the recommendations is improved with the identification and analysis of feeling hash tags. In each cluster, a user item-by-part network and then collaborative filtering methods will be useful for the prediction of the recommended product, The Community Recommendation Detection User Item (UICDR) method group the users and cluster stuff. The benefits and disadvantages of both contents-based and collaborative filtering methods are own, and thus Liang Feng and other [12] have developed a hybrid approach and both approaches are beneficial. Another hybrid recommendation model was developed by Liu *et al.* [11], and this model provides recommendations through the use of an advance learning approach, referring both information and explicit feedback obtained through the user reviews. When there are a large number of users and products, the rating matrix suffers. This methodology uses implicated feedback rather than explicit feedback evaluations.

In addition to converging on the only sentiment label, the proposal in Liang *et al.* [12] is to create a multi-class sentiment analytical procedure that studies all feelings available in the post review. Karthik and Sannasi [13] suggested a novel feature and method for product ranking, as well as a recommendation system (FBPRA). Each characteristic in their method for sentimental analysis, where feelings for each product opinion are computed, is tested in online customer reviews.

Several significant aspects of the type of goods have been selected manually or automatically, and phrases about each feature have been obtained from web reviews. Furthermore, for each attribute statement, a technique similar to that described in the literature is applied to generate a product ranking. In order to encourage consumer procurement decisions, a system should be established to determine the positive, negative and neutral orientations of online evaluations, along with the rank of alternative items based on selected sentimental guidelines and product weights provided by the consumer. This reference scheme used contextual information such as time, location, etc. to enhance the accuracy of predictions. However, in the recommendation systems, many contextual dimensions are to be taken into account which could be important for predicting the rating. The contextual information is identified the relevant influencing factors between all the important contextual dimensions. To find out what the consumer likes or is interested in, the authors applied flush logic. In paper [14] planned a common feeling model, which extracts online user reviews, their views as well as the feeling of polarity of opinions, primarily. The system used contextual data, such as time, location, etc., to improve the accuracy of the predictions. However, in the recommendation systems, many contextual dimensions are to be taken into account, which could be important for predicting the rating. It is identified the relevant influencing factors between all the important contextual dimensions. The authors used flush logic to achieve the user preferences or interests. It have projected a common thematic sentiment model that draws mainly online user reviews and their associated views and then calculates the polarity of feeling for opinions.

Rules are used to mine the function and their consistent terms of opinion using the linguistic relations amid dissimilar word in a phrase. The paper [15] have developed SenticNet addiction rules to mine product structures explicitly from online reviews. They use a marked corpus as well as their own categories to extract implicit characteristics. The rules for the mining of product structures based on online assessments were suggested by Qiu *et al.* [16]. After online preprocessing reviews, the proposed technique uses a double propagation method to extract features of subjective phrases.

The polarities and uncertainty of fuzzylogic is used to model concept related to different domains. The graph of recognition is based on WordNet and SenticNet resources. The gram is used to propagate sentiment information learned fromlabeled data sets using graph-continuous propagation gorithm. The graph contains two levels; the former depicts semantic connections between concepts, and the latter contains connections among the idea of membership and the various domains.

They have developed rules for finding product features in comparative phrases. Syntactical rules to detect a part-to-part relationship of product topographies in online reviews are defined to handle objective sentences. In order to increase the accuracy with which features are extracted, different pruning strategies are proposed. In a given document, the established an method to the spread of iterative mine characteristics and opinions. A seed feeling lexicon is used to bootstrap the algorithm. The algorithm mine more features and terms of opinion by means of syntactic rules. The hybrid rules-based procedure [17] projected to extract features and opinions from film opinions. The sentiment analysis in microblogs, the authors are proposing a fuzzy-based approach called Public Sense Discriminator.

The technique is built on the hypothesis of correlating feelings, allowing calculation of sentiment direction on the level of feelings, microblogs and the level of public sentiment.

Using a frequency-based technique, the candidate features are initially extracted as seed words. Synonyms are then identified with WordNet for each extracted function. Finally, the syntactic principles are questioned by looking at the seed terms' dependencies in the reviews. Algorithm for automatic rule selection According to Liu [18], a subset of the best accurate algorithms for identifying product features from social media content should be chosen. They were assessed based on their precision and reminder in order to test the correctness of the rules. The F1-score is finally used to choice the most powerful rules for feature extraction, as the performance evaluation measure the reviews of the clients. A system for formulating phrases, determining their perception scores and polarity using the SentiWordNet and the fluffy linguistic covers, is proposed by the authors. It also allows the use of the fuszy entropy and k mean clustering to extract relevant key sentence for sentimental analyses. The paper [19] proposed a two-fold rule based method for extracting product reviews features. In the first fold, grammar rules have been developed that can extract domain independent feature sentences. In the second fold, however, SenticNet 4 lexicons have tracked the domain-dependent features. The frequency and similarity-based approaches are used for measuring unrelated results. The [20] proposed a regulatory framework for the analysis of restaurant reviews for pros and cons. They used language designs to extract associated adverbs, adjectives and substantials from reviews. They produce a list of adjectives and adverbs in order to calculate the polarity. When they contain an adjective/adverb and question its polarity, the average assessments of the detailed exams are taken into account. Finally, they follow various approaches to calculate a sentence's final polarity score based on the positive or negative behavior of the adjective. SenticNet is one of the leading regulations for the performance of various linguistic tasks, including features and concepts, naming and polarity detection.

It created Weakness Finder, an expert system for analyzing consumer attitudes in Chinese language online texts, in a recent study. The system derives attitudes to aspects of products including quality and pricing from a morphemesis-based analysis. In the process of determining the Polarity of each sentiments in relation to product flaws, explicit and involving sentiments were taught to. Because it takes into account numerous language features such as degree adverbs and negation, this study built on prior work by Ding et al. [6]. Consumer attitudes can be utilized to categorize and prioritize automotive issues, according to the authors. Pekar and Ou

[7] proposed to evaluate 268 reviews of major hotels using sentiment analysis techniques based on customer reviews posted on the website epinions. com. Food, room service, facilities, and price were employed by the writers to automatically assess attitudes expressed toward those items.

The TF-IDF and FPCDA phrase FE methodology for product review SA. The local patterns of feature vectors were determined by considering the varying lengths of product reviews using the OPSM bi-clustering algorithm. Finally, an algorithm for detecting frequent and pseudo-consecutive phrases with a strong discriminative power (such as FPCD phrases) has been developed. Furthermore, various critical factors, including separation and the discriminative capability of words, were used to improve the discriminative capability of Sentiment Polarity (SP). The extraction of text features was then completed. The SA's performance on product review improved as a result of the sequence of experience and analogue outcomes. However, it has a worse classification accuracy when extracting textual features.

The sentiment analysis has recently also been carried out in microvideo and hashtag with multimodal data. Fuzzylogic helps improve the predictive accuracy of the recommendation list with the online shopping system and offers customers highly personalized products and products of interest. Recently, in government fields [9], fuzzy-based recommendations have been applied to applications such as tax payment, providing some confidence to increase public awareness of tax payments. A fuzzy-based strategy for multi-domain sentiment analysis was put forward by Dragoni *et al.* [21]. The approach benefits from possible overlaps of conceptual fields for the construction of arbitrary arbitrary domains. Fuzzy logic represents the learned polarities and is then incorporated in SenticNet and the General Inquirer vocabulary with conceptual knowledge. The findings prove that the proposal is feasible.

On paper [8], the SLCABG SA model was established, which was based on the SL, BIGRU and Convolutionary Neural Network (BNN). SLCABG SL was an SLCABG Model (CNN). In the SLCABG idea the advantages of SL and DL technology are combined. In review processes, the SL was employed to improve the feelings (SF). In order to remove the major SF and background items from examination using the attention mechanics, the CNN and the network Gated Recurrent Unit (GRU) were utilized. Finally, a categorization was awarded to the weighted SF. This method could, however, only categorize feelings into bad and positive categories, which was insufficient when feeling refining was needed. Finally, a categorization was awarded to the weighted SF. This method could, however, only categorize feelings into bad and positive categories, which was insufficient when feeling refining was needed. Hybridization approaches are used in paper [9] to classify the twitter streaming of data based on sentiment analysis.

The presented a multifunctional sentiment analysis strategy is used in the study of Dragoni *et al.* [21]. The approach takes advantage ofthe possible overlaps of conceptual domains for building general models to compute the sentiment polarity of texts from arbitrary domains. The fuzzy logic represents the polarities learned, and is integrated in SenticNet's and General Inquirer's vocabulary with conceptual knowledge. The results show that the proposal is feasible.

Research has substantially helped to the sentiment analysis and ranking of products through internet reviews. Though just two types of sentiment orientations are revealed in most of the current sentiment analysis investigations, i.e., that the direction of each sentence or text is either positive or negative. In addition, in the present product rating research online reviews neutral sentiment guidelines are neglected. This will result in the departure of key decision makers. In order to promote the purchase decisions of consumers, a system should therefore be established. This can impact whether internet reviews are positive, neutral, or negative.

9.3   Methodology

For sentiment analysis, fuzzy logic has been widely used. The author analyzes the progress and difficulties in the field in Dragoni *et al.* [21]. Our method incorporates fluidized logic in order to represent the polarity of linguistic characteristics of a particular field. The fundamental references to the fuzzy logical elements used in the rest of the article are provided here. The mathematical description accompanied by a more detailed presentation of these fuzzy logic elements is available in the study of Karthik and Sannasi [13] The lexicon contains the total number of times the word pair appears in a single ID and offset pair. The Fuzzy sets then generalize the crisp set, obtained by substituting the characteristic Z, μZ function that takes value in $\{0, 1\}(\beta(x) = 1$iff x x entirely Z, $\check{z}Z(x) = 0)$ with μZ membership, which is capable of assuming any value in $[0, 1]$. The $\mu Z(x)$ or, more simply, $Z(x)$ is the element xin Z, that is to say the x belongs to Z. The lexicon contains the total data for each word pair, with a single id and an offset, including how many times the word pair appears. The framework proposed as seen in Figure 9.1 comprises two parts: (1) Inverted wordpair index table construction (2) a categorizing of reviews technique.

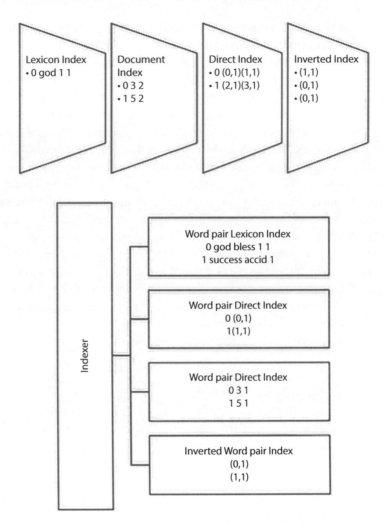

Figure 9.1 Inverted index stucture stucture with other indexted index structure.

9.3.1   Construction of Inverted Wordpair Index

Types of index table:

Consider {term$_d$} where c=1,2,. . . m and d=1,2,3,. . . n. The word pair of documents is formed
as (term$_d$, term$_{+1}$). so,the document Doc$_m$ = {(term$_1$, term$_2$) , (term$_2$, term$_3$) . . .(term$_n$, null)}

Wordpair Lexicon Index: In the lexicon the total data for each pair of words are registered in the corpus, with a single id and an offset, including how many times the pair of words is appearing.

Wordpair Direct Index: The word sequence is properly ordered in the document collection. The sequence of words was broken in pairs of words instead of a single word. The lexicon list is made up of these word pairs. The document identification and its accompanying word pair are stored in the word pair direct index. $Doc1= (term_1, term_2), (term_2, term_3), (term_n, null)$, etc.

Inverted Wordpair Index: The reversed index is created on the terrier platform to quickly and efficiently recover. The terrier creates a lexicon and document index reversed index. The index of the word pair was built as a work modified. Information on the word pairings is available in the collection of documents. The number of indexed data decreased to below 40%, but the time required to produce an index has increased due to the word pair collection technique. When you establish a word-pair inverted index, the number of disc visits is decreased also by two. The reversed wordpair index structure is displayed in Figure 9.1.

The current technique focuses on identifying sentiment and categorizing review patterns at the phrase level in terms of positive, negative, and neutral orientation. For review recognition, the suggested methodology takes into account sentiment terms, co-occurrence terms, and connected sentences. For classification, the suggested method employs Part of Speech Tagging and sentiment Actifiers. Here, sentence patterns are split down into phrases, and a Neuro-Fuzzy model is employed to classify them, yielding 8 different review phrase patterns. For capturing the degree of sentiment content that exists in the semantics of patterns, appropriate intensities are assigned. These sentiment expressions are given weights, which help determine whether the sentiment is good, negative, or neutral. The method is tested on web documents, and the proposed categorization method performs well and achieves high F-Scores.

9.3.1.1 Sentiment Analysis Design Framework

This section provides a framework for the analysis of the design sentiment with regard to input data for Online Product Reviews and appropriate NLP techniques (see the Online Product Reviews section for Data Source) (see section "Techniques for natural language processing"), as well as algorithms for machine learning. Amazon.com was chosen as the source of data for online review (OPRs). Amazon.com offers a wide selection of products and millions of OPRs as one of the world's biggest e-commerce platforms to analyse. It may be applied to millions of additional products by proving the applicability of the created framework for one single Amazon product. Criticisms made on Amazon.com include beneficial information such as the identity reviser, credibility revisor, rating of products, timeliness of review, the capacity of other reviewers to assess helpfulness and late editing of comments. Amazon's culture of promoting consumer input assures that it is a high-quality data source in addition to the enormous amount of information. This is illustrated by Amazon's "Hall of Fame," a page that glorifies its most useful customers. The quality of the examinations has to be strictly assessed. The "hilfefulness" of reviews as voted by other customers is a basic metric of quality on Amazon reviews. A study carried out by Hu *et al.* [22] has shown that the Amazon "helpfulness" rating does not necessarily relate to the designers' helpfulness rating. Four essential factors for evaluating aid were identified by Hu *et al.* [22] as language, product, quality of information and theory of information.The product features include product imports, qualitative characteristics related to sensitivity and subjectivity and characteristics related to the examination's divergence of opinion Elements, such as number of descriptive words and grammar include language characteristics.

Because customer-written content consists of product reviews, the system contains several fundamental NLP approaches. NLP combines linguistic studies and the application of human language through several statistical approaches. In order to comprehend the definitions and how similar they are to a different word, WordNet is an online lexical database. These relate words, which consist of linked groups of nouns, adjectives, verb and adverbs are referred to by WordNet as "synsets." Synsets for WordNet include degrees of relationship based on linguistic approaches. WordNet can identify synonyms that are similarly meaningful words, and anthonyms are less related. It is also able to distinguish hyponyms and hypernyms. For instance, "robin" means the "bird" hyponym, while "bird| means "rolling." Hyponyms refer to the general class of the particular type. Also measured are meronyms and holoniams, with meronyms belonging to a group and holonyms all pieces.

9.3.1.2   Sentiment Classification

Sentiment analysis is a new research field, which primarily focuses on the sentiments, emotions and/or feelings of people on a product/service from a text. A view can be defined as an entity or aspect of that entity in simple way as a positive or negative feeling or emotion. This section provides details on the preprocessing data, feeling calculation and product evaluation processes used in the proposed model.

9.3.1.3   Preprocessing of Data

Data preprocessing is done by tokenization, POS tag and parsing. The first is that the stage of tokenization and morphological analytical analysis divides the review comment into flags. The subjective terms will also be removed and adjectives taken into account during the POS tagging process for a further process. Lastly, for every annotation, the parsing process is used to build a tree. The review comment also identifies the links between the words. Tokenization is a term used to describe the process of converting a Tokens, often known as terms, are used to separate the contents. The works are arranged in such a way that they provide relevant semantic units for subsequent processing. To do tokenization and morphological analysis, we used custom POS Tagging.

Tagging

POS provides information on the manner in which terms are used in a sentence. This procedure tags speech tags like nouns, pronouns, adjectives, and verbs. Adjectives are essential to establish the point of view in a comment. POS tagging simply labels the word with the appropriate POS tag, so that the sentence/comments contain a further analysis. We used customer reviews like "Awesome Product," "My son loved it very much" and "Worth for money" as part of speaking tagging. The reviews, including "Awesome Product," "Fine Look," "My son really loved it" and "My money is worth it."

Despite the fact that sentiment analysis of internet texts has piqued the interest of academics, research on ranking products based on online reviews is still in its infancy. There are only a few research that directly or indirectly address this topic. The paper Ding *et al.* [6] proposed an online review-based system for ranking products. In their method for identifying subjective and qualified sentences in online product reviews, they propose a dynamic programming technique, where a subjective phrase represents a subjective product opinion for the consumer, and a comparative phrase represents a comparative relation between two products. Furthermore, depending on the emotion orientations collected, the amount of different types of words is computed.

Subjective and objective sentences are the two sorts of sentences. Subjective sentences usually have more emotion than objective sentences. For instance, the objective sentence is that milk is white, while the subjective sentence is that milk tastes wonderful. The subjectivity of words is determined by the context in which they are used. A subjective sentence may appear in an objective document. We utilize the recommended system strategy to address these challenges, which also improves the accuracy of the reviews. To test the accuracy, we employ Recall, F-measure, and Precision parameters as metrics. Precision provides better accuracy than other methods. Finally, the system determines the Polarity of the reviews. This paper outlines a method for classifying reviews as either negative, good, or neutral. This method takes the Amazon dataset as input and returns a positive or bad review based on the user's input.

In this paper, we have used hierachical tree structure to classifiy the sentence into difference class is shown in Figure 9.2. The paired inverted index table used to extract the cooccurence team along with feature term.

The first level of classification is based on the nature of the sentence, which divides it into Simple and Complex classes. Some sentence have single verb term and some of the sentence have multiple verb term. Complex sentnece have a "conjunction" word to cnnect two noun and verb. At the next level, sentence are classified based on co-occurence of FT. The co-occurence is positive or negative word.

Rule :

Rule 1: if $(s = \text{Simple})$ && $(ft_{(i-1)} = \text{Adverb})$ && $(ft_{(i+t)} = JJ)$ then $C = \text{Class1}$
else if $(s = \text{Simple})$ && $(ft_{(i-1)} = \text{No Adverb})$ && $(ft_{(i+t)} = JJ)$ then $C = \text{Class2}$
Rule 2: if $(s = \text{Complex})$ && $(ft_{(i-1)} = \text{Adverb})$ && $(ft_{(i+t)} = JJ)$ then $C = \text{Class3}$
else if $(s = \text{Complex})$ && $(ft_{(i-1)} = \text{No Adverb})$ && $(ft_{(i+t)} = JJ)$ then $C = \text{Class4}$

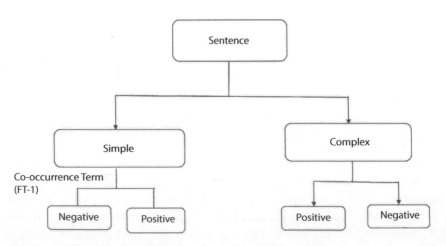

Figure 9.2 Hierarchical structure of sentence classification.

For each pre-processed review in this section, the objective user-based product rating calibration technology will generate a product rating score. First, by taking into account the polarity of each customer review, the sentiment score (SS) is generated. Second, by adding all the feelings for the target user category in question, the product rating score is generated. In order to improve the calculation accuracy of the feelings, we employed five feeling polarity levels, including positive, very positive, neutral, negative and very negative. The easiest way of representing human knowledge is by converting it in the form of IF-THEN rules into natural language terms .As the background and consequence of linguistic variables is that the fuzzy rule-based system is particularly useful in the simulation of some complicated systems that people can look at. These linguistic variables can naturally be expressed in fluid sets and logical connections of these set. The three most prevalent deductive methods of reasoning for the fuzzy systems based on language rules are (1) the Mamdani systems, (2) the Sugeno models and (3) the Tsukamoto models.

The first step in building the sentiment pattern is to extract relevant information from the documents analyzed. This step is called Extraction of Features (FE). The lexical and syntactic features that may relate to computing text polarity or the domain the text belongs to are taken out of all the documents included in the training. The functions are taken from the Stanford Core NLP Toolkit by analyzing document contents [5]. Every term is lemmatized, listed with a portion of the POS language tagger and extracted from the Stanford core NLP toolkit the reliance tree related to each sentence in this document. We extract from the output provided by Stanford Core NLP Toolkit two types of features: "Simple" or "Complex." The building blocks for our sensation model are these characteristics. The words of opinion in the text (noun, verb, adverb or adjective) are the simple features. For simple characteristics, in the two above phrases, the names "joy" and "deception" and the adjectives "stunning" and "snarling" are examples of opinions. In order to support the domain detection task, in particular those not related to the value of polarity in the resources used, nouns are also used to produce the sentiment model. The "laptop" in the fir is an example.

The complex characteristics are taken from a subset of the dependency relationships detected by the Stanford Core NLP Toolkit dependency parser. These features train the model for links between ideas in certain fields and how they allow specific polarities to be inferred. The subset of dependencies for extracting "Complex" functionality consists of: the "noun-adjective" and the "noun-verb" and "adjective-verb" combinations.

Experiment and Result Analysis

To conduct these trials, a huge number of comments from Amazon's ten product categories were gathered. Three-fourths of the product subcategories were used for training, and one-fourth of the subcategories were maintained for testing. For categorical reviews, summary and rating, and review classification, these findings were obtained.

9.3.1.4   Algorithm to Find the Score

(i)   Pre-processed review $S_i = \{d_1, d_2 \ldots \ldots dn\}$

(ii)   Identify sentiment term using NLP

(iii)   Compute score of each review

if $(x \leq 0.125)$ then y = Highly Negative sentence

If $(x \geq 0.125$ and $x \leq 0.25$) then y = less intentive Negative sentence

If $(x \geq 0.25$ and $x \leq 0.50)$ then y= Neutral sentence

if $(x \geq 0.50$ and $x \leq 0.75)$ then y=Positive sentence

if $(x \geq 0.75$ and $x \leq 1)$ then y =Highly Positive sentence

(iv)   Sort score in amending order

9.3.1.5   Fuzzy System

The initial stage of a fuzzy system is the identification of input and output variables. Following the definition of the input variables and Membership Function, the rule-based design (or fuzzy knowledge-based decision matrix) must be defined, which is comprised of expert IF-THEN rules. Using these principles, the input variables are transformed into an output. This will indicate whether the likelihood of operational issues is low, normal, or high. Figure 9.3 depicts the fuzzification system.

The Membership Function (MF) converts the crisp values of the linguistic variables into the provided fuzzy sets [9]. Appropriate membership functions for linguistic variable partitions map the inputs into degrees of membership. Membership functions come in a variety of shapes and sizes. In a fuzzy system that correctly replicates fuzzy modelling, choosing appropriate membership functions for fuzzy sets is critical. In the proposed study, the categorization labels for the intensity of semantic orientation and positive or negative polarity of a specific sentence are as follows:

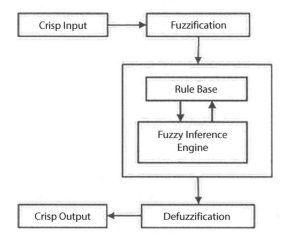

Figure 9.3 Fuzzy system.

1) positive review
2) negative review
3) neutral review

9.3.1.6 Lexicon-Based Sentiment Analysis

To begin, a seed list of sentiment terms is created based on the needs of the study questions. Then, either statistical or semantic approaches are used to find the opinion terms in the phrases. Furthermore, the opinion terms are based upon the sentiment terms in the seed list, and with a weighted summation based on several parameters, like various terms, polarity and degrees the feeling word score for the whole phrase is calculated. In the end, the sentiment score determines whether the sentence is positive, negative or neutral. Different ways of formulating a sentiment based on Lexicon can further be divided into two groups: Analysis of dictionary emotions and corpus-based analysis of sentiments. Finally, the sentiment score is used to determine if the sentence has a positive, negative, or neutral sentiment orientation. Lexicon-based sentiment analysis can be further separated into two groups depending on distinct ways of sentiment word set construction: Analysis of the dictionary sentiment and analysis of the corpus sentiment.

Hu and Liu had previously used the dictionary-based sentiment analysis approach and a vocabulary word creation process. A trivial number of sentiment words is manually designated as a seed list first. Subsequently, synonyms and antonyms of sentimental terms are identified in a sentiment dictionary, such as WordNet or HowNet. If no new word(s) is found, it will end the search and will be used as the final set of sentimental words for the current seed list. Dictionary sentiment analysis is often used by academics at this time. Based on the HowNet sentiment dictionary, in a paper by Liu *et al.* [20] suggested a technique for creating a product feature dictionary. The sentiment analysis method based on dictionaries that enables for the processing of context-related opinion terms. The paper by Xu *et al.* [23] used WordNet's synonym and antonym of adjectives to create a collection of emotion words to examine the sentiment of the mined opinion terms in online reviews. Customers' sentiment orientations for competitive products were captured using a dictionary-based sentiment analysis technique.

A variety of approaches to deal with negated neutral sentences and terms with degree adverbs. The user review guidelines for each product feature were also identified to determine the product failure. For the sentence level, Liu and Seneff [20] suggested a sentence analysis method. It should be noted that constructing a sentiment term set based on a vocabulary is simple, since many Sentiment Dictionaries, such as HowNet and the WordNet Sentiment Lexicons, can be used to directly increase the Seed List. As a consequence, dictionary sentiment analysis is used in most existing sentiment analysis studies. The dictionary-based sentiment analysis methodologies or procedures, on the other hand, have several drawbacks. One is that such approaches are unable to take into account sentiment terms in a context-specific setting. Because certain phrases can reflect either positive or negative directions in dissimilar circumstances, this would degrade the correctness of sentiment analysis. The additional is that the final seed list is primarily made up of broad language terms that lack technical jargon and colloquial idioms, despite the fact that the seed list can be expanded using the current emotion dictionary. The co-occurrence patterns of terms can be utilized to recognize the sentiment direction of a term or phrase using corpus-based sentiment analysis approaches. The major method for constructing sentiment word sets from corpus data. A trivial number of sentiment terms is manually designated as a seed list first. The seed list's significant words are then entered into a big corpus. The seed list is expanded to provide a final feeling word list. The context is assessed.

9.3.1.7   *Defuzzification*

Defuzzification is the process of converting a fuzzy amount to a definite quantity. The area of the generated figures for each MF must be calculated in three stages. Keeping in mind that these areas are usually triangles and trapezoids. If the degree of membership is not equal to one, the region will have a trapezoidal shape rather than a triangle.

if (x ≤ 0.125) then y = Highly Negative sentence
If (x ≥ 0.125 and x ≤0.25) then y = less intensive Negative sentence
If (x≥0.25 and x ≤ 0.50) then y= Neutral sentence
if (x ≥ 0.50 and x ≤ 0.75) then y=Positive sentence
if (x ≥ 0.75 and x ≤ 1) then y =Highly Positive sentence

9.3.2   Performance Metrics

The input: positive and negative results are shown in low, medium, and high fuzzy sets for each review, resulting from a negative, neutral, or positive feeling, according to our fuzzy technique. Whereas the previous work does not detect the neutral feeling. The fluent components of words are modified with a linguistic hedge in their approach. Take the average sum of scores as a total aggregated output. The final polarity of the tweet is determined by a flush-based rule-based system. The aggregation includes a combination of low, medium and high activation level.

To assess the success of an aspect extraction technique, we employ precision, recall, F-score, and accuracy.

$$precision = \frac{True\ Positive}{(True\ Positiv + False\ Positive)} \tag{9.1}$$

$$Recall = \frac{True\ Positive}{(True\ Positive + False\ Neagtive)} \tag{9.2}$$

$$F - Score = 2 * \frac{(Precision * Recall)}{(Precision + Recall)} \tag{9.3}$$

Table 9.1 Comparsion of our approah with other bench mark approach.

Model	Precision	Recall	F-score
Entropy model	70.4	68.7	72.5
Paired Inverted index with fuzzy	86.4	64	73.1

Table 9.1 shows a performance comparison of our technique with state-of-the-art results. As shown in Table 9.1, we acquire findings that are comparable to other product review datasets.

9.4   Conclusion

Because it incorporates natural language processing, sentiment analysis emerges as a difficult field with numerous challenges. Its results can be used in a wide range of applications, including news analytics, marketing, and question answering. Existing expert systems and applications literature advocates for both machine learning and lexicon-based techniques. Despite the fact that the former strategy performs better, it is not always favored over the latter due to a shortage of labeled training datasets. In this approach we have uses paired inverted index to extract the sentiment word. The Artificial Neuro-Fuzzy Inference System (ANFIS) model was then built to categorize review patterns in order to capture the degree of product present in review, and the fuzzy rule was evaluated using the member function. The proposed system is more efficient, with an accuracy of over 85%. The proposed technique for simulating fuzzy linguistic hedges could be used to solve the sentiment categorization problem.

References

1. http://www.amazon.cn/
2. https://www.taobao.com/
3. Vishwanath, J. and Aishwarya, S., User suggestions extraction from customer reviews: A sentiment analysis approach. *Int. J. Comput. Sci. Eng.*, 3, 3, 2, 2011.
4. Turney, P.D., Learning to extract keyphrases from text. arXiv preprint cs/021,2013, 1–41, 2002.
5. Blair-Goldensohn, S., Hannan, K., McDonald, R., Neylon, T., Reis, G., Reynar, J., Building a sentiment summarizer for local service reviews, pp. 5–33, Morgan and Claypool Publishers, 2008.
6. Ding, X., Liu, B., Yu, P.S., A holistic lexicon-based approach to opinion mining, in: *Proceedings of the 2008 International Conference on Web Search and Data Mining*, pp. 231–240, 2008.
7. Pekar, V. and Ou, S., Discovery of subjective evaluations of product features in hotel reviews. *J. Vacat. Mark.*, 14, 2, 145–155, 2008.
8. Yang, L., Li, Y., Wang, J., Sherratt, R.S., Sentiment analysis for E-commerce product reviews in Chinese based on sentiment lexicon and deep learning. *IEEE Access*, 8, 23522–23530, 2020.

9. Murugan, N.S. and Usha, D.G., Feature extraction using LR-PCA hybridization on twitter data and classification accuracy using machine learning algorithms. *Cluster Comput.*, 22, 6, 13965–13974, 2019.

10. Yang, C.-S. and Shih, H.-P., A rule-based approach for effective sentiment analysis, 1–5, 2012.

11. Liu, H., Wang, Y., Peng, Q., Wu, F., Gan, L., Pan, L., Jiao, P., Hybrid neural recommendation with joint deep representation learning of ratings and reviews. *Neurocomputing*, 374, 77–85, 2020.

12. Liang, F., Pan, Y., Gu, M., Guan, W., Tsai, F., Cultural tourism resource perceptions: Analyses based on tourists' online Travel notes. *Sustainability*, 13, 2, 519, 2021.

13. Karthik, R.V. and Ganapathy, S., A fuzzy recommendation system for predicting the customers interests using sentiment analysis and ontology in e-commerce. *Appl. Soft Comput.*, 108, 107396, 2021.

14. Tang, F., Fu, L., Yao, B., Xu, W., Aspect based fine-grained sentiment analysis for online reviews. *Inf. Sci.*, 488, 190–204, 2019.

15. Poria, S., Majumder, N., Hazarika, D., Cambria, E., Gelbukh, A., Hussain, A., Multimodal sentiment analysis: Addressing key issues and setting up the baselines. *IEEE Intell. Syst.*, 33, 6, 17–25, 2018.

16. Qiu, G., Liu, B., Bu, J., Chen, C., Expanding domain sentiment lexicon through double propagation, in: *Twenty-First International Joint Conference on Artificial Intelligence*, 2009.

17. Zhuang, L., Jing, F., Zhu, X.-Y., Movie review mining and summarization, in: *Proceedings of the 15th ACM international conference on Information and knowledge management*, pp. 43–50, 2006.

18. Liu, B., Sentiment analysis and subjectivity, in: *Handbook of Natural Language processing*, vol. 2, pp. 627–666, 2010.

19. Rana, T.A. and Cheah, Y.-N., Aspect extraction in sentiment analysis: Comparative analysis and survey. *Artif. Intell. Rev.*, 46, 4, 459–483, 2016.

20. Liu, J. and Seneff, S., Review sentiment scoring via a parse-and-paraphrase paradigm, in: *Proceedings of the 2009 Conference on Empirical Methods in Natural Language Processing*, pp. 161–169, 2009.

21. Dragoni, M., Poria, S., Cambria, E., OntoSenticNet: A commonsense ontology for sentiment analysis. *IEEE Intell. Syst.*, 33, 3, 77–85, 2018.

22. Hu, X., Tang, J., Gao, H., Liu, H., Unsupervised sentiment analysis with emotional signals, in: *Proceedings of the 22nd International Conference on World Wide Web*, pp. 607–618, 2013.

23. Xu, H., Liu, B., Shu, L., Yu, P.S., BERT post-training for review reading comprehension and aspect-based sentiment analysis. arXiv preprint arXiv:1904.02232, 2019.

10

Semantic Technology Pillars:
The Story So Far

Michael DeBellis¹*, Jans Aasman² and Archana Patel³

¹Consultant, San Francisco, CA
²Franz. Inc., Lafayette, CA
³Department of Software Engineering, Eastern International University,
Binh Duong, Vietnam

Abstract

In 2001 Tim Berners-Lee published a paper that charted a vision for an Internet based on semantic concepts and relations rather than hypertext links and keywords. Since that time, work in knowledge representation in artificial intelligence has matured from laboratories to public standards with implementations capable of scaling up to handle the big data that modern organizations rely on. This paper discusses these semantic pillar technologies, their roots in research and the current standards and implementations. The semantic pillars are as follows: Internationalized Resource Identifiers for indexing resources, the Resource Description Framework (RDF) and Resource Description Framework Schema (RDFS) for describing graphs of resources in terms of triples, the Web Ontology Language (OWL) for defining sophisticated logical models that describe resources, the SPARQL query language for querying knowledge graphs, and the Shapes Constraint Language (SHACL) for defining data integrity constraints on resources. Together, these pillars provide the tools for a new kind of Internet and new kinds of systems that can leverage big data and provide synergy with Machine Learning algorithms. This chapter will describe the research that paved the way for semantic technology. It will then describe each of the semantic pillars with examples and explanations of the business value of each technology.

Keywords: OWL, RDF, SPARQL, SHACL, SWRL, Semantic Web

---

*Corresponding author: mdebellissf@gmail.com; michaeldebellis.com

Archana Patel, Narayan C. Debnath and Bharat Bhusan (eds.) Data Science with Semantic Technologies: Theory, Practice, and Application, (247–276) © 2022 Scrivener Publishing LLC

10.1   The Road that Brought Us Here

The roots of semantic technology and data science are as old as the modern digital computer. In 1945 Vannevar Bush was the director of the United States Office of Scientific Research and Development. This federal agency coordinated scientific research in the second world war. Bush wrote a report describing a "future device" in which an individual stores all his books, records, and communications, and which is mechanized so that it may be consulted with exceeding speed and flexibility. It is an enlarged intimate supplement to his memory" [1] Bush's vision was further elaborated by Doug Engelbart at the Stanford Research Institute (SRI). In 1962, Engelbart published a paper titled Augmenting Human Intellect where he described many of the capabilities that would lead to the Internet. Engelbart also created a prototype system which he demonstrated in what has come to be known as the "Mother of all Demos" in 1968 at the ACM/IEEE Computer Society's Joint Computer Conference [2]. Engelbart's demo showed capabilities that we now take for granted, such as multimedia, hypertext, GUIs, and teleconferencing at a time when most people were still programming with punch cards.

Although the ideas of these visionaries have in many ways been made reality with the Internet, there was also a fundamental concept behind them that we are just now bringing to fruition. The gap between the initial Internet and this vision was described by Tim Berners-Lee in a 2001 paper published in Scientific American titled "The Semantic Web: A new form of Web content that is meaningful to computers will unleash a revolution of new possibilities" [3]. Berners-Lee described how the initial vision for the Internet was a web of knowledge rather than a web of documents.

The functionality that Berners-Lee required for a Semantic Web are that it must be:

- Distributed: The Semantic Web (like the Internet) must be highly distributed. It must be able to support information stored in many different sources and formats.
- Open: Conventional databases and software assume that all the information available to the system is already in the system. If some information cannot be found in the current system, we assume that information does not exist. A semantic web, on the other hand, must be open with no assumptions about completeness since no model can encompass all the information on the Internet.

- Explicit knowledge representation: This is the most important difference between the traditional Internet and the semantic web. In the traditional Internet, a link from one document to another may mean many things. The link could provide the form for a user to register in the system or to the web site of the author of a paper or countless other things. However, this information is implicit in the documentation or code. In the Semantic Web, such information is made explicit via *semantic* models that can be understood by both humans and machines.

The technology available at the birth of the Internet did not provide the capability for this vision. Instead, a compromise was accepted to focus on hypertext documents indexed by keywords. In his seminal Scientific American paper Berners-Lee described the research in process that would lead to a Semantic Web rather than a document web. The technologies described by Berners-Lee have now been implemented and are yielding a true semantic approach to data science both within organizations and in the public Internet. This chapter describes the technologies that provide the pillars for this semantic approach to data science.

10.2   What is a Semantic Pillar?

To begin, we need to define what we mean by semantic technology for data science. What makes a technology semantic as opposed to other approaches to data science? The distinction is best seen by contrasting the research approaches in artificial intelligence applied to data science. This research can be broadly divided into two categories: machine learning (ML) and semantic technology.

10.2.1   Machine Learning

Machine learning consists of a collection of mathematical models, such as linear regression, gradient descent, and artificial neural networks. With ML we are generating a model based on sample data called training sets.

For example, one of the most basic but still useful ML techniques is linear regression. With linear regression we find the line that is the best fit to the training set. Then, when we have new input data, we position it on the X axis and find the point on the Y axis that intersects the line created by our training set. That value is the predicted value from the ML algorithm.

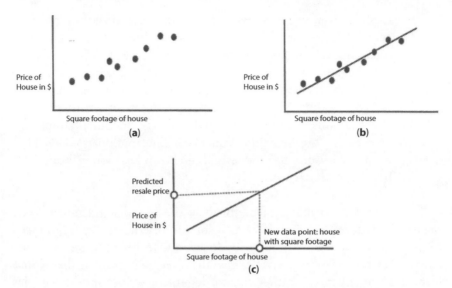

Figure 10.1 (a), (b) and (c) Predict the cost of a house based on square feet.

Figures 10.1(a), (b) and (c) show a simple example of using linear regression to predict the cost of a house based on square feet.[1]

10.2.2 The Semantic Approach

Machine learning is a powerful tool for data science. The alternative approach is to use Semantic rather than mathematical models to represent knowledge. Semantic models are defined using concepts such as class hierarchies, property hierarchies, and rules. Early research in artificial intelligence found that experts often used such concepts when asked to verbalize how they solve a problem. These two approaches complement each other. It is rare that a problem is equally a good fit for an ML and a semantic solution. Typically, the kinds of problems (e.g., recognizing a signal in noisy data) that are appropriate for an ML solution are not well suited to a semantic approach and vice versa.

The advantages of ML are:

- The algorithms are determined by the training sets (data). Although choosing the appropriate ML technique can require significant knowledge once a technique has been selected developing the model is mostly automatic.

---

[1]This example is based on the introductory lecture from Andrew Ng's Coursera class on Machine Learning: https://www.coursera.org/learn/machine-learning.

- They are good at separating signals from noisy data. For example, taking an input stream of sound and recognizing the words spoken by one or more people. In the last few decades, there have been great strides in AI due to progress in ML which provide the ability to solve problems that were difficult to solve with the semantic approach.

The advantages of the semantic approach are:

- It is a "white box" as opposed to a "black box" approach as ML is. With ML the result is determined by the mathematical model. Such models can be difficult for domain experts to understand and are not amenable to changes based on feedback from domain experts. Typically to improve an ML system the only options are better or more training sets, i.e., they are difficult to incrementally improve by manually editing the model.
- It provides a new foundation for enterprise data that is more integrated, consistent, and understandable than existing data based on relational models. This is commonly described in the semantic community as eliminating data silos.
- It can provide explanations for the inferences that the system makes. This is difficult to do with ML because the models are mathematical and not directly relevant to domain experts. With the semantic approach models are defined in terms of hierarchies and rules that are intuitive to humans and can be improved by feedback from such experts. They are not constrained by the existing data but can often provide ways to improve and go beyond it.
- It provides models that can define and enforce criteria for valid data. This is an example of how the two technologies are synergistic. In a recent talk on ML Andrew Ng one of the foremost experts in the ML field emphasized that improving the quality rather than the quantity of the data was often the best way to improve the accuracy of an ML system [4]. Using semantic technology such as SHACL (described below) is a way to improve the integrity of enterprise data.

The technologies seldom compete. Indeed, most systems that work with big data and solve complex AI problems such as IBM's Watson integrate both technologies for different aspects of the problem [5]. In the chapter on application of semantic technology to the Covid-19 pandemic, the majority of the systems described also utilized Machine Learning for part of the system. The art of the data scientist is to understand the strengths and weaknesses of each technology and to select the appropriate technology for the appropriate problem. This book and the rest of this chapter will focus on the semantic approach and the technology pillars that enable semantic models. Our focus will be on W3C standard technologies. However, where appropriate, we will also discuss alternative technologies.

The first applications of AI to industry problems were primarily driven by semantic technology. This was the first "AI Boom" in the 1980s. These systems primarily used rules and inference engines to build expert systems that solved problems, such as medical diagnosis, mortgage loan analysis, and computer configuration that were difficult to solve with traditional structured programming [6]. After the expert system boom researchers in semantic AI developed more sophisticated languages that went beyond rules to represent complex data and logic. These systems integrated frames or objects with rules. Frames/objects were modeled as is-a hierarchies that defined concepts as trees going from the most general concepts (e.g., animal) to more specific (e.g., mammal, dog and cat) and finally to the leaves of the trees which were instances of the concepts (e.g., fido, whiskers). KL-One was the first system to formally define the axioms for why one concept was more general or more specific than another. It was followed by more powerful languages, such as NIKL and Loom [7]. Loom was one of the essential technologies to the DARPA knowledge sharing initiative which investigated how to use logical models to represent large knowledge bases that facilitated storing information so that it could be easily found and reused [8]. These initiatives were some of the most important research that led to the pillars for the semantic web.

10.3   The Foundation Semantic Pillars: IRI's, RDF, and RDFS

Preliminaries (definitions and semantic stack architecture): Before we begin, it is useful to define some important terms.

- Ontology: An ontology is a model of concepts. It defines the overall structure of the system: the class hierarchy, the properties, etc. It is similar to a data model in relational databases or a UML model in OOP systems. The primary difference is that ontologies provide models with a formal semantics based in logic and set theory that support automatic validation and reasoning.

- Vocabulary: A vocabulary is an ontology designed to be reusable rather than for a specific application. The Friend of a Friend (FOAF)[2] vocabulary is one of the first and most widely used vocabularies. Other important vocabularies are the Dublin Core[3] vocabulary which models meta-data and the Simple Knowledge Organization System (SKOS) vocabulary[4] for defining concepts to organize information, such as taxonomies, classification schemes, and glossaries.
- Knowledge Graph: A knowledge graph is the application level of a semantic system. It adds large amounts of application data described by ontologies and vocabularies.
- Triplestore. A graph database that utilizes triples as the fundamental data structure rather than tables. Although ontologies can store data in relational databases, the preferred technology is the triplestore because the mapping from graph structures to the database is direct and straight forward.
- Data Silo. A standalone data source such as a database that has a data model which may be inconsistent with other data sources in an organization and data that may be redundant

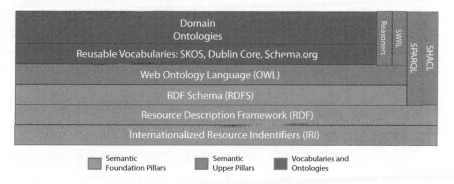

Figure 10.2 Semantic stack architecture.

[2]http://www.foaf-project.org/
[3]https://dublincore.org/
[4]https://www.w3.org/TR/swbp-skos-core-spec/

or inconsistent with other data sources. One of the goals of semantic technology is to eliminate data silos.

The complete stack architecture is shown in Figure 9.2. The foundation pillars that are utilized by all the other pillars are in green, the upper level pillars in light blue, and the vocabularies and ontologies in dark blue. This is an idealized stack. In actual use, it is common to utilize only some parts of this stack, for example to build vocabularies and knowledge graphs purely in RDF. Several of the most commonly used vocabularies, such as SKOS and Dublin Core, are implemented in RDF rather than in OWL.

10.3.1   Internationalized Resource Identifier (IRI)

Everyone is familiar with a Uniform Resource Locator (URL). These are addresses, such as https://protege.stanford.edu/ that point to web sites and (typically) hypertext documents on those sites. An IRI looks similar to a URL; however, it is used differently. For example, the IRI for the RDF language (described in the next section) is: http://www.w3.org/1999/02/22-rdf-syntax-ns#, whereas a URL typically points to a fairly large-grained artifact, such as a hypertext document or a video, an IRI can point to any resource that is useful to find on the Internet (or behind the firewall of an Intranet). A URL is a specialized type of IRI meant to point to documents and other artifacts that can be displayed in a browser. An IRI is a more general identifier that can point to ontologies and even individual classes, properties, or instances in an ontology. All URLs are IRIs but many IRIs (and virtually all of the ones described below) are not URLs. Rather than being meant to be viewed in a browser an IRI can point to any resource meant to be utilized by tools, such as ontology editors, knowledge graphs, SPARQL queries, or Semantic Web systems.

You may also see the term uniform resource identifier (URI) in older documents about the semantic web. This is the original term for identifiers. The only difference between a URI and an IRI is that URIs are restricted to only ASCII characters, whereas IRIs can also accommodate character sets, such as Kanji, Cyrillic, and Arabic. The standard typically used now is that we always use the term IRI for these types of resources, whether they are made up of only ASCII characters or not.

10.3.2   Resource Description Framework (RDF)

The basic data structure for Semantic data science is the triple. A triple consists of a Subject, a Predicate, and an Object. RDF is the language that provides the basic capability to define graphs of triples. The contents of an RDF file are what is known in mathematical graph theory as an undirected graph. That means there is no general flow from top to bottom or from left to right. Triples result in undirected graphs because the object of one triple can be the subject of another and vice versa.

A vocabulary defines the terminology for a specific domain in a way that is meant to be re-usable across many different systems. One of the most important goals of the semantic approach to data science is to enable reuse and eliminate data silos. Vocabularies are one tool that facilitates these goals. The Friend of a Friend (FOAF) vocabulary is one of the first vocabularies. It defined people, contact data, and relations between them. An example RDF triple from FOAF would be:

1. Michael knows Jans
   In this example Michael is the subject, knows is the predicate, and Jans is the object. Other triples could be:
2. Jans knows Yan
3. Biswanath knows Michael
4. Michael knows Yan

In the second triple, Jans is now the subject whereas he was the object in the first triple. In the third triple Michael is the object whereas he was the subject in the first triple. We can illustrate all these triples with a simple graph (Figure 10.3):

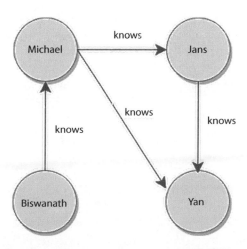

Figure 10.3 RDF graph.

The reason that RDF builds on IRIs is that most[5] resources described in an RDF triple (the subject, predicate, and object) are IRIs. The first triple described above would more accurately be represented as:

> http://example.org/Michael http://xmlns.com/foaf/0.1/knows http://example.org/Jans

This will yield files that are extremely verbose and difficult to read. For that reason, a useful RDF construct is the prefix. A prefix has the following form (anything in *italics* is meant to be instantiated by a specific name when used):

<div align="center">@Prefix <em>Prefix_name</em>: <<em>Prefix base IRI</em>>.</div>

Once we have prefixes defined, we can just use the prefix name followed by a colon in front of the resource name. This makes files much more concise and readable. To make the triples above conform to IRIs but still be readable we could add prefixes and then describe the triples as follows:

> @Prefix foaf: <http://xmlns.com/foaf/0.1/>.
> @Prefix ex: <http://example.org/>.
> ex:Michael foaf:knows ex:Jans.
> ex:Jans foaf:knows ex:Yan.
> ex:Biswanath foaf:knows ex:Michael.
> ex:Michael foaf:knows ex:Yan.

The RDF vocabulary is itself a resource that has an IRI: http://www.w3.org/1999/02/22-rdf-syntax-ns. In addition to providing the foundation for defining triples, RDF provides some important predicates used by languages that are built on it such as RDFS and OWL. One of the most important predicates is rdf:type. This is a predicate for defining the datatype of a resource.

10.3.2.1   *Alternative Technologies to RDF: Property Graphs*

An alternative technology to RDF is property graphs [9]. There currently is no standard for property graphs. The name is a bit confusing because an RDF graph is also a property graph. The predicate (link) in an RDF graph is known as a property as will be discussed below in the sections on RDFS

---

[5]With the exception of literals to be described shortly.

and OWL. The difference is that properties in property graphs have structure, i.e., where as an RDF predicate can only link two nodes a property graph can link multiple nodes. Property graphs have their roots in Frame-based knowledge representation. In frames, a property was called a *slot* and each slot could also have one or more *facets*. The facets defined additional information about the relation between the subject and object of the slot. For example, a facet called certainty could be associated with each slot that was a rational number between 0 and 1 that described the level of certainty for the relation between the subject and object [10].

A proposed standard that extends RDF is RDF* [11]. This allows RDF predicates to have additional predicates as property graphs do. Most triple-store vendors that have RDF compliant implementations also have optional extensions that provide the equivalent capabilities of property graphs.

A formal way to understand property graphs is that they allow for the direct definition of n-ary relations. In RDF and the languages built on it, only binary relations are possible. However, it is possible using a common design pattern to replicate the functionality of n-ary relations with binary relations and an additional class [12].

10.3.3   RDF Schema (RDFS)

RDF schema (RDFS) is the final part of our semantic foundation. It is built on top of RDF. RDF provides a model for describing graphs in terms of triples. RDFS provides the basic concepts to provide meaning to these graphs.

RDFS is itself an RDF resource with an IRI: http://www.w3.org/2000/01/rdf-schema. All files that leverage RDFS will begin with a prefix that maps this IRI to the preface "rdfs." This is just a convention. One could map the IRI to "foo" and as long as the prefix was used consistently things would still work.

The most important additions that RDFS adds to RDF are:

1. Definition of *classes*
2. Definition of *super* and *sub-classes*.
3. Definition of predicates which are called *properties*. From this point on *predicate* and *property* are synonyms and used interchangeably.
4. Definition of the *domain* and *range* of properties.
5. Definition of *super* and *sub* properties.
6. Definition of some common *meta-data properties* that should be standardized across all models such as rdfs:label and rdfs:comment.

Note that items 1 to 5 make RDFS a meta-model, i.e., a model used to define other models.

In RDFS a class is similar to a class in OOP. It can have super and sub-classes. The RDFS class provides the foundation for OWL classes which have a richer semantics, so further discussion of classes will be postponed for the section on OWL.

In order to discuss the domain and range of a property, we first need to explain the distinction between literals and classes. In most object-oriented languages, not everything is represented as a class, e.g., in the Common Lisp Object System (CLOS), Java, and C++ there are libraries of predefined datatypes such as strings, integers, characters, etc. This is because there is extra overhead with a class that a simple datatype does not require. The same principle applies to RDFS. It would be wasteful to instantiate a class every time one utilized an integer such as 1 or a string such as "Tim." Thus, the objects of a triple (but not the subject or predicate) can be what is called a *Literal*. A literal is a simple datatype. Semantic systems typically re-use literal datatypes from XML.[6]

Properties have a domain and range just as they do in object-oriented programming.[7] The domain for a property is the set of classes that can be the subject of the property. The range is the set of datatypes (classes or Literals) that can be the object. One of the differences between OOP and semantic objects is that the domain and range for a property are both optional. It is usually a best practice to define both of them; however, there are use cases, such as vocabularies meant to be reusable, where it is best to not define the domain and/or range.

An example of properties that have literal values rather than IRIs from the FOAF vocabulary are name and title. For example, the name for the http://example.org/Biswanath resource would be the string "Biswanath Dutta," and the title would be the string "Dr." Note the difference between ex:Biswanath as an IRI resource and the string "Biswanath." In the first case the object is a resource which can be the subject or object of other triples. In the second case, the object is a string which can only be the object of

---

[6]Most commonly from the XML Schema datatypes. Hence, many of the most common datatypes have a preface of "xsd" such as xsd:string and xsd:integer.

[7]We use OOP as a way to explain semantic constructs because most developers are familiar with it. However, while there are many similarities between OOP and Semantic objects there are also important differences. We will describe some of the most important differences but for a detailed overview of the differences see: https://www.w3.org/TR/sw-oosd-primer/

a triple. If we wanted to have "Dr." be the subject of a property we would make "Dr." an IRI.

One of the differences between properties in RDFS and OOP is that properties in OOP depend on some class for their definition. They must be defined within the definition of some class and can then be inherited to sub-classes of that class. In RDFS, this is not the case. A property is a first class resource that has an independent definition. This is one of the ways that RDFS meets one of the design goals for the Semantic Web [13], that is, the Semantic Web should be an open system capable of being extended. In most OOP languages, in order to add to the definition of a class (e.g., to define a new property), one needs to change the original definition of the class. Having properties as independent resources allow developers to add new properties without changing (or even able to access) the original definition of the class that is the domain for that property.

Another difference in semantic web properties and traditional OOP is that properties can have super and subproperties. Although these are defined in RDFS, their semantics are typically enforced by OWL reasoners so we shall postpone detailed discussion for the discussion on OWL below.

10.4   The Semantic Upper Pillars: OWL, SWRL, SPARQL, and SHACL

The upper pillars built on top of the foundation pillars are:

- The Web Ontology Language (OWL). The language defined on top of RDFS that adds powerful semantics based on set theory and logic. OWL is also supported by reasoners that are similar to the classifiers of previous AI languages, such as KL-One and Loom.
- The Semantic Web Rule Language (SWRL). SWRL extends OWL with a rule language to define relations that are difficult or impossible to define with OWL. SWRL can also automate the computation of the value for properties and change the class of an instance.
- SPARQL. The query language. SPARQL is to semantic technology as SQL is to relational databases. SPARQL is a powerful query language because it can match any or all parts of a triple. It also has many predefined functions for math, string, aggregate, and other types of common data manipulation and analysis.

- The Shapes Constraint Language (SHACL). SHACL defines data integrity constraints. At a first glance SHACL and OWL seem to overlap significantly. For example, both can define that a property must have a minimum or maximum number of values. However, they are very different not because of *what* they express but *how* they are used. OWL is designed for *reasoning* about data and SHACL is designed to define and enforce *constraints* about data.

OWL builds on top of RDFS. SWRL can only be used with OWL. SPARQL and SHACL on the other hand can function either at the OWL level or at levels below it (i.e., RDFS or RDF). The reason for this distinction is that in some cases developers may wish to forego the enhanced semantics of OWL for reasons of efficiency. It is desirable in those situations to still be able to leverage SPARQL for queries and SHACL for data integrity constraints.

10.4.1   The Web Ontology Language (OWL)

OWL is the language that is the most similar to previous logic-based AI languages, such as NIKL and Loom. However, unlike Loom and other languages, OWL does not provide a mechanism for implementing methods to define business processes. It focuses exclusively on data. In so doing it provides the capability for a powerful semantic language that implements many of the concepts from set theory and logic that in the past were confined to research systems that could not scale to the enterprise level.

An OWL model is called an ontology although as described above an ontology can also be implemented in RDF. An OWL ontology consists of a set of logical axioms. These axioms all map to triples in an RDF graph. However, it is most intuitive to think of them as logical axioms.

An important distinction in the type of axioms is between what for historical reasons are known as Terminological (or T-Box) and Assertional (or A-Box) axioms. Terminological axioms define the structure of the ontology: classes, properties, and logical definitions and restrictions on them such as a property's domain or range. Assertional axioms describe individuals and property values. In the standard OOP model terminological axioms are the definitions of classes and properties and assertional axioms are the instances of classes and the values of each instance's properties. In the Entity-Relation model terminology corresponds to the definition of the data model (entity, relation, and attribute definitions) and the assertions correspond to rows in the tables, i.e., terminology is the abstract definition of the data model and assertions are the actual data itself.

Another name for an ontology is a knowledge graph. The term was first coined by Google [14] and has since come to dominate the use of semantic technology in industry. An OWL ontology is fundamentally an RDF graph. However, another common way these terms are distinguished is that *ontology* is often used to refer to the terminological (T-Box) model whereas *knowledge graph* often is used to refer to the T-Box and large application data sets (A-Box). A triplestore is a special kind of database designed for knowledge graphs, where the foundational data structure is a triple rather than a table as in relational databases.

The logical model for OWL is description logic. Description logic (DL) is a subset of first-order logic that provides far more expressive power than rule-based systems and other previous semantic technology but still supports automated reasoning. The roots of description logic go back to the database community because it is focused on defining the data model rather than a complete model that includes process logic.

The power of OWL is in the reasoner. In precursor languages, such as Loom, this was called the classifier because the primary purpose was to automatically define the class hierarchy. The name was changed because the automated reasoning provided by the OWL reasoner goes well beyond validating and restructuring the class hierarchy. The primary capabilities of the OWL reasoner are:

1. Validating the ontology: The reasoner first ensures that the ontology is *consistent*, i.e., that there are no logical contradictions in the axiom definitions.
2. Restructuring the ontology: The reasoner can restructure the *terminology* of the ontology, e.g., class and property hierarchies can be re-arranged.
3. Inferences about individuals: The reasoner can also make new *assertions* about the individuals in the ontology, e.g., it can infer that an individual is an instance of additional classes from those defined by the user and it can infer additional property values based on definitions of classes and properties and their logical implications.

There are four fundamental constructs in OWL:

1. Classes: OWL defines a richer concept for class than RDFS based on Description Logic and the power to automatically restructure the class hierarchy and infer that individual are instances of classes.

2. Properties: OWL extends RDFS with three types of properties and new capabilities that are dependent on the type of OWL property.
3. Individuals: In RDF/RDFS there is not a strong distinction between instances and classes. Everything is just a resource (an IRI) which has one or more types, and which has links (RDFS properties) to other resources. OWL adds set theoretic semantics and thus requires a rigorous distinction between classes which are sets and individuals which are elements (instances) of sets. In OWL property values can only be asserted on individuals not on classes.[8]
4. Rules: The Semantic Web Rule Language (SWRL) extends OWL with a powerful forward chaining rule system.

We use the term *entity* when we want to refer to *any* OWL construct, i.e., an entity can be a class, property, individual, and/or rule. Note: this is very different than the definition in Entity/Relation models.

10.4.1.1   *Axioms to Define Classes*

A complete explanation of all the capabilities of OWL is beyond the scope of this chapter. Instead, we will focus on only a very few capabilities and point the reader to resources at the end of the chapter for more detail. One of the most important capabilities of OWL, that traces back to languages such as Loom and KL-One is the ability to define necessary and sufficient conditions on classes. These axioms are often defined in terms of properties that have the class in their domain. For example, an axiom may constrain a class to have a certain number of values for a property or that a property must have a specific value. A class that has necessary and sufficient conditions is known as a defined class. The reasoner can automatically infer that individuals are instances of defined classes.

To illustrate defined classes and other capabilities of OWL, we have created a small sample People_Example ontology that describes people and their family and social relationships. The sample ontology as well as instructions for those who wish to explore it in Protégé can be found at: https://tinyurl.com/PillarsExamples.

---

[8]The exception to this is punning which is a simple meta-class capability. It is beyond the scope of this chapter. For details see: https://www.w3.org/TR/owl2-new-features/#F12:_Punning.

10.4.1.2   The Open World Assumption

Recall that one of the essential design goals for the semantic web is that it is an open system meant to model information on the Internet. For this reason, it has a different model regarding values that are not found. Traditional databases and programming languages assume that if a value is missing, then it does not exist. It is common in traditional database and programming languages such as Python to equate a null value with false. If a record does not exist for someone in the Customer database, then the assumption is that there is no customer with the matching key yet. This is what is known as the Closed World Assumption (CWA). It is so prevalent that most developers simply take it for granted.

To model the web this is not appropriate. It is possible that there is information that exists somewhere on the Web that has not been incorporated into the ontology yet. Thus, OWL reasoners utilize the Open World Assumption (OWA). The default assumption is that absence of information does not imply that the information does not exist.

As an example of the OWA in the People_Example ontology, one of the defined classes is Hermit with the definition:

Person and has_Social_Relation_With max 0 Person

In the ontology there is an individual Miss_Havisham (a hermit from the novel Great Expectations). Miss_Havisham has no social relations. However, while the reasoner can find instances of the defined class Social_ Person (a Person with 5 or more social relations) it cannot find instances of the class Hermit including Miss_Havisham who we would think certainly qualifies. This is an example of the OWA. Even though Miss_Havisham has no social relations defined in the ontology the reasoner cannot infer that there are not additional values that exist but that have not yet been discovered. Although the reasoner would signal an error if someone was defined to be an instance of Hermit and had more than 0 social relations it cannot recognize instances with no values as Hermits. Due to the OWA there are some axioms such as those regarding maximum number of values that are difficult to utilize to recognize instances of defined classes. There are ways around this by utilizing SPARQL or SHACL to be discussed below.

10.4.1.3   No Unique Names Assumption

Another difference due to the open nature of the Semantic Web is that names (IRIs) are not assumed to be unique. In the People_Example ontology examine any individual and you will see that in its description there is a list of Different Individuals that lists all the individuals in the ontology. There is a command in Protégé to declare that all individuals are different from each other. Or one can individually declare certain individuals to be different. Without this axiom the defined class for Social_Person would not infer that *any* individual was a Social_Person because it could be the case that although the various individuals have different IRIs that some or all of them are actually the same person.

10.4.1.4   *Serialization*

Serialization is the process of taking some data structure that exists in memory, such as an array or an instance of a class and saving it in a text format that can be stored in a file or sent across the network in a text stream. When working in an OWL ontology editor such as Protégé, you are changing definitions of entities that are in memory. In order to save the ontology to a file you have to serialize the various entities into some format that is portable and that other tools besides Protégé can read. For example, you may wish to take your ontology and load it into a triplestore. This is where serialization comes in.

When you first save an ontology in Protégé you will be given several serialization options to choose from. The two most widely used are RDF/XML and Turtle. RDF/XML is the most portable and least likely to cause problems when going from one tool to another. However, it is rather verbose. Turtle is also very portable and less verbose. The FOAF example in the section on RDF was in Turtle format. It is best to avoid manually editing these serialized files directly and to leverage ontology editors such as Protégé whenever possible as one small change can make the entire file incapable of being parsed.

10.4.2   The Semantic Web Rule Language

OWL is a very powerful language, however, there are certain types of inferences that are difficult or impossible to define with it but are still useful for definition of the semantics of data. In order to extend the semantics of OWL the Semantic Web Rule Language (SWRL) was created.

The easiest way to explain SWRL is with a simple example. One classic example that cannot be defined with normal OWL is an aunt or uncle relation. In the People_Example ontology there are two SWRL rules to define these. The SWRL rule that defines the has_Aunt relation is:

has_Child(?p, ?c) ^ has_Sister(?p, ?s) -> has_Aunt(?c, ?s)

The "^" symbol is used to specify the AND logical relation. All expressions in a SWRL rule are connected with just this operator meaning that in order for a SWRL rule to succeed every expression must succeed for some binding of the variables (the symbols with a "?" before them). To understand SWRL rules it is useful think in First Order Logic and the concept of quantification. The left-hand side of a SWRL rule (all the expressions on the left of the "->") are implicitly universally quantified and the right side is implicitly existentially quantified, i.e., every variable on the left-hand side that begins with a "?" is a wildcard and SWRL will match every possible permutation that satisfies the property values on the left-hand side. Similarly, for every "?" value on the right-hand side, every time the left-hand side is satisfied, SWRL will match an existing appropriate binding if one exists or will create a new property value if the binding does not currently exist.

In this example, the reasoner will find all individuals that satisfy the has_Child property, e.g., in the People_Example it will bind ?p to John_Doe and ?c to Mary_Doe. It will then see if any of the bindings for ?p also satisfy the has_Sister property. In this example since ?p is already bound to John_Doe it will check all the individuals that are sisters of John_Doe and bind those to ?s. Thus, ?s will bind to Sarah_Doe. Since the reasoner has found bindings that satisfy all the expressions on the left-hand side it

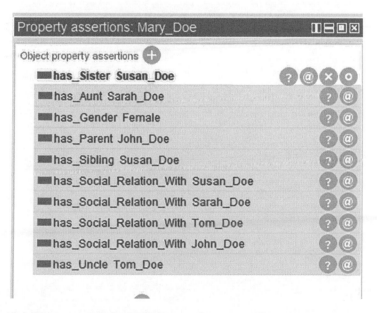

Figure 10.4 Property values for Mary_Doe.

will see if there exists a binding that satisfies the right-hand side has_Aunt. Since there is none, it will assert a new value for has_Aunt, i.e., that Mary_Doe has_Aunt Sarah_Doe. Figure 10.4 shows the property assertions for Mary_Doe in Protégé. In Protégé, any assertion inferred by the reasoner is highlighted in yellow. Note that in Figure 10.4 almost all of the values have been inferred by the reasoner. The only value explicitly defined by the user is that Mary_Doe has_Sister Susan_Doe. One of the inferences (due to the SWRL rule) is that Mary_Doe has_Aunt Sarah_Doe.

This is also a good time to highlight another advantage of the OWL reasoner: the ability to generate explanations. We can see all the inferences of the reasoner highlighted in yellow, but we can get more information than that as a benefit of the reasoner. Note that every assertion has a "?" next to it. We can click on this for any assertion and the reasoner will generate an explanation for the inference.

Figure 10.5 shows the window that results when we click on the "?" next to the has_Aunt assertion for Mary_Doe. The system displays the SWRL rule that was utilized, and the assertions: that John_Doe has_Daughter Mary_Doe and has_Sister Sarah_Doe and the fact that has_Daughter is a sub-property of has_Child. This also demonstrates the power of property

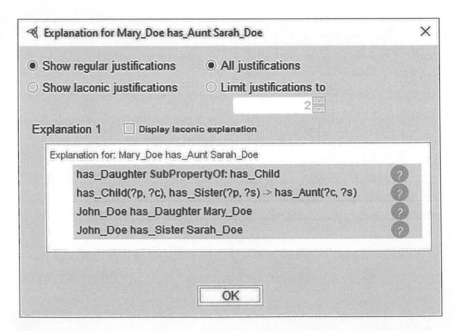

Figure 10.5 Explanation for inference that Mary_Doe has_Aunt Sarah_Doe.

hierarchies. Since has_Daughter is a sub-property of has_Child if x has_ Daughter y then the reasoner can infer that x has_Child y.

SWRL also has a library of what are called built-in functions [15]. These look similar to property expressions except they can often have more than 2 values. These can be used for standard types of mathematical, string, date-time, and other computations and comparisons. This makes SWRL a very powerful rule language similar to forward chaining rules in expert system shells.

10.4.2.1   The Limitations of Monotonic Reasoning

Due to the fact that SWRL is based on a logical reasoner (a version of what is called a theorem prover), it has some limitations in the types of reasoning it can perform. If you have ever done a logical proof, you know that one way to disprove something is to show that the results of the logical formulas result in two different values for a variable. A common proof technique is to assume that the theorem you wish to prove is false and then show that a contradiction (e.g., $p = 0$ and $p = 1$) results. This means that your assumption that the theorem is false must itself be false, i.e., you've proved the theorem to be true.

This means that the reasoning in SWRL (and OWL) are what is called *monotonic*, i.e., the OWL reasoner cannot change the value of a property because if the property has two different values that is a logical contradiction. This means that certain types of reasoning cannot be performed in SWRL. For example, if you want to have a rule that adds 1 to the age of a Person every year, such a rule cannot be defined in SWRL. In general, any type of reasoning that requires counting or summing is difficult or impossible in SWRL due to monotonic reasoning. In the SWRL tutorial in [16] there is an example of how to get around this restriction when adding the times of sub-tasks to get the total time of a task. However, this technique will not always work. One simpler way to work around this is to use SPARQL, SHACL or a programming language. None of these are restricted to monotonic reasoning.

10.4.2.2   Alternatives to SWRL

Of all the pillars SWRL is currently the one that has the least traction in industry at this point. It is an incredibly elegant language. After working with it just a bit, it is soon apparent how to write powerful rules quickly and succinctly. However, a result of this power is that reasoning with SWRL can be slow for large knowledge graphs and as a result some commercial triplestores do not support it yet. There are several alternative rule languages that can be used such as the Java Expert System Shell (JESS).[9] Another alternative is to simply use SPARQL as well as an extension to SPARQL known as SPARQL Inferencing Notation (SPIN).[10] Any rule defined in SWRL can be defined in SPARQL, although what typically requires a few expressions that could fit on one line of SWRL code requires several lines of SPARQL code. Prolog is also still a popular language that can define rules and there are implementations of it that are well integrated with semantic technologies such as triplestores.

10.4.3   SPARQL

SPARQL (pronounced "sparkle") is a recursive acronym. It stands for SPARQL Protocol and RDF Query Language. SPARQL is to RDF as SQL is to relational databases. SPARQL works at the level of RDF, however since OWL is mapped very directly to RDF, SPARQL can also be used with OWL ontologies.

The power of SPARQL is its ability to match any or all parts of an RDF triple. There are 3 parts of any SPARQL query:

1. Prefix mappings: These are identical to the mappings discussed in the section on RDF. Just as with RDF they allow the developer to access IRIs by typing a prefix followed by a colon rather than the entire IRI.
2. The action clause: This can be one of several keywords: SELECT, CONSTRUCT, INSERT, DELETE, etc. This tells the SPARQL processor what to do with the data that is matched in the WHERE clause. The most straight forward is the SELECT clause which lists variables of the WHERE clause and displays them.
3. The WHERE clause: This describes one or more triples to match as well as other constructs to further constrain (or expand) the query such as FILTER and OPTIONAL. Each triple can contain 0 to 3 wildcards. A triple with all wildcards will retrieve every resource in the graph.

10.4.3.1   The SERVICE Keyword and Linked Data

One of the powers of SPARQL is that it can bring in data from many diverse sources such as DBpedia and integrate them as if they were all in

---

[9]http://alvarestech.com/temp/fuzzyjess/Jess60/Jess70b7/docs/index.html
[10]https://www.w3.org/Submission/2011/SUBM-spin-sparql-20110222/

the same database. Essentially, it allows your computer to have the entire web as one huge, distributed database right at your fingertips. This is a concept called Linked Data.

DBpedia[11] is a resource that is part of the Wikipedia family of free crowd sourced tools. If you examine most Wikipedia pages you will see a rectangle in the upper right corner. It usually has a picture of the subject of the article along with the most essential information about the subject. These are called InfoBoxes and there is a hierarchy of various classes of InfoBox that provides default properties that are usually required for kinds of subjects. For example, in the Wikipedia article for Alan Turing, the InfoBox is of type Scientist which is a subclass of the InfoBox Person. Person has properties such as date and place of birth. Scientist inherits all properties for Person as well as additional properties such as Field (the areas that the scientist specialized in). DBpedia is created by programs called bots that regularly search through the Wikipedia site and extract information from InfoBoxes and save them in the DBpedia knowledge graph. Recall in the introduction we mentioned that sophisticated AI systems such as IBM's Watson utilized semantic data as well as machine learning. One of the primary knowledge sources for Watson was DBpedia. Another useful free resource is Geonames[12] which provides a knowledge graph of places: nations, states, cities, etc. along with information such as their latitude and longitude.

One way to access these linked data resources is just to include additional IRIs in your prefixes that give you access to open datasets. Another way is to use the SERVICE keyword. The difference is that using a preface assumes that all the data and actions for that IRI are available to all users. For very large knowledge graphs such as DBpedia this would not be practical. For example, a user could request the entire DBpedia knowledge graph which would put a strain on the DBpedia server. Or even worse, a user might either via vandalism or ignorance attempt an INSERT or DELETE query which could corrupt the knowledge graph.

Thus, large open knowledge graphs are typically available via SPARQL endpoints. An endpoint requires that you use the SERVICE keyword. SERVICE sends the query to the SPARQL endpoint (which of course is an IRI) and leaves it to the server at the endpoint to determine how to reply to the query. For example, the server may have ways to optimize the query that the client is not aware of. Or there may be restrictions on the amount

---

[11]https://www.dbpedia.org/
[12]http://www.geonames.org/

of data or the kinds of changes available to users based on their authorization credentials.

The following illustrates a SPARQL query that takes advantage of linked data. To start we want to answer the question: "What is the average income for the place where Barack Obama was born?" For this query we first go to DBpedia to find his birthplace and the corresponding Geonames ID. Then we go to Geonames to find all the other Geonames-ids that are populated places within 10 miles of President Obama's birthplace, with this list of Geonames we then go to the 2000 census and find the average income for each place (each Geonames ID).

Here is the SPARQL query:

```
PREFIX geo: <http://franz.com/ns/allegrograph/3.0/geospatial/>
PREFIX geonames: <http://sws.geonames.org/>
PREFIX dbpedia_rsrc: <http://dbpedia.org/resource/>
PREFIX dbpedia_onto: <http://dbpedia.org/ontology/>
PREFIX dbpedia_prop: <http://dbpedia.org/property/>
PREFIX census: <tag:govshare.info,2005:rdf/census/>
PREFIX  census_samp:  <tag:govshare.info,2005:rdf/census/details/
samp/>
SELECT distinct ?censusplace ?income {
 dbpedia_rsrc:Barack_Obama dbpedia_onto:birthPlace ?birthplace .
 ?birthplace dbpedia_prop:hasGeonamesID ?geonamesresource .
       SERVICE      <https://localhost:10000/catalogs/demos/repositories/
geonames>
        { ?geonamesresource geonames:isAt5 ?location .
        ?otherplace geo:inCircleMiles (geonames:isAt5 ?location 10) .
        ?otherplace geonames:feature_code "PPL" .
        ?geonamesresource geonames:feature_code "PPL" .
          SERVICE  <https://localhost:10000/catalogs/demos/repositories/
census>
        { ?censusplace dbpedia_prop:hasGeonamesID ?otherplace .
        ?censusplace census:details ?detail .
        ?detail census_samp:population15YearsAndOverWithIncomeIn1999 ?d .
        ?d census_samp:medianIncomeIn1999 ?income .}}}
```

To see this query in action, the reader can do the following:

1. Go to: https://tinyurl.com/LDExample
2. Click on the demos catalog link. There will be several demo repositories. Select the dbpedia repository.

3. Under "Pre-Defined Queries" click on the link: barack-obama-query-using-service. This will take you to the query listed above displayed in the AllegroGraph SPARQL query window.

4. Click on the "Execute" button beneath the window where the query is displayed. This will execute the query. There is some overhead to start the server so be patient it may take a bit of time. After a while you will see the answer. If you click on execute again, now that the server is warmed up it should be about a second.

5. This returns the average income of all the populated places within ten miles of Obama's birthplace. To see the answer to our question you can edit the first line of the query after the prefixes so that rather than "SELECT distinct ?censusplace ?income" it is: "SELECT (AVG(?income) AS ?avgincome)." This will give the average of the four median incomes returned by the initial query.

This shows the true power of SPARQL. We have utilized data from 3 different large data sources: DBpedia, Geonames, and the 2000 Census. All of these were developed independently with no explicit design for integration.

10.4.4   SHACL

The final semantic pillar is the Shapes Constraint Language (SHACL). SHACL is a somewhat newer standard than the other semantic pillars. The reason for this is that in the early days of the Semantic Web it was viewed as a technology that was focused primarily on the Internet where the OWA is most appropriate. However, in the past decade the leading technology vendors such as Google, Microsoft, Amazon, Facebook, and IBM have embraced knowledge graphs in a big way and many other enterprises have followed these technology leaders [17]. As a result, semantic technology is becoming as important behind the firewalls of large organizations as it is for the Internet. This caused a demand to validate enterprise data in a way that OWL could not accommodate.

The concept of a *shape* in SHACL has nothing to do with a geometric shape. It is a metaphor for defining the outline of a class via constraints on its property values, i.e., you are not defining the actual class or any instances of the class but the various rules that constrain the data for each instance.

At a first glance there seems to be significant overlap between SHACL and OWL. Both can define concepts such as cardinality, legal values, etc. However, whereas these constraints are used for reasoning in OWL, in

SHACL they are used to validate that the data conforms to constraints and to trigger warnings when they do not.

The reasons that a different language is required for constraints are:

1. The Open World Assumption (OWA) and monotonic reasoning are not appropriate for constraint validation.
2. The real world is messy. When an OWL axiom is violated, the entire ontology is inconsistent and cannot be used for reasoning until the inconsistency is resolved. Anyone who has experience with large databases knows that it is common to find data that does not conform to integrity constraints. Using OWL for such constraints could mean that for enterprise data the ontology was often invalid due to bad data and the reasoner was useless for inferencing. SHACL does not make the ontology inconsistent when it finds a constraint violation. Instead, it triggers a warning. In some cases SHACL may also attempt to fix the problem.

The OWA is very limiting for certain kinds of data integrity constraints. The whole point of the OWA is that the system is open, and that the reasoner recognizes that some data may not yet be included in the ontology. However, for data integrity constraints this is not acceptable. For example, a common constraint is that an employee must have a social security number, or an online customer must have an email. While it is possible to define those axioms in OWL the OWA means that the OWL reasoner will not enforce them.[13]

Monotonic reasoning also interferes with constraint checking. One common feature of constraint validation is to not just signal a problem but attempt to fix it. For example, if the datatype for a property is an integer and the value is the string "1" the constraint checker may attempt to coerce the string into an integer. In order to do this, it must change the value of the property which is not possible with monotonic reasoning.

10.4.4.1   *The Fundamentals of SHACL*

SHACL consists of two fundamental components:

---

[13]The reader might wonder why have them If the reasoner can't enforce them? There are ways to still utilize these axioms, for example to determine that one class is a subclass of another.

1. An RDF vocabulary that provides the model to define constraints.
2. A validation reasoner that can apply the constraints defined in the SHACL vocabulary to graphs and can detect constraint violations. The reasoner triggers a warning and/or attempts to repair the violation.

The SHACL vocabulary is defined in RDF rather than in OWL because for some purposes developers may choose to only use RDF or RDFS for their data rather than OWL. The primary reason for doing this is that the extra semantics of OWL bring with it some extra overhead. For most purposes the extra overhead is not that excessive, and the extra semantic power and reasoning are well worth it. However, for some systems where efficiency is paramount developers may wish to forego OWL. In these cases, they can still use SHACL to define constraints for their data since SHACL is defined in RDF rather than OWL.

Like all other resources the SHACL vocabulary has an IRI: http://www.w3.org/ns/shacl_The convention is to define a prefix that maps this IRI to "sh." This allows names like sh:property to be used and not conflict with the resources named property in RDF and OWL.

The most important concepts in the SHACL vocabulary are:

1. The Shape class: An sh:NodeShape defines constraints for a specific RDFS or OWL class.
2. The Target property: Each Shape has an sh:targetClass property. This property points to the class that the Shape defines constraints for.
3. The Property property: Each shape has a set of properties that are just called sh:property. The value of each sh:property is what is called a blank node. A blank node is an object that is defined on the fly and that does not have a name. This contrasts with named individuals in OWL that have IRIs and are meant to be persistent. A blank node also has properties. In the case of SHACL the properties of each of these blank nodes define the specific constraints on the property, e.g., that a property must have a certain number of values, that a numeric property must be within a certain range, or that a string property must match a certain pattern.

10.5   Conclusion

This chapter has introduced the semantic pillars. These pillars are an emerging field that is showing enormous benefits in the information technology world and hold even more promise for the future. This chapter has just scratched the surface. For a hands-on tutorial with the Protégé ontology editor, see [18]. For more details on SPARQL, see DeBellis [19]. For more theoretical background on the pillars and how they can be used in the enterprise, see DuCharme [20].

References

1. Bush, V., As we may think. *Atl. Mon.*, 176, 1, 101–108, 1945, https://doi.org/10.3998/3336451.0001.101.
2. Engelbart, D., *Augmenting Human Intellect: A Conceptual Framework*. SRI Summary Report AFOSR-3223, Stanford Research Institute, Menlo Park, CA, October 1962, https://www.dougengelbart.org/content/view/138. For the demo see: https://www.youtube.com/watch?v=yJDv-zdhzMY.
3. Berners-Lee, T., Hendler, J., Lassila, O., The semantic web: A new form of web content that is meaningful to computers will unleash a revolution of new possibilities. *Sci. Am.*, 284, 5, 1–5, May 2001.
4. Ng, A.A., Chat with Andrew on MLOps: From model-centric to data-centric AI, DeepLearning, AI, Palo Alto, CA, March 24, 2021, https://www.youtube.com/watch?v=06-AZXmwHjo.
5. Ferrucci, D., Brown, E., Chu-Carroll, J., Fan, J., Gondek, D., Kalyanpur, A.A., Lally, A., Murdock, J.W., Nyberg, E., Prager, J., Schlaefer, N., Welty, C., Building Watson: An overview of the DeepQA project. *AI Mag.*, 31, 3, 59–79, 2010, https://doi.org/10.1609/aimag.v31i3.2303.
6. Hayes-Roth, F., Waterman, D., Lenat, D., *Building Expert Systems*, Addison-Wesley, Reading, MA, 1983.
7. MacGregor, R., *Retrospective on Loom*, Information Sciences Institute (ISI), Marina del Rey, CA, 1991, https://web.archive.org/web/20131025063241/http://www.isi.edu/isd/LOOM/papers/macgregor/Loom_Retrospective.html.
8. Neches, R., Enabling technology for knowledge sharing. With Richard Fikes, Tim Finin, Thomas Gruber, Ramesh Patil, Ted Senator, and William T. Swartout. *AI Mag.*, 12, 3, 36–56, 1991.
9. Polikoff, I., Knowledge graphs vs. Property graphs, TopQuadrant, Inc. Raleigh, NC. August 19, 2020, https://tdan.com/knowledge-graphs-vs-property-graphs-part-1/27140.

10. Felix, R., Reasoning with Uncertainty in the Knowledge Engineering Environment (KEE). *1991 IEEE/ACM International Conference on Developing and Managing Expert System Programs*, vol. 1.

11. RDF-star: Home of RDF-star, a part of the RDF-DEV community group, World Wide Web Consortium, Cambridge, MA, https://w3c.github.io/rdf-star/.

12. Defining N-ary Relations on the Semantic Web. W3C Working Group Note, 12 April 2006, World Wide Web Consortium, Cambridge, MA, https://www.w3.org/TR/swbp-n-aryRelations/.

13. Berners-Lee, T., What the Semantic Web Can Represent, World Wide Web Consortium, Cambridge, MA, 1998, http://www.w3.org/DesignIssues/RDFnot.html.

14. Singhal, A., Introducing the knowledge graph: Things, not strings, May 16, Google, Inc. Mountain View, CA, 2012, https://blog.google/products/search/introducing-knowledge-graph-things-not/?_ga=2.255959499.1183610525.1632524921-1030216246.1632524921.

15. SWRL: A semantic web rule language combining OWL and RuleML. W3C Member Submission, World Wide Web Consortium, Cambridge, MA, 21 May 2004, https://www.w3.org/Submission/SWRL/.

16. DeBellis, M., Semantic Web Rule Language (SWRL) Process Modeling Tutorial, San Francisco, CA, https://www.michaeldebellis.com/post/swrl_tutorial.

17. Noy, N., Gao, Y., Jain, A., Narayanan, A., Patterson, A., Taylor, J., Industry-scale knowledge graphs: Lessons and challenges. *Commun. ACM*, 62, 8, 36–43, 2019 August 2019.

18. DeBellis, M., A Practical guide to building OWL ontologies using protégé 5.5 and Plugins Edition 3.0, 2021, San Francisco, CA, https://www.michael-debellis.com/post/new-protege-pizza tutorial.

19. DuCharme, B., *Learning SPARQL: Querying and Updating with SPARQL 1.1*, Second Edition, O'Reilly Media, Sebastopol, CA, July 30, 2013.

20. Uschold, M., *Demystifying OWL for the Enterprise*, 1st edition, Morgan & Claypool Publishers, San Rafael, CA, May 29, 2018.

## 11

Evaluating Richness of Security Ontologies for Semantic Web

Ambrish Kumar Mishra[1], Narayan C. Debnath[2] and Archana Patel[2*]

[1]School of Management, Gautam Buddha University, Greater Noida,
Uttar Pradesh, India
[2]Department of Software Engineering, School of Computing and Information
Technology, Eastern International University, Binh Duong, Vietnam,

Abstract

This chapter first describes the ontology evaluation tools and then focuses on the evaluation of the security ontologies. We classify the existing ontology evaluation tools under two categories namely domain-dependent ontology evaluation tools and domain-independent ontology evaluation tools. For the evaluation of the security ontologies, we use ontometric tool which is a domain-independent tool and it calculates the richness of the ontology in terms of five metrics. This chapter addresses various questions related to the ontology evaluation and security ontologies like, How many ontology evaluation tools are available on the web? How to calculate the richness of an ontology? Which ontology is suitable for the security of semantic web? How many security ontologies are available?

Keywords: Ontology, security, ontology evaluation, ontometric, semantic web

11.1 Introduction

Ontologies are used in various applications for the representation of the domain knowledge. It provides a way to represent knowledge in machine understandable manner. An ontology consists at least classes, properties (data and object properties), instances and axioms. The latest ontology development language is Web ontology Language (OWL) [1].

Corresponding author: archana.patel@eiu.edu.vn

Archana Patel, Narayan C. Debnath and Bharat Bhusan (eds.) Data Science with Semantic Technologies: Theory, Practice, and Application, (277–298) © 2022 Scrivener Publishing LLC

OWL Classes: OWL classes are built on top of and add additional semantics to RDFS classes. Whereas classes in most other languages only have heuristic definitions OWL classes have a rigorous formal definition. An OWL class is a set. A superclass is a superset, i.e., a set that is more general and contains more elements than its subset. Individuals in OWL are elements of sets. When an individual is an instance of a class, then that individual is an element of the set represented by that class. The properties that describe sets in set theory also apply to OWL classes and can be asserted by various axioms. The intersection of two classes are all the individuals that are instances of both classes. The union of two classes is the set formed by combining all the instances of each class. There are three types of OWL classes [2]:

- Primitive classes—These are classes that have axioms that provide necessary but not sufficient conditions for an individual to be an instance of the class. The reasoner can infer information about an instance based on the fact that it is declared as an instance of a primitive class, but it cannot infer that an individual is an instance of a primitive class.
- Defined classes—These are classes that have both necessary and sufficient conditions. The reasoner can both infer new information about an individual defined to be an instance of a defined class and it can also infer that an individual is an instance of a defined class even if the user has not explicitly asserted that it is.
- Anonymous classes—Anonymous classes are created by the reasoner based on various other axioms, e.g., if the definition for the domain or range of a property is that it must be an instance of human or an instance of animal the reasoner will create an anonymous class that is the union of the classes human and animal.

OWL Properties: Relations between individuals are described by OWL properties. There are three types of OWL properties: object properties, data properties, and annotation properties [3].

- Object properties. Object properties are properties that have other classes as their range, i.e., the value of the property will be an instance of an OWL class. Since defining the domain and range of a property is optional if the domain or range of an object property are not defined, they default to owl:Thing.

- Data properties. Data properties are properties that have Literals such as strings and integers as their range, i.e., the value of these properties will be a Literal rather than an instance of a class. As with object properties if the domain is not defined for a data property it defaults to owl:Thing. If the range is not defined it defaults to the literal datatype. Any datatype, such as a string or integer, is also an instance of the literal datatype.
- Annotation properties. Object and data properties describe the domain of the ontology. Their domain must be an OWL class, i.e., only instances of classes can have object or data property values. This is more restrictive than RDFS properties which can be applied to anything with an IRI. Annotation properties relax this restriction and can be applied to anything in the ontology, such as a class or even a property. This is because annotation properties are for meta-data and meta-data such as comments need to be used for everything in the ontology. Because annotation properties are for meta-data they cannot be utilized by the reasoner. The default domain for an annotation property is any resource with an IRI. The default range is Literal.

OWL provides additional ways to describe a property that can then be utilized by the reasoner for automatic inferencing. The most commonly used definitions are: functional properties, symmetric properties, inverse properties, transitive properties, reflexive properties, super and sub properties. All properties can have super and sub properties. Only object and data properties can be functional. The rest of the characteristics can only apply to object properties.

OWL Axioms: One of the most powerful features of OWL is the ability to provide formal definitions of classes using the description logic (DL) language. These axioms are typically asserted on property values for the class. There are three kinds of axioms that can be asserted about OWL classes [4]:

- Quantifier restrictions. These describe that a property must have some or all values that are of a particular class or datatype.
- Cardinality restrictions. These describe the number of individuals that must be related to a class by a specific property.

- Value restrictions. These describe specific values that a property must have.

Due to reasoning power of ontology, it is utilized in various domains, resultantly different users create so many separate ontologies in the same or different domains that create a problem to the users in choosing the best ontology from the available ontologies. The selection of the best or suitable ontology as per need depends on the ontology evaluation process. Ontology evaluation provides the approaches and criteria to examine the quality and quantity of the ontology. Many security ontologies have been developed for secure communication. The main characteristics of security are confidentiality (allowing only authorized users to access the information), integrity (only authorized users must alter the information), and availability (the information must be available as per user request) [5]. The available security ontologies can hold the different characteristics of the security. These ontologies play a vital role in securing the information on the semantic web. However, the evaluation of security ontologies is missing in the literature that create a problem when user need to asses quality ontology.

The aim of this chapter is to present the ontology evaluation tools and evaluate the security ontologies to detect the suitable ontology among the available ontologies. The rest of the chapter is divided as follows: Section 11.2 shows the ontology evaluation tools under two categories namely domain dependant and domain-independent tools. Section 11.3 focuses on the available security ontologies. Section 11.4 depicts the evaluation of the security ontologies that calculate their richness. The last section concludes this chapter.

11.2   Ontology Evaluation: State-of-the-Art

In the existing literature, there are 13 ontology evaluation tools available. These tools are: SSN Ontology Validator, OntoMetrics, FoEval, OntoKeeper Validator, Ontology Pitfall Scanner!, OntologyFixer, OQuaRE, OntoQA, OWL Validator, W3C RDF/XML Validator, OntoClean, S-OntoEval, and OntoVal. We have grouped these tools into two categories namely domain-dependent and domain-independent ontology evaluation tools. Figure 11.1 shows the classification of the available ontology evaluation tools.

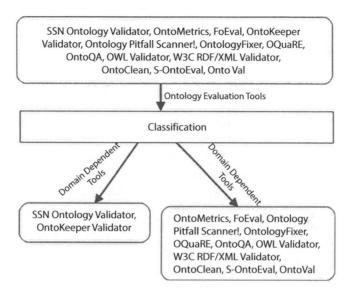

Figure 11.1 Ontology evaluation tools.

11.2.1 Domain-Dependent Ontology Evaluation Tools

The domain-dependent ontology evaluation tools are able to evaluate only domain-oriented ontology. There are two tools (SSN ontology validator and OntoKeeper validator) available that evaluate domain ontologies.

- **SSN Ontology Validator**—The Semantic Sensor Networks (SSN) validator are used to evaluate the IoT-related domain ontologies. It has sensors and observation-related data in OWL2 language which is latest ontology language. The validator takes the input ontology and validate it with SSN ontology as well as other ontologies that are associated with it. The online version of SSN validator is available at URL: http://iot.ee.surrey.ac.uk/SSNValidation/ and SSN ontology is available at URL: https://www.w3.org/2005/Incubator/ ssn/ssnx/ssn [6].
- **OntoKeeper Validator**—This validator evaluates the biodiversity domain-related ontologies. It uses semiotic metrics (syntactic, pragmatic and semantic) to evaluate the biodiversity ontologies. The validator shows quality of the ontology based on the different parameters namely richness, accuracy, interpretability, and comprehensiveness [7].

11.2.2   Domain-Independent Ontology Evaluation Tools

The domain-independent ontology evaluation tools are used to evaluate all types of ontologies (ontologies belong to the different domains). There are 11 domain-independent ontology evaluation tools available till now. These tools are Ontology Pitfall Scanner!, OntoMetrics, OntologyFixer, OQuaRE, OntoQA, OWL Validator, W3C RDF/XML Validator, OntoClean, S-OntoEval, OntoVal, and FoEval.

- **Ontology Pitfall Scanner! (OOPS!)**—This tool shows the pitfalls or anomalies of an ontology. These pitfalls are categories into three groups namely minor pitfalls, important pitfalls and critical pitfalls. The most dangerous pitfalls are critical pitfalls that need to remove from the ontologies before using them otherwise result will get damage [8].

- **OntoMetrics**—This tool shows the statistical information of an ontology. The statistical information is calculated based on five metrics namely Base metrics (addresses quality of an ontology element), Schema metrics (addresses design or schema of an ontology), Knowledge base metrics (addresses the amount of knowledge encoded in an ontology), Class metrics (addresses the classes and relationships of an ontology), and Graph metrics (addresses the structure of an ontology) [9].

- **OntologyFixer**—This tool measures the quality of an ontology based on the ten metrics namely ANOnto (shows annotation richness), CBOnto (shows coupling between objects), CROnto (shows class richness), INROnto (shows number of relations per class), LCOMOnto (shows lack of cohesion in methods), NOMOnto (shows number of properties per class), RCOnto (shows distribution of instance across class), RFCOnto (shows response measure for a class), and RROnto (shows relationship richness). This tool also integrates the OOPs! tool to detect the anomalies of an ontology [10].

- **OQuaRE**—It evaluates the quality of an ontology on the basis of both quality model and quality metrics. OQuaRE adapts and reuses five characteristics from the SQuaRE namely Structural (it specifies the formal and semantic important properties of an ontology), functional adequacy (it includes the degree of accomplishment of functional requirements), reliability (it checks level of performance under stated conditions), operability (it shows effort needed for building an ontology and individual assessment), maintainability (it shows the ability of ontologies to be modified for changes in environments) [11].

- **OntoQA**—The OntoQA evaluates the design and representation of knowledge of an ontology as well as the placement of the instances within the ontology and its effective usage. The OntoQA categories the quality of the ontology into three groups namely schema metrics (shows the design of an ontology), knowledgebase metrics (describes the encoded KB) and class metrics (it describes each class that defined in the schema) [12].

- **OWL Validator**—It validates the ontologies against OWL2, OWL2DL, OWL2RL, OWL2EL, and OWL2QL profiles. The aim of OWL validator is to ensure that all the concepts and properties in an ontology are specified as per the W3C standard. It shows an error message with the detailed report when an input ontology does not support the selected profile [13].

- **W3C RDF/XML Validator**—This tool is being used for the validation of RDF documents by tracking the RDF issues. It shows a warning message when an error occurred during validation of the RDF document. W3C RDF validator shows the number of tuples (subject-object-predicate) that are encoded in the ontology, as well as its graphical representation. This validator aims to ensure that the document is syntactically valid [14].

- **OntoClean**—It validates the adequacy of ontology hierarchy based on general ontological notions namely essence, unity and identity. The correctness of the ontology hierarchy is checked via the principles of metaproperties namely rigidity, unity, identity, and dependence. Later on, two more metaproperties, namely permanence and actuality have been added to validate the ontolog of OntoVal is divided into three stages namely class evaluation (evaluates the classes of an ontology), property evaluation (evaluates the properties of an ontology), overall evaluation (evaluates an ontology based on the important criteria like agreement on the name of an ontology and its description) [17].

- **FoEval**—This is a ranking and selection tool that has three features, namely: it allows the user to select a set of metrics that help in the evaluation process, this tool allows user to evaluate the locally stored and searched ontologies from the different search engines or repositories, it captures the structural and semantic information of a domain. It includes rich set of metrics namely coverage (It covers class and relation coverage), richness (it measures by three different levels namely relation richness, attribute richness, detail level), comprehensiveness (it evaluates content comprehensiveness of ontologies with the help of average number of annotated classes, annotated relations and instance per class), and computational efficiency (it measures the speed of the reasoner that need to fulfil the required tasks) [18].

11.3   Security Ontology

Various authors have developed the security ontologies to manage the security information over the web. These ontologies are summarized below:

- **Credential Ontology:** Denker *et al.* [19] have introduced credential ontology which is represented in DAML-S. The authentication process determines whether access will be granted or not. When the authentication depends on the token, then it is known as a credential. Credentials can use different authentication techniques like public and private keys, passphrase login, and certificates. Credential ontology aims to provide access to the web pages or services only to the authorized request. It defines those credentials that are commonly used in internet security. The main class of this ontology is credential (top class), which has one subclass, namely ComposedCredential, which is three subclasses: IDCard, SmartCard, and SimpleCredential. The SimpleCredential has four subclasses: Login, Cookie, BioMetric, Certificate, OneTimePassword, and Key. All subclasses are pairwise disjoint like class key has two disjoint subclasses, namely public key, and symmetric key. The certificate class has subclass

"X509Certificate," which has a specific class of X509 certificates in the XML Signature.

- **OWL-S [20, 21]:** It is a web ontology language that provides essential constructs for web services. To describe the web services, it offers three ontologies, namely

    a) *Profile Ontology:* It provides a higher level of description of services.
    b) *Process Ontology:* It describes the detailed description of service's operation.
    c) *Grounding Ontology:* It specifies the details about how an agent can access the services.
    The profile, process, and grounding define the services in terms of 'what the services do', 'how to use it', and 'how to interact with it', respectively.

- **Agent Security Ontology [22]:** This ontology allows to query of the web resources based on the requestor's requirements and capabilities. It has an agent class that presents the service requestor. This class has two properties, namely securityRequirement and securityCapability, that take values from classes, namely SecurityObjective and SecurityConcept.
- **Information Object Ontology (InfoObj) [23]:** This ontology is designed to capture web services' encrypted input and output data. It has a class Information Object (InfObj) that has two subclasses, signed Information Object (SigInfObj) and Encrypted Information Object (EncInfObj). The class InfObj is marked as a range for input/output parameters of services mentioned in OWL-S. It uses the cryptoAlgUsed property to specify the algorithm that used in encryption.
- **Main Security Ontology [22]:** This ontology is designed for the security purpose of having information about the assets, threats, countermeasures, and vulnerabilities. It also contains information about defense strategies like prevention and detection as well as security goals such as confidentiality, integrity, etc.
- **Security Ontology:** Denker *et al.* [24] have developed a security ontology that describes a high level of abstraction of security mechanisms by accommodating various security standards and notations. The class SecurityMechanism has six main subclasses: Syntax, Signature, Encryption, Protocol,

KeyFormat, SecurityNotation, and Protocol, whereas the Protocol class has two subclasses: KeyProtocol and DataTransferProtocol. The KeyProtocol has three subclasses, namely KeyRegistrationProtocol, KeyInformationProtocol, and KeyDistributionProtocol. Many properties and instances are also defined as per the requirement of the security mechanism.

- **Security View Ontology [22]:** This ontology imports the main security ontology to provide the view of security. The defined classes sort threats and countermeasures according to assists, defense strategies, and security goals.
- **Service Ontology [25]:** It defines general concepts of service. Service ontology uses three vocabulary GoodRelations, Schema.org and FOAF. There are three main classes, namely ServiceProvider (provides the service), ServiceConsumer (consumes the service), and ServiceLimitation (imposes the constraints on the services), which are used to define the service.
- **Service Security Ontology [26]:** This ontology has extended the OWL-S profile ontology. The ServiceParameter class has two subclasses, namely SecurityConcept and SecurityObjective; these classes are taken from the security ontology. It has a property, namely serviceParameter, which has two properties, securityRequirement, and secuirtyCapability. These properties describe the security requirements and capabilities in its service description. All the subproperties are associated with range and domain that define the security requirements and capabilities in terms of security objective or mechanism.

Apart from these ontologies, three ontologies, namely security algorithm ontology, security assurance ontology, and NRL security ontology, are also available. However, they are not accessible because not available on the web.

Security algorithm ontology describes the various security algorithms, which support security-related protocols and specify what algorithm would be used to encrypt the data on the web [27]. This ontology groups the security ontology into key exchange algorithm, encryption algorithm, checksum algorithm, and signature algorithm. The encryption algorithm and signature algorithm have two subclasses: symmetric algorithm and asymmetric algorithm; Hash algorithm and MAC algorithm, respectively.

This ontology uses isNISTStandard property to check whether the algorithm is standard or not and uses hasNSALevel property to ensure the algorithm's encryption. Other properties of this ontology provide descriptions of key lengths and modes of operation.

Security assurance ontology provides standardized assurance methods for algorithms, security protocols, and mechanisms [28]. It uses the hasAssurance property of security ontology to describe the terms based on their assurance level. The assurance class of this ontology has four subclasses, namely standard, evaluation, certification, and accreditation.

NRL security ontology combines seven ontologies: information object ontology, security ontology, security assurance ontology, credential ontology, agent security ontology, service security ontology, and OWL-S ontology [29]. The focus of this ontology is on the annotation of the resources rather than web services. It describes the different types of security information, like protocols, algorithms, mechanisms, objectives credentials. The NRL Security ontology is well organized and contains comprehensive information about the security aspects. It can represent different types of security statements, and the class hierarchy makes it easy to use and extend. NRL Security ontology is a collective representation of all security-related ontologies. This ontology overcame the limitation of DAML-based security ontology.

11.4   Richness of Security Ontologies

The evaluation of an ontology shows the richness of that ontology. Richness determines the quantity of the ontology elements like classes, properties, instances, etc. We use the Ontometric tool for the calculation of the richness of the security ontologies. It is a web-based tool that calculates the statistical information about an ontology. The current version of the OntoMetric tool is available at https://ontometrics.informatik.uni-rostock.de/ontologymetrics/. It has five types of metrics, namely Base metrics, Schema metrics, Knowledge base metrics, Class metrics, and Graph metrics.

- **Base metrics:** These metrics show the quantity of ontology elements by calculating class Axioms (Axioms, Logical Axiom, and Class), property (data and object), individual axioms, annotation axioms, and DL expressivity.
- **Schema metrics:** It addresses the design (schema) of an ontology based on eight parameters, namely attribute richness (measures the average number of attributes per class

in ontology), inheritance richness (measures the distribution of information across the different levels of ontology's hierarchy), relationship richness (measures the diversity of the types of relations in an ontology), attribute-class ratio (measures the ratio between the classes that have attributes and all classes in ontology), equivalence ratio (measures the ratio between similar classes and all classes in ontology), axiom class ratio (measures the ratio between axioms and classes), Inverse relations ratio (measures the ratio between the inverse relations and all relations in an ontology), class relation ratio (measures the ratio between the classes and the relations in an ontology).

- **Knowledge base metrics:** It measures the amount of knowledge represented by an ontology and shows the effectiveness of an ontology design. It calculates average population (measures average distribution of instances across the classes), class richness (measures how instances are distributed across classes), cohesion (measures the degree of relatedness between the different entities).

- **Class metrics:** It measures the classes and relationships of an ontology. It shows class connectivity, class fullness, class importance, class inheritance richness, class readability, class relationship richness, class children, class instances, and class properties.

- **Graph or Structure metrics:** It calculates the structure of an ontology based on 10 parameters, namely cardinality (which shows the graph-related number of elements. It can be absolute root, leaf, and sibling cardinality), depth (shows cardinality of paths that exist in a graph. It can be absolute, average, and maximum depth), breadth (shows the cardinality of level. It can be absolute, average, and maximum breadth), fan-outness (shows the dispersion of graph nodes), tangledness (shows the multihierarchical nodes of a graph), Total and average number of paths, density (measure the clusters of classes with various non-taxonomical relations existing among them), logical adequacy (measure the formal semantics with the help of directed or conceptual relations), modularity (related to the asserted modules of a graph).

Table 11.1 Richness of security ontologies via ontometric tool (a) security ontologies namely agent security, credential, grounding, infObj, mainsecurity, process, profile (b) security, securityview, service, serviceview.

Ontologies→ metrics↓		Agent security	Credential	Grounding ontology	InfObj	MainSecurity	Process	Profile
Base Metrics	Axioms	9	146	144	31	1953	322	70
	Logical axioms count	4	83	74	16	1131	180	40
	Class count	3	30	13	13	460	41	11
	Object properties	2	4	13	2	29	42	10
	Data properties	0	11	14	0	1	9	9
	Instances	0	0	0	6	30	4	0

(Continued)

Table 11.1 Richness of security ontologies via ontometric tool (a) security ontologies namely agent security, credential, grounding, infObj, mainsecurity, process, profile (b) security, securityview, service, serviceview. (*Continued*)

Ontologies→ metrics↓		Agent security	Credential	Grounding ontology	InfObj	MainSecurity	Process	Profile
Schema metrics	Attribute richness	0.0	0.366667	1.076	0.0	0.002	0.219	0.818
	Inheritance richness	0.0	1.2	1.384	0.384	1.630	1.487	0.818
	Relationship richness	1.0	0.454545	0.419	0.285	0.25	0.483	0.526
	Attribute class ratio	0.0	C.0	0.0	0.0	0.0	0.0	0.0
	Equivalence ratio	0.0	0.0	0.0	0.0	0.278	0.146	0.0
	Axiom/class ratio	2.666	4.866667	11.076	2.384	4.245	7.853	6.363
	Inverse relations ratio	0.0	0.0	0.0	0.0	0.448	0.047	0.0
	Class/relation ratio	1.5	0.454545	0.419	1.857	0.46	0.347	0.578

(*Continued*)

Table 11.1 Richness of security ontologies via ontometric tool (a) security ontologies namely agent security, credential, grounding, infObj, mainsecurity, proces, profile (b) security, securityview, service, serviceview. (Continued)

Ontologies→ metrics↓		Agent security	Credential	Grounding ontology	InfObj	MainSecurity	Process	Profile
Knowledgebase Metrics	Average population	0.0	0.0	0.0	0.461	0.065	0.097	0.0
	Class richness	0.0	0.0	0.0	0.384	0.010	0.048	0.0
Graph metrics	Absolute root cardinality	3	6	6	8	121	14	8
	Absolute leaf cardinality	3	21	8	11	281	20	8
	Absolute sibling cardinality	3	30	11	13	373	25	9
	Absolute depth	3	88	16	18	2386	43	10
	Average depth	1	2.933	1.454	1.384	3.873	1.72	1.111
	Maximal depth	1	5	2	2	8	3	2
	Absolute breadth	3	30	11	13	616	25	9

(Continued)

Table 11.1 Richness of security ontologies via ontometric tool (a) security ontologies namely agent security, credential, grounding, infObj, mainsecurity, process, profile (b) security, securityview, service, serviceview. *(Continued)*

Ontologies→ metrics↓		Agent security	Credential	Grounding ontology	InfObj	MainSecurity	Process	Profile
	Average breadth	3	3.0	2.75	4.333	4.219	4.166	4.5
	Maximal breadth	3	6	6	8	121	14	8
	Ratio of leaf fan-outness	1	0.7	0.615	0.846	0.610	0.487	0.727
	Ratio of sibling fan-outness	1	1.0	0.846	1.0	0.810	0.609	0.818
	Tangledness	0	0.2666	0.307	0.0	0.267	0.146	0.090
	Total number of paths	3	30	11	13	616	25	9
	Average number of paths	3	6.0	5.5	6.5	77.0	8.333	4.5

(a)

Table 11.1 Richness of security ontologies via ontometric tool (a) security ontologies namely agent security, credential, grounding, infObj, mainsecurity, process, profile (b) security, securityview, service, serviceview.

Ontologies→ metrics↓		Security	Securityview	Service	Servicesecutiy
Base Metrics	Axioms	148	55	55	10
	Logical axioms count	93	34	23	5
	Class count	57	30	5	2
	Object properties	6	2	11	3
	Data properties	0	0	0	0
	instances	54	0	0	0
Schema metrics	Attribute richness	0.0	0.0	0.0	0.0
	Inheritance richness	0.228	0.633	0.4	0.5
	Relationship richness	0.606	0.472	0.846	0.75
	Attribute class ratio	0.0	0.0	0.0	0.0
	Equivalence ratio	0.245	0.5	0.0	0.0
	Axiom/class ratio	2.596	1.833	11.0	5.0
	Inverse relations ratio	0.0	0.0	0.363	0.0
	Class/relation ratio	1.727	0.833	0.384	0.5
Knowledgebase Metrics	Average population	0.947	0.0	0.0	0.0
	Class richness	0.210	0.0	0.0	0.0

(Continued)

Table 11.1 Richness of security ontologies via ontometric tool (a) security ontologies namely agent security, credential, grounding, infObj, mainsecurity, process, profile (b) security, securityview, service, serviceview. (*Continued*)

Ontologies→ metrics↓		Security	Securityview	Service	Servicesecutiy
Graph metrics	Absolute root cardinality	44	11	3	1
	Absolute leaf cardinality	51	20	3	1
	Absolute sibling cardinality	57	30	3	2
	Absolute depth	76	69	3	3
	Average depth	1.333	2.3	1.0	1.5
	Maximal depth	4	5	1	2
	Absolute breadth	57	30	3	2
	Average breadth	8.142	2.727	3.0	1.0
	Maximal breadth	44	11	3	1
	Ratio of leaf fan-outness	0.894	0.666	0.6	0.5
	Ratio of sibling fan-outness	1.0	1.0	0.6	1.0
	Tangledness	0.0	0.0	0.0	0.0
	Total number of paths	57	30	3	2
	Average number of paths	14.25	6.0	3.0	1.0

(b)

We have calculated base metrics, schema metrics, knowledgebase metrics, and graphs metrics of the security ontologies. We did not calculate the class metrics because all the important information about the classes is already covered in other metrics. Table 11.1 shows the value of these metrics for available security ontologies, which are listed above.

Table 11.1 shows the MainSecurity ontology contains highest number of classes, process ontology contains highest number of object property, and grounding ontology contains highest number of data properties. Hence, based on the different metrics, only these three ontologies are rich.

11.5 Conclusion

Ontologies are used in various domains for the representation of domain knowledge. Developed ontologies need to be evaluated to check their quality. Ontology evaluation determines the suitable ontology among available ontologies. This study has presented considerable work related to ontology evaluation and security ontologies developed for the semantic web. The evaluation of these accessible and downloadable security ontologies is shown via Ontometric tools to check the quality in term of richness.

References

1. Patel, A. and Jain, S., A novel approach to discover ontology alignment. *Recent Adv. Comput. Sci. Commun. (Formerly: Recent Pat. Comput. Sci.)*, 14, 1, 273–281, 2021.
2. Antoniou, G. and Van Harmelen, F., Web ontology language: Owl, in: *Handbook on Ontologies*, pp. 67–92, Springer, Berlin, Heidelberg, 2004.
3. Patel, A. and Debnath, N.C., Development of the InBan_CIDO ontology by reusing the concepts along with detecting overlapping information. *3rd International Conference on Inventive Computation and Information Technologies (ICICIT 2021)*, Springer, 2021.
4. Haase, P. and Stojanovic, L., Consistent evolution of OWL ontologies, in: *European Semantic Web Conference*, Springer, Berlin, Heidelberg, pp. 182–197, 2005.
5. Gonzalez-Gil, P., Martinez, J.A., Skarmeta, A.F., Lightweight data-security ontology for IoT. *Sensors*, 20, 3, 801, 2020.
6. Kolozali, S., Elsaleh, T., Barnaghi, P.M., A validation tool for the W3C SSN ontology based sensory semantic knowledge, in: *TC/SSN@ International Semantic Web Conference*, pp. 83–88, 2014.

7. Amith, M., Manion, F., Liang, C., Harris, M., Wang, D., He, Y., Tao, C., Architecture and usability of OntoKeeper, an ontology evaluation tool. *BMC Med. Inform. Decis. Mak.*, 19, 4, 1–18, 2019.

8. Mishra, A.K., Patel, A., Jain, S., Impact of Covid-19 outbreak on performance of Indian Banking Sector, in: *CEUR Workshop Proc*, 2021.

9. Lozano-Tello, A. and Gómez-Pérez, A., Ontometric: A method to choose the appropriate ontology. *J. Database Manage. (JDM)*, 15, 2, 1–18, 2004.

10. Roldan-Molina, G.R., Mendez, J.R., Yevseyeva, I., Basto-Fernandes, V., Ontology fixing by using software engineering technology. *Appl. Sci.*, 10, 18, 6328, 2020.

11. Duque-Ramos, A., Fernández-Breis, J.T., Iniesta, M., Dumontier, M., Aranguren, M.E., Schulz, S., Stevens, R., Evaluation of the OQuaRE framework for ontology quality. *Expert Syst. Appl.*, 40, 7, 2696–2703, 2013.

12. Tartir, S. and Arpinar, I.B., Ontology evaluation and ranking using OntoQA, in: *International Conference on Semantic Computing (ICSC 2007)*, IEEE, pp. 185–192, 2007.

13. OWL Validator. URL: http://mowl-power.cs.man.ac.uk:8080/validator/

14. RDF/XML Validator. URL: https://www.w3.org/RDF/Validator/.

15. Guarino, N. and Welty, C.A., An overview of OntoClean, in: *Handbook on Ontologies*, pp. 151–171, 2004.

16. Dividino, R.Q., Romanelli, M., Sonntag, D., Semiotic-based Ontology Evaluation Tool (S-OntoEval), in: *LREC*, 2008.

17. Avila, C.V.S., Maia, G., Franco, W., Rolim, T.V., da Rocha Franco, A.D.O., Vidal, V.M.P., OntoVal: A Tool for Ontology Evaluation by domain specialists, in: *ER Forum/Posters/Demos*, pp. 143–147, 2019.

18. Bouiadjra, A.B. and Benslimane, S.M., FOEval: Full ontology evaluation, in: *2011 7th International Conference on Natural Language Processing and Knowledge Engineering*, IEEE, pp. 464–468, 2011.

19. Denker, G. and Kagal, L., Security Annotation for DAML web services, in: *Proc. 2nd International Semantic Web Conference (ISWC2003)*, Sanibel Island, Florida, USA, 2003.

20. Martin, D., Burstein, M. *et al.*, Bringing semantics to web services with OWL-S. *World Wide Web*, 10, 3, 243–277, 2007.

21. Kagal, L., Finin, T., Paolucci, M., Srinivasan, N., Sycara, K., Denker, G., Authorization and privacy for semantic web services. *IEEE Intell. Syst.*, 19, 4, 50–56, 2004.

22. OWL-S Ontology. URL: http://www.daml.org/services/owl-s/security.html.

23. Bhaumik, A., *An approach in defining Information Assurance Patterns based on security ontology and meta-modeling*, University of Nebraska at Omaha, 2012.

24. Ekelhart, A., Fenz, S., Klemen, M.D., Weippl, E.R., Security ontology: Simulating threats to corporate assets, in: *International Conference on Information Systems Security*, Springer, Berlin, Heidelberg, pp. 249–259, 2006.

25. Wang, H.H., Gibbins, N., Payne, T.R., Redavid, D., A formal model of the semantic web service ontology (WSMO). *Inf. Syst.*, 37, 1, 33–60, 2012.
26. Blanco, C., Lasheras, J., Fernández-Medina, E., Valencia-García, R., Toval, A., Basis for an integrated security ontology according to a systematic review of existing proposals. *Comput. Stand. Inter.*, 33, 4, 372–388, 2011.
27. Vorobiev, A. and Bekmamedova, N., An ontology-driven approach applied to information security. *J. Res. Pract. Inf. Technol.*, 42, 1, 61–76, 2010.
28. Kim, A., Luo, J., Kang, M., Security ontology for annotating resources, in: *OTM Confederated International Conferences "On the Move to Meaningful Internet Systems"*, Springer, Berlin, Heidelberg, pp. 1483–1499, 2005.
29. Blanco, C., Lasheras, J., Valencia-García, R., Fernández-Medina, E., Toval, A., Piattini, M., A systematic review and comparison of security ontologies, in: *2008 Third International Conference on Availability, Reliability and Security*, IEEE, pp. 813–820, 2008.

12

Health Data Science and Semantic Technologies

Haleh Ayatollahi[1,2]

[1]*Health Management and Economics Research Center, Heath Management Research Institute, Iran University of Medical Sciences, Tehran, Iran*
[2]*Department of Health Information Management, School of Health Management and Information Sciences, Iran University of Medical Sciences, Tehran, Iran*

Abstract

In the health care industry, a large amount of health data is produced on a daily basis. These data can be found in various sources, such as electronic health records (EHR) and wearable medical devices. However, collecting, processing, and analyzing such a huge amount of data in order to extract useful knowledge are challenging for health care organizations and health care professionals. One of the emerging disciplines to deal with a vast amount of data is health data science, which applies mathematics, computer science, statistics, and medicine together to make better use of health data. Artificial intelligence (AI) techniques, including machine learning (ML) and natural language processing (NLP), are important approaches in health data science. In this chapter, initially, the main concepts of health data, data science, health data science, examples of the application of health data science and related challenges, are discussed. These sections are followed by highlighting the application of semantic technologies in health data science and challenges ahead of using these technologies. The next sections of this chapter belong to the application of data science for COVID-19 and related data challenges, and the last section is devoted to presenting an overview of biomedical data science.

Keywords: Heath, data science, health data, semantic technology, COVID-19, biomedical data

Email: ayatollahi.h@iums.ac.ir

Archana Patel, Narayan C. Debnath and Bharat Bhusan (eds.) Data Science with Semantic Technologies: Theory, Practice, and Application, (299–322) © 2022 Scrivener Publishing LLC

12.1   Health Data

Every day, a huge amount of health data is generated and stored in various sources and databases. Some of these sources are wearable medical devices, clinical information systems, electronic health records (EHRs), administrative and billing databases, IoT devices, mobile health (mhealth) and telemedicine applications, surveillance systems, genomic sequencing, and research databases. There are also other sources of data, such as social media, occupational, geographical, economic, and environmental data, that can be used along with other types of health data to provide valuable opportunities for better patient care and healthcare services [1, 2]. In addition to the substantial increases in the volume of health care data, they are highly complex, their types and standards are different and about 80% of them are unstructured which constraint semantic interoperability [3]. As a result, health care industry has faced a lot of challenges related to collecting and processing these data, especially in terms of extracting new knowledge. To be able to deal with such a huge volume of data, new methods and cutting-edge technologies have emerged and evolved overtime [1, 4].

It is notable that the use of health related data have great potentials to improve healthcare services, patient care, and the health status of the communities. These potentials can only be realized, if data are made available and accessible across clinical settings and scientific communities. In order to better use of health data, a better understanding of its nature, data sources and data types is necessary [5]. Moreover, a number of new research opportunities can be proposed by innovative, efficient, and secure use of data. For example, a number of new datasets can be created via data linkage. In addition, data from new sources, such as biosensors, smart phone applications, social networks, commercial databases, and wearable devices, can be linked together. These data can be used to make informed decisions by policy makers and health care practitioners to improve patients' and community health conditions. Some good examples of using health data are identifying disease outbreaks, such as COVID-19, adverse drug reaction, and predicting clinical outcomes after hospital discharge [6]. It is notable that not only for managing the routine health care data but also for organizing the large volume of health care data generated through new technologies, such as the Internet of Things (IoT) devices, electronic health (e-health) and mobile health (mhealth) applications, the use of new methods and approaches for data processing and management needs to be taken into account [5].

12.2 Data Science

The term "data science" is increasingly used along with the term "big data." Therefore, it can be implied that data science has a focus around data and their organization, properties, analysis, and their role in inference [7]. Data science is a set of principles that support the process of information and knowledge extraction from data, and data mining is a close concept related to data science. According to another definition, data science is a set of concepts, processes, and techniques that are used to analyze data and make inferences much easier [8]. It is an interdisciplinary discipline, which collects and analyses data from structural and unstructured sources using computational procedures, algorithms, techniques, and systems [9]. Eventually, data science aims to improve decision making based on the analysis of data rather than using intuition [8].

Data science also refers to the use of computational and statistical techniques in a specific domain of knowledge. However, in addition to the theoretical skills, practical skills are necessary for data scientists. These skills include the ability to generate models to answer research questions, retrieve and clean data, present results visually, and perform data analyses. Obviously, the process of data analysis may not be straightforward and sometimes may need to pass several cycles before reporting the final results [10].

It is notable that data science emerged from the scientific methods; however, they are different in some aspects. Similar to the scientific methods, a number of principles and techniques are used in data science to be able to discover knowledge and data patterns. In terms of differences, it can be said that sometimes the quality of data is not guaranteed in different databases, while in the scientific methods more controlled environment is required to reach precise results. The theories and models used in the scientific methods have a long history of development; however, data science models are generated on demand for different studies. In fact, the scientific methods have been developed slowly, whereas data science models are developed rapidly. Moreover, the number of variables in data science analysis can be unlimited, while in the scientific methods, researchers need to work with specific type of data [11].

12.3 Health Data Science

Health data science is a relatively new discipline in which statistics, mathematics, computer science, and medicine are used together to provide solutions for complex health problems [1]. As health data have a great role in revolutionizing the health care industry, advanced analytics technologies are used by data scientists in different areas, such as diagnostics, medical imaging, disease prediction, public health, genomics, drug discovery, real-time monitoring, cost reduction and staffing to improve health care services, public health, and well-being [2]. Not only data scientists but also the experts and professionals in various related fields, such as health informatics, biomedical informatics, and bioinformatics, have been engaged in developing methods to analyze data and extract knowledge in the fields of medicine, health, and biology [12].

It is notable that the use of data science technologies in health care is useful for both patients and health care professionals and results in progress in diagnosing and treating different types of diseases [13]. Health care managers and decision makers have also been encouraged to gain better use of health data by increasing the use of technology and making more effective decisions [14].

While a number of tools and techniques have been developed in the last twenty years to facilitate data processing and analysis [15], it seems that data science in health care has been applied in three common ways: (a) analyzing big data collected in large data sets including electronic heath records (EHR) and social media; (b) getting access to new data sources which are available via data sharing and health information exchange (HIE); and (c) using analytic techniques, such as machine learning and artificial intelligence to analyze both structured and unstructured data to provide predictive models in clinical and administrative practices [15, 16]. Each of these approaches is explained below.

In the health care settings, big data are generated and collected via different data sources on a daily basis. These data can be analyzed by using data techniques, such as data mining, machine learning, mathematical and statistical modeling [16, 17]. Some sources of big data are health care or bio-medical applications, epidemiological databases and health care statistics [18]. The knowledge gained from these data is valuable for epidemiologists, researchers, and policy makers to get a better understanding of a health phenomenon. COVID-19 epidemiological data is an example of big data which inherit the common characteristics of big data. These characteristics consist of 7 Vs, i.e., the volume of data (high number of cases), velocity (adding new data on a daily basis), variety (heterogeneous data and data sources), veracity (some data are precise and some are not), valuable (making better decisions to control the disease), visibility (visual analysis is demanding), and validity (lots of efforts are being made to show the validity of data) [17].

As data science tools need to use massive collections of different types of data, strong data acquisition systems need to be designed and implemented to get access to these data. Electronic health records systems (EHRs) and electronic medical records (EMR) are examples of these systems. However, the use of EHRs in the globe has faced a number of technical and nontechnical challenges, such as low level of usability, staff resistance, high cost of design and implementation, and the exhaustion and shortage of workforce. These challenges have negatively affected the integration and maintenance of EHR systems [14].

Health information exchange (HIE) provides an opportunity to transfer electronic health data within and across health care organizations through interoperable health information systems. Data can be transferred securely and patients and health care providers can be assured about respecting the confidentiality issues. However, the lack of reliable terminology and unified classifications has been considered as major barriers ahead of successful data transfer. As a result, new technologies, such as blockchain technology has been applied to improve interoperability and data security [1, 14].

Another technology is artificial intelligence (AI) which can be used to improve clinical assessments, monitor drug adherence, predict disease outbreaks, etc. AI is the use of computer algorithms and statistical models to enhance the understanding of complicated medical issues by analyzing medical data. AI includes machine learning (ML), natural language processing (NLP), and computer vision applications. These techniques help to use a large amount of data to design, depict, and predict new models and associations. AI can be used in medical disciplines for making reliable and accurate predictions about clinical circumstances and assisting clinicians to make better decisions, especially in acute conditions or for rare diseases [14].

Machine learning is a subfield of artificial intelligence (AI), which can be used for generating prediction models and discovering unknown or hidden associations between different variables [1]. Machine learning techniques are categorized into three methods, which include supervised, unsupervised, and reinforcement learning methods. In supervised learning method, a predicting model is generated based on the previous labeled training data, while in unsupervised learning method, a model is produced to identify hidden patterns without labeling data. The third category which is reinforcement learning method is like a game and uses feedback as a reward or penalty to improve its performance [19].

Although a large part of medical records consists of narrative and textual data, it is still a rich source of data for conducting research. To analyze this type of data, natural language processing (NLP) is used as a set of rules and computational techniques and machine learning algorithms are applied along with NLP techniques to learn and predict models of associations. The supervised learning method is a common method of machine learning used in this field [20].

Computer vision is another subfield of artificial intelligence that has been utilized in medical research to analyze and interpret digital images, such as computed tomography (CT) images, x-rays images, etc. It can be used in disease diagnosis, prognosis and treatment, and recently, a substantial amount of research applied this technique in relation to the challenges of COVID-19, for example, to recognize social distancing and wearing masks [21].

12.4   Examples of Health Data Science Applications

The use of data science in medicine and health care has been reported in numerous studies. Here, a limited number of these studies are presented to provide a better understanding and insight into the research opportunities that are available for data scientists in these fields.

Hueso *et al.* discussed the application of data science in hemodialysis. They noted that this type of treatment includes various types of data related to extracorporeal circuit, hydraulic circuit, chemistry, physiology, and machines. These data can be linked to other datasets, such as biomedical research, pathology laboratories, genome sequencing databanks, and health environmental records and need to be analyzed by using data science techniques [22].

The application of data science in genomics was addressed by Navarro *et al.* The huge amount of data generated by genomics researchers, the velocity of data in terms of speed in data generation and data analysis, and the variety of data in terms of phenotype and sequencing data are some characteristics of genomics data, which require data science techniques to conduct large scale data analyses. However, concerns over privacy issues in genomics related data and data ownership are some challenges that data scientists may face when working in genomics discipline [23].

Intensive care unit (ICU) is another setting in which a large amount of data is produced and data scientists can make the most of it to create prognostic and predictive models using machine learning algorithms. Prognosing the risk of mortality, predicting the likelihood of responding to a particular therapy, and calculating the risk of developing sepsis and septic shock are some examples of data science research in critical care. Moreover, unstructured clinical data such as discharge summaries, progress reports and nursing notes can be analyzed by natural language processing (NLP) for different purposes. Physiological waveform data collected by wearable devices and radiographic images are other sources of data useful for data science studies in critical care [24].

Radiotherapy is another field of medicine, which can benefit from data science studies. In this field, the technology and the principles of radiotherapy are combined together to verify cancer patient's requirements for being exposed to the radiations. Although the primary data, such as dosage, time, and the number of fractions are collected routinely, most of these details might be stored in the related department and in the separate systems. Like other fields of medicine, radiotherapists need to know predictive models of risk factors, toxicity, adjustment for disease stage, and survival rate. Analyzing data derived from patient-reported outcomes (PROs), ensuring the interoperability of databases, and developing ontology for procedures are of particular interest in radiation oncology, which can be addressed by data science research studies [25].

Data science for child health was proposed by Bennett et al. [26]. As congenital conditions mainly present in childhood, there are many opportunities to conduct research in the fields of proteomics, genomics, and metabolimics to identify diseases and their related issues by using data science methods. Identifying phenotypes, predicting models of care for patients hospitalized in the neonatal or pediatric ICU, identifying physiomarkers, genetic diagnosis of rare diseases, and medication management are examples of research topics in which data scientists can collaborate with pediatricians. Moreover, as clinical trials in the field of pediatrics are much fewer than this type of research among adults, it seems that data science can provide high-quality evidence for the current and future research [26].

In terms of injuries and violence prevention, data science can help to overcome a number of challenges such as the lack of access to real-time data, inability to recognize health threats, and the lack of integration between clinical information systems. Developing data sources, accelerating data collection, processing, and disseminating data via integrated information systems, predicting future changes in injury and violence burden, developing data visualization techniques, and detecting outbreaks are some activities expected to be realized by using data science techniques [27].

Public health data science includes data-driven processes which focus on protecting and promoting public health. Similar to other applications of data science in medicine, big data, statistical and computational approaches, prediction models, and interdisciplinary work are the fundamental aspects of public health data science. Data analytics techniques can help to identify the burden of diseases, disparities, causal effects and the impact of interventions [28].

Surgical data science has brought new insight to surgical care. It means that surgical care needs to be evolved over time not only to be updated by medical knowledge, but also to involve patients, information technology and care givers. Moreover, evidence-based decision making should be used along with the surgeon's experience. This evidence derives from large-scale data and various databases. Surgical data science aims to improve the quality of interventional procedures, which are performed to diagnose, prognose, or treat a disease or a condition. Therefore, a large amount of data is produced which are related to the patient's condition before intervention, the intervention-related data, and the outcome and care process data after intervention. Developing decision support systems, especially by using artificial intelligence techniques, providing surgical training and context-aware assistance are some areas that data science can be used in surgical domain [29].

The application of data science in genomic nursing is another example. In this field, the main aim is to use omics data in different aspects of nursing care. In fact, omics data can be regarded as big data due to their inherent characteristics, such as complexity and size. These data are also used in genomics, proteomics, prenatal screening, pharmaceutical safety, oncology therapeutics, and metabolomics research. The genomic nursing data science focuses on using big omics data to explore a variety of disease-related phenotypes biology. Analyzing gene expression patterns, identifying transcriptomes, and comparing epigenome DNA methylation patterns are some research activities that can be supported by the use of data science techniques in this field [30].

12.5   Health Data Science Challenges

Although there are many datasets and the new ones are quickly created, challenges ahead of using health data science should not be underestimated. Some of these challenges are related to data accessibility, data quality especially in the unstructured data, current skills and capability for data analysis, and managing public trust in health data sharing and research [6, 14]. Each of these challenges is discussed below.

The accessibility of data might be hindered by "hard" and "soft" barriers. Hard barriers include legal, technological and financial constraints and "soft" barriers are related to the ethical issues over data sharing [31]. Regarding ethical issues, some researchers believe that health care data should be made available to them without any limitations, while data custodians are concerned about compromising data privacy and confidentiality. Moreover, the digitization of health records has caused new ethical concerns over data sharing. Therefore, it is necessary for the data users to reach an agreement about the type of data that can be collected and the purposes and methods that the data will be used [6, 31]. Providing standardized consents for different databases and encrypting datasets to make calculations on the encrypted data without getting access to the personal identification data are some recommendations to overcome privacy concerns. As data privacy is related to a larger issue, which is data ownership, it seems that more clarification on the value of data, especially when they are shared and analyzed, will be helpful to prepare public and health care organizations to adopt this approach [23].

Data quality can also influence the process of data analysis. In fact, data collection is a fundamental part of a research project, and the quality of the results and the extracted knowledge is highly dependent on the quality of the collected data. However, the quality of data in databases might be low mainly due to the inconsistency and redundancy of data or missing values in a database. Therefore, before conducting data analysis, data quality verification and preprocessing is necessary [22]. The quality of data collected by new data sources, such as sensors and the quality of linked data bases are of high importance, too. Data linkage between different data sources may cause negative impact on data quality due to a lack of unique identifiers to share data across different sources [6, 31]. Therefore, these data need to be harmonized before analysis to be able to use and compare them [22].

Although health data science is a new emerging and demanding field of knowledge, there is a lack of training opportunities to offer effective courses in this field. As a result, there is a shortage of skilled workers and experts in this area which should be taken into account. Apart from the mentioned challenges, it seems that obtaining public trust to get access to health records on a large scale is difficult. In fact, people need to be reassured about respecting data privacy, while their data are shared and used for other purposes [6, 31].

Other concerns are related to the appropriateness of data for research and analysis. For example, there is a dispute over the weaknesses of retrospective data for assessing causal effects. Moreover, the available data might be useful for patient care, but not for being used in research. Despite these concerns, the researchers believe that routine data can be collected and used in low cost, and they usually show a representative sample and setting. So, they can be used for different types of research [32]. Apart from data collection, clinicians expect to see successful implementation of data-driven systems. These systems must produce effective outputs to help clinicians to make a right decision, at the right time and for the right patient. Therefore, not only the quality of data but also the quality of systems is important to be safely used for patients. To achieve this, collaboration between clinicians and data scientists can help to focus on the vital issues which are important in clinical practices. Although perceived loss of autonomy due to the use of sophisticated data science techniques may arise among some clinicians, most of them acknowledge the fact that medicine is complex and the cognitive capacity of clinicians is limited. Therefore, they need some extra assistant to consider different influencing factors and make the best clinical decisions for patients [24].

12.6   Health Data Science and Semantic Technologies

In healthcare settings, current and relevant data should be collected and many decisions should be made in a short time. While a large volume of data and information is available in these settings, it is important to make relevant data and information accessible for anyone who needs to use them [33]. As a result, the issues of data and database integration as well as data linkage have to be taken into account. To achieve this, semantic technology and semantic web technology are used to enable data interoperability and provide more powerful information services. The development of ontologies, semantic interoperability, information sharing, system integration, and knowledge management are some examples of using semantic technologies in health care [34]. However, the characteristics of health care data, a considerable amount of knowledge in each domain and the traditional environment of health care delivery are real challenges which need to be taken into account before using new technologies [6].

Semantic technologies are used as a knowledge representation paradigm to encode the meaning of data. The use of semantic technologies is also popular to support decision making; however, most automated systems use syntactic rules [34]. Semantic technologies are technical methods that facilitate the interpretation of meaning by machines and their goals are to help machines to understand data. Some of the well-known technologies to achieve these goals are ontologies, web ontology language (OWL) and resource description framework (RDF). These technologies are used to explore the meaning of data [35].

Similarly, semantic web (SW) is another technology which refers to the meaning of data, when they are linked together. While basic semantics are used in the search engines with tags and may not be useful when data are linked, semantic web makes a web of data linked together to build a context that follows a language construct [36]. Semantic web is the extension of the current web which enables better interoperability between health information systems and better interaction between human and computers. Ontology is a fundamental part of semantic web to represent the knowledge of domain and to facilitate connection between information systems [37].

The semantic web architecture includes five layers. These are uniform resource identifier (URI), which identifies the available resources on the Internet, extensible mark-up language (XML), which helps users to create web pages and supports information sharing across the web, and resource description framework (RDF), which is used to describe objects and resources. RDF schema is used to provide basic elements for ontology and web ontology language (OWL) is applied to facilitate interoperability among different sources. The proof layer is related to the representation of logics to identify documents and the trust layer supports the use of digital signatures [36].

According to He *et al.* semantics technologies in health care engineering and data analytics can be divided into three categories of a) natural language processing and data mining, (b) clinical data sharing and data integration, and (c) ontology engineering and quality assurance (QA) [38]. These technologies are discussed in the following sections.

12.6.1   Natural Language Processing (NLP)

As mentioned before, natural language processing (NLP) can explore knowledge from semi-structured or unstructured medical data and is applied to support clinical research and practices [39]. NLP includes a set of techniques to transform narrative text into datasets that can be analyzed by statistical methods and machine learning algorithms. The sources of data can be patients' medical records, social media, and patients' experiences and preferences, which are documented in different data sources [40]. NLP techniques are used in various domains, such as identifying at risk populations, health interventions, health outcomes, disease surveillance, knowledge translation, environmental scanning, and health promotion [41]. Automated text classification is another popular application of NLP [39]. However, despite the advantages of NLP techniques, the unavailability and low data quality may hinder using this technology [41]. Data mining is another popular type of research in health care, which helps to identify causes of diseases, appropriate medical interventions, and efficient health care policies. It also helps to cluster patients or health issues with similar conditions. This approach facilitates making decisions by clinicians and policy makers [42].

12.6.2   Clinical Data Sharing and Data Integration

With an increase in the use of electronic health records (EHRs) and health information systems (HIS) in the health care settings, health data are produced and stored more than before [35]. This amount of data needs to be explored and transformed into valuable information to improve health care processes. However, data sharing is not easy, and there are various challenges ahead of this process. Some of these challenges are associated with data integration, system interoperability, ontology development and its visualization, increasing the volume of health data and semantic data repositories, and the need for developing new user friendly interfaces. Therefore, semantic technologies, such as semantic web have been used to overcome these challenges [36].

It is notable that data sharing and data integration can support meaningful data analytics [38]. However, clinical data deals with signs, symptoms, medications, and lab results. These data can be shared if they are collected in a standard and structured format. Moreover, many data analysis techniques need to use structured data [36]. As big data is coming from different sources, the traditional methods of data collection and designing health information systems may not be appropriate anymore and need to be replaced with new methods to make effective use of information technology in both collecting and analyzing health data [39].

To overcome data sharing issues, the interoperability standards are used as a bridge to integrate and exchange data among multiple sources. The process of interoperability can be categorized into functional and semantic processes. Functional interoperability deals with common procedures and semantic interoperability deals with a language that a machine can understand in a communication. To make applications fully interoperable developing standards, such as vocabulary or ontology, data interchange and integration standards, and health record maintenance standards are necessary. Moreover, it is necessary to develop good interfaces for semantic web applications. Semantic interoperability of data can help different users and organizations to get the maximum benefits from the collected data [36].

12.6.3 Ontology Engineering and Quality Assurance (QA)

In healthcare environment, most of data are narrative or provided in an unstructured format. Therefore, the use of ontologies has been suggested as a method for collecting and sharing data in a defined format [43]. Ontology describes concepts, relationships between things, and categories within a domain [35, 43]. In fact, without well-defined metadata, it is not possible to manage and analyze large health datasets and ontologies are required to organize health datasets semantically [36]. While a thesaurus provides expanded terms of a basic taxonomic classification, ontology defines concepts with their semantic meaning and relations to other concepts for better interoperability between multiple vocabularies [42]. Ontology can also be used for semantic similarity measurement, improving system performance and semantic web applications, eliminating or decreasing conceptual and terminological confusions in a domain, and providing a common understanding of the concepts to facilitate interoperability, communication and reusability [36, 43, 44]. Furthermore, ontologies are essential for developing knowledge-based and expert systems [45, 46].

Ontology is a model or an abstraction of a domain, which is understandable by both humans and machines [39]. In addition, a case-base ontology can be used to improve semantic retrieval algorithms. However, the development of ontology is a labor-intensive task and various methodologies can be used for ontology development [45]. The use of ontologies in biomedical research and clinical applications are limited mainly due to the complexity of the related ontologies, missing relationships, and missing concepts [36].

Generally, ontologies can be classified into upper-level and domain ontologies based on the level of specificity. Upper-level ontology includes general concepts, which are not dependent of a particular domain. However, a domain ontology shows the concepts which are related to a particular domain [45]. Upper-level ontologies are usually used as a starting point for developing other ontologies. These ontologies include general classes of a domain. The ontology for general medical science (OGMS) is an example of a top-level ontology, which includes general classes, such as doctor, patient, disorder, and disease in medicine [47].

Upper-level ontologies can be divided into basic formal ontology (BFO) and general formal ontology (GFO). BFO can be used to facilitate the integration of information and GFO is used to integrate objects and processes in a coherent framework [41]. Descriptive ontology for linguistic and cognitive engineering (DOLCE) and object-centered high-level reference

(OCHRE) are other types of top-level ontologies. DOLCE makes the distinctions and the domain will be limited to the particulars, and OCHRE helps to integrate heterogeneous data from different sources with different terminologies [48]. The benefit of using upper-level ontology is supporting semantic interoperability and harmonizing the domain knowledge in different ontologies. The ontological reduction and the large scale ontology development method are other methods of ontology development [44].

Ontologies can be divided into two groups of application and reference ontologies based on the purposes of development. The application ontology includes a set of concepts required for a special application, and the reference ontology consists of the theories of a domain and the application purposes are not considered [44].

There are several methodologies for ontology development, some of them are well-structured, such as the Noy and McGuinness methodology and methontolog and some others, have been customized by the ontology developers. The semiautomatic methodology is also another method for ontology development in which different technologies, such as natural language processing (NLP), formal concept analysis (FCA), and universal networking language (UNL) are used to extract the main concepts. NLP can help to improve the linguistic comprehension of ontology. The FCA method deals with the mathematical concepts, and the UNL method transforms natural language into the computer language in a semantic network [44].

A formal ontology language for expressing ontologies is web ontology language (OWL), which is based upon a description language (DL). The latter is a language for knowledge representation and reasoning. The Manchester, RDF/XML and OWL/XML are other approaches to write ontologies. Query languages, such as SPARQL Protocol and RDF Query Language (SPARQL), are used to make queries over the ontology. The query languages can return information semantically and reduce information redundancy [44]. The study conducted by Kaur and Khamparia is an example of using SPARQL to query a liver ontology [49].

In the process of ontology engineering, the evaluation stage should not be neglected, as it helps to identify ontology problems and improves the development process [44]. In the process of evaluation, different automated, and semiautomated quality assurance methods can be used to identify the errors in ontology and improve its application [36]. Ontology evaluation methods can be divided into two groups of syntactic and logic-based approaches. In the syntactic approach, lexical structures of the ontology are explored and in the logic-based approach, the accuracy of the domain knowledge is investigated. The most common approaches of ontology evaluation are task-based approach, gold standard approach, criteria-based approach, and data-driven approach. The criteria-based approach includes expert-based and structure-based methods [44].

12.7   Application of Data Science for COVID-19

The use of data science techniques in relation to COVID-19 outbreak and biomedical data is also remarkable. While numerous research have been conducted in this area, there are still a number of challenges that need be addressed and many opportunities that can be used for future research. The SARS-CoV-2 virus has caused the outbreak of COVID-19 which was first identified in China in December 2019, and turned to be a pandemic on March 11, 2020. Many countries started to create databases and collected the disease-related data to be able to visualize the spread of COVID-19 and to generate predictive models of the disease outbreak. These data-sets usually include the data related to the COVID-19 cases at the local and national levels, patient demographics, locations, case reporting date, recoveries, and deaths. Not only the numerical data but also the textual data have been used to understand the nature and spread of COVID-19 [40]. Morcover, different technologies have been utilized to manage health care resources, treat patients, inform policy makers, handle uncertainties, and clinical trials [9].

Similar to other technologies, data science techniques played a significant role in developing computer vision algorithms to accelerate the process of disease detection and analyzing computed tomography (CTs) and chest x-rays [17, 46]. In addition, other techniques, such as artificial intelligence (AI) [50], deep learning algorithms [18], machine learning [51], natural language processing (NLP) and data and pattern mining [16] have been applied to improve health care professionals' and individuals' understanding about COVID-19. Overall, AI has helped to identify, track and forecast outbreaks, as well as diagnosing the virus and alerting. It is also used in computational biology and disease modeling, processing the health care claims, developing drugs, and coronavirus vaccine [18].

The risk assessment of potential patients and mortality rate is another opportunity to use data science and semantic technologies [46]. This approach is important, especially in the countries that the resources are limited. As the lack of proper screening is a major issue in many countries, using computational diagnostic tools would be helpful, particularly in developing countries that face with a shortage of staff and health care facilities or in large population areas, such as airports. Developing a system to calculate mortality risk for hospitalized COVID-19 patients [52] and screening and evaluation of COVID-19 by using CT images [53] are some examples of a large number of studies conducted in this domain. Contact tracing and monitoring social distancing, monitoring patients' conditions, as well as medications and vaccinations, are other applications of data science during COVID-19 outbreak. Not only predicting and screening the disease but also predicting the consumption of medical supplies can be performed by using data science techniques and different prediction models [46].

12.8   Data Challenges During COVID-19 Outbreak

There are some challenges associated with data collection and data analysis of infectious diseases, such as COVID-19. While the availability of big data in the health care settings may have a number of benefits for conducting research and reaching new models and results, in public health and especially in critical conditions, data are usually collected manually and cannot be disseminated easily. Moreover, there might be severe time lags to collect and present the correct data [54]. Since data collection process varies across different data sources, integrating them is another major challenge. A lack of well-defined and uniform data reporting mechanism may also hinder getting access to the data and timely data dissemination [53].

Another challenge might be related to the level of uncertainty about the data, which raises doubts about the accuracy of the results and models [55]. Even, data sources may provide the data with different level of precision [53]. Therefore, data uncertainty needs to be taken into account during data analysis [55]. Inconsistency and the lack of standard definitions regarding concepts, such as recovery from COVID-19, the prolonged symptoms of the disease and its impact on an individual's health status, and probable cases in different regions are other challenges. Although a number of definitions have been approved by World Health Organization (WHO), it is not clear how definitions are practically applied. Moreover, the definitions may change over time. Data privacy is another issue, which needs to be considered. In fact, the data should be anonymized to be analyzed and published [53].

Other challenges are related to a lack of ontology-based data integration, limited use of graph-based models, inefficient data analysis workflows, inadequate analysis of virus variants and their impact, and limited use of deep learning and other artificial intelligence models for drug discovery and timely disease prediction [56].

12.9   Biomedical Data Science

Biomedical data science refers to new insights into the biological knowledge for being used in medical diagnosis, treatment, and disease prevention [10]. Similar to other fields of health care and medicine, biomedical researchers including clinical research scientists and biologists can use their huge amount of data using data science techniques. They have access to big data and various datasets which can make research about DNA sequencing, molecular and cellular proteomics easier. However, the complexity of data in biomedical data science is much more than other health related data and any judgments or results interpretation need to be based on sufficient collaboration between data scientists and biomedical researchers [12].

There are some common aspects between biomedical data science and biomedical informatics. In fact, both of these fields deal with powerful techniques and tools to understand biological and health related issues. There are two arguments regarding these fields. The first one indicates that biomedical informatics has evolved over time and concentrated on using data science techniques to analyze biological data and to introduce a new field as biomedical data science [57]. The second one considers data science as a contributing discipline to biomedical informatics. In this perspective, adequate knowledge of data science is necessary for biomedical informaticians and the diversities between these two fields should be taken into account [58]. Although differences between these two are highlighted by some researchers, it seems that the collaboration between the scientists of both fields can facilitate gaining new knowledge in biomedical sciences.

Currently, biomedical data science is evolving to use the new technologies. For example, knowledge-based biomedical data science (KBDS) is an emerging theme in biomedical data science. The main concepts of this field are ontologies, semantic web standards, and knowledge graphs (KGs) [59]. KBDS involves the use of computer science in biomedicine, for example to interpret data, infer, and answer a natural language question. The computational methods for analyzing data depend on the internal and external knowledge representation and the knowledge representation is based on the ontology. To make the construction of ontologies clear, reusable and understandable, a set of international standards called semantic web standards has been developed. By using these standards, linking web-based elements is possible while their meanings are shared, too. Currently, the basis of most knowledge representation systems in biomedicine is semantic web standards along with biomedical ontologies [60].

Knowledge graphs are the knowledge bases that are represented as graphs. Although all knowledge bases are not implemented as graphs (because sometimes tables are used to organize the knowledge), sometimes the terms of "knowledge graph" and "knowledge base" are used interchangeably. Knowledge graphs help to create alternative representations of the main entities, infer new knowledge, and improve information retrieval. In biomedical data science, knowledge graphs can be applied to biological, clinical, and natural language processing concepts. However, some barriers of using knowledge graphs are related to data unavailability, a lack of standards for creating knowledge graphs, dependency upon the current resources, and data licensing issues [59].

It is notable that currently, with respect to the advancement of biological and medical sciences and in particular personalized medicine, big biomedical data are created that require appropriate technology to be handled and analyzed. Therefore, the next generation of biomedical data scientists needs to be trained specifically in biomedicine, data management, statistical analysis, data science and artificial intelligence techniques [10].

12.10   Conclusion

The huge amount of health care data has caused significant challenges in data management and analysis. This becomes more complex when data are coming from heterogeneous sources. It seems that semantic technologies can help to condense structured and unstructured data to generate new knowledge and overcome these challenges. As a result, different approaches such as data mining, natural language processing, and ontology engineering, are used to facilitate effective use of health care data. In addition, many new methods, platforms, and algorithms are developed to integrate, process, and analyze different types of health data and convert them to knowledge for better healthcare services. However, there are still certain challenges that need to be overcome via future research. Semantic data integration of IoT devices, developing new interfaces for searching and exploring semantic web technologies, and integration of machine learning algorithms or deep learning techniques into semantic technologies can be considered as future areas for research in health data science.

As the world is combating with COVID-19 outbreak, more multidisciplinary research is needed. Moreover, there are many opportunities to use modern technologies and COVID-19 big data to deal with the clinical and nonclinical difficulties caused by the disease. More attentions need to be paid to the quality of COVID-19–related data and creating a uniform data reporting system to improve data collection processes and support future data analysis. Biomedical data science can also help to reach a deeper understanding about COVID-19 and the methods of disease prevention, medication, and vaccination.

References

1. Zhan, Q., Health data science-A new science partner journal dedicated to promoting data for better health. *Health Data Sci.*, Article ID 9843140, 2021, 2021.
2. Thalhah, S.Z., Tohir, M., Nguyen, P.T., Shankar, K., Rahim, R., Mathematical issues in data science and applications for health care. *Int. J. Recent Technol. Eng.*, 8, 2S11, 4153–4156, 2019.
3. McPadden, J., Durant, T.J., Bunch, D.R., Coppi, A., Price, N., Rodgerson, K., Torre, C.J., Jr, Byron, W., Hsiao, A.L., Krumholz, H.M., Schulz, W.L., Health care and precision medicine research: Analysis of a scalable data science platform. *J. Med. Internet. Res.*, 21, 4, e13043, 2019.
4. Syed, L., Jabeen, S., Manimala, S., Elsayed, H.A., Data science algorithms and techniques for smart healthcare using IoT and big data analytics, in: *Smart Techniques for a Smarter Planet. Studies in Fuzziness and Soft Computing*, M. Mishra, B. Mishra, Y. Patel, R. Misra, (Eds.), pp. 211–241, Springer, Cham, Switzerland, 2019.
5. Jones, K.H., Laurie, G., Stevens, L., Dobbs, C., Ford, D.V., Lea, N., The other side of the coin: Harm due to the non-use of health-related data. *Int. J. Med. Inform.*, 97, 43–51, 2017.
6. MacPherson, Y. and Pham, K., Ethics in health data science, in: *Leveraging Data Science for Global Health*, L.A. Celi, M.S. Majumder, P. Ordóñez, J.S. Osorio, K.E. Paik, M. Somai, (Eds.), pp. 365–372, Springer, Cham, Switzerland, 2020.
7. Dhar, V., Data Science and Prediction. Working paper CeDER-12-01, 2012. http://hdl.handle.net/2451/31553.
8. Provost, F. and Fawcett, T., Data science and its relationship to big data and data-driven decision making. *Big Data*, 1, 1, 51 59, 2013.
9. Rehman, A., Saba, T., Tariq, U., Ayesha, N., Deep learning-based COVID-19 detection using CT and X-Ray images: Current analytics and comparisons. *IT Prof.*, 23, 3, 63–68, 2021.
10. Moore, J.H., Boland, M.R., Camara, P.G., Chervitz, H., Gonzalez, G., Himes, B.E., Kim, D., Mowery, D.L., Ritchie, M.D., Shen, L., Urbanowicz, R.J., Holmes, J.H., Preparing next-generation scientists for biomedical big data: Artificial intelligence approaches. *Per. Med.*, 16, 3, 247–257, 2019.

11. Brodie, M.L., What is data science?, in: *Applied data science, lessons learned for the data-driven business*, M. Braschler, T. Stadelmann, K. Stockinger, (Eds.), pp. 101–130, Springer, Cham, Switzerland, 2019.

12. Altman, R.B. and Levitt, M., What is biomedical data science and do we need an annual review of it? *Annu. Rev. Biomed. Data Sci.*, 1, 1, i–iii, 2018.

13. Abedjan, Z., Boujemaa, N., Campbell, S., Casla, P., Chatterjea, S., Consoli, S. *et al.*, Data science in healthcare: Benefits, challenges and opportunities, in: *Data Science for Healthcare: Methodologies and Applications*, S. Consoli, D. Reforgiato Recupero, M. Petković, (Eds.), pp. 3–38, Springer, Cham, Switzerland, 2019.

14. Agha-Mir-Salim, L. and Sarmiento, R.F., Health information technology as premise for data science in global health: A discussion of opportunities and challenges, in: *Leveraging Data Science for Global Health*, L.A. Celi, M.S. Majumder, P. Ordóñez, J.S. Osorio, K.E. Paik, M. Somai, (Eds.), pp. 3–15, Springer, Cham, Switzerland, 2020.

15. Bhavnani, S.P., Muñoz, D., Bagai, A., Data science in healthcare: Implications for early career investigators. *Circ. Cardiovasc. Qual. Outcomes*, 9, 6, 683–687, 2016.

16. Dash, S., Shakyawar, S.K., Sharma, M., Kaushik, S., Big data in healthcare: Management, analysis and future prospects. *Big Data*, 6, 54, 2019.

17. Leung, C.K., Chen, Y., Shang, S., Deng, D., Big data science on COVID-19 data, in: *14th International Conference on Big Data Science and Engineering (BigDataSE)*, Guangzhou, China, 31 Dec.-01 Jan, IEEE, pp. 14–21, 2021.

18. Kumar, A., Gupta, P.K., Srivastava, A., A review of modern technologies for tackling COVID-19 pandemic. *Diabetes Metab. Syndr.*, 14, 4, 569–573, 2020.

19. Le Glaz, A., Haralambous, Y., Kim-Dufor, D., Lenca, P., Billot, R., Ryan, T.C., Marsh, J., DeVylder, J., Walter, M., Berrouiguet, S., Lemey, C., Machine learning and natural language processing in mental health: Systematic review. *J. Med. Internet. Res.*, 23, 5, e15708, 2021.

20. Afshar, M., Phillips, A., Karnik, N., Mueller, J., To, D., Gonzalez, R., Price, R., Cooper, R., Joyce, C., Dligach, D., Natural language processing and machine learning to identify alcohol misuse from the electronic health record in trauma patients: Development and internal validation. *J. Am. Med. Inform. Assoc.*, 26, 3, 254–261, 2019.

21. Ulhaq, A., Khan, A., Gomes, D., Paul, M., Computer vision for COVID-19 control: A survey, in: *Electrical Engineering and Systems Science*, 2020.

22. Hueso, M., de Haro, L., Calabia, J., Dal-Ré, R., Tebé, C., Gibert, K., Cruzado, J.M., Vellido, A., Leveraging data science for a personalized haemodialysis. *Kidney Dis.*, 6, 385–394, 2020.

23. Navarro, F.C.P., Mohsen, H., Yan, C., Li, S., Gu, M., Meyerson, W., Gerstein, M., Genomics and data science: An application within an umbrella. *Genome Biol.*, 20, 1, 109, 2019.

24. Sanchez-Pinto, L.N., Luo, Y., Churpek, M.M., Big data and data science in critical care. *Chest*, 154, 5, 1239–1248, 2018.

25. Vogelius, I.R., Petersen, J., Bentzen, S.M., Harnessing data science to advance radiation oncology. *Mol. Oncol.*, 14, 7, 1514–1528, 2020.
26. Bennett, T.D., Callahan, T.J., Feinstein, J.A., Ghosh, D., Lakhani, S.A., Spaeder, M.C., Szefler, S.J., Kahn, M.G., Data science for child health. *J. Pediatr.*, 208, 12–22, 2019.
27. Ballesteros, M.F., Sumner, S.A., Law, R., Wolkin, A., Jones, C., Advancing injury and violence prevention through data science. *J. Saf. Res.*, 73, 189–193, 2020.
28. Goldsmith, J., Sun, Y., Fried, L., Wing, J., Miller, G., Berhane, K., The emergence and future of public health data science. *Public Health Rev.*, 42, 1604023, 2021.
29. Maier-Hein, L., Vedula, S., Speidel, S., Navab, N., Kikinis, R., Park, A. *et al.*, Surgical data science for next-generation interventions. *Nat. Biomed. Eng.*, 1, 691–696, 2017.
30. Dreisbach, C. and Koleck, T.A., The state of data science in genomic nursing. *Biol. Res. Nurs.*, 22, 3, 309–318, 2020.
31. Ford, E., Boyd, A., Bowles, J.K.F., Havard, A., Aldridge, R.W., Curcin, V. *et al.*, Our data, our society, our health: A vision for inclusive and transparent health data science in the United Kingdom and beyond. *Learn. Health Syst.*, 3, e10191, 2019.
32. Peek, N. and Rodrigues, P.P., Three controversies in health data science. *Int. J. Data Sci. Anal.*, 6, 3, 261–269, 2018.
33. Angele, J., Mönch, E., Nierlich, A., Oppermann, H., Rudat, H., Schnurr, H.P., Applications and good practices of semantic technologies, in: *Semantic Web*, T. Pellegrini, and A. Blumauer, (Eds.), Springer, Berlin, Heidelberg, 2006.
34. Leenen, L. and Meyer, T., Semantic technologies and big data analytics for cyber defence, in: *Information Retrieval and Management: Concepts, Methodologies, Tools, and Applications*, pp. 1375–1388, IGI Global, 2018.
35. Fürber, C., Semantic technologies, in: *Data Quality Management With Semantic Technologies*, pp. 56–68, Springer, Gabler, Wiesbaden, 2016.
36. Nagpal, P., Chaudhary, D., Singh, J., Knowing the unknown: Unshielding the mysteries of semantic web in health care domain. *ACI'21: Workshop on Advances in Computational Intelligence at ISIC 2021*, Delhi, India, February 25-27, 2021.
37. Alamri, A., Ontology middleware for integration of IoT healthcare information systems in EHR systems. *Computers*, 7, 4, 51, 2018.
38. He, Z., Tao, C., Bian, J., Dumontier, M., Hogan, W.R., Semantics-powered healthcare engineering and data analytics. *J. Healthc. Eng.*, 7983473, 2017, 2017. https://doi.org/10.1155/2017/7983473
39. Kukhtevich, I.I., Goryunova, V.V., Goryunova, T.I., Zhilyaev, P.S., Medical decision support systems and semantic technologies in healthcare, in: *Advances in Economics, Business and Management Research, Proceedings of the Russian Conference on Digital Economy and Knowledge Management (RuDEcK 2020)*, Feb 27-29, ATLANTIS Press, 2020.

40. Harrison, C.J. and Sidey-Gibbons, C.J., Machine learning in medicine: A practical introduction to natural language processing. *BMC Med. Res. Methodol.*, 21, 158, 2021.

41. Baclic, O., Tunis, M., Young, K., Doan, C., Swerdfeger, H., Schonfeld, J., Challenges and opportunities for public health made possible by advances in natural language processing. *Can. Commun. Dis. Rep.*, 46, 6, 161–168, 2020.

42. Tomar, D. and Agarwal, S., A survey on data mining approaches for healthcare. *IJBSBT*, 5, 5, 241–266, 2013.

43. Shojaee-Mend, H., Ayatollahi, H., Abdolahadi, A., Developing a mobile-based disease ontology for traditional Persian medicine. *Inform. Med. Unlocked*, 20, 100353, 2020.

44. Shojaee-Mend, H., Ayatollahi, H., Abdolahadi, A., Development and evaluation of ontologies in traditional medicine: A review study. *Methods Inf. Med.*, 58, 6, 194–204, 2019.

45. Shojaee-Mend, H., Ayatollahi, H., Abdolahadi, A., Ontology engineering for gastric dystemperament in Persian medicine. *Methods Inf. Med.*, 60, 1/2, 162–170, 2021.

46. Latif, S., Usman, M., Manzoor, S., Iqbal, W., Qadir, J., Tyson, G. *et al.*, Leveraging data science to combat COVID-19: A comprehensive review. *IEEE Trans. Artif. Intell.*, 1, 1, 85–103, 2020.

47. Ochs, C., Perl, Y., Geller, J., Arabandi, S., Tudorache, T., Musen, M.A., An empirical analysis of ontology reuse in BioPortal. *J. Biomed. Inform.*, 71, 165–177, 2017.

48. Machno, A., Jannin, P., Dameron, O., Korb, W., Scheuermann, G., Meixensberger, J., Ontology for assessment studies of human–computer-interaction in surgery. *Artif. Intell. Med.*, 63, 2, 73–84, 2015.

49. Kaur, P. and Khamparia, A., Diagnosis of liver cancer ontology using SPARQL. *Int. J. Appl. Eng. Res.*, 10, 69, 15–18, 2015.

50. Vinod, D.N. and Prabaharan, S.R.S., Data science and the role of artificial intelligence in achieving the fast diagnosis of Covid-19. *Chaos Solitons Fractals*, 140, 15-18, 110182, 2020.

51. Kim, M., Gu, Z., Yu, S., Wang, G., Wang, L., Methods, challenges, and practical issues of COVID-19 projection: A data science perspective. *J. Data Sci.*, 19, 2, 219–242, 2021.

52. Bertsimas, D., Lukin, G., Mingardi, L., Nohadani, O., Orfanoudaki, A., Stellato, B. *et al.*, COVID-19 mortality risk assessment: An international multi-center study. *PloS One*, 15, 12, e0243262, 2020.

53. Xie, H., Li, Q., Hu, P.F., Zhu, S.H., Zhang, J.F., Zhou, H.D., Zhou, H.B., Helping roles of artificial intelligence (AI) in the screening and evaluation of COVID-19 based on the CT Images. *J. Inflamm. Res.*, 14, 1165–1172, 2021.

54. Callaghan, S., COVID-19 is a data science issue. *Patterns (NY)*, 1, 2, 100022, 2020.

55. Saxena, N., Gupta, P., Raman, R., Rathore, A.S., Role of data science in managing COVID-19 pandemic. *Indian Chem. Eng.*, 62, 4, 385–395, 2020.

56. Kumar Das, J., Tradigo, G., Veltri, P., Guzzi, P.H., Roy, S., Data science in unveiling COVID-19 pathogenesis and diagnosis: Evolutionary origin to drug repurposing. *Brief. Bioinform.*, 22, 2, 855–872, 2021.
57. Brennan, P.F., Chiang, M.F., Ohno-Machado, L., Biomedical informatics and data science: Evolving fields with significant overlap. *J. Am. Med. Inform. Assoc.*, 25, 1, 2–3, 2018.
58. Payne, P.R.O., Bernstam, E.V., Starren, J.B., Biomedical informatics meets data science: Current state and future directions for interaction. *JAMIA Open*, 1, 2, 136–141, 2018.
59. Callahan, T.J., Tripodi, I.J., Pielke-Lombardo, H., Hunter, L.E., Knowledge-based biomedical data science. *Annu. Rev. Biomed. Data Sci.*, 3, 23–41, 2020.
60. Hunter, L.E., Knowledge-based biomedical data science. *Data Sci.*, 1, 1-2, 19–25, 2017.

## 13

Hybrid Mixed Integer Optimization Method for Document Clustering Based on Semantic Data Matrix

Tatiana Avdeenko* and Yury Mezentsev

Novosibirsk State Technical University, Novosibirsk, Russia

Abstract

Solving the problem of document clustering involves two fundamental stages. The first stage is preprocessing a text document and representing it as a data table suitable for subsequent application of data analysis methods. The second stage is actually the optimization clustering algorithm, which allows to achieve best dividing the document collection by thematic content. In present paper, we use a new approach to conceptual indexing of documents by transformation of a set of key terms to a weighted set of concepts of a certain hierarchical knowledge model of the application domain. The semantic matrix of document relationships with taxonomy concepts can be used as a data matrix for solving the clustering problem. For this purpose, we propose an original hybrid optimization approach based on two different mixed integer programming statements. The first statement is based on minimizing the sum of pairwise distances between all objects (PDC clustering), while the second statement is based on minimizing the total distance from objects to cluster centers (CC clustering). Computational experiments showed that the developed hybrid method for solving clustering problem combines the advantages of both approaches—the speed of the k-means method and the accuracy of PDC clustering, which makes it possible to get rid of the main drawback of the k-means, namely the lack of guaranteed determining the global optimum.

Keywords: Optimal document clustering, conceptual indexing, mixed integer programming, NP-hard problem

Corresponding author: tavdeenko@mail.ru

Archana Patel, Narayan C. Debnath and Bharat Bhusan (eds.) Data Science with Semantic Technologies: Theory, Practice, and Application, (323–346) © 2022 Scrivener Publishing LLC

13.1   Introduction

The work of modern organizations is accompanied by the creation, accumulation and use of a variety of electronic documents related to various business processes. With a huge number of documents, the urgent task is to increase the speed and relevance of searching for documents necessary for employees of the organization in their professional activities. Semantic technologies and machine learning are modern approaches to solving this problem.

Semantic technologies are a set of standards and methods which allow to describe the meaning of data (their semantics) and provide working with it. This scientific area has many overlapping terms with areas, such as information retrieval (IR), natural language processing (NLP). Data science uses methods of analyzing large amounts of data to solve problems of forecasting, classification, regression, clustering. The combination of semantic technologies with data science methods when working with unstructured data in the form of text documents can significantly improve the quality of the results obtained.

In this chapter, we consider the process of clustering the documents, which is aimed at finding natural clusters (subsets) of documents, and thus grouping them according to semantic topics in a collection of documents for their subsequent more efficient (quick and relevant) retrieval. In the field of data science, the data clustering problem belongs to the topic of unsupervised machine learning, when the distribution of objects by classes is not known in advance, in contrast to the classification problem, referred to supervised machine learning, when the belonging of objects to classes is known in the training set.

Document clustering is defined in [1] as an optimization process that is aimed at determining the partition of a collection of documents in such a way that the documents within each cluster are most similar (cluster compactness), but the resulting clusters would be as different as possible in semantic content (distinguishability of clusters). The process of document clustering can be broken down into two fundamental steps. The first stage is associated with preprocessing the documents and aims to transform them into a form suitable for data analysis. The second stage (clustering algorithm itself) is aimed directly at analyzing the data prepared at the first stage and dividing the documents into clusters.

Despite the importance of the clustering algorithm, one cannot underestimate the first stage of the clustering process, which is at least as important as the optimization algorithm itself [2]. Indexing is traditionally used as the first stage of document preprocessing, in which a collection of documents is replaced with a sequence of index terms (keywords). Index terms can be obtained directly from the document or generated indirectly using more complex algorithms. The existing methods of indexing differ, first, in different ways of defining index terms, and second, in different methods of calculating the importance of a term relative to the document under consideration [3]. Most of the indexing methods use traditional approaches using a set of terms (keywords), and the method of calculating the term frequency [TF]. In the process of applying these approaches, a plurality of index terms is defined and their weights is calculated based on the frequency of repetition of the term in the document. As a result, each document D is indexed by the vector TF. The higher is the weight of the term in the TF vector, the higher its importance in the document.

Despite widespread application methods using this approach to indexing suffer from the following disadvantages:

- do not make it possible to differentiate the semantic importance of each term in the document, since they assign weights based on the frequency of occurrence of the term, without taking into account the semantic importance of words in the document;
- do not take into account synonyms, polysemous words, etc., therefore, the document and centroid vectors may contain various index terms, which are, for example, synonyms [4];
- most likely lead to vectors of very large dimensions (full-text indexes).

To overcome the above disadvantages of classical indexing methods, the literature suggests approaches that add a semantic component to indexing techniques in various ways. Thus, in the study by Scott and Stan [5], a method is proposed that uses the Ripper algorithm, which was adapted to overcome the problem of multidimensionality and ambiguity to solve the problem of document classification. The authors use WordNet to extract a variety of synonyms and hyperonyms for each noun and verb in the corpus, and use this information to overcome the ambiguity problem. In addition, in this work, the hierarchy depth parameter is used for the first time to control the generalization level of a set of subordinate concepts. In the paper by Rajman *et al.* [6], EDR (electronic dictionary) is used to define the relationship of concepts with the keywords of the document. However, like the previous method, this approach does not completely solve the problem of eliminating ambiguity. The most advanced results are proposed in Barresi *et al.* [7]. The authors propose a conceptual indexing method, which consists in pairwise comparison of the document's keywords in order to find the most suitable concept (meaning) corresponding to the shortest path from one word to another on the graph corresponding to the taxonomy of knowledge. This article uses WordNet as the taxonomy of knowledge. As a result of applying this approach, for each document indexed by keywords according to the classical methodology, the authors receive a vector of "meanings" (concepts of the WordNet ontology) and corresponding weights for these concepts, which determine how closely this "meaning" matches the content of the document.

In present paper, we propose an approach that offers further improvement of the procedure for conceptual indexing of documents based on a knowledge model in the form of a taxonomy of concepts, and the presentation of information in a form convenient for subsequent clustering and retrieval of related documents. (As the specified taxonomy, the hierarchical basis of any subject ontology can be used.) We assume that each document has weighted relationships with some concepts of the specified taxonomy. The relationships can be determined either manually, by an expert in the relevant subject area, or automatically, for example, using the above-described document preprocessing approach proposed in [7]. Based on this information, it is proposed to construct a semantic matrix of document links with terminal (final) concepts of taxonomy, which can then be used as a data matrix for the subsequent application of data analysis methods, in particular, to solve the problem of document clustering.

To perform the second stage of document clustering, an optimization algorithm is proposed in present chapter, in which the formal statement of the problem is used in the form of computationally laborious mixed integer programming problem. The application of the proposed approach (see, for example, [8, 9]) is justified by obtaining the theoretically best (in the sense of a given optimality criterion) solution to the clustering problem. This was experimentally confirmed in comparison with the use of traditional clustering tools (for example, the k-center method [10]). In present work, we propose an improved version of the optimization method, which, on the one hand, can be applied to large-scale problems by reducing the computational complexity, secondly, gives the best values of the optimality criterion in comparison with traditional clustering techniques.

13.2   A Method for Constructing a Semantic Matrix of Relations Between Documents and Taxonomy Concepts

Suppose we have a collection of documents that need to be grouped, i.e. divided into clusters according to their semantic content. Each document is identified by a set of keywords that define its content. In addition, suppose we have some hierarchical model of knowledge representation (taxonomy or ontology, for example, WordNet) describing the application domain to which the documents belong.

Further, we assume that each document is assigned the required number of concepts (meanings) from the hierarchical knowledge model. This can be done either manually, for example, by application domain experts, or automatically. For example, the conceptual indexing method proposed in Kelmanov and Pyatkin [7] makes it possible to automatically determine a weighted set of concepts describing a separate document based on a finite set of document keywords:

$$D = \{ (C_1, v_1), (C_2, v_2), , \ldots, (C_I, v_I) \}.$$

We use notation C_i for the name of the concept and its weight value $v_i, 0 \leq v_i, \leq 1, \sum_{i=1}^{I} v_i = 1$, determining the strength of the relationship between the document and corresponding concept. The higher is the weighting factor v_i, the closer is the semantic meaning of the document to the corresponding taxonomy concept. We emphasize the possibility of determining a link between the document not only with one, but with several taxonomy concepts. This expands the expressive possibilities of the proposed approach, since it implies the possibility of describing an interdisciplinary problem at the junction of several concepts.

The concept selected for indexing a document C_i can be either a terminal taxonomy concept (having no subordinate child concepts) or a non-terminal (intermediate) concept. The need to determine a connection with a non-terminal (more general) concept may be due to the fact that this document describes a more general aspect of the concept.

Suppose we have J terminal concepts and for each terminal $kw_j, j = \overline{1, J}$ it is necessary to calculate the weight $w_j, j = \overline{1, J}, \sum_{j=1}^{J} w_j = 1$, based on the initial weights v_i connecting the document with the taxonomy, and also taking into account the hierarchical structure of the taxonomy. The procedure for calculating the weights $w_j, j = \overline{1,J}$ for terminal concepts $kw_j, j = \overline{1,J}$ can be constructed as follows. Suppose we have the document D related to taxonomy concepts $C_1, C_2, \cdots, C_I$.

1. First, we assign initial values to the weights of terminal concepts $w_j = 0, \forall j = \overline{1,J}$.
2. Cycle through all concepts $C_i, i = \overline{1,I}$, associated with the document:
   - if C_i is terminal concept $\left(kw_j = C_i = C_i^{(0)} \right)$, then $w_j = v_j$;
   - if C_i is non-terminal concept, i.e. terminal concept kw_j is a descendant of the L-th level of the intermediate concept $C_i, kw_j = C_i^{(L)}$, then $w_j = v_i \cdot \prod_{l=1}^{L} v_i^{(l)}$,

where $v_i^{(l)}$ is the weight of the hierarchical relationship $R_{ISA}\left(c_i^{(l-1)}, c_i^{(l)} \right)$ between the concept parent $C_i^{(l-1)}$ and the concept child $C_i^{(l)}$ on the path from the concept C_i, associated with the document to the terminal concept kw_j, as seen in Figure 13.1. If there are no weights of hierarchical relations in the taxonomy, then we can set the weights of the links emerging from one parent concept equal to 1/p, where p is the number of child concepts.

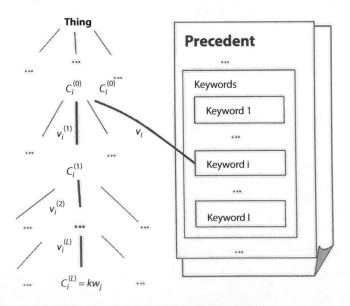

Figure 13.1 Calculation of the elements of the semantic matrix.

As a result of applying the above algorithm to each document from the analyzed collection, we obtain a semantic matrix of links, for which the number of lines is equal to the number of documents (objects in the data table), the number of columns is equal to the number of terminal concepts of the taxonomy. The elements of this table are numeric (values vary from 0 to 1), the sum of the elements in the row equals 1 according to the calculation procedure. It is possible to directly apply data analysis algorithms to this data table for the subsequent structuring of the document space, or for structuring the space of terminal concepts with the aim of a possible redesign of the taxonomy.

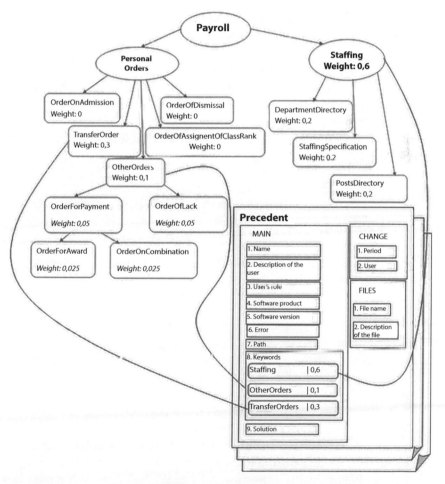

Figure 13.2 An example of calculating the strength of the semantic relationship of a document with terminal concepts of knowledge taxonomy.

As an example of the application of the proposed approach, let us consider the problem of clustering the documents concerning IT support of organization's information system. In [11], an ontology in the field of IT support was built, the hierarchical basis of which can be used as a taxonomy of concepts for indexing the documents. Figure 13.2 illustrates a fragment of a taxonomy (with three links, respectively, with weights $v_1 = 0.6$, $v_2 = 0.1$ and $v_3 = 0.3$ from the document Precedent to the concepts that are transitive closure of a concept *Payroll*. For this fragment of taxonomy, we have the following subvector of weights $\tilde{w} = \left(0 \ 0.3 \ 0.025 \ 0.025 \ 0.05 \ 0 \ 0 \ 0.2 \ 0.2 \ 0.2\right)^T$.

In a similar way, all documents were indexed with the corresponding concepts of the ontology (120 documents, 20 terminal concepts of the ontology common to the set of documents under consideration). As a result, a 120x20 semantic matrix was generated with the values of the weights as rows, which was further used as a data matrix for cluster analysis.

In the following sections, we will describe a general clustering method based on formal statements of mixed integer programming problems, which will be used to cluster documents. In this case, a semantic matrix obtained by applying the document indexing procedure is used as a data matrix.

13.3   Mathematical Statements for Clustering Problem

13.3.1   Mathematical Statements for PDC Clustering Problem

To perform clustering of a discrete number of objects, mathematical formulations were used in the form of intractable mixed integer programming problems. The application of this approach was substantiated, for example, in Kelmanov and Pyatkin [8], by obtaining the theoretically best (in the sense of a given optimality criterion) solution to the clustering problem. This has been confirmed experimentally in comparison with traditional clustering tools, for example, the k-means method [10].

The results of present paper are based also on the authors' results obtained in Mezentsev and Estraykh [9]. In the proposed method, after normalizing the initial data, a matrix of distances between all pairs of objects is calculated. We refer to this formulation of the problem as Pairwise Distance Clustering (PDC). In the experimental model, two criteria for the clustering quality were applied: minimax (for minimizing the maximum sum of distances between all pairs of objects in each cluster) and additive (for minimizing the total sum of distances between all pairs of objects across all clusters). Accordingly, the content of PDC problem consists in such a partition of the set of objects in the metric space into disjoint subsets, which minimizes the maximum sum of distances between all pairs of objects in each cluster (minimax criterion), or minimizes the total sum of distances over all clusters (additive criterion).

Let us present a formal statement of the PDC problem for given number of clusters m. Introduce the following notations. Let $i, j = \overline{1,n}$, be the object numbers; $l, k = \overline{1,m}$ - cluster numbers; $p_{i,t}$ - the value of the t - th coordinate (t - th indicator) for the i-th object, $t = \overline{1,T}$,; $c_{i,j}$ - distance between the objects i and j, $i, j = \overline{1,n}$, $c_{i,j}^k$ - distances between the objects i and j in cluster k, for example, Euclidean distance $c_{i,j}^k = \left(\sum_{t=1}^{T} \left(p_{i,t}^k - p_{j,t}^k \right)^2 \right)^{1/2}$.

First, we define the variables y_i^k identifying the belonging of objects $i, j = \overline{1,n}$ to cluster $k, k = \overline{1,m}$:

$$y_i^k = \begin{cases} 1, & \text{if object } i \text{ belongs to cluster } k, \\ 0 & \text{otherwise, } i = \overline{1,n}. \end{cases} \tag{13.1}$$

$$\sum_{k=1}^{m} y_i^k = 1, \quad i = \overline{1,n}, \tag{13.2}$$

We also define the dependent variables $x_{i,j}^k = y_i^k \cdot y_j^k, i = \overline{1,n}$, i.e.

$$x_{i,j}^k = \begin{cases} 1, & \text{if the objects } i, j: (y_i^k = 1, y_j^k = 1) \text{ belong to cluster } k, \\ 0 & \text{otherwise, } i, j = \overline{1,n}, \ i \neq j, \end{cases} \tag{13.3}$$

Thus, the introduced Boolean variables of the problem mean the inclusion or non-inclusion of an object or any pair of objects in a particular cluster. To introduce variables $x_{i,j}^k$ into the model, we will linearize the corresponding equations, replacing them with inequalities
$0 \leq y_i^k + y_j^k - 2x_{i,j}^k \leq 1, k = \overline{1,m}, i, j = \overline{1,n}, \ i \neq j$, which, for an asymmetric distance matrix, can be generalized to the inequalities

$$0 \le y_i^k + y_j^k - x_{i,j}^k - x_{j,i}^k \le 1, k = \overline{1,m}, i,j = \overline{1,n}, \ i \ne j. \qquad (13.4)$$

Now we add conditions that implement minimax criterion, which makes sense to minimize the maximum sum of distances between all objects in each cluster:

$$\sum_{j=1}^{n} \sum_{i=1}^{n} c_{i,j} x_{i,j}^k \le \lambda, k = \overline{1,m}, \ i \ne j. \quad \lambda \to \min \qquad (13.5)$$

As a result, we get a mathematical model (13.1)-(13.5) for solving clustering problem.

The minimax criterion (13.5) can be used to partition the initial set of objects into maximally homogeneous subsets with the simultaneous minimization of the sums of distances between the objects. In addition to criterion (13.5), in some cases, an additive criterion is more acceptable, which can be represented in the form:

$$\sum_{j=1}^{n} \sum_{i=1}^{n} c_{i,j} x_{i,j}^k = \lambda^k, k = \overline{1,m}, i \ne j. \qquad (13.6)$$

$$\sum_{k=1}^{m} \lambda^k \to \min, \qquad (13.7)$$

where λ^k is the sum of the distances between all pairs of objects in the cluster $k, k = \overline{1,m}$. The relations (13.6)-(13.7) can be presented in the equivalent form

$$\Lambda = \sum_{k=1}^{m} \sum_{j=1}^{n} \sum_{i=1}^{n} c_{i,j}^k x_{i,j}^k \to \min.$$

The solution of problem (13.1)-(13.4), (13.6), (13.7) makes it possible to find partitions of the set of objects into a given number (m) of clusters, which guarantees minimization of the sum of the minimum total distances between all pairs of objects across all clusters.

Let us discuss the complexity of both mathematical statements (13.1)-(13.5) and (13.1)-(13.4), (13.6), (13.7) of the clustering problem. We do not provide a formal proof of the NP-hardness of the presented formulations of the statements, since it requires their reduction to any known NP-complete problem, which in itself may turn out to be a hard problem. Only note that with a significant simplification of the limiting conditions of any of the above statements, we obtain an NP-hard mixed integer programming problem. In particular, subproblem (13.1)-(13.2), (13.5) is interpreted as NP-hard problem of optimizing the schedules of unconnected parallel machines by criterion $C_{max} = \max\{C_1, C_2,...,C_n\}$, where C_j is the completion time of job j. The proof of its NP-hardness can be found, for example, in [12, 13]. Taking into account additional limiting conditions, the complexity of the above statements increases many times, as evidenced from computational experiments.

Let us show how we can somewhat weaken the complexity of the statements (13.1)-(13.5) and (13.1)-(13.4), (13.6), (13.7). For this, we use relaxation with respect to auxiliary Boolean variables $x_{i,j}^k$, removing the integer conditions (13.3). Instead, we introduce the variation limits for continuous variables:

$$0 \le x_{i,j}^k \le 1, k=\overline{1,m}, i,j=\overline{1,n},\ i \neq j. \tag{13.8}$$

Relaxations of the statements (13.1)-(13.5) and (13.1)-(13.4), (13.6), (13.7) we denote, respectively, as (13.1), (13.2), (13.4), (13.5), (13.8) and (13.1), (13.2), (13.4), (13.6)-(13.8).

Since the prospects for the development of efficient approximation algorithms acceptable in terms of accuracy for the formulated models are rather vague, we will use conditionally exponential algorithms, the success of which in practice strongly depends on the actual number of integer variables. In this sense, relaxations (13.1), (13.2), (13.4), (13.5), (13.8) and (13.1), (13.2), (13.4), (13.6)-(13.8) have significant advantages over statements (13.1)-(13.5) and (13.1)-(13.4), (13.6), (13.7). Indeed, we note a decrease in the number of Boolean variables in relaxed problems by the value $m \cdot n^2$. The total number of Boolean variables (13.1) in the statements (13.1), (13.2), (13.4), (13.5), (13.8) and (13.1), (13.2), (13.4), (13.6)-(13.8) equals $m \cdot n$ in the presence of $m \cdot n^2 + 1$ continuous variables (13.7) and (13.8), against $m \cdot n (1 + n)$ Boolean variables in the statements (13.1)-(13.5) and (13.1)-(13.4), (13.6), (13.7).

Let us assume the equivalence of the statements (13.1)-(13.5) and the statements (13.1), (13.2), (13.4), (13.5), (13.8), as well as the statements

(13.1)-(13.4), (13.6), (13.7) and the statements (13.1), (13.2), (13.4), (13.6)-(13.8) from the finding the optimal values of the variables y_i^k point of view. The above equivalence immediately follows from the hypothesis that the relations $x_{i,j}^k = y_i^k \cdot y_j^k$ and $0 \le y_i^k + y_j^k - x_{i,j}^k - x_{j,i}^k \le 1$ are equivalent not only for integer $x_{i,j}^k$, but also for $0 \le x_{i,j}^k \le 1$. In fact, the equivalence of conditions $0 \le y_i^k + y_j^k - x_{i,j}^k - x_{j,i}^k \le 1$ and $x_{i,j}^k = y_i^k \cdot y_j^k$, for $0 \le x_{i,j}^k \le 1$, has been confirmed only experimentally. More than 100 experiments with large-scale PDC problems have been carried out, in which no cases were recorded that refute the hypothesis.

Due to the universality of the presented formulations, standard mixed programming tools implemented in the latest versions of GUROBI and IBM CPLEX software systems are quite applicable for computations. However, as shown above, the proposed mathematical statements are NP-hard; therefore, there are no theoretically efficient algorithms, i.e., there are restrictions on the dimensions of the implementations. Nevertheless, for practical applications, algorithms have been sufficiently developed that can be designated as conditionally exponential. That is, despite the lack of efficiency evidence, these algorithms allow finding optimal, or close to optimal, solutions to hard problems in a reasonable time. An example of such an algorithm is the binary cutting and branching algorithm [14]. Its software implementation was used to find a solution to the clustering problems formulated above (13.1), (13.2), (13.4), (13.5), (13.8) and (13.1), (13.2), (13.4), (13.6)-(13.8).

13.3.2   Mathematical Statements for CC Clustering Problem

The use of the PDC mathematical tools presented in previous section has led to encouraging practical results. For a number of special cases, it was possible to achieve acceptable performance with an estimate of deviations from the optimum not exceeding 4%. However, in the general case, the problem of dimension for a variety of applied clustering problems remains relevant.

In the PDC mathematical statements (13.1), (13.2), (13.4), (13.5), (13.8) and (13.1), (13.2), (13.4), (13.6)-(13.8), metrics λ^k and λ are applied, being the sum of the distances between all pairs of objects in all clusters $k, k = \overline{1,m}$. However, quite often, the measures of distances of objects to the centers of clusters are used as a criterion for clustering. An example of such a criterion is the sum of squares of the Euclidean distances to the centers of the clusters with maximization of distances between the centers, which are implemented in the k-means method [10].

Let us consider the mathematical formulation of the clustering problem, focused on the cluster centers (CC clustering), and also compare the two presented formulations with each other. Denote

$z^k = \|z_t^k\|$ be a coordinate of cluster k center, $k = \overline{1,m}, t = \overline{1,T}$, T- dimension of the object description vector;

$p_i = \|p_{i,t}\|$ be a coordinate t of T-dimensional object $i, i = \overline{1,n}, t = \overline{1,T}$;

n^k be the number of elements in cluster;

$r_{i,t}^k = p_{i,t}^k - z_t^k$ be a coordinate t of vector r_i^k with origin in the center of the cluster k;

$r_i^k = \|r_{i,t}^k\|$ be Euclidean distance of the object i to the center of the cluster $k, k = \overline{1,m}, i = \overline{1,n}$,

$$r_i^k = \left(\sum_{t=1}^{T} \left(p_{i,t}^k - z_t^k \right)^2 \right)^{1/2} = \left(\sum_{t=1}^{T} r_{i,t}^k {}^2 \right)^{1/2}. \tag{13.9}$$

Based on the introduced notations, the clustering problem can be formulated as follows:

Find $y_i^k, i = \overline{1,n}, k = \overline{1,m}$, and $z_t^k, k = \overline{1,m}, t = \overline{1,T}$ such that

$$\sum_{i=1}^{n} \sum_{t=1}^{T} \left(p_{i,t} - z_t^k \right)^2 y_i^k \leq \beta^k, \quad \sum_{k=1}^{m} \beta^k \to \min \tag{13.10}$$

under conditions

$$y_i^k = \begin{cases} 1, & \text{if object } i \text{ belongs to cluster } k, \\ 0 & \text{otherwise,} \quad i = \overline{1,n}. \end{cases} \tag{13.11}$$

$$\sum_{k=1}^{m} y_i^k = 1, \; i = \overline{1,n}, \tag{13.12}$$

$$z_t^k \geq 0, k = \overline{1,m}, t = \overline{1,T}. \tag{13.13}$$

In some cases, it is possible to supplement the statement with a restriction on the number of elements in clusters:

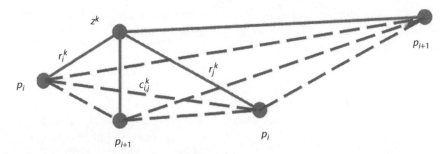

Figure 13.3 Relations of the distances r_i^k (r_j^k) of objects i, j to the center of the cluster z^k and the distances $c_{i,j}^k$ between pairs of object.

$$\sum_{i=1}^{n} y_i^k \geq n^k, \; k = \overline{1, m}. \tag{13.14}$$

An illustration of the variables $z^k, p_i, r_i^k, c_{i,j}^k$ for the 2-dimensional case is shown in Figure 13.3.

Thus, mathematical statement for CC clustering is defined by the relations (13.10)-(13.13). Formulations that are formally close to (13.10)-(13.13) are used in a number of clustering algorithms. It is known that problem (13.10)-(13.13) is NP-complete. For it, there are no approximation algorithms with a priori estimates of the proximity of solutions to optimal ones. However, there are many heuristic algorithms to solve it, including the k-means method.

13.3.3   Relations between PDC Clustering and CC Clustering

The hybrid clustering algorithm presented in the paper includes decision stages using both PDC clustering and CC clustering statements. Therefore, in this section, we analyze the relationship between the statement (13.10)-(13.13) and the statement (13.1), (13.2), (13.4), (13.6)-(13.8), as well as the relations between the coordinates of optimal solutions to the problem in both clustering statements.

We denote by $\tilde{y}^k = \left\| \tilde{y}_i^k \right\|, \tilde{x}^k = \left\| \tilde{x}_{i,j}^k \right\|, \tilde{\lambda}^k$, - the coordinates of the optimal solution to the PDC clustering problem (13.1), (13.2), (13.4), (13.6)-(13.8), by $\tilde{n}^k$ - the number of elements of the cluster k in the optimal solution, and then calculate the coordinates of the cluster centers $\tilde{z}^k$ for these solutions: $\tilde{z}^k = \dfrac{1}{\tilde{n}^k} \sum_{i=1}^{n} \sum_{t=1}^{T} p_{i,t}^k \tilde{y}_i^k$. Also let the optimal solution to the

C-problem (13.10)-(13.13) be known. Let us show its connection with the optimal solution of the PDC problem (13.1), (13.2), (13.4), (13.6)-(13.8).

If the cluster centers $\tilde{z}^k = \dfrac{1}{\tilde{n}^k} \sum\limits_{i=1}^{n} \sum\limits_{t=1}^{T} p_{i,t}^k \tilde{y}_i^k$ (it is quite obvious that

$p_{i,t}^k = p_{i,t}^k, k = \overline{1,m}$) calculated after solving the optimization problem (13.1), (13.2), (13.4), (13.6)-(13.8) are included into the set of clustering objects, then it is quite obvious that with the additional PDC partitioning each of the centers $\tilde{z}^k$ will be included into the corresponding cluster, and the centers of the clusters $\tilde{z}^k$ themselves will not change from such an extension. We will call this task extended PDC clustering.

Let us denote the coordinates of complementary objects (for which we put $i = 0$) and paired distances between the original and complementary objects by $p_0^k = \tilde{z}^k, c_{i,0}^k = r_i^k, k = \overline{1,m}$. The corresponding changes are shown in Figure 13.4.

The solutions to the extended PDC clustering problem will be denoted by $\tilde{\tilde{y}}^k = \left\| \tilde{\tilde{y}}_i^k \right\|, \tilde{\tilde{x}}^k = \left\| \tilde{\tilde{x}}_{i,j}^k \right\|, i, j = 0, \tilde{n}^k, k = \overline{1,m}$. It is quite obvious that

$\tilde{\tilde{y}}_i^k = \tilde{y}_i^k, \tilde{\tilde{x}}_{i,j}^k = \tilde{x}_{i,j}^k, i, j = \overline{1, \tilde{n}^k}, \tilde{\tilde{z}}^k = \tilde{z}^k = \dfrac{1}{\tilde{n}^k} \sum\limits_{i=0}^{n} \sum\limits_{t=1}^{T} p_{i,t}^k \tilde{\tilde{y}}_i^k, k = \overline{1,m}$, i.e., solu-

tions to the original and extended PDC clustering problems are the same for all $i, j = \overline{1, \tilde{n}^k}, k = \overline{1,m}$.

All distances between the calculated cluster centers $\tilde{z}^k(\hat{z}^k)$ can be set equal to infinity $\left(c_{0,0}^k = \infty \right)$ and further excluded from consideration. Then we can formulate the following problem of the minimum edge coverage of the complete graph for the original PDC clustering problem:

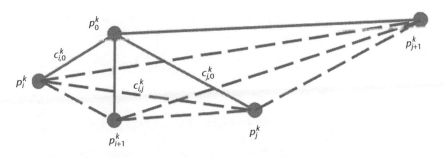

Figure 13.4 Geometric representation of cluster **k** objects for the extended PDC clustering.

$$\Lambda_0 = \sum_{k=1}^{m} \sum_{i=1}^{n} c_{i,0}^{k} x_{i,0}^{k} \rightarrow \min \tag{13.15}$$

$$\sum_{k=1}^{m} x_{i,0}^{k} = 1, \ i = \overline{1,n}, \tag{13.16}$$

$$\sum_{i=1}^{n} x_{i,0}^{k} \geq n^{k}, \ k = \overline{1,m}. \tag{13.17}$$

$$x_{i,0}^{k} = \begin{cases} 1, \textit{if the object i belongs to cluster k}, \\ 0, \textit{ otherwise} \end{cases} \tag{13.18}$$

The formulated problem is polynomially solvable, since it is a special case of the assignment problem, according to which constraints on variables (13.18) can be replaced by:

$$0 \leq x_{i,0}^{k} \leq 1, k = \overline{1,m}, i = \overline{1,n}. \tag{13.19}$$

The formulated problem (13.15)-(13.17), (13.19) has relations with both PDC and CC clustering problems. Indeed, on the one hand, it is equivalent to the above formulated CC clustering problem (13.10)-(13.14) with known cluster centers $\hat{z}^{k}$, where $y_{i}^{k} = x_{i,0}^{k}, k = \overline{1,m}, i = \overline{1,n}$. On the other hand, the problem (13.15)-(13.17), (13.19) can be considered as a special case of PDC clustering problem (13.1), (13.2), (13.4), (13.6)-(13.8), when the definition of m cliques with the minimum sum distance is replaced by the definition of m minimal edge coverings of these cliques.

We denote by $\hat{x}_{i,0}^{k}, k = \overline{1,m}, i = \overline{1,n}., \hat{\Lambda}_0 = \sum_{k=1}^{m} \sum_{i=1}^{n} c_{i,0}^{k} \hat{x}_{i,0}^{k}$ the optimal solution and its estimate for the problem (13.15)-(13.17), (13.19). Taking into account the above notations (13.10), one can also write $\hat{\Lambda}_0 = \sum_{k=1}^{m} \hat{\beta}^{k}$, where $\hat{\beta}^{k}$ is the calculated estimate for the cluster k.

Note the following properties of solutions to problems (13.1), (13.2), (13.4), (13.6)-(13.8), and (13.15)-(13.19) according to optimality criteria (13.6)-(13.7) and (13.15):

1. <u>Admissibility.</u> $\widehat{y}_i^k = \widehat{x}_{i,0}^k, k = \overline{1, m}, i = \overline{1, n}$ are the coordinates of the feasible solution to the problem (13.1), (13.2), (13.4), (13.6)-(13.8), due to the fulfillment of constraints (13.1), (13.2). Then conditions (13.4) and (13.8) ensure the fulfillment of the equalities: $\widehat{x}_{i,j}^k = \widehat{y}_i^k \cdot \widehat{y}_j^k, k = \overline{1, m}, i, j = \overline{1, n}, \ i \neq j,$, which means the fulfillment of all constraints (13.1), (13.2), (13.4), (13.8) for the values $\widehat{y}_i^k, \widehat{x}_{i,j}^k, k = \overline{1, m}, i, j = \overline{1, n}, \ i \neq j.$

2. <u>Optimality.</u> Let us show that the minimum of the criterion (13.6)-(13.7) is achieved on these admissible solutions under a number of conditions. To do this, consider the modified objective function Λ in comparison with Λ_0:

$$\widetilde{\Lambda} = \sum_{k=1}^{m}\sum_{j=1}^{n}\sum_{i=1}^{n} c_{i,j}^k \widetilde{x}_{i,j}^k, \ \widehat{\Lambda} = \sum_{k=1}^{m}\sum_{j=1}^{n}\sum_{i=1}^{n} c_{i,j}^k \widehat{x}_{i,j}^k, \ \widehat{\Lambda}_0 = \sum_{k=1}^{m}\sum_{i=1}^{n} c_{i,0}^k \widehat{x}_{i,0}^k$$

$$\widetilde{\Lambda}_0 = \sum_{k=1}^{m}\sum_{i=1}^{n} c_{i,0}^k \widetilde{x}_{i,0}^k$$

Note that for $\widetilde{x}_{i,j}^k = \widehat{x}_{i,j}^k$ and, $\widetilde{x}_{i,0}^k = \widehat{x}_{i,0}^k, \widetilde{\Lambda} = \widehat{\Lambda}$ and $\widetilde{\Lambda}_0 = \widehat{\Lambda}_0$ is true. The converse is also true under the assumption of non-uniqueness of optimal solutions.

At the same time, taking into account the linear relationship between the values of $c_{i,0}^k$ and $\widetilde{x}_{i,j}^k, k = \overline{1, m}, i, j = \overline{1, n}, \ i \neq j$ (see Figure 13.4), it can be assumed that there is a close relationship between the optimal solutions of both clustering problems (PDC and CC) $\widetilde{y}_i^k$ and $\widehat{x}_{i,0}^k, k = \overline{1, m}, i = \overline{1, n}$, which is confirmed experimentally. This does not mean equality of optimal solutions in general case, but indicates the proximity of estimates of optimal solutions measured in terms of performance criteria $\widetilde{\Lambda}$ and $\widehat{\Lambda}, \widetilde{\Lambda}_0$, and $\widehat{\Lambda}_0$.

The latter directly implies, first, the correctness of comparisons of the results of both PDC and CC clustering solutions; secondly, the possibility of applying linearized formulation of PDC statement (13.1), (13.2), (13.4), (13.6)-(13.8), with obtaining the initial values of the cluster centers coordinates from the training sample for the effective approximate solution of the problems of clustering big data.

13.4   Heuristic Hybrid Clustering Algorithm

The main drawback of the used CC clustering formulations of the form (13.10)-(13.14) is the use of heuristic algorithms (for example, the k-means algorithm), which not only do not guarantee the optimality of the partitions of the initial sets of objects into clusters, but can also lead to arbitrarily bad results [8]. On the other hand, the advantage of the heuristic algorithms is that its complexity does not actually depend on the dimensions of the problem, while solution of problems even of relatively low dimensions by the exact algorithms described in previous sections is often impossible.

In this regard, we propose a hybrid algorithm that combines optimization advantages of the exact methods at the initial stage with the speed of heuristic algorithms for solving simplified CC clustering problems at the final stage. Using the above-mentioned PDC clustering property of the statement (13.1), (13.2), (13.4), (13.6)-(13.8), to find close-to-optimal solutions for implementations containing up to 400 variables y_i^k, as well as the revealed relation between PDC and CC clusterings, the following algorithm can be proposed with the following two-stage computation scheme.

Algorithm A_e. (clustering n objects into m clusters)

1. Input of initial data: the size n_v of the training sample, the number of clusters m, zeroing the initial values of the clusters centers for the implementation of the original CC clustering problem (13.10)-(13.14). Setting the initial values of the clustering quality criteria $\hat{\Lambda} = 0, \widehat{\Lambda} = 0, \tilde{\Lambda}_0 = 0, \widehat{\Lambda}_0 = 0$.

   I stage of Algorithm

2. A representative base subsample of n_v objects is selected from the initial set of n objects, on which the implementation of direct algorithms for solving PDC clustering problems (13.1), (13.2), (13.4), (13.6)-(13.8) will be carried out to preliminary determine the centers of the clusters used at stage II. The number of bound Boolean variables y_i^k, equal to $m \cdot n_v$, has to, on the one hand, be large enough to ensure the accuracy of the optimal solution, and on the other hand, satisfy the upper constraints to overcome the complexity of the algorithms for solving PDC clustering problems. The representativeness of the base subsample is ensured by the equal choice probability.

3. Solving the PDC clustering subproblem (13.1), (13.2), (13.4), (13.6)–(13.8) with characteristics

$$y_i^k \in \{0,1\}, 0 \le x_{i,j}^k \le 1, k = \overline{1,m}, i, j = \overline{1,n_v} \; i \ne j \Lambda_v = \sum_{k=1}^{m} \sum_{j=1}^{n_v} \sum_{i=1}^{n_v} c_{i,j}^k x_{i,j}^k \to \min,$$

and accordingly, determining optimal or close to optimal solutions, which we denote as

$$\tilde{y}_i^k \; \tilde{x}_{i,j}^k, k = \overline{1,m}, i, j = \overline{1,n_v}, \; i \ne j, \tilde{\Lambda}_v = \sum_{k=1}^{m} \sum_{j=1}^{n_v} \sum_{i=1}^{n_v} c_{i,j}^k \tilde{x}_{i,j}^k.$$

4. Calculation of cluster centers in the base subsample

$$\tilde{z}_{vt}^k = \frac{1}{\tilde{n}_v^k} \sum_{i=1}^{n_v} p_{i,t}^k \tilde{y}_i^k, t = \overline{1,T}, k = \overline{1,m}, \tilde{z}_v^k = \frac{1}{\tilde{n}_v^k} \sum_{i=1}^{n_v} \sum_{t=1}^{T} p_{i,t}^k \tilde{y}_i^k,$$

where $\tilde{n}_v^k$ is the number of elements in the cluster $k, k = \overline{1,m}$.

II stage of Algorithm
5. Setting the initial values of the coordinates of the clusters centers for the implementation of the CC clustering problem (13.10)–(13.14): $\hat{z}^k = \tilde{z}_v^k, k = \overline{1,m}$, iteration number $l = 0$, criterion $\hat{\Lambda}_0^l := \hat{\Lambda}_0$.
6. Increasing the iteration number $l: = l + 1$.
7. Calculation of new values $c_{i,0}^k, k - 1, m, i = \overline{1,n}$. Solution of the polynomially solvable problem (13.15)–(13.17)

(13.19): $\hat{x}_{i,0}^k, k = \overline{1,m}, i = \overline{1,n}, \hat{\Lambda}_0^l = \sum_{k=1}^{m} \sum_{i=1}^{n} c_{i,0}^k \hat{x}_{i,0}^k$, calculation of new values of cluster centers

$$\hat{z}_t^k = \frac{1}{\hat{n}^k} \sum_{i=1}^{n_v} p_{i,t}^k \hat{x}_{i,0}^k, t = \overline{1,T}, k = \overline{1,m}.$$

8. Comparison of values $\hat{\Lambda}_0$ at the current and previous step. If $\hat{\Lambda}_0^l - \hat{\Lambda}_0^{l-1} = 0$, then go to 9. Otherwise, return to 6.
9. Found a solution to the original problem $\hat{y}_i^k(\hat{x}_{i,0}^k), k = \overline{1,m}, i - \overline{1,n}, \hat{\Lambda}_0, \hat{\Lambda}$.

Note that the algorithm does not guarantee the optimality of solutions to the problems (13.10)–(13.14) and (13.1), (13.2), (13.4), (13.6)–(13.8) in the general case. However, on real data it shows good results in comparison with other methods of optimal clustering in terms of accuracy and speed, which allows us to hope for its wide application for practical purposes.

13.5   Application of a Hybrid Optimization Algorithm for Document Clustering

This section presents the results of applying the hybrid clustering method to the considered problem of automatically partitioning a collection of documents into groups of similar topics. The semantic matrix of document links with ontology concepts obtained as a result of the proposed method of document indexing is used as a data matrix for solving the problem of cluster analysis.

The original meaningful statement of the clustering problem contains 120 objects, 20 features (terminal concepts of ontology). The number of clusters $m = 10$ was preliminarily agreed upon, consistent with the topics of the documents.

Initially, the PDC clustering model was directly applied to this problem. Direct application of the model (13.1),(13.2),(13.4),(13.6)-(13.8) for 10 clustering with limiting the computation time to an acceptable value led to the following results. Vector of total distances between the objects within clusters equals: λ = (45.262; 63.264; 49.271; 51.967; 48.968; 45.81; 54.579; 25.674; 49.976; 61.137) with a total criterion value of $\tilde{\Lambda} = 495.908$. The number of elements in the clusters (12; 13; 12; 12; 12; 11; 12; 8; 11; 17). This result, due to the high dimension of the NP-difficult PDC clustering problem, did not guarantee any measure of proximity to the optimum, which mediated the need to reduce the dimension dimensionality reduction by applying decomposition. The decomposition was carried out according to the following two-stage hierarchical scheme:

1) selection of two clusters (disjoint subsets of objects);
2) sequential 5 clustering of each of the subsets formed at the first stage.

The final result of clustering with decomposition according to this two-stage hierarchical scheme was about 20% better than the initial one: $\tilde{\lambda} = (30.94; 44.18; 44.37; 32.76; 42.65; 40.88; 39.92; 46.12; 45.97; 32.90)$ with general criterion value $\tilde{\Lambda} = 400.68$ and the number of elements in the clusters (12; 13; 13; 10; 11; 11; 11; 16; 12; 11). The improvement in the result is explained by the possibility of a significantly larger approximation to the optima local for subproblems, due to the reduction in the dimensions of PDC implementations.

On the obtained solution $\tilde{y}_i^k \tilde{x}_{i,j}^k, k = \overline{1,m}, i, j = \overline{1,n}, i \ne j$, the follow-ing values of the extended PDC clustering problem $\tilde{\beta}^k, k = \overline{1,m}$ and $\tilde{\Lambda}_0 = \sum_{k=1}^{m} \tilde{\beta}^k$ were achieved:

$$\tilde{\beta} = (3.82; 5.08; 5.10; 5.20; 6.01; 5.69; 5.58; 4.21; 5.85; 4.45), \tilde{\Lambda}_0 = 50.98.$$

The use of the hybrid algorithm A_e made it possible, based on the obtained result, to test experimentally the above assumptions regarding the solutions of the PDC and CC problems. In particular, it turned out that when using the initial centers of the clusters determined with the A_e, we obtained the following solutions in four steps

$$\hat{x}_{i,0}^k \left(\hat{y}_i^k \right), k = \overline{1,m}, i = \overline{1,n}:$$

$$\hat{\beta} = (3.73; 6.61; 3.18; 3.60; 6.42; 6.08; 4.90; 5.00; 6.57; 3.60), \hat{\Lambda}_0 = 49.69,$$

$$\hat{\lambda} = (30.27; 71.59; 20.74; 17.00; 50.39; 48.05; 27.38; 62.48; 56.50; 23.77),$$

$$\hat{\Lambda} = 408.17,$$

with the number of elements in the clusters (12; 16; 10; 8; 12; 12; 9; 18; 13; 10).

Minor differences in the results are clearly visible. The improve-ment $\hat{\Lambda}_0 = 49,69$ versus $\tilde{\Lambda}_0 = 50,98$ is about 2.6%. Deterioration $\hat{\Lambda} = 408,17$ versus $\tilde{\Lambda} = 400.68$ is about 1.9%. The composition of the clus-ters is also slightly different. The number of mismatches across the clusters is determined by the vector (2; 3; 3; 2; 1; 1; 4; 2; 1; 1).

Further, the results obtained were compared with the clustering results using the k-means algorithm implemented in Statistica 12 Advanced. Its direct application leads to the following results:

$$\hat{\beta} = (12.72; 4.23; 7.12; 5.58; 4.03; 1.71; 2.95; 7.97; 3.84; 2.12), \hat{\Lambda}_0 = 50.27,$$

$$\hat{\lambda} - (254.0; 37.28; 76.60; 14.63; 20.03; 6.70; 10.94; 79.26; 25.50; 8.12), \hat{\Lambda} = 533.04.$$

Using k-means, the following distribution of elements by clusters was obtained: (29; 13; 16; 10; 8; 7; 6; 15; 10; 6).

Thus, one can see a significant difference in the k-means solution com-pared to the results obtained using the hybrid algorithm. If the value of the criterion $\hat{\Lambda}_0 = 50.27$ turned out to be close to the obtained estimate of the solution by the hybrid algorithm $\left(\hat{\Lambda}_0 = 49.69 \right)$, then the parameter (in fact, the second criterion $\hat{\Lambda} = 533.04$) turned out to be almost 25% worse.

If we take into account the vector of the number of discrepancies in the distribution of solutions over clusters (41; 29; 26; 18; 8; 19; 7; 33; 23; 16), the unevenness of such a distribution, as well as its interpretation in terms of content, one can be convinced of the significant advantage of the clustering results obtained with use of the proposed hybrid algorithm.

13.6   Conclusion

The chapter proposes a hybrid exact clustering algorithm that combines mathematical statements of PDC and CC clusterings. The method was applied to the semantic matrix of document links with ontology concepts, obtained as a result of the document indexing method proposed by the authors. Based on the result of applying the method, the following conclusions can be drawn.

1. Optimal solutions to the PDC and CC clustering problems (mathematical statements (13.1), (13.2), (13.4), (13.6)-(13.8) and (13.10)-(13.14)) generally do not coincide.
2. Criterion Λ of the PDC clustering problem (13.1), (13.2), (13.4), (13.6)-(13.8) is much more informative than the criterion Λ_0. This follows from their geometric considerations (any clique in the graph carries more information than its edge cover).
3. The combined use of both formulations using two criteria and a hybrid algorithm that consistently uses them brings undoubted benefits, which is expressed in eliminating the shortcomings of the k-means method.

Acknowledgment

The research for this chapter is supported by Ministry of Science and Higher Education of Russian Federation (project FSUN-2020-0009).

References

1. Bolelli, L., Ertekin, S., Lee, G.C., Clustering scientific literature using sparse citation graph analysis. Proc. 10th European Conference on Principles and

Practice of Knowledge Discovery, in: *Databases (PKDD 2006)*, Germany, pp. 30–41, 2006.

2. Sedding, J. and Kazakov, D., WordNet-based text document clustering, in: *Proc. COLLING-2004 3rd Workshop on Robust Methods in Analysis of Natural Language Data*, pp. 104–113, 2004.

3. Sebastiani, F., Machine learning in automated text categorization. *ACM Comput. Surv.*, 34, 1–47, 2001.

4. Boubekeur, F. and Azzoug, W., Concept-based indexing in text information retrieval. *IJCSIT*, 5, 1, 1, 119–136, 2013.

5. Scott, S. and Stan, M., Text classification using WordNet hypernyms, in: *WordNet@ACL/COLING*, 1998.

6. Rajman, M., Andrews, P., Almenta, M.D., Seydoux, F., Conceptual document indexing using a large scale semantic dictionary providing a concept hierarchy, in: *Proc. Applied Stochastic Models and Data Analysis (ASMDA 2005)*, France, pp. 88–105, 2005.

7. Barresi, S., Nefti-Meziani, S., Rezgui, Y., A Concept based indexing approach for document clustering. *2008 IEEE International Conference on Semantic Computing*, Santa Clara, CA, pp. 26–33, 2008.

8. Kelmanov, A.V. and Pyatkin, A.V., NP-difficulty of some Euclidean problems of partitioning a finite set of points. *Comp. Math. Math. Phys.*, 58, 5, 852–856, 2018.

9. Mezentsev, Y.A. and Estraykh, I.V., On problems and algorithm of clustering and constructing optimal routes by speed criterion, in: *14th International Scientific-Technical Conference on Actual Problems of Electronic Instrument Engineering, APEIE 2018*, DOI: 10.1109/APEIE.2018.8546185 https://doi.org/10.1109/APEIE.2018.8546185.

10. MacQueen, J., Some methods for classification and analysis of multivariate observations, in: *Proc. 5th Berkeley Symp. on Math. Statistics and Probability*, p. 281—297, 1967.

11. Avdeenko, T.V. and Makarova, E.S., The case-based decision support system in the field of IT-consulting. *J. Phys. Conf. Ser.*, 803, 6, 2017.

12. Pincdo, M., *Scheduling Theory, Algorithms, and Systems*, 3rd. ed, p. 672, Springer, Springer Dordrecht Heidelberg, London, New York, 2008.

13. Lenstra, J.K., Shmoys, D.B., Tardos, E., Approximation algorithms for scheduling unrelated parallel machines. Report OS-R8714, Centre for Mathematics and Computer Science, Amsterdam, 1987.

14. Mezentsev, Y.A., Binary cut-and-branch method for solving linear programming problems with Boolean variables. *2016 CEUR Workshop Proceedings*, EID: 2-s2.0-85019596857 http://ceur-ws.org/Vol-1623/paperco12.pdf.

## 14

Role of Knowledge Data Science During COVID-19 Pandemic

Veena Kumari H. M.* and D. S. Suresh

Department of ECE, Channabasaveshwara Institute of Technology, Gubbi, Tumkur, VTU Belagavi, Karnataka, India

Abstract

Corona virus disease 2019 (COVID-19) episode that was proclaimed as a pandemic by the World Health Organization (WHO) on March 11, 2020, has effectively had serious results in all parts of individuals' lives around the world. The pandemic has influenced more than 215 nations and has become a significant concern. As per the global data received on August 27, 2021, 5:33 pm CEST from WHO, there have been 214,468, 601 confirmed cases, and 4470969 deaths of the COVID-19. The global effect of the novel corona virus (COVID-19) necessitates precise forecasting of confirmed cases, as well as analysis of death and recovery rates. Prediction of the COVID-19 outbreak is an exceptionally important challenge. In this research work, a model fbprophet is used for the analysis of time series data which highly depend on the novel coronavirus 2019 dataset (https://www.kaggle.com/sudalairajkumar/novel-corona-virus-2019-dataset). This model is predicting the future trend of confirmed, recover, active, and death cases based on the available data from January 22, 2020 to May 29, 2021. The present model predicted the spread of COVID-19 for a future period of 30 days. The RMSE, MSE, MAE, and MdAPE metrics are used for the model evaluation. The outcome of this investigation would assist the concerned specialists with anticipating and contain future COVID-19 spreads productively.

Keywords: COVID-19, World Health Organization, time series forecasting, pandemic, fbprophet model, future prediction

---

*Corresonding author: veenasudhi30@gmail.com

Archana Patel, Narayan C. Debnath and Bharat Bhusan (eds.) Data Science with Semantic Technologies: Theory, Practice, and Application, (347–392) © 2022 Scrivener Publishing LLC

14.1   Introduction

On December 31, 2019, in Wuhan, China total of 27 pneumonia cases were identified [2]. Wuhan is the hottest city in China with a population of 11 million people. Infected cases were 20,000 in the middle of February but it is raised to 80,000 in March and around 4,000 deaths. In Europe by the beginning of March, 20,000 people got infected with 1,000 deaths [3]. The World Health Organization (WHO) stated corona virus disease 2019 (COVID-19) as a public health emergency on January 30, 2020. (WHO) was named this disease as COVID-19 [3]. It is named severe acute respiratory syndrome coronavirus 2 (SARS-CoV-2) by the International Committee on Taxonomy of Viruses (ICTV) on February 11, 2020, and officially named COVID-19. The illustration of SARS is shown in Figure 14.1. On January 15, 2020, the Ministry of Health Taiwan CDC, also named this disease as severe pneumonia with novel pathogens, and it could be the fifth category. Seventeen years ago, SARS-2003 a modifiable disease, which is caused by another beta coronavirus. On March 11, 2020, WHO announced COVID-19 disease as a global pandemic [3].

These patients have clinical symptoms of fever, dry cough, lung infiltrates on imaging, and fatigue. It happened in Wuhan's seafood wholesale market. Once the epidemiologic alert was announced, the market was shut down on January 1, 2020 [4]. January resulted in a very terrible outbreak in most of the cities in China. Further, the disease traveled and started to spread in other countries, like Thailand, Japan, the US, Vietnam, Korea, Germany, and Singapore. The disease has spread to 25 countries [6]. The first case was reported in India was on January 21, 2020. On January 7, 2020, Chinese

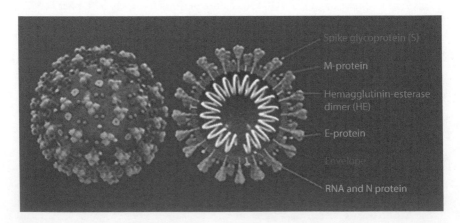

Figure 14.1 Illustration of the SARS-CoV-2 virion.

Center for Disease Control and Prevention (CCDC) conducted throat swab samples and identified the first causative agent. World Health Organization documented on February 6, 2020, a total of 28,276 confirmed cases and 565 deaths. It spread to a minimum of 25 countries [5].

Background

Coronavirus is a positive single-strand RNA virus and is a subfamily of orthocoronavirinae, which has "crown-like" spikes on its surfaces. The characteristic of the COVID-19 informs that transmission may be from droplets from an infected person to another person's nose and eyes [6]. Once the other person got infected, the person does not have any symptoms because of an incubation period. Generally, this incubation period is between 5 and 14 days [6, 7]. However, the person who got infected but had no symptoms may transmit the virus. The asymptomatic persons may also spread the disease.

Generally, the symptoms are fever, sore throat, cough, fatigue, headache [6, 7]. The rate of the infection is mild then 80% to 90% recovers without any major impacts and about 10% suffer from short breathing, and reduced oxygen saturation level need hospitalization. A 5% of people may suffer from respiratory malfunction and/or multiorgan failure, which leads to death. More common symptoms are shortness of breath of 31% to 55%, cough of 76% to 82%, and fever of 83% to 98%. The infected COVID-19 patients may die because of suffering from other diseases 5% got infected but it translates to 8,000,000 to hospitalize and occurred around 200,000, such as heart disease, asthma, and diabetes [8]. In Bangladesh, even with less population, say deaths. Because of these reasons, the hand sanitization, wearing a face mask, and social distancing have become important parameters in controlling the disease spread. Noticing the spread and critical wellbeing impacts, most of the researchers the assessed possible effect of the COVID-19 pandemic to give inputs to policymakers to get readies their particular nation's frameworks to confront this pandemic. The primary purpose of these assessments has been a support to strategy producers to execute solid nonpharmaceutical intervention (NPI), for example, social separating, hand cleanliness, and wearing of face masks, self-isolating, all to lessen the likely spread of the pandemic. Exploration has likewise discovered the testing, segregating, or isolating with the contaminated people might moderate the spread of the disease [9].

Many researchers attempted to comprehend the example of spread, in light of accessible information. In China, one model is created to plan the spread of COVID-19, and the equivalent is thought to be sufficiently exact for both reverse affirmation and forward extrapolation. In one more article, numerical devices are taken advantage of to comprehend the conduct of contaminations and foundation of forecast apparatuses if there should arise an occurrence of epidemics [10]. The forecasting procedure is likewise stretched out to the spread of COVID-19 in the Western World, and significant parameters like attack rate, turning point, and durations are considered for modeling. Generally, accessible information is displayed by different remarkable components, and the equivalent is utilized to foresee the idea of illness in the future. These assessments utilize epidemiologic models like the Suspected Infected Recovery (SIR) model [11–13] to extend the number of contaminated cases, the number of passing and expected interest for medical care, exceptionally clinic ICU use during the pandemic peak. Further researchers concentrated on the impact of NPI on the unexpected spread of the disease.

14.1.1   Global Health Emergency

The emergency committee has informed that the spreading of the COVID-19 is also interrupted by isolation, timely detection, and contacts. The WHO announces this is an epidemic Public Health Emergency of International Concern [PHEIC] [4, 8]. As per the global data received on August 27, 2021, 5:33 pm CEST from WHO, a total of 214,468,601 infected cases and 44,70,969 deaths of COVID-19 [14].

WHO classified the pandemic situation into four stages: stage 1 is the reported cases based on travel history. Stage 2 is people contacted with the affected area. The third stage situation is worse, the contamination becomes spread to the not traveled and the one who does not have contact with the infected person. This situation requires lockdown to reduce social contact to control the rate of infection [16, 17]. Figure 14.2 explains the transmission stages of coronavirus. Stage 4 becomes the epidemic. However, the initial place of infection is Wuhan, China, and it infected the USA, Italy, UK, Spain, and other countries. The unimaginable spreading of this disease can be able to calculate using machine learning models. Machine learning techniques are able to predict the epidemic forecasting if huge amounts of past data [18–29].

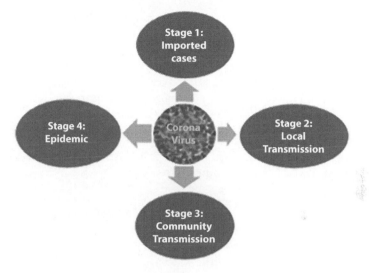

Figure 14.2 Transmission stage of corona virus.

14.1.2   Timeline of the COVID-19

Think Global health website is launched on January 21, 2020. It is a mul-
ticontributor site that inspects the manners by which changes in the
well-being are reshaping economies, social orders, and the regular daily
existences of individuals all over the world. This group has been intently
checking the development of COVID-19, the COVID-19 pandemic, and
its monetary and social outcomes. This timetable is a running record, accu-
mulated continuously [3]. According to Think Global Heath, as of 5:33 pm
CEST, August 27, 2021, total 214,468,601 confirmed cases and 4,470,969
deaths reported to WHO globally.

The timeline of the COVID-19 pandemic from January 2020 to
December 2020 is framed in Table 14.1, and the timeline from January
2021 to June 2021 is charted in Table 14.2.

This chapter is structured in the following manner: Section 14.1 contains an introduction. In Section 14.2, a brief discussion about related work
is carried out. Model discussion and implementation are in Section 14.3.
The experimental results are analyzed in Section 14.4 and Section 14.5 the
contribution of this research work is summarized.

Table 14.1 COVID-19 pandemic timeline from January 2020 to December 2020.

January 2020 – December 2020	
January	• Wuhan city is closed. • United States and Europe confirms first cases. • First cases appeared in many other countries. • India confirms its first case on January 30.
February	• Outbreaks started to grow in Iran, South Korea, and Italy. • New outbreaks in the Europe and America. • Outside China more deaths. • Travel restrictions increase.
March	• Nearly 1/3 of the population in the world started living under the coronavirus boundaries. • Worldwide, 1/5 of all students outside the school. • Europe becomes the epicentre. • Italy: the highest death tool country.
April	• Worldwide corona virus cases exceed one million. • The more deaths recorded in the united states in the world. • Americans unemployment is over 10 million. • China pledges 530 millions to the WHO.
May	• The global total cases reaches 4 million. • More than 10,000 health care workers tested positive in Iran. • The Coronavirus death cases in United states pass 100,000. • China flattens the curve.
June	• Global coronavirus death surpasses 500,000. • The total of daily new coronavirus cases highest report is in India and the United States. • China publishes white paper. • Vaccine trails in Africa begin.
July	• WHO announces independent coronavirus review. • Cases in United States and Brazil continue to Spike. • India passes one million cases. • South Korea's largest daily case reported, since from the March. • Worldwide 3rd highest death toll recorded in Mexico.
August	• India become third worst effected country. • COVID-19 cases in the Philippines passes 100,000. • Cases reached to March levels in Europe.

(Continued)

Table 14.1 COVID-19 pandemic timeline from January 2020 to December 2020. (*Continued*)

January 2020 – December 2020	
September	• An immune response was generated by Russian vaccine. • Over 500,000 children are diagnosed with COVID-19 in United states. • India reports over 83,000 daily new cases. • United States passes 7 million corona cases. • Global death passes one million.
October	• Global reported cases pass 40 million. • United States passes 100,000 in 1 day. • Less than 50,000 cases reported in India. • Singapore and Indonesia open their borders. • European Union become the new Epicentre of the pandemic.
November	• World Records 50 million cases. • Oxford and Astrazeneca announce interim results, which shows that the vaccine candidates are reduced the risk of symptomatic COVID-19 on an average 70 percentage.
December	• The United States grants emergency use of Pfizer BioNTech vaccine. • Pfizer BioNTech vaccine approved by EU. • SinoVac phase three trials completes in Brazil. • SputniK V vaccine registered by Belarus.

Table 14.2 COVID-19 pandemic timeline from January 2021 to June 2021.

January 2021 to June 2021	
January	• Turkey vaccinates over 600,000 people in two days • US COVID cases decline 16% • The AstraZeneca vaccine, first found in the United Kingdom, is very effective against the coronavirus • Global death poll passes 2 million
February	• The US ordered 70.5 million vaccine doses for COVID-19 • Russia's Sputnik V is confirmed over 90 percent effective • United states passes 500,000 deaths
March	• US 7-day vaccine passes 2 million • Johnson and Johnson wins WHO approval • AtraZeneca vaccine is safe • Covax vaccination deliveries are delayed

(*Continued*)

Table 14.2 COVID-19 pandemic timeline from January 2021 to June 2021. (*Continued*)

January 2021 to June 2021	
April	• India records over 100,000 new cases in a day • Vaccine expires in Africa • John Johnson is paused
May	• India become the first country: more than 400,000 cases recorded in a single day • Vaccine inequity widens • An Indian government panel decided to recommend the gap widening between first and second dose vaccines
June	• G7 nations promise to donate: a total of one billion vaccines to the world • WHO announces that the very soon the delta variant is likely to become globally dominant • The world reaches one billion vaccine dose administered

Source*: Think Global Health Pandemic.

14.2   Literature Review

Over the past decade, artificial intelligence played a key role in critical and epidemic issues of health care. Forecasting is the most promising area of machine learning. A variety of standard ML algorithms are used to predict the future which actions are required in many applications in different major areas like forecasting, stock market, and weather forecasting, as well as disease prognosis and disease forecasting in healthcare. Various models like regression, classification, and NN models have been widely used in future prediction for understanding the conditions of the patient with a specific disease. The research work has been carried out for the prediction of noncommunicable diseases using ML techniques, such as coronary artery disease, diabetes cardiovascular disease, and breast cancer. Machine learning (ML) has gained attention in developing epidemiological seek models for building outbreak prediction models [26–43].

This research study is mainly concentrated on COVID-19 live forecasting of active, confirmed, recovered, and death cases. These ML prediction systems can be exceptionally useful in decision making to deal with the current scenario to plan early interventions to control these diseases and to avoid disease spread. To contribute to this kind of information, various researchers are involved in the investigation of various patterns of the pandemic and produce the outcomes to help humankind. The prophet model is used for business forecasting like cash flow, air pollution, and also in emergency healthcare departments using time series data. This model is also used earlier to forecast other epidemics of diseases such as seasonal flu, influenza [18]. As of January 5, 2021, a year later worldwide, COVID-19 cases reached 90 million, and 2 million people last their life. However, the recovered numbers increased to 120,627,647 people.

Kucharski *et al.* [9] presented a logical model of SARS-CoV-2 spread by considering the different information to examine since Wuhan COVID-19 episodes. The investigation continued for disease outbreaks even outside Wuhan. Junyi Lu and Sebastian Meyer, 2020 [10] demonstrated that ML and Deep learning models are extensively used for the prediction of the outbreak. These models try to predict future trends based on historical data. Chen *et al.* [11] suggested that, by the influence of available huge data, machine learning can offer healthier results. The author concentrated on the compartment model to infectious diseases and model viruses epidemiologically. The SIR model most accepted model (S means susceptibility, I for infectious, and R represents recovered). Bhatnagar [12] proposed an updated mathematical model for the spread of COVID-19. The author concluded that Italy and the USA are in the 3rd stage of COVID-19 by the available data, whereas India will be in the second stage during April 2020. Estimation of new cases can be performed by using the proposed model easily. Ndiaye *et al.* [15] compared the model performances of different models polynomial regression, support vector regression prophet, linear regression, and MLP for the forecasting of COVID-19 in Senegal. They concluded that prophet and MLP give better performance based on the root mean square error. Tulshyan *et al.* [14] proposed a prophet model using data from March 2, 2020 to May 24, 2020, to predict the deaths in India. In this study, prediction accuracy was 87%.

Ndiaye *et al.* [23] proposed a model which gives better performance for the time series data which have seasonal effects. The model includes parameters like trend, holidays, and seasonality. Kumar and Susan [24] proposed Prophet and ARIMA model for forecasting the cases of COVID-19 in the ten most infected countries like the USA, France, Italy, Spain, Russia, Germany, UK, Iran, Turkey, and India. They concluded that ARIMA gave better performance based on MAE, RMSE, and other performance metrics. Lu and Meyer [25] suggested that Long Short-Term Memory networks (LSTM), Auto Regressive Integrated Moving Average (ARIMA), and Prophet are used in forecasting pandemic diseases. Wang *et al.* [26] proposed a hybrid logistic model and prophet model to calculate the peak, turn end, and the fastest growthing point of recovered cases. The author also concentrated on epidemic size in the world and also the rest of the high-risk countries, like Brazil, India, Russia, Indonesia, and Peru. Shek [27] proposed a regression model for predicting and forecasting the COVID-19 outbreak in India. The author used linear and poly nominal models for prediction. The model is predicted the number of confirmed, deaths, and recovered cases based on the dataset available from March 12 to October 31, 2020. Benvenuto *et al.* [28] proposed a model Auto Regressive Integrated Moving Average (ARIMA) for forecasting the COVID-19 spread. The Johns Hopkins epidemiological data is used to predict the trend COVID-19 incidence.

Literature reviews elucidate very clearly that data analysis exploits a better understanding of the current trends of the COVID-19 epidemic [26–43]. Machine learning techniques based on predictive models can predict the consequences of future dates. To add to this pandemic circumstance control, this review endeavors to perform future estimating on the death rate, the daily confirmed cases, and the number of daily recovery cases in the forthcoming 30 days.

14.3 Model Discussion

The major aim of this article is to collect the dataset, process, analyze, and visualize the result into its geographical form for easy understanding and further usages. The implementation methodology is as shown in Figure 14.3.

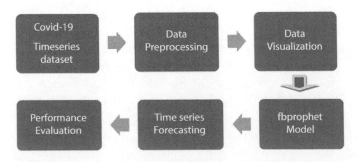

Figure 14.3 Flowchart of the implementation methodology.

14.3.1   COVID-19 Time Series Dataset

Any knowledge (data) to the time that is passionate about time-related information is called time series data. It could be a sequence of observations in time order. In such kind of data, we can see the trends, seasonality, and nonstationary supported on a daily, weekly, yearly basis. Time series analysis is the analysis of time data and the extraction of salient features from the data. Generally speaking, the idea behind the time series analysis is to build a model to describe the time series pattern. Time series forecasting is usually a complex task because the structure is already univariate data. This category of data is badly affected when any of the parameters is hampered. The data scientists research these data and can get valuable predictions out of it. Further, this can be used for future predictions or forecasting [24, 27].

In the present work, a novel coronavirus 2019 dataset (https://www.kaggle.com/sudalairajkumar/ novel corona-virus-2019-dataset) is taken from Kaggle (machine learning and data science community), which was taken from daily reports a huge dataset repository [1]. This dataset is last updated on 26.04.2021. This dataset contains data divided by country/region, describing all the daily cases in each country/region. The dataset contains information from the date of 22.01.2020 to 29.05.2021 in the data frame [1]. The objective is to know about the confirmed cases, recovered cases, number of deaths, and active cases. The dataset consists of one, and a half year daily recorded COVID-19 cases which have eight columns, i.e., observation date, state country, last updated, confirmed cases, recovered cases, and death cases. It has 306,040 rows, which covered global data of daily wise, state wise, country wise information the total active cases is equal to the number of confirmed cases minus the number of recovered cases and the number of death cases.

$$Active\ Cases[AC] = Confirmed\ Cases[CC] - Recovered\ Cases[RC] - Death\ Cases[DC].$$

$$(14.1)$$

The calculation of death rate (DR), active rate (AR), and recovered rate (RR) by using the mentioned equations:

$$AR = \frac{AC}{CC} * 100 \qquad DR = \frac{DC}{CC} * 100 \qquad RR = \frac{RR}{CC} * 100$$

$$(14.2)$$

(all the cases are taken in time from the initial day to....).

14.3.2   FBProphet Forecasting Model

AI strategies for forecasting algorithms are a part of software engineering that is trained from past data, such as decision trees, artificial neural networks, and deep learning [29]. The idea is to choose a reasonable preparing model as per the attributes of recorded information and use it to anticipate future perception results. We applied this method to COVID-19 estimating in reality. Predictive analysis of time series data can be analyzed by different machine learning models like long short term memory (LSTM), ARIMA, AR model, exponential smoothing, etc. The input data is provided to these models, and the prediction depends upon certain tweaking and fine tuning, which require suitable knowledge about the time series models [28]. The time series data models are also adapted for the COVID-19 disease since the cases and deaths are daily recorded. Among these models, auto regressive integrated moving average (ARIMA), LSTM networks, and Prophet are the most commonly used in forecasting epidemic diseases [29] [30]. They are widely used and accepted due to their more accurate forecasting capability. However, Prophet is much faster and simpler to implement than ARIMA and LSTM models [29, 30].

A Prophet is an open source time series forecasting algorithm released by Facebook's Core data science team. Even people who lack extensive experience with time series prediction models can be used to generate predictions for various problems. The current model has an advantage over other models that are accurate, and fast, because it is built in Stan (written in C++), a programming language for statistical inference. The models get fit in Stan, the forecasts will be in a very few seconds. Fully automatic, Prophet detects changes in trends automatically by selecting change points. It has an additive regression model. The nonlinear trends are fit with yearly, weekly, and daily seasonality, plus holiday effects. The tunable procedure includes many tweaks and adjusts forecasts possibilities. Available in Python or R. Prophet is very strong to outliers, dramatic changes, and missing data in the time series data [31, 32].

The Prophet is an open source structure of Facebook for time series estimating dependent on an additive model which is opened up to people in 2017. The Prophet is a time series model fitted with three main nonlinear trends (model components), such as yearly, weekly, daily seasonality, and with holiday effects. Prophet builds a model by finding the best smooth line the superposition y(t) which can be represented as a sum of the following components:

$$y(t) = g(t) + s(t) + h(t) + \epsilon(t) \qquad (14.3)$$

g(t): represents the trend for nonperiodic changes in time series, s(t): reflects the periodic changes of a week or a year (seasonality), h(t): effects of special day/days such as holidays, ε(t): error term, which occurs because of any unusual changes. The model could be overfitting or underfitting while working with the trend component [28, 29]. Because of built in change point inputs, the model fit is more flexible. In this review, we just consider the nonintermittent changes of time series. The study first explains the nature of epidemic growth and analyzes the growth and analyzes the preliminary exponential growth of the virus and calculates the growth ratio and growth factor [GF] of the epidemic. Generally, epidemics follow exponential growth because of the nature of the virus where infected people in turn infect others. The measurement of this growth with a positive constant is called the epidemic growth factor. This exponential growth is not continued throughout the epidemic but it will start to stabilize (growth factor =1) and gradually decreasing. This point is called the infection point [22, 23].

The pandemic growth factor can be calculated between two consecutive days by the number of cases yesterday divided by the cases of today.

$$GF \; for \; day(N) = \frac{Number \; of \; cases \; on \; day \; (N)}{Number \; of \; cases \; on \; day(N-1)} \qquad (14.4)$$

It will give an idea about the spreading of the virus, if the growth factor is equal to 1, it indicates yesterday and today cases are the same. If the growth factor is greater than 1 indicates growing and less than 1 indicates decreasing. For ex: the number of confirmed cases for January 25, 2021, is 936,426, and the number of confirmed cases for January 26, 2021, is 936,955. This gives a PGF of 936,955/936,426 = 1.00056 ~1. If the growth factor is 1, it indicates that both day's cases are almost the same (936955 − 936426 = 529) on January 26. The curve is flattening.

For predicting the number of future cases, the relationship is as follows:

Number of cases in future N days $= (number \; cases \; today) * (Pandemic \; growth \; factor) \wedge N$

$$(14.5)$$

The number of confirmed cases in West Bank and Gaza is on May 29, 2021, is 307,838. But in the future, 5 days cases are increasing. The confirmed cases are greater than projected cases. This sign indicates the average growth factor increases [33].

14.3.3   Data Preprocessing

The input to Prophet is constantly a data frame with two columns: the date and the target column and the remaining column ignored. Convert the date column to date time format and, then rename the two columns to date for "ds" and the target for "y." In our study. ds is the date of the day and "y" is the number of cases. The column 'ds' preferably YYYY-MM-DD format for date (date stamp) or YYYY-MM-DD HH:MM:SS for a timestamp [33]. Timestamp ("2021-05-29 00:00:00"). The target "y" column must be a numeric value that we wish to forecast. The prophet is used to generate a future dates forecast of all kinds of COVID-19 cases. Preferably, the forecast interval is 95 percentage [34].

14.3.4   Data Visualization

The COVID-19 dataset can be grouped country/region wise e confirmed, recovered, deaths, and active cases in Table 14.3. It consists of a total of 195 rows and 5 columns.

The above table illustrates that as of May 29, 2021, COVID-19 cases in Algeria 128456 infected cases, 89419 recovered cases and deaths are 3460. Likewise, 195 countries' cases are displayed [35–40].

The disease has been spread to 100 countries all over the world. The COVID-19 active cases are indicated in the world map as shown in Figure 14.4. The shaded color bar shown on the right side of the world map represents the country wise number of active cases in millions. The darker color indicates more active cases in the country. The US is having the highest five million cases, and India is having around three million cases [37]. The dataset used in this research is *covid_19_data.csv* from the kaggle repository [1]. The dataset has the trend and seasonality of the world data. COVID-19 has become a pandemic because it is contagious and can be transmitted through contact with the vector [38]. The number of future cases depends on the current cases. This is the main reason that past data can be fit into a machine learning model and used to predict new cases. From the graphical representation of the data shown in Figure 14.5, it can be seen that the data set has an upward trend.

Table 14.3 The country wise display of confirmed, recovered, deaths, and active cases.

	Country/ Region	Confirmed	Recovered	Deaths	Active
0	Afghanistan	70111	57281	2899	9931
1	Albania	132297	129215	2449	633
2	Algeria	128456	89419	3460	35577
3	Andorra	13693	13416	127	150
4	Angola	34180	27646	757	5777
.	.	.	.	.	–
.	.	.	.	.	–
.	.	.	.	.	–
190	Vietnam	6908	2896	47	3965
191	West Bank and Gaza	307838	300524	3492	3822
192	Yemen	6,731	3,399	1,319	2,013
193	Zambia	94,751	91,594	1276	1,881
194	Zimbabwe	38,933	36,578	1,594	761
195 rows × 5 columns					

From the above trend, we can observe that confirmed cases are exponentially increasing, which is indicated by a yellow line. It is good to see that recovery cases are shown in green areas in parallel with confirmed cases due to precautionary measures taken by WHO, government sectors, frontline warriors specifically medical professionals, and the public the ones who strictly followed the rules. The major reason for the increased recovery rate is due to vaccination. The active trend shown in the blue line just below the recovery cases shows that both infected and recovery is side by side, the active cases have a less exponential trend. Lastly, the death cases shown in red color indicates that, globally, it is constant.

Countries with Active Cases

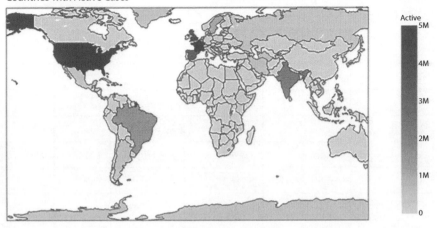

Figure 14.4 World map of COVID-19 active cases as of 29.05.2021. The darker the color indicates the more active cases in the country.

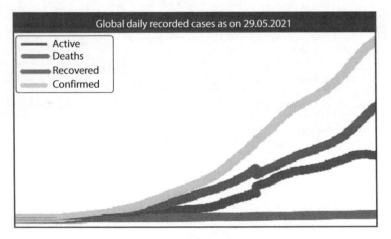

Figure 14.5 The graph depicts the observed date Vs data frame (because of the huge dataset, the data points are merged and invisible in the graph) The trend lines for active, confirmed, death, and recovered cases from the dataset worldwide daily recorded cases from the date of 22.01.2020 to 29.05.2021.

14.4 Results and Discussions

14.4.1 Analysis and Forecasting: The World

We try to build a framework using machine learning techniques for the potential prediction of cases caused by the coronavirus. The analysis provides details of regular estimates of total active cases, the total recovered cases and death occurred from corona virus.

This research is an attempt to estimate the number of the human being who could be affected by a new infection person, death and the total predicted recovery for the upcoming 30 days. In this study the dataset used for forecasting the trend of COVID-19 in global based on the epidemiological data from the date 2020-01-22 to 2021-05-29 [1], which will analyze the effectiveness of our proposed model. The most concerned countries worldwide and the countries' with highest COVID-19–infected cases are Brazil, India, the US, Russia, Peru, and Indonesia [38]. However, more data is required to predict the more detailed information. This fbprophet model will help us to predict confirmed, active, recovered and death cases for the future period of 30 days up to 2021-06-28. The new data frame consists of 584 rows and one column including the past data from 2020-01-22 to future data up to 2021-06-28 a forecasting of 30 days [35–40].

The yhat is the future predicted value based on historical dates and will provide an in sample fit. A new data frame will generate which includes a forecast value with the column **yhat** and well as columns **yhat_lower** and **yhat_upper** for components and uncertainty intervals.

The Table 14.4 (a), 14.4 (b), 14.4 (c), and 14.4 (d) depict the predicted output yhat of Active, death, Recovered, and Confirmed cases along with yhat_lower and yhat_upper boundaries respectively till 28th June 2021. The **yhat** is predicted output based on the input (historical data.). Yhat_lower and yhat_upper values are the intervals, i.e., predicted output fluctuations shown in the shaded area.

Figure 14.6 (a), Figure 14.6 (b), Figure 14.6 (c), and Figure 14.6 (d) show the actual, predicted dataset and also forecasting of the active, confirmed, recovered, and death cases respectively for the next 30 days. The predictions were made by the fbprophet library till June 2021. The solid blue line represents the actual historical data, and the light blue line is the predicted values yhat. The extension of light blue lines is the prediction of unseen data or future data on the extreme right ended curve and also light blue shaded area is an interval between the Yhat_lower and yhat_upper values. The forecasting may vary between these two values. In Figure 14.9 (a) and Figure 14.9 (c), the discontinuity in the solid blue line indicates that the active cases and recovered cases are almost minimal, in December 2020.

Figure 14.7, Figure 14.8, Figure 14.9, and Figure 14.10 show the trend, weekly and daily active, confirmed, recovered, death cases respectively. The daily fluctuations are almost similar in the graph because of the timely basis for the cases, but the weekly cases are different in each case. The graph indicates that the number of active cases least on Monday, whereas peak

Table 14.4 14.4 (a), 14.4 (b), 14.4 (c), and 14.4 (d) depict the predicted output yhat of Active, death, Recovered, and Confirmed cases along with yhat_lower and yhat_upper boundaries respectively till June 28, 2021.

(a)

	World: Active cases		
	ds	yhat_lower	yhat	yhat_upper
494	2021-05-30	6.172988e+07	6.310620e+07	6.461445e+07
495	2021-05-31	6.166504e+07	6.320948e+07	6.460629e+07
496	2021-06-01	6.200678e+07	6.343538e+07	6.484136e+07
....	....	....	....	....
521	2021-06-26	6.559461e+07	6.761228e+07	6.948117e+07
522	2021-06-27	6.569009e+07	6.778500e+07	7.015837e+07
523	2021-06-28	6.571191e+07	6.788829e+07	7.017920e+07

(b)

	World: Death cases		
	ds	yhat_lower	yhat	yhat_upper
494	2021-05-30	3.482382e+06	3.507186e+06	3.531838e+06
495	2021-05-31	3.491834e+06	3.516713e+06	3.541515e+06
496	2021-06-01	3.505323e+06	3.528786e+06	3.554801e+06
....	....	....	....	....
521	2021-06-26	3.741947e+06	3.805014e+06	3.876199e+06
522	2021-06-27	3.750157e+06	3.813376e+06	3.884599e+06
523	2021-06-28	3.755758e+06	3.822902e+06	3.896423e+06

(Continued)

Table 14.4 14.4 (a), 14.4 (b), 14.4 (c), and 14.4 (d) depict the predicted output yhat of Active, death, Recovered, and Confirmed cases along with yhat_lower and yhat_upper boundaries respectively till June 28, 2021. (*Continued*)

(c)

	World: Recovered cases			
	ds	yhat_lower	yhat	yhat_upper
494	2021-05-30	9.918581e+07	1.021795e+08	1.050268e+08
495	2021-05-31	9.968009e+07	1.026216e+08	1.056624e+08
496	2021-06-01	1.003324e+08	1.029938e+08	1.056910e+08
....	....	....	....	....
521	2021-06-26	1.106101e+08	1.138086e+08	1.166485e+08
522	2021-06-27	1.110728e+08	1.141594e+08	1.172026e+08
523	2021-06-28	1.111766e+08	1.146015e+08	1.178035e+08

(d)

	World: Confirmed cases			
	ds	yhat_lower	yhat	yhat_upper
494	2021-05-30	1.675364e+08	1.694723e+08	1.713928e+08
495	2021-05-31	1.679842e+08	1.700435e+08	1.720763e+08
496	2021-06-01	1.686320e+08	1.706675e+08	1.724697e+08
....	....	....	....	....
521	2021-06-26	1.825493e+08	1.864000e+08	1.905269e+08
522	2021-06-27	1.828668e+08	1.869600e+08	1.908155e+08
523	2021-06-28	1.834774e+08	1.875311e+08	1.921187e+08

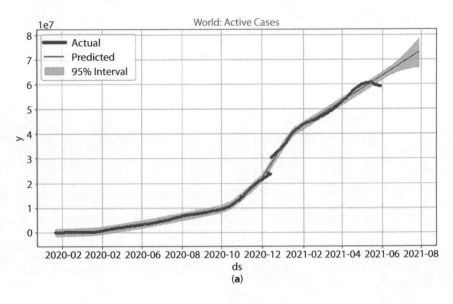

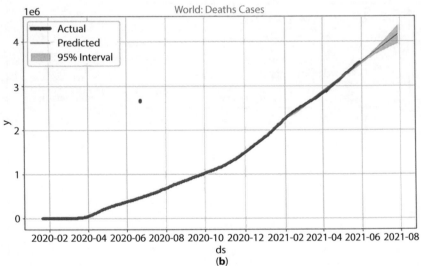

Figure 14.6 (a–b) shows the actual and predicted cases active, death, recovered, and confirmed cases till June 28, 2021.   (*Continued*)

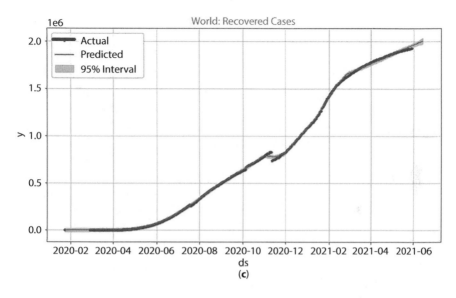

(c)

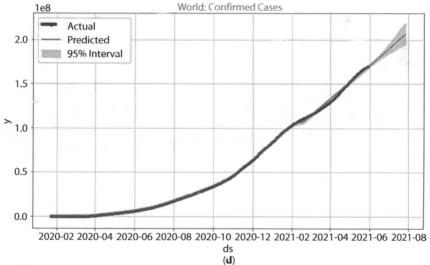

(d)

Figure 14.6 (Continued) (c–d) shows the actual and predicted cases active, death, recovered, and confirmed cases till June 28, 2021.

on Friday and decreasing on Saturday as shown in Figure 14.7. The confirmed cases are the same on Monday and Tuesday, whereas the maximum is on Friday as shown in Figure 14.8. The recovered cases are almost nil on Monday, minimum on Tuesday, and the recovery rate increases as the week grow as shown in Figure 14.9. The death cases are minimum on Monday, peak on Friday, and decreasing on Saturday. The curve is almost linear between Monday and Friday as shown in Figure 14.10.

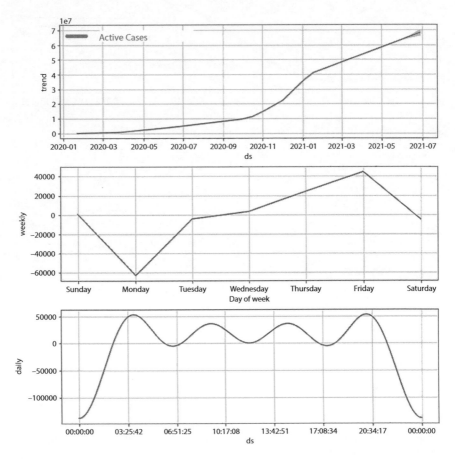

Figure 14.7 Trend, weekly, and daily cases of active case.

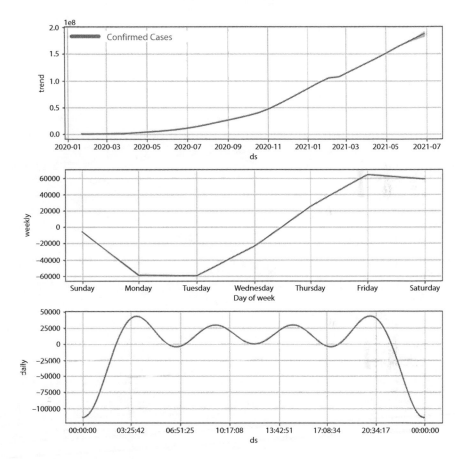

Figure 14.8 Trend, weekly, and daily cases of confirmed cases.

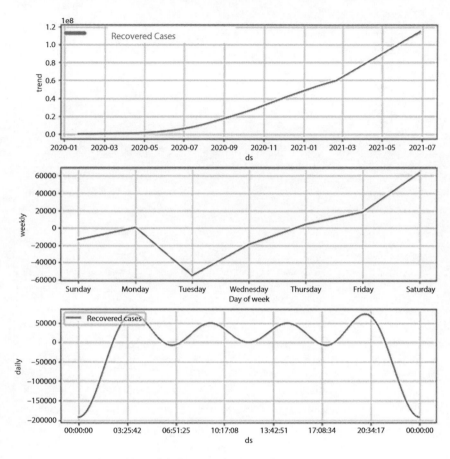

Figure 14.9 Trend, weekly, and daily cases of recovered cases.

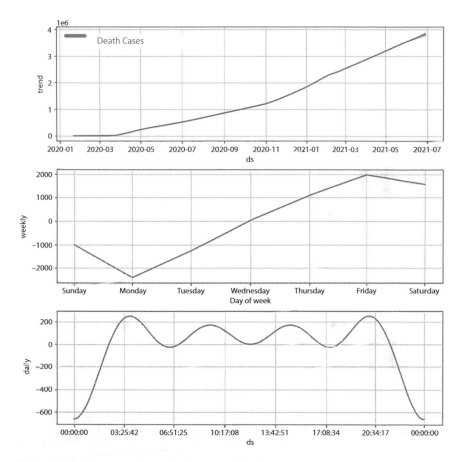

Figure 14.10 Trend, weekly, and daily cases of death cases.

14.4.2   Performance Metrics

The standard statistical metric used for the measure of model performance is the root mean square error (RMSE) in research studies and the other useful measure widely used for the model evaluation is the mean absolute error (MAE). For many years, both metrics are used for the calculation model performance. When both metrics are used for evaluating the MAE assigns the same weights to all errors but the RMSE assigns more weight for the errors with large absolute values and less weight for small absolute values. It is not limited to RMSE and MAE, MSE and MdAPE are also used to assess the model performance. In this study, we evaluate the model performance in terms of MSE, RMSE, MAE, and MAPE [41, 42].

Mean Square Error (MSE)

It estimates to determine the mean response time of the error and average square difference between the predicted values and real values. MSE is a risk function that corresponds to the expected [E] value of the loss of squared error. The error is almost pure positive values. The bigger value of MSE means the closest you are to finding the right match side [29].

$$MSE = \frac{1}{m} \sum_{j=1}^{m} (y_j - y_j)2 \tag{14.6}$$

where m = observed points, y_j = actual value and y_j =predicted points.

Root Mean Square Error (RMSE)

RMSE is the standard residual deviation. It is defined as the square root of differences between the observed and predicted values. The lower the RMSE the better a given model can "fit" a dataset. RMSE is sensitive to outliers. It is an error rate defined as follows

$$RMSE = \sqrt{\frac{1}{n} \sum_{j=1}^{n} (p - a)2} \tag{14.7}$$

N = observed data, p = estimated value and a = actual value.

Mean Absolute Error (MAE)

It is commonly used in model assessments. It is the calculation of errors that reflects certain performances expressing the same phenomenon like expected Vs actual, concurrent time Vs original time. MAE is suitable to illustrate the uniformly distributed errors. Model errors generally have normal distribution tan uniform distribution.

$$MAE = \frac{1}{m} \sum_{i}^{m} |y_j - y_j| \tag{14.8}$$

m = Total number of data points and $|y_j - y_j|$ = absolute value of residual.

Mean Absolute Percentage Error

The Median Absolute Percentage Error **(MdAPE)** is found by ordering the absolute percentage error (APE) from the smallest to largest using its middle value when N is odd or the average of the middle two values when N is even, as the median.

In this study, different model accuracy parameters used to analyze the performance of the fbprophet model are as shown in Table 14.4, Table 14.5, Table 14.6, and Table 14.7 for all the cases. If the MSE value is very high, then the

Table 14.5 Model performance for active cases.

	Horizon	MSE	RMSE	MAE	MAPE	MdAPE	C
0	9 days	4.067316e+12	2.016759e+06	1.137440e+06	0.089397	0.038832	
1	10 days	4.379153e+12	2.092643e+06	1.192019e+06	0.091284	0.044381	
2	11 days	4.683779e+12	2.164204e+06	1.245580e+06	0.093687	0.051808	
3	12 days	1.098935e+09	33150.186646	22901.408122	0.060927	0.053928	
4	13 days	1.237053e+09	35171.765573	24631.911531	0.065949	0.262222	

Table 14.6 Model performance for confirmed cases.

	Horizon	MSE	RMSE	MAE	MAPE	MdAPE
0	9 days	2.891632e+12	1.700480e+06	1.081914e+06	0.050139	0.029477
1	10 days	3.278147e+12	1.810565e+06	1.163599e+06	0.055113	0.031183
2	11 days	3.683958e+12	1.919364e+06	1.245885e+06	0.060132	0.033188
3	12 days	4.114823e+12	2.028503e+06	1.328824e+06	0.065100	0.035503
4	13 days	4.567764e+12	2.137233e+06	1.412593e+06	0.069997	0.037645

Table 14.7 Model performance for recovered cases.

	Horizon	MSE	RMSE	MAE	MAPE	MdAPE
0	9 days	8.855292e+11	9.410256e+05	565598.591861	0.049883	0.033770
1	10 days	9.372691e+11	9.681266e+05	596129.857684	0.055142	0.038910
2	11 days	9.973695e+11	9.986839e+05	627135.812520	0.060285	0.043208
3	12 days	1.101161e+12	1.049362e+06	663798.762800	0.065564	0.047667
4	13 days	1.207159e+12	1.098708e+06	699768.496180	0.070746	0.051617

model is a good one. The RMSE value is lower informs that the model is fit to the dataset. MAPE is inversely proportional to the accuracy of the model. The lower the value of MAPE, the higher is the model accuracy. The coverage is the difference between lower boundary y_hat lower and upper boundary y_hat upper, the spread area. The trend of the performance measures are shown in Figure 14.11, Figure 14.12, Figure 14.13, and Figure 14.14 for all cases.

Cross validation

It is a method of measuring forecast error by comparing the predicted value with the actual value using historical data. In this process, a cutoff point is selected from the last data, and the model is fitted with selected data up to the cutoff point, and then compares the actual value with the predicted value. In our study, we selected the horizon = 30 days, period = 15 days and Initial days = 90 days [43]. Computation for the forecast begins from end-horizon works backward and until initial is reached.

The RMSE scores are 2016759 to 3517176, and MdAPE scores are 0.038832 to 0.262222 from 9 days to 13 days by the horizon 30 days for active cases are as shown in Table 14.5. The RMSE scores are 1700480 to

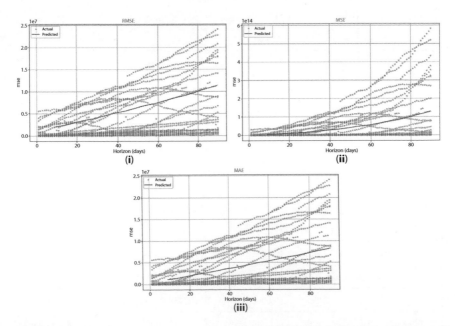

Figure 14.11 Trend of the performance measures (i) MSE, (ii) RMSE, (iii) MAE for active cases.

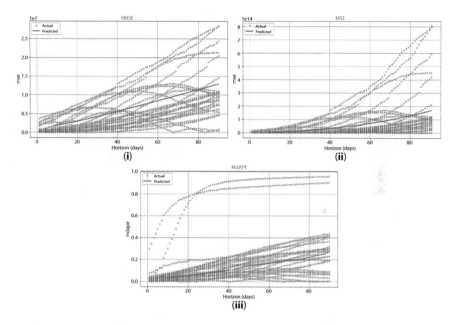

Figure 14.12 Trend of the performance measures (i) MSE, (ii) RMSE, (iii) MdAPE for confirmed cases.

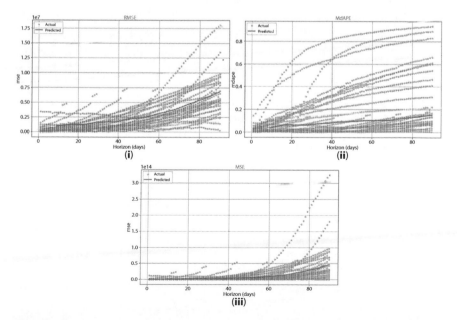

Figure 14.13 Trend of the performance measures (i) MSE, (ii) RMSE, and (iii) MAPE for recovered cases.

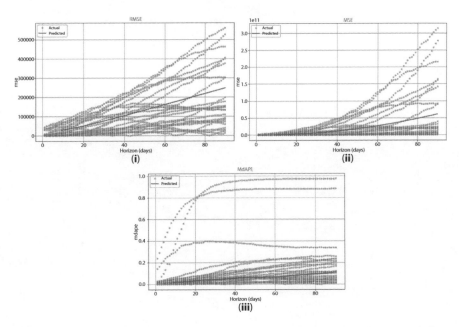

Figure 14.14 Trend of the performance measures (i) MSE, (ii) RMSE, and (iii) MAPE for death cases.

2137233, and MdAPE scores are 0.029477 to 0.037645 from 9 days to 13 days by the horizon 30 days for confirmed cases are as shown in Table 14.6. The RMSE scores are 9,410,256 to 1,098,708, and MdAPE scores are 0.033770 to 0.051677 from 9 days to 13 days by the horizon 30 days for recovered cases are as shown in Table 14.7. The RMSE Scores are 27549.30 to 35171.76, and MdAPE scores are 0.016248 to 0.019579 from 9 days to 13 days by the horizon 30 days for death cases are as shown in Table 14.8.

Table 14.8 Model performance for death cases.

	Horizon	MSE	RMSE	MAE	MAPE	MdAPE
0	9 days	7.589642e+08	27549.305379	18300.020931	0.045901	0.016248
1	10 days	8.622515e+08	29364.119708	19727.422174	0.050813	0.017158
2	11 days	9.741436e+08	31211.274217	21249.890385	0.055895	0.017880
3	12 days	1.098935e+09	33150.186646	22901.408122	0.060927	0.018857
4	13 days	1.237053e+09	35171.765573	24631.911531	0.065949	0.019579

14.4.3   Analysis and Forecasting: The Top 20 Countries

The top 20 countries of confirmed and recovered cases as of 29.05.2121 are displayed in Figure 14.15 and the corresponding bar graph of confirmed versus recovered cases in Table 14.9.

The US has the highest, with 33,251,939 infected persons, India has 27,894,800, Brazil has 16,471,600 cases, and Netherland, Czech Republic has the least infected cases among 20 countries.

From the graph, it is clear that the recovered cases are very promising in India, Brazil, Turkey, Russia, Italy, Argentina, Germany Colombia, Iran, Poland, Mexico, Ukraine, Peru, Indonesia, and the Czech Republic because of the proper execution of nonpharmaceutical intervention (NPI) [34]. For example, social separating, hand cleanliness and wearing of face covers, self isolating, whereas in US recovery rate is nil but poor recovery rate in France, UK, and Spain and in the Netherlands [14].

Analysis
The COVID-19 patients actual and predicted confirmed, deaths, recovered and actives cases of US, UK, Brazil, France, Colombia, Argentina, Spain, Peru, India, Italy, turkey, Germany, Russia, Poland, and Mexico on dated May 25, 2021, May 27, 2021, and May 29, 2021 listed in Table 14.10. As per the observation, the actual and predicted values are the same. Similarly, the future forecasting values of next 15 days by considering 5th day, 10th day, and 15th day are listed in Table 14.11.

Figure 14.16 depicts the actual, predicted, and 95% intervals in different countries. In Figure 14.16 (a) the active cases are peak in the month of

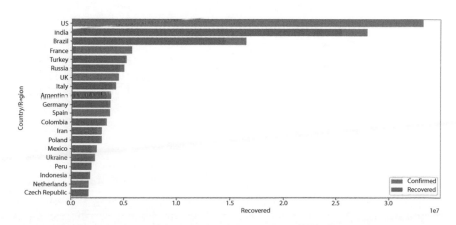

Figure 14.15 The world's top 20 countries recovered vs confirmed cases as on 29.05.2021.

Table 14.9 Display of top 20 countries confirmed and recovered cases as on 29.05.2021.

	Country/region	Confirmed	Recovered
0	US	33,251,939	0
1	India	27,894,800	25,454,320
2	Brazil	16,471,600	14,496,224
3	France	5,719,877	390,878
4	Turkey	5,235,978	5,094,279
5	Russia	4,995,613	4,616,422
6	UK	4,496,823	15,481
7	Italy	4,213,055	3,845,087
8	Argentina	3,732,263	3,288,467
9	Germany	3,684,672	3,479,700
10	Spain	3,668,658	150,376
11	Colombia	3,363,061	3,141,549
12	Iran	2,893,218	2,425,033
13	Poland	2,871,371	2,636,675
14	Mexico	2,411,503	1,924,865
15	Ukraine	2,257,904	2,084,477
16	Peru	1,947,555	1,897,522
17	Indonesia	1,809,926	1,659,974
18	Netherlands	1,671,967	26,810
19	Czech Republic	1,660,935	1,617,498

January 2021 in Argentina, in Figure 14.11 (c), the death cases are exponentially raising in Brazil, Active cases are flattening in Colombia in Figure 14.16 (d), but death cases are exponentially raising in Colombia (e) and France (f). Simultaneously, recovered cases are increasing in India (g), Indonesia (h), Poland (n) ,and Mexico (r). The death cases increasing in Spain (o), UK (p), and Italy (j). The active cases are increasing in US (q).

Table 14.10 COVID-19 patients actual and predicted confirmed, deaths, recovered and actives cases time series worldwide top countries on May 25, 2021, May 27, 2021, and May 29, 2021.

Country	Date	Confirmed		Deaths		Recovered		Active	
		Actual	Predicted	Actual	Predicted	Actual	Predicted	Actual	Predicted
UK	2021 - 05 - 25	4,483,177	4,515,878	128,001	129,010	15,453	15,681	4,339,723	4,371,713
	2021 - 05 - 27	4,489,552	4,522,906	128,020	129,315	15,480	15,776	4,346,052	4,378,375
	2021 - 05 - 29	4,496,823	4,530,998	128,037	129,461	15,481	15,871	4,353,305	4,386,258
US	2021 - 05 - 25	33,166,418	33,376,500	590,941	598,142	20,450,517	20,389,275	12,124,960	12,389,083
	2021 - 05 - 27	33,217,995	33,486,910	593,288	600,644	21,631,206	21,555,799	10,993,501	10,993,501
	2021 - 05 - 29	33,251,939	33,607,010	594,306	602,544	23,482,714	22,578,798	9,174,919	10,425,698
Brazil	2021 - 05 - 25	16,194,209	16,263,260	452,031	457,587	1,423,1991	14,356,170	1,510,187	1,447,676
	2021 - 05 - 27	16,342,162	16,411,850	456,674	462,890	14,455,810	14,475,470	1,429,678	1,472,961
	2021 - 05 - 29	16,471,600	16,550,710	461,057	467,807	14,496,224	14,586,080	1,514,319	1,495,602
Russia	2021 - 05 - 25	4,960,174	4,971,086	117,197	117,561	4,579,421	4,606,484	263,556	244,022
	2021 - 05 - 27	4,977,332	4,988,422	117,990	118,353	4,598,014	4,627,395	261,328	239,506
	2021 - 05 - 29	4,995,613	5,006,557	118,781	119,131	4,616,422	4,647,661	260,410	236,422

(Continued)

Table 14.10 COVID-19 patients actual and predicted confirmed, deaths, recovered and actives cases time series worldwide top countries on May 25, 2021, May 27, 2021, and May 29, 2021. (*Continued*)

Country	Date	Confirmed		Deaths		Recovered		Active	
		Actual	Predicted	Actual	Predicted	Actual	Predicted	Actual	Predicted
Peru	2021 - 05 - 25	1,932,255	1,957,144	68,470	67,580	1,881,421	1,908,228	−17,636	−10,295
	2021 - 05 - 27	1,942,054	1,971,510	68,816	68,114	1,892,794	1,923,565	−19,556	−11,472
	2021 - 05 - 29	1,947,555	1,987,437	68,978	68,682	1,897,522	1,940,109	−18,945	−12,025
Indonesia	2021 - 05 - 25	1,786,187	1,793,334	49,627	49,469	1,642,074	1,659,657	94,486	82,266
	2021 - 05 - 27	1,797,499	1,804,166	49,907	49,792	1,642,074	1,671,275	98,405	81,013
	2021 - 05 - 29	1,809,926	1,814,845	50,262	50,087	1,659,974	1,682,495	99,690	80,025
Italy	2021 - 05 - 25	4,197,892	4,357,387	125,501	127,914	3,804,246	3,848,537	268,145	376,748
	2021 - 05 - 27	4,205,970	4,389,186	125,793	128,619	3,826,984	3,884,151	253,193	372,734
	2021 - 05 - 29	4,213,055	4,422,120	126,002	129,300	3,845,087	3,917,708	241,966	370,700
India	2021 - 05 - 25	27,157,795	23,507,500	311,388	257,795	24,350,816	1,980,796	2,495,591	3,152,991
	2021 - 05 - 27	27,555,457	23,831,930	318,895	260,568	24,893,410	2,004,931	2,343,152	3,152,991
	2021 - 05 - 29	27,894,800	24,154,150	325,972	263,306	25,454,320	2,029,378	2,114,508	3,282,230

(*Continued*)

Table 14.10 COVID-19 patients actual and predicted confirmed, deaths, recovered and actives cases time series worldwide top countries on May 25, 2021, May 27, 2021, and May 29, 2021. (*Continued*)

Country	Date	Confirmed		Deaths		Recovered		Active	
		Actual	Predicted	Actual	Predicted	Actual	Predicted	Actual	Predicted
Germany	2021 - 05 - 25	3,662,568	3,706,012	87,733	88,013	3,439,570	3,355,685	135,265	206,906
	2021 - 05 - 27	3,673,990	3,740,775	88,192	88,529	3,463,130	3,383,544	122,668	208,775
	2021 - 05 - 29	3,684,672	3,770,203	88,413	88,865	3,479,700	3408447	116,559	211,386
France	2021 - 05 - 25	5,670,486	6,104,453	109,040	110,615	386,798	386,425	5,174,648	5,608,595
	2021 - 05 - 27	5,697,076	6,155,891	109,327	111,124	389,105	389,651	5,198,644	5,656,443
	2021 - 05 - 29	5,697,076	6,209,364	109,518	111,665	390,878	392,306	5,219,481	5,706,569
Argentina	2021 - 05 - 25	1,786,187	179,334	49,627	49,469	1,642,074	1,659,657	94,486	82,266
	2021 - 05 - 27	1,797,499	1,804,166	49,907	49,792	1,649,187	1,671,275	98,405	81,013
	2021 - 05 - 29	1,809,926	1,819,892	50,262	50,087	1,659,974	1,682,492	99,690	80,025
Spain	2021 - 05 - 25	3,652,879	3,647,946	79,801	81,079	150,376	150,401	15,048	3,416,210
	2021 - 05 - 27	3,663,176	3,663,845	79,888	81,418	150,376	150,269	3,432,912	3,430,813
	2021 - 05 - 29	3,668,658	3,668,593	79,905	81,590	150,376	150,228	3,438,377	3,436,514

(Continued)

Table 14.10 COVID-19 patients actual and predicted confirmed, deaths, recovered and actives cases time series worldwide top countries on May 25, 2021, May 27, 2021, and May 29, 2021. (*Continued*)

Country	Date	Confirmed		Deaths		Recovered		Active	
		Actual	Predicted	Actual	Predicted	Actual	Predicted	Actual	Predicted
Colombia	2021 - 05 - 25	3,270,614	3,160,805	85,666	81,733	3,063,330	2,928,843	3,422,702	3,416,210
	2021 - 05 - 27	3,319,193	3,185,908	86,693	82,333	3,101,390	2,950,557	3,432,912	3,430,893
	2021 - 05 - 29	3,363,061	3,210,506	87,747	82,922	3,141,549	2,970,132	3,438,377	3,436,514
Poland	2021 - 05 - 25	2,867,187	3,061,380	73,096	74,696	2,629,626	2,775,552	3,422,702	3,416,210
	2021 - 05 - 27	2,869,652	3,092,034	73,440	75,568	2,632,483	2,804,378	3,432,912	3,430,893
	2021 - 05 - 29	2,871,371	3,122,352	73,682	76,364	2,636,675	2,836,774	3,438,377	3,436,514
Mexico	2021 - 05 - 25	2,867,187	3,061,380	221,960	225,589	1,917,958	1,940,541	3,422,702	3,416,210
	2021 - 05 - 27	2,869,652	3,092,934	222,661	226,602	1,921,510	1,944,736	3,432,912	3,430,893
	2021 - 05 - 29	2,871,371	3,122,352	223,455	227,570	1,924,865	1,952,017	3,438,377	3,436,514

Table 14.11 Forecast values for 5th day, 10th day, and 15th day new infected cases, death cases, recovered, and active cases of COVID-19 Worldwide Top countries.

Country	Date	Forecasting the number of cases after 5th day, 10th day and 15th day			
		Confirmed	Deaths	Recovered	Active
UK	2021 - 06 - 03	4,547,675	129,730	16,114	4,402,519
	2021 - 06 - 08	4,565,416	129,840	16,357	4,420,002
	2021 - 06 - 13	4,584,463	130,249	16,602	4,423,267
US	2021 - 06 - 03	33,860,600	607,172	22,389,275	3,347,233
	2021 - 06 - 08	34,032,450	611,198	23,555,799	3,377,130
	2021 - 06 - 13	34,105,340	616,124	23,578,798	3,399,301
Brazil	2021 - 06 - 03	16,872,830	479,765	14,879,790	1,513,322
	2021 - 06 - 08	17,185,220	491,338	15,164,870	1,528,399
	2021 - 06 - 13	17,526,390	503,613	15,443,833	1,578,778
Russia	2021 - 06 - 03	5,050,501	120,996	4,693,349	232,257
	2021 - 06 - 08	5,095,245	122,849	4,738,464	229,523
	2021 - 06 - 13	5,139,836	124,771	4,787,645	222,507
Peru	2021 - 06 - 03	2,023,355	69,941	1,979,563	−15,828
	2021 - 06 - 08	2,060,834	71,234	2,020,225	−19,007
	2021 - 06 - 13	2,099,892	72,597	2,060,918	−20,496
Indonesia	2021 - 06 - 03	1,840,583	50,875	1,711,656	70,469
	2021 - 06 - 08	1,866,168	51,634	1,740,420	71,177
	2021 - 06 - 13	1,887,679	52,397	1,769,138	67,842
Italy	2021 - 06 - 03	4,499,733	131,020	4,001,905	362,579
	2021 - 06 - 08	4,578,480	132,716	4,084,045	356,437
	2021 - 06 - 13	4,661,382	134,427	4,168,701	352,649
Germany	2021 - 06 - 03	3,844,802	89,976	3,476,254	208,496
	2021 - 06 - 08	3,914,066	90,908	3,541,107	203,201
	2021 - 06 - 13	3,990,342	91,868	3,605,403	205,313

(Continued)

Table 14.11 Forecast values for 5th day, 10th day, and 15th day new infected cases, death cases, recovered, and active cases of COVID-19 Worldwide Top countries. (*Continued*)

Country	Date	Forecasting the number of cases after 5th day, 10th day and 15th day			
		Confirmed	Deaths	Recovered	Active
France	2021 - 06 - 03	6,337,516	113,047	399,838	5,826,144
	2021 - 06 - 08	6,467,703	114,461	406,801	5,947,996
	2021 - 06 - 13	6,606,346	115,715	411,565	6,021,226
Argentina	2021 - 06 - 03	1,840,583	50,875	1,711,656	75,469
	2021 - 06 - 08	1,866,168	51,634	1,740,420	71,177
	2021 - 06 - 13	1,892,726	52,397	1,769,138	67,842
Spain	2021 - 06 - 03	3,704,713	82,309	150,268	3,471,813
	2021 - 06 - 08	3,731,682	82,860	150,400	3,498,050
	2021 - 06 - 13	3,751,474	83,405	150,451	3,519,514
India	2021 - 06 - 03	24,888,010	269,130	2,081,494	3,451,638
	2021 - 06 - 08	25,619,680	274,920	2,133,922	3,614,833
	2021 - 06 - 13	26,368,590	280,824	2,186,590	3,793,400
Colombia	2021 - 06 - 03	3,267,794	84,307	3,017,363	3,471,813
	2021 - 06 - 08	3,324,578	85,683	3,062,454	3,498,050
	2021 - 06 - 13	3,383,942	87,096	3,110,656	3,517,214
Poland	2021 - 06 - 03	3,195,941	78,164	2,914,428	3,471,813
	2021 - 06 - 08	3,269,195	79,887	2,995,652	3,498,050
	2021 - 06 - 13	3,347,962	81,879	3,075,661	3,505,207
Mexico	2021 - 06 - 03	3,195,945	229,626	1,967,652	3,471,813
	2021 - 06 - 08	3,269,195	231,636	1,986,372	3,498,050
	2021 - 06 - 13	3,347,962	233,845	2,001,333	3,517,214

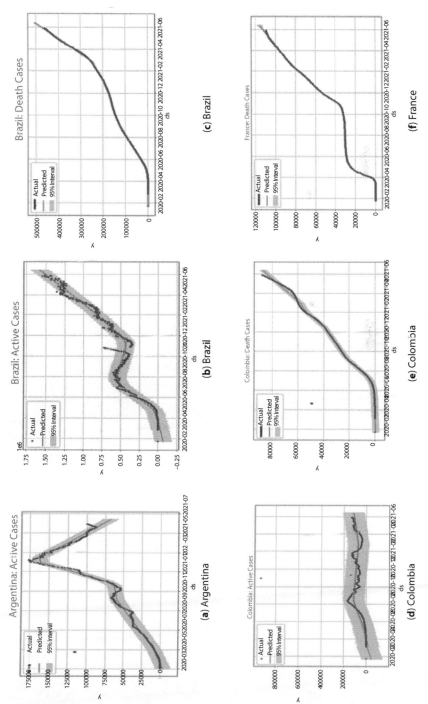

Figure 14.16 Worldwide top countries daily COVID-19 cases of actual vs predicted with future prediction starting from 30.05.2021.   (*Continued*)

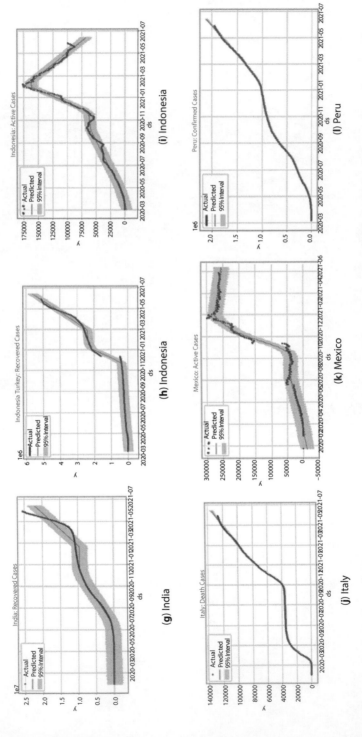

Figure 14.16 (Continued) Worldwide top countries daily COVID-19 cases of actual vs predicted with future prediction starting from 30.05.2021.

(Continued)

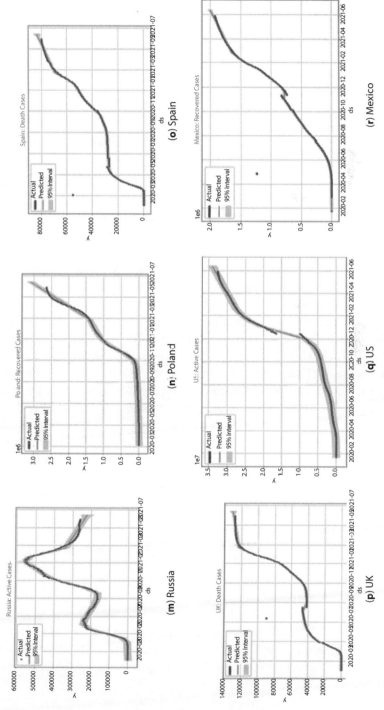

Figure 14.16 (Continued) Worldwide top countries daily COVID-19 cases of actual vs predicted with future prediction starting from 30.05.2021. (*Continued*)

Active cases are increased in Mexico (K) up to February 2021 and flattened. Especially in Russia (m) observes that active cases are raised in June 2020, next decreased again exponentially rose in the month of January 2021 and onward decreases. We observe that in (h), (k), (q), and (r), there is a discontinuity in the graph, which indicates that the cases were minimized in the month of December 2020.

14.5   Conclusion

COVID-19, caused by SARS-COV-2, is turned into a global pandemic. The government sectors and researchers around the world are concerned about this pandemic impact. The ML approaches for the prediction of the COVID-19 outbreaks are remarkable.

The research paper successfully shows the analysis of the gathered global COVID-19 data, which contains the past data, and the data is available in the day, month, and year format and can be used to predict the future dates. Compared to SIR, LSTM, ARIMA, and other models, the fpprophet model is fast and automating tuning for time series data which does not require an expert data analyst. Facebook prophet model includes the parameters trend, holiday's weekly, yearly and daily seasonality, which gives better performance using time series COVID-19 data. Unlike other models, the splitting of the dataset into training and testing is not required, whereas the whole dataset is fed to predict and forecast. In our study, we have done a prediction of the next one month for all active, confirmed, recovered, and death cases based on the available historical data from January 22, 2020 to May 29, 2021. In light of the outcomes revealed here, and because of the exceptionally complicated nature of the COVID-19 outbreak and variety in its conduct from country to country. In this study, analysis has been done in two ways. First, the analysis done on entire global data and secondly analysis separately done top countries like US, Brazil, France, UK Argentina, Spain, Italy Peru, India, Turkey, Germany, Colombia, Poland, Russia, and Mexico on total cases. The overall, based on these experimental results and performance metrics RMSE, MSE, MAE, MAPE, and MDAPE, from this research work we recommend that fbprophet is a viable tool for predicting and forecasting COVID-19, which will help the government sectors and medical practitioners to manage this pandemic crisis and to plan for public safety. These results may guide the health authorities to estimate major requirements, ventilators, hospital beds, masks, and other medical needs.

References

1. Kaggle Repository, Novel Corona Virus 2019 Dataset. https://www.kaggle.com/sudalairajkumar/novel-corona-virus-2019-dataset.
2. WHO, Coronaviruses (COVID 19). https://www.who.int/emergencies/diseases/novel-coronavirus-2019.
3. Think Global Health, Updated timeline of the coronavirus. https://www.thinkglobalhealth.org/article/updated-timeline-coronavirus.
4. Coronavirus updates, 2020 Accessed on January 5, 2021. *IEEE Transactions on Network Science and Engineering.*, 7, 4, 3279–3294, Feb. 2020, Available at: https://www.worldmeter.info/coronavirus.
5. Sohrabi, C. *et al.*, World Health Organization declares global emergency: A review of the 2019 novel coronavirus (COVID-19). *Int. J. Surg.*, 76, 71–76, 2020.
6. Guan, W. *et al.*, Clinical characteristics of Coronavirus Disease 2019 in China. *N. Engl. J. Med.*, 382, 18, 1708–1720, 2020.
7. Wu, Y.C., Chen, C.S., Chan, Y.J., The outbreak of COVID-19: An overview. *J. Chin. Med. Assoc.*, 83, 3, 217–220, Wolters Kluwer Health, 2020.
8. Ying, S. *et al.*, Spread and control of COVID-19 in China and their associations with population movement, public health emergency measures, and medical resources, 2020.
9. Kucharski, A.J. *et al.*, Early dynamics of transmission and control of COVID-19: A mathematical modelling study. *Lancet Infect. Dis.*, 20, 5, 553–558, May 2020.
10. Lu, J. and Meyer, S., Forecasting flu activity in the united states: Benchmarking an endemic-epidemic beta model. *Int. J. Environ. Res. Public Health*, 17, 4, 2020.
11. Chen, Y.-C., Lu, P.-E., Chang, C.-S., Liu, T.-H., A time-dependent SIR model for COVID-19 with undetectable infected persons, *IEEE Trans. Netw. Sci. Eng.*, 7, 4, 3279–3294, Feb. 2020.
12. Bhatnagar, M. and Bhatnagar, M.R., COVID-19: Mathematical modeling and predictions spatial modulation view project COVID-19: Mathematical modeling and predictions, 2020.
13. Menon, A., Rajendran, N.K., Chandrachud, A., Setlur, G., Modelling and simulation of COVID-19 propagation in a large population with specific reference to India, medRxiv, 2020.
14. Tulshyan, V., Sharma, D., Mittal, M., An eye on the future of COVID'19: prediction of likely positive cases and fatality in India over a 30 days horizon using prophet model. *Disaster Med. Public Health Prep.*, 2020.
15. Ndiaye, B.M., Balde, M.A.M.T., Seck, D., Visualization and machine learning for forecasting of COVID-19 in Senegal, 2020, [Online]. Available: http://arxiv.org/abs/2008.03135.
16. Baloch, S., Baloch, M.A., Zheng, T., Pei, X., The coronavirus disease 2019 (COVID-19) pandemic. *Tohoku J. Exp. Med.*, 250, 4, 271–278, 2020.

17. Sun, P., Lu, X., Xu, C., Sun, W., Pan, B., Understanding of COVID-19 based on current evidence. *J. Med. Virol.*, 92, 6, 548–551, 2020.
18. Huang, X., Wei, F., Hu, L., Wen, L., Chen, K., Epidemiology and clinical characteristics of COVID- 19. *Arch. Iran. Med.*, 23, 4, 268–271, 2020.
19. Shekhar, H., Prediction of spreads of COVID-19 in India from current trend, medRxiv, June, 2020.
20. Chen, B. *et al.*, Visual data analysis and simulation prediction for COVID-19. *International Journal of Educational Excellence (IJEE)*, 6, 1, pp. 95–114, 2020 [Online]. Available: http://cfcs.pku.edu.cn/.
21. Dey, S.K., Rahman, M.M., Siddiqi, U.R., Howlader, A., Analyzing the epidemiological outbreak of COVID-19: A visual exploratory data analysis approach. *J. Med. Virol.*, 92, 6, 632–638, Jun. 2020.
22. Yadav, R.S., Mathematical modeling and simulation of SIR model for COVID-2019 epidemic outbreak: A case study of India. *INFOCOMP J. Comput. Sci.*, 19, 2, 01–09, 2020.
23. Ndiaye, B.M., Tendeng, L., Seck, D., Analysis of the COVID-19 pandemic by SIR model and machine learning technics for forecasting, 2020, [Online]. Available: http://arxiv.org/abs/2004.01574.
24. Kumar, N. and Susan, S., COVID-19 pandemic prediction using time series forecasting models. *2020 11th Int. Conf. Comput. Commun. Netw. Technol. ICCCNT 2020*, 2020.
25. Duarte, D., Walshaw, C., Ramesh, N., A comparison of time-series predictions for healthcare emergency department indicators and the impact of COVID-19. *Appl. Sci.*, 11, 8, 2021.
26. Wang, Y., Predictions of US COVID-19 Pandemic: Comparisons Among Different Models, February, 2021.
27. Shaikh, S., Gala, J., Jain, A., Advani, S., Jaidhara, S., Edinburgh, M.R., Analysis and prediction of COVID-19 using regression models and time series forecasting, in: *Proceedings of the Confluence 2021: 11th International Conference on Cloud Computing, Data Science and Engineering*, pp. 989–995, Jan. 2021.
28. Benvenuto, D., Giovanetti, M., Vassallo, L., Angeletti, S., Ciccozzi, M., Application of the ARIMA model on the COVID-2019 epidemic dataset. *Data Br.*, 29, Apr. 2020.
29. Li, W.T. *et al.*, Using machine learning of clinical data to diagnose COVID-19: A systematic review and meta-analysis. *BMC Med. Inform. Decis. Mak.*, 20, 1, Sep. 2020.
30. Deb, S. and Majumdar, M., A time series method to analyze incidence pattern and estimate reproduction number of COVID-19, Mar. 2020, [Online]. Available: http://arxiv.org/abs/2003.10655.
31. Bhadana, V., Jalal, A.S., Pathak, P., *A comparative study of machine learning models for COVID-19 prediction in India*, Dec. 2020.
32. Krishna, A., Forecasting COVID-19 confirmed cases in major Indian Cities and their connectedness with mobility and weather-related parameters. *Vision*, 2021.

33. Darapaneni, N., Maram, S., Kour, M., Singh, H., Nagam, S., Paduri, A.R., Predicting the impact of Covid-19 pandemic in India. *2021 IEEE Int. IOT, Electron. Mechatronics Conf. IEMTRONICS 2021 - Proc*, vol. 2020, 2021.

34. Ardabili, S.F. *et al.*, COVID-19 outbreak prediction with machine learning. *Algorithms*, 13, 10, 2020.

35. Belkacem, S., COVID-19 data analysis and forecasting: Algeria and the World, pp. 1–11, 2020, [Online]. Available: http://arxiv.org/abs/2007.09755.

36. Kodge, B.G., A review on current status of COVID19 cases in Maharashtra state of India using GIS: A case study. *Spat. Inf. Res.*, 29, 2, Springer Science and Business Media B.V., 223–229, Apr. 01, 2021.

37. Yadav, R.S., Data analysis of COVID-2019 epidemic using machine learning methods: A case study of India. *Int. J. Inf. Technol.*, 12, 4, 1321–1330, Dec. 2020.

38. Rustam, F. *et al.*, COVID-19 future forecasting using supervised machine learning models. *IEEE Access*, 8, 101489–101499, 2020.

39. Zoabi, Y., Deri-Rozov, S., Shomron, N., Machine learning-based prediction of COVID-19 diagnosis based on symptoms. *NPJ Digit. Med.*, 4, 1, Dec. 2020.

40. Solanki, A. and Singh, T., COVID-19 epidemic analysis and prediction using machine learning algorithms, in: *Studies in Systems, Decision and Control*, vol. 324, pp. 57–78, Springer Science and Business Media, Deutschland GmbH, 2021.

41. Punn, N.S., Sonbhadra, S.K., Agarwal, S., COVID-19 epidemic analysis using machine learning and deep learning algorithms, medRxiv, 2020.

42. Sengupta, S. and Mugde, S., Covid-19 pandemic data analysis and forecasting using machine learning algorithms, medRxiv, 2020, [Online]. Available: https://doi.org/10.1101/2020.06.25.20140004.

43. Chai, T. and Draxler, R.R., Root mean square error (RMSE) or mean absolute error (MAE)? -Arguments against avoiding RMSE in the literature. *Geosci. Model Dev.*, 7, 3, 1247–1250, Jun. 2014. doi: 10.5194/gmd-7-1247-2014.

Semantic Data Science in the COVID-19 Pandemic

Michael DeBellis[1]* and Biswanath Dutta[2]

[1]Consultant, San Francisco, CA
[2]DRTC, Indian Statistical Institute, Bangalore, India

Abstract

The COVID-19 pandemic created many opportunities for semantic data science. There was a deluge of information about the spread of the virus. In addition, there were many opportunities to use semantic technology to analyze the virus and investigate potential treatments. The semantic data science community stepped up to this challenge and many researchers ignored bureaucratic boundaries and volunteered their time to rapidly collaborate and develop systems to combat the pandemic. This paper is an exploratory survey of these systems. Our emphasis was on systems that incorporated real-world data and were utilized by actual users. We first describe our methodology for the survey. We then describe the various domains where semantic technology was applied and some of the most impressive systems developed in each domain. Finally, we conclude with some tentative conclusions for future research based on our survey.

Keywords: Ontology, knowledge graph, semantic, data science, application, COVID-19, healthcare, survey

15.1 Crises Often Are Catalysts for New Technologies

Many of the most important technology innovations can trace their origins to crises. The modern digital computer was facilitated by work done by the US and UK in WWII. The cold war created a requirement (thankfully never tested) for a highly distributed network that had no central point of

---

*Corresonding author: mdebellissf@gmail.com; michaeldebellis.com

Archana Patel, Narayan C. Debnath and Bharat Bhusan (eds.) Data Science with Semantic Technologies: Theory, Practice, and Application, (393–426) © 2022 Scrivener Publishing LLC

failure and could survive a nuclear war. This resulted in the ARPANET, which evolved into the Internet.

In the same way one of the few positive results of the COVID-19 pandemic is that it served as a catalyst for researchers in semantic data science to apply the technology to help combat the pandemic. This chapter will provide a survey of these applications.

15.1.1   Definitions

The definitions we use for various formal concepts such as class, property, entity, etc. are the same definitions described in detail in the Semantic Pillars chapter. In addition, we define technical terminology that we will use in this chapter that have somewhat specific definitions in the healthcare domain:

- Model. The most generic term, which can include ontologies, vocabularies, taxonomies, knowledge graphs, and machine learning.
- Ontology. A semantic model in some format that goes beyond simply defining nodes and links in a graph. Unless otherwise indicated all ontologies are defined in the W3C Web Ontology Language (OWL).
- Vocabulary. A vocabulary is a model that is not designed for a specific system but rather to be shared across a domain. Vocabularies may be defined as ontologies (e.g., SNOMED CT) but many healthcare vocabularies (e.g., UMLS) are not ontologies.
- Taxonomy. A taxonomy is a tree structure that defines terminology for a domain. It is less semantically rich than an ontology, which typically includes many different taxonomies as well as other logical definitions. All ontologies include taxonomies but not all taxonomies are ontologies.
- Knowledge graph. A knowledge graph is defined in some graph language that defines data in terms of nodes and links, such as RDF or property graphs. Also, we use the term knowledge graph to refer to ontologies that have been populated with significant amounts of real world data.
- Corpus. A large collection of documents relevant to a specific domain. Often a corpus will also be stored in a format with meta-data that facilitates using a knowledge graph to index and search the corpus.

- FAIR Principles.[1] The standard for scientific data. It should be: Findable, i.e., easy for humans and machines to discover such as a URL. Accessible, i.e., unconstrained by licenses or proprietary data formats. Interoperable, i.e., able to be easily integrated other data sources and Reusable. Reuse is the ultimate goal, to eliminate data silos and to enable developers and users to reuse models and data.

Also, since some readers may not be familiar with biological and medical terminology, we define some common terms that will be used:

- EMHR. Electronic Medical Healthcare Record. The records of a patient's healthcare history, current status, prescribed drugs, etc. In the past these were stored in paper format but in most industrialized nations they are now stored in electronic format.
- BioPortal hub. A repository for medical and biological ontologies: https://bioportal.bioontology.org/ The vast majority of the ontologies described below are available on the BioPortal site.
- Phenotype. In a medical context phenotypes refer to traits associated with an illness such as nausea, headache, etc. Essentially a synonym for symptom.

15.1.2   Methodology

The present study is based on exploratory review. As defined in [1], a systematic review is meant to be exhaustive and repeatable whereas an exploratory review is neither but rather provides a broad overview of the topic and focuses on specific types of research.

A systematic review is not desirable for the following reasons:

- There is so much material that a systematic review is beyond the scope of what we could accomplish.
- Some of the best work in the field has happened so rapidly that in some cases (e.g., the COVID*GRAPH semantic search tool) there are no peer reviewed journal or conference papers available. In a systematic search these examples

---

[1]See: https://www.go-fair.org/fair-principles/

would have to be eliminated whereas an exploratory review can be more flexible.
- An exploratory review can also focus on specific issues. In our case we focus on research that made its way out of the lab and incorporated real data and/or was used by medical professionals or the general public.

Our methodology for this study was:

1. Initial Search: We searched Google Scholar for the keywords: "Ontology COVID-19" and "Knowledge graph COVID-19". We used the first three pages of each search.
2. Expanded search: We followed references from the initial papers that looked to be especially of value. We also included papers from colleagues that seemed of high value. We define high value to be systems that met both of the following criteria:
   a. The primary technology in the research was semantic technology, i.e., ontologies or knowledge graphs
   b. The system utilized real world data and/or was utilized by actual users (health professionals or the general public)
3. Exclusion. Our expanded search resulted in 61 papers. We formulated exclusion criteria (see below) and used these to exclude certain papers. This reduced the number of papers from 61 to 32.
4. Initial Analysis. We read each paper and created our COVID-19 application domains based on this initial analysis. We excluded additional papers that seemed to match our exclusion criteria after our initial analysis. This left us with 26 papers that are described in this survey.
5. Analysis. After our initial analysis We read each paper in depth and summarized the major contributions of each.

Our exclusion criteria were:

- Papers that were not available in English.
- Duplicate papers that covered the same research.

- Papers where the ontology or knowledge graph was a minor part of the research, e.g., the primary emphasis was on Machine Learning or some other technology.
- Papers where the emphasis was on a technical problem and not primarily on the COVID-19 pandemic. For example, one paper utilized a COVID-19 ontology to test out an ontology validation tool.
- References to GitHub code sites rather than papers. We made exceptions for these criteria if the system had significant real world data or use.

15.2   The Domains of COVID-19 Semantic Data Science Research

We identified seven classes of semantic applications related to the pandemic. These categories are not mutually exclusive, some systems address more than one of the following domains:

1. Survey. Survey papers on semantic technology and COVID-19.
2. Semantic Search. Semantic search in general is one of the first and most common applications. Semantic search allows researchers to search for papers related to the pandemic using ontologies rather than keywords.
3. Statistics. Statistical models take data and represent it in a graph model such as RDF. Often using higher-level models, such as the Web Ontology Language (OWL). The data is provided by governments and public health organizations on the number of people who have contracted the virus in a specific area over given time intervals. In addition, they record data such as the number of patients who recover, die, have been vaccinated, etc.
4. Surveillance. Surveillance systems aid in monitoring patients. These papers typically focus on an Internet of Things (IoT) architecture. They take input from mobile devices as well as stationary medical devices. This includes the domain of risk detection: systems that identify people in specific communities (e.g., older people in residential care facilities) who are most at risk from the pandemic.
5. Vocabularies. These are ontologies designed to model specific domains such as the COVID virus in order to be reused by other researchers rather than for specific applications.

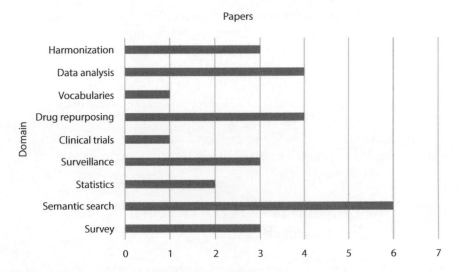

Figure 15.1 Semantic technology COVID-19 domains.

6. Data analysis. Papers that utilized semantic technology to integrate data from various data sources and/or to provide additional understanding of the data.
7. Harmonization. One of the biggest problems in medical research are the disparate taxonomies and vocabularies utilized to describe symptoms, diseases, treatments, lab results, etc. These ontologies attempt to provide integrated models for medical domain models such as SNOMED CT, LOINC, ICD, UMLS, HL7, etc. Harmonization includes efforts by different researchers to standardize, integrate, and reuse their ontologies.

Figure 15.1 shows a graph of the papers for each topic.

15.2.1 Surveys

We encountered three survey papers on semantic technology and COVID-19.

1. The work in Lei *et al.* [2] was equal parts about harmonization (discussed below), as well as a survey of some ontologies developed in response to the pandemic.

2. The work in Kejriwal [3] is an excellent introduction to the concepts and history of the semantic web as well as a general discussion of some of the most significant opportunities for applying it to the pandemic. We will leverage this paper in our conclusion. For those looking for a good executive overview paper to introduce the semantic data concept to a healthcare business audience or to technical executives, this is an excellent paper.

3. For our purposes, [1] was by far the most useful paper. It provided information about several very impactful systems that did not show up in our Google scholar search and in general provided us with a significant starting point as a model exploratory survey paper and we leveraged it considerably in this paper and are indebted to the authors for their excellent work.

15.2.2   Semantic Search

Semantic search is one of the most successful applications of semantic technology to the COVID-19 pandemic. It is vital because the amount of information generated about the pandemic is truly staggering. Several papers surveyed emphasized the problem of information overload, i.e., there is so much information about the pandemic that it can be overwhelming to find the actual information that is needed. All of the systems discussed in this section have been utilized by actual users. Most of them have public URLs or SPARQL endpoints that we will illustrate with screen captures.

The most useful input data for semantic search systems is the CORD-19 corpus of research documents on the COVID-19 pandemic developed by the Allen Institute. The CORD-19 data set includes over 500,000 research articles about COVID-19, SARS-CoV-2, and related coronaviruses [4]. Some of the semantic search systems below use additional data sets besides CORD-19 but all of them utilize CORD-19.

15.2.2.1   *Enhancing the CORD-19 Dataset with Semantic Data*

In Steenwinckel *et al.* [5], the goal was not to create a semantic search tool but rather to take the tabular data of the CORD-19 dataset and to enhance it with semantics. This transformed the CORD-19 dataset from raw data to a knowledge graph. This resulting graph is then available as a starting point for other semantic researchers who wish to develop tools that utilize the data.

The researchers used several technologies, both machine learning and semantic to enhance this data. They restricted their project to the subset of CORD-19 data available in JSON format. First, they enhanced the JSON data structures with additional information from various vocabularies including ORCID [6] (for data about the authors of each paper), DBpedia [7] (for data about geographic locations and general concepts found in the title, abstract, and body of each paper), and Bioportal [8] (for biological and medical terminology from the COVID-19 surveillance (COVID-19), Coronavirus Infectious Disease (CIDO) and Influenza (FLU) vocabularies [9].

After enhancing the JSON data, the researchers created mapping rules to map the JSON to RDF. A tool called YARRML [10] was utilized to define the human readable version of the rules. The YARRML parser than transformed these human readable rules into the RDF Mapping Language (RML) [11] format and the RML rules transformed the enhanced JSON to RDF.

15.2.2.2   CORD-19-on-FHIR -- Semantics for COVID-19 Discovery

HL7 is an ANSII approved messaging standard founded in 1987 by health-care organizations in order to facilitate the integration of healthcare systems, especially via Message Oriented Middleware. It is coordinated by the non-profit HL7.org. HL7 focuses on the interfaces between systems and attempts to be as neutral as possible on the structure of the data. The seven in HL7 is for the seventh layer (the highest layer for application domains) in the ISO OSI reference model.

The Fast Healthcare Interoperability Resources (FHIR pronounced "fire") standard is a more recent addition to the HL7 set of standards. Unlike traditional HL7, FHIR defines an HTTP RESTful data model that can be implemented in XML, JSON, or RDF [12].

CORD-19-on-FHIR [13] adds semantic annotations to the CORD-19 dataset by parsing the titles and abstracts of articles and adding FHIR RDF annotations for conditions, medications, and procedures. It also utilizes the PubTator [14] ML tool to further annotate the data with meta-data from PubMed.

15.2.2.3   Semantic Search on Amazon Web Services (AWS)

The work done by Wise *et al.* [15] utilizes the Amazon Web Services (AWS) platform including proprietary software so unlike the majority of work in this chapter, the source for this project is not available and it does not meet

FAIR principles. However, there is a publicly available web site: https://www.cord19.aws/ for the general public and researchers. Figure 15.2 shows a screen capture taken on August 17, 2021. The interface is a text entry field and there are several sample questions provided as suggestions, from simple question such as "What are COVID-19 symptoms?" to sophisticated medical questions such as "Are IL-6 inhibitors key to COVID-19?" In order to provide a better test, rather than asking one of these predefined questions, we entered a question that was in the news at the time, the issue of "booster" vaccine shots. The retrieved papers were very relevant.

The knowledge graph for this system contains five top level classes: paper, author, institution, concept, and topic. For the concept class, they used their Comprehend Medical Detect Entities V2 software which utilizes natural language processing (NLP) to recognize medical concepts and relations. They worked with medical experts to define 10 subclasses of the topic class: vaccines/immunology, genomics, public health policies,

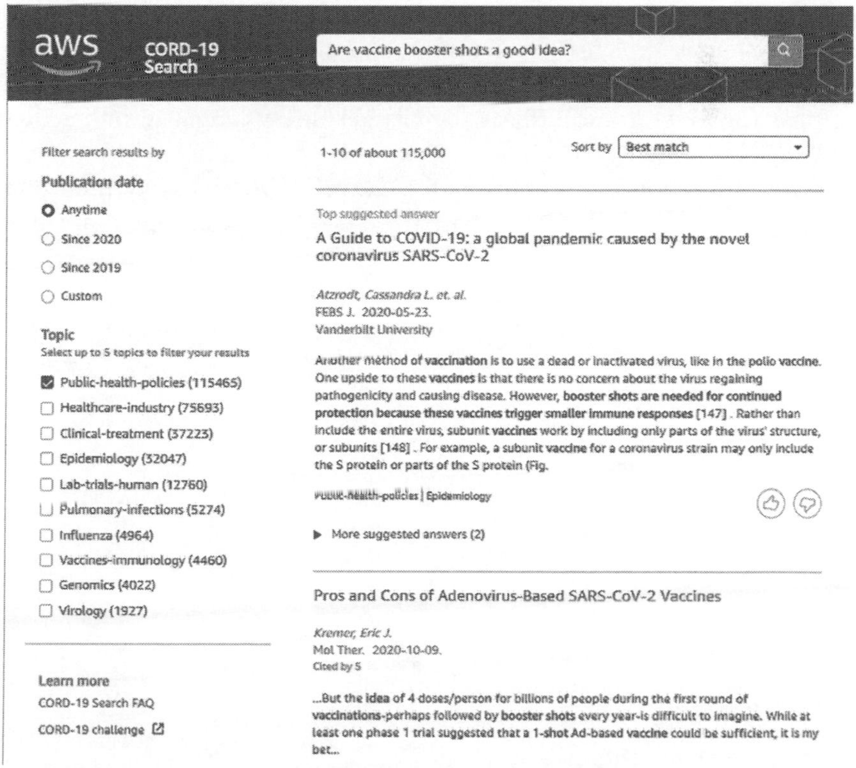

Figure 15.2 Amazon semantic search tool.

epidemiology, clinical treatment, virology, influenza, healthcare industry, lab trials (human) and pulmonary infections. They manually labeled a small subset of the papers and then used this subset as the training set for a machine learning classifier, which automatically labeled the rest.

In addition, they utilized SciBERT [16] to perform semantic embedding. This is an NLP technique to embed important keywords with definitions in the form of real valued vectors of words that have similar meanings, i.e., the vector space represents the degree to which two words have similar meanings.

15.2.2.4   COVID*GRAPH

The CovidGraph project began in March 2020 as a group of volunteers developed a knowledge graph as a response to the pandemic. The original work combined a number of data sources including PubMed articles, patent data, clinical trials, and biomedical concepts. In April 2021, as the project began to show results a non-profit called HealthECCO was formed [17].

The system is implemented in Python and utilizes the Neo4J graph database platform. Rather than W3C standards such as RDF it utilizes property graphs. The system also utilizes the Cypher query language rather than SPARQL.

Figure 15.3 shows an example of the COVID*GRAPH semantic search tool. The nodes are displayed based on their classes. Papers are blue

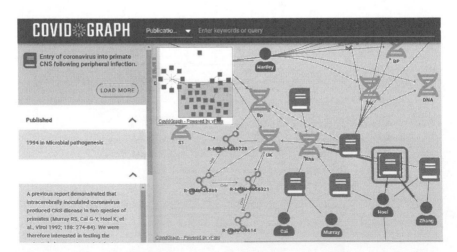

Figure 15.3 COVID*GRAPH semantic search tool.

rectangles, authors of each paper are linked and are purple people icons, molecules such as DNA and RNA and their synonyms referenced in the paper are light green and have the shape of the double helix and nucleotides referenced in the paper are light blue and in the shape of circles and lines.

15.2.2.5   Network Graph Visualization of CORD-19

In Cernile *et al.* [18], the researchers constructed a knowledge graph that can be used to navigate and find relevant papers to topics from CORD-19. The user begins with a view of the network that can be zoomed in or out. One can then click on any node in the graph and find relevant papers and related concepts.

Figure 15.4 shows an example of the user interface. The user has zoomed in to a subset of the network and selected the *Ebola virus* node. In the right panel the detailed information for this node is displayed.

Selecting any of the links in the panel displays a pop-up window with links to papers related to Ebola virus and the selected link. For example,

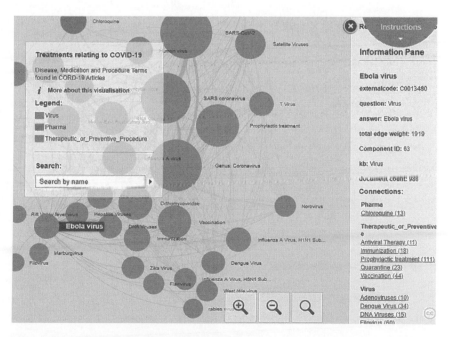

Figure 15.4 Knowledge graph visualization of COVID-19 concepts and relevant papers.

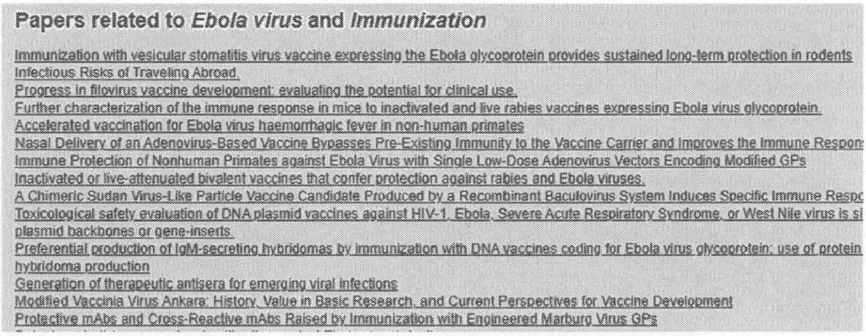

Papers related to *Ebola virus* and *Immunization*

Immunization with vesicular stomatitis virus vaccine expressing the Ebola glycoprotein provides sustained long-term protection in rodents
Infectious Risks of Traveling Abroad.
Progress in filovirus vaccine development: evaluating the potential for clinical use.
Further characterization of the immune response in mice to inactivated and live rabies vaccines expressing Ebola virus glycoprotein.
Accelerated vaccination for Ebola virus haemorrhagic fever in non-human primates
Nasal Delivery of an Adenovirus-Based Vaccine Bypasses Pre-Existing Immunity to the Vaccine Carrier and Improves the Immune Respon-
Immune Protection of Nonhuman Primates against Ebola Virus with Single Low-Dose Adenovirus Vectors Encoding Modified GPs
Inactivated or live-attenuated bivalent vaccines that confer protection against rabies and Ebola viruses.
A Chimeric Sudan Virus-Like Particle Vaccine Candidate Produced by a Recombinant Baculovirus System Induces Specific Immune Respc
Toxicological safety evaluation of DNA plasmid vaccines against HIV-1, Ebola, Severe Acute Respiratory Syndrome, or West Nile virus is si
plasmid backbones or gene-inserts.
Preferential production of IgM-secreting hybridomas by immunization with DNA vaccines coding for Ebola virus glycoprotein: use of protein
hybridoma production
Generation of therapeutic antisera for emerging viral infections
Modified Vaccinia Virus Ankara: History, Value in Basic Research, and Current Perspectives for Vaccine Development
Protective mAbs and Cross-Reactive mAbs Raised by Immunization with Engineered Marburg Virus GPs

Figure 15.5 Example of papers discovered via network graph semantic search.

in Figure 15.5, the user has clicked on the immunization link and a list of papers related to Ebola virus and immunization is displayed.

This system is also not open source and hence not FAIR. It was developed using a cloud based NLP product from Inspira [19]. The researchers used 10 Knowledge Bases (KB): one core KB and nine domain specific KBs developed using the Unified Medical Language System (UMLS) terms supplemented with terms specific to COVID-19. The title and abstract of all the papers in the CORD-19 corpus were processed against the ontologies to extract relevant data from each paper and add it to the knowledge graph. In addition, all relevant meta-data such as publication date, authors, etc. was stored in the graph. The open source tool Gephi was used to visualize the network [20].

15.2.2.6   COVID-19 on the Web

The COVID on the Web project [21] supplemented the CORD-19 dataset with two knowledge graphs:

1. Named entities in CORD-19 discovered in DBpedia, Wikidata, and BioPortal vocabularies.
2. Arguments extracted using ACTA, a tool that automates the extraction and visualization of argument graphs.

In order to visualize this enhanced knowledge graph, the project utilized the Corese Semantic Web platform [22], the MGExplorer visualization library [23] as well as the Jupyter Notebook [24]. In addition to standard semantic search, this enables various statistical analyses and visualization of the corpus. Also, this is the first tool to enable not just search but automated construction of arguments for or against various hypotheses.

The system is publicly available at: http://ns.inria.fr/covid19/covidontheweb-1-1.

15.2.3   Statistics

The statistics domain encompasses systems that use semantic technology to record and visualize the spread of the pandemic. The two dimensions that are typically used are the status of patients (e.g., infected, cured, deceased) for various geographic areas (e.g., nations, states, cities) and various temporal intervals (e.g., daily, weekly, monthly).

15.2.3.1   The Johns Hopkins COVID-19 Dashboard

One of the best examples of collecting and displaying statistical data is that collected by the Johns Hopkins University of Medicine [25].

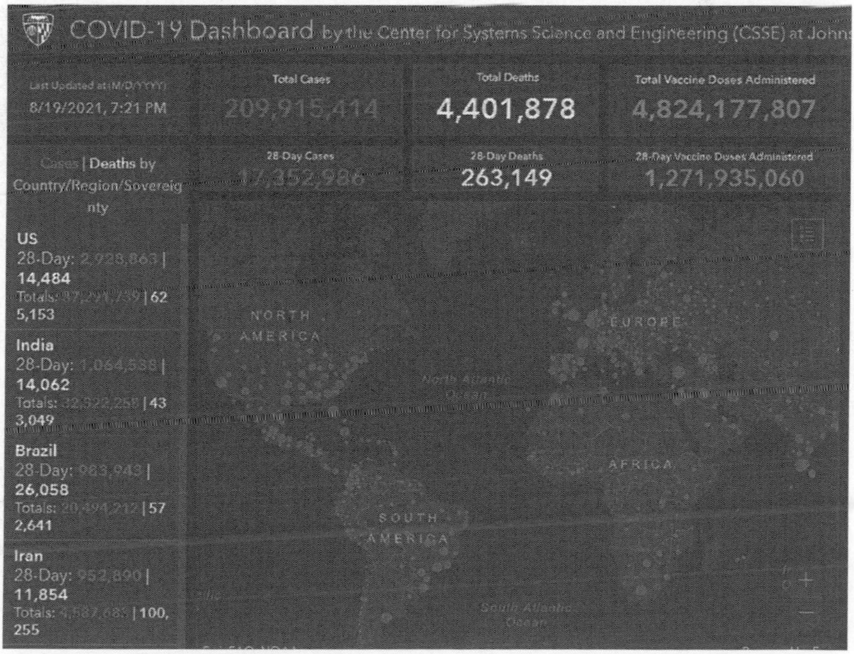

Figure 15.6 The Johns Hopkins dashboard.

The information they collect is shown via a global dashboard[2] hosted by the Center for Systems Science and Engineering (CSSE) at Johns Hopkins University (see Figure 15.6). They take in data from several sources in real time including DXY (an online source run by members of the Chinese medical community), Twitter feeds, online news services, and direct communication submitted via the dashboard. The data is validated with regional health organizations such as Centers for Disease Control (CDC) local organizations in China and Europe and the World Health Organization (WHO). The Dashboard is just one resource on a very valuable web site[3] that serves as a resource both for the general public and healthcare professionals and researchers. In addition to providing useful information to help combat the disinformation about the pandemic that has unfortunately flourished on various social media sites the site is a strong advocate for the FAIR principles of data sharing.

15.2.3.2   *The NY Times Dataset*

The New York Times maintains statistical data on the pandemic in the United States [26]. The data is collected from US state and county governments and health departments. The data is stored in CSV format. Stardog, a leading vendor of semantic technology tool, created an RDF model and makes this available via their Stardog Sandbox[4] [27]. Figure 15.7 shows a screen print of the NY Times dataset with a SPARQL query executed in the Stardog Sandbox. The query matches the total deaths and total cases for each US state.

15.2.4   Surveillance

Surveillance is the domain of monitoring patients and individuals. The Internet of Things (IoT) concept and the fact that most people carry mobile devices with them, such as smart watches, enable many new possibilities for monitoring health data in real time. These new capabilities bring with them increased issues of privacy.

15.2.4.1   *An IoT Framework for Remote Patient Monitoring*

The researchers in Sharma *et al.* [28] developed an IoT ontology-based architecture for continuous indoor and outdoor monitoring of COVID-19

---

[2]https://coronavirus.jhu.edu/map.html
[3]https://coronavirus.jhu.edu/
[4]https://www.stardog.com/stardogexpress/

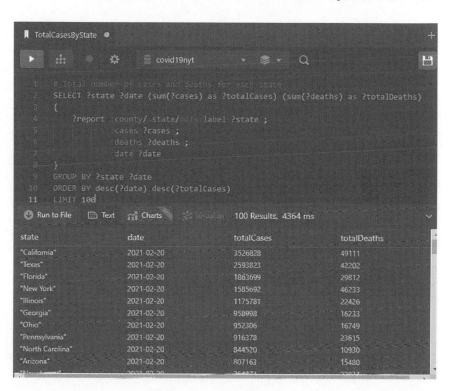

Figure 15.7 The NY times dataset in the Stardog cloud.

patients as well as the general public. One of the innovative aspects of the architecture was to incorporate wearable devices, such as smart watches and other devices from vendors, such as Apple, Fitbit, and Bio-strap. In addition, the authors incorporated support for data, such as electrocardiogram (ECG) and arterial oxygen separation (SpO2). They point out that although none of the commercially available wearable devices currently support this type of monitoring this data is crucial for early warning of possible COVID-19 infection and hence vendors should consider adding these capabilities. They also utilized machine learning to automatically identify undiagnosed people who show symptoms of infection in real time. The advantages of this are obvious, the sooner an infected person can be identified, the sooner they can be treated which will minimize the severity of the disease. Perhaps more importantly, identifying infected people in real time minimizes the chance that they will spread the virus to others. They simulated the performance of their architecture using real data and software designed to simulate real time data input into a network from external sources such as wearable computing devices. In their simulation, they showed a 96% accuracy rate to recognize infected individuals in real time.

15.2.4.2   Risk Factor Discovery

A different approach to surveillance was the work of Bettencourt-Silva *et al.* [29]. They utilized a knowledge-graph approach to analyze risk factors for COVID-19. In addition to traditional healthcare metrics, they also focused on Social Determinants of Health (SDoH), such as employment and access to nutritious foods. They point out that these types of factors can be quite impactful in predictions and outcomes for a patient; however, they are typically not included in traditional EMHRs nor in traditional vocabularies such as SNOMED CT and ICD-10. They utilized a WHO defined set of SDoH keywords and developed their knowledge graph by text mining the PubMed database and Google Trends. They utilized a machine learning tool to perform supervised sentence classification. To train the model, they manually annotated 550 of the extracted context sentences and used those as their training set. The resulting knowledge graph illustrated the importance of SDoH factors in the pandemic.

15.2.4.3   COVID-19 Surveillance in a Primary Care Network

Another semantic approach was used for surveillance in a primary care network [30]. The researchers created a COVID-19 surveillance ontology for the Oxford Royal College of General Practitioners (RCGP) Research and Surveillance Centre (RSC). The RCGP RSC is a primary care network. which extracts pseudorandomized data two times a week from a representative sample of over 500 general practices in the Public Health England (PHE) network. They began by creating a testable use case for the COVID-19 virus working with medical experts. They developed their ontology based on anonymized EMHR data from COVID-19 cases. The scope of the ontology included:

- Demographic data. such as age and gender
- Recording of monitored conditions and key clinical symptoms
- Relevant comorbidities and risk factors
- Tests and test results
- Outcome measures including hospitalization, oxygen therapy, intensive care admission, and mortality

They evaluated their ontology by conducting a Delphi study with nine clinicians and informaticians. After revision based on this evaluation, they developed a surveillance dashboard system that utilized the ontology. The dashboard included metrics on respiratory conditions, infection, and integration with the SNOMED CT coding system used in the network. The dashboard also provided weekly summary data so that healthcare professionals could monitor the spread of the virus across the network. In addition to the Delphi study, the researchers conducted a panel review of the revised ontology, and there was a strong consensus that the majority of the issues had been addressed.

The project was a model for research with strong empirical validation and illustrated the advantages of an iterative agile[5] approach to ontology development.

15.2.5   Clinical Trials

The only system to address clinical trials was the COVID-NMA project. Their goal is to integrate all COVID-19 data on clinical trials into one open, browsable site. The site can be found at: https://covid-nma.com/. Figure 15.8 shows an example of one of the ways to browse the data. The map of the world shows each nation. The lines on the map indicate trials that were coordinated between two or more nations. As one moves over a nation, that nation is highlighted, and the nations that coordinated with that nation are displayed in a white box below. In the figure, the mouse is hovering over the nation of India illustrating that India has conducted 243 trials with partners including Argentina, Australia, etc.

When one clicks on the nation, the clinical trials are shown in displays below the map (not visible in the figure) and each trial can be selected for detailed inspection. The majority of work involved in maintaining the database is conducted by volunteers.

The COVID-NMA process is based on three pillars:

1. A living mapping of registered trials.   COVID-NMA searches the WHO International Clinical Trials Registry Platform (ICTRP) once a week to extract registered clinical trials (RCTs) and evaluate the effectiveness of interventions

---

[5]Although the researchers did not explicitly mention Agile methods, their approach utilized many of the key concepts of Agile methods such as test-based development, iterative development, rapid development cycles, and inclusion of business stake holders in all parts of the development process.

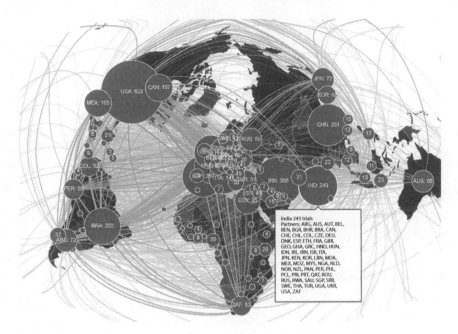

Figure 15.8 COVID trials visualization.

for preventing and treating COVID-19. This feeds into data visualizations of treatments and vaccines developed jointly with the LIRIS Laboratory (CNRS/École Centrale de Lyon). These are updated once a week. Studies can be filtered by their status, country, design, and many other factors.

2. A living systematic review of trial results. COVID-NMA searches the L.OVE platform[6] and the Cochrane COVID-19 Study register platform[7] every day to identify new RCTs with results. They collect data from all RCTs identified and access its risk of bias, judge its accuracy, and incorporate this into their evidence synthesis.

3. A living monitoring of trials transparency. An ongoing monitoring process assesses outcomes, completeness of reporting, and sharing of results.

The results of each pillar are fed back to funders, regulatory authorities, and guideline developers. This enables a decision making process of continuous improvement based on the best available evidence.

---

[6]https://iloveevidence.com/
[7]https://covid-19.cochrane.org/

15.2.6   Drug Repurposing

Drug repurposing is the process of taking a medication initially used to treat one disease and utilize it to treat a different disease. One example is the drug Sildenafil. It was originally developed for the treatment of coronary and artery diseases by Pfizer in the 1980s. It was later discovered to be an effective treatment for erectile dysfunction and was rebranded as Viagra.

The researchers in Stebbing *et al.* [31] utilized a proprietary knowledge graph called BenevolentAI to enable identification of drugs that could be repurposed for use against the COVID-19 virus. The BenevolentAI system is a combination of machine learning algorithms and knowledge graph data. The system identified baricitinib, fedratinib, and ruxolitinib as potential candidates based on their anti-viral and anti-inflammatory properties. Baricitinib emerged as the best candidate because it only required a once only oral dosage, showed potential to combine well with other antiviral drugs, and had acceptable side effects compared to the alternatives. A clinical trial of baricitinib plus remdesivir was conducted and showed that the combination was superior to remdesivir alone in reducing recovery time [1].

The second example [32] created a cause and effect knowledge graph which could then be utilized for drug repurposing. They utilized machine learning techniques for clustering and classification which was then used to identify potential drugs to repurpose to treat COVID-19. As input to their knowledge graph, they were one of the few projects to not rely on the CORD-19 corpus but rather retrieved relevant articles from PubMed, Europe PMC, LitCovid, and other sources. The corpus was filtered based on information about drug targets for COVID-19, biological pathways, and viral proteins and their functions. The articles were prioritized based on the information in the knowledge graph. Evidence from the prioritized articles was then manually encoded in the Biological Expression Language (BEL) as triples including metadata and provenance information. The authors felt that manual encoding, although more tedious resulted in higher quality information.

Their knowledge graph summarizes cause and effect information on COVID-19 published in 160 articles. It includes 10 classes (e.g., proteins, genes, and biological processes) and over 10K relations (e.g., increases, decreases, association). The researchers have used this knowledge graph to identify over 300 candidate drugs for repurposing to combat COVID-19 which are under various states of evaluation including several clinical trials.

The third example of drug repurposing [33] utilized a knowledge graph to generate reports required to repurpose a medication. Such a report must address 11 questions:

1. Current indication. What is the drug currently approved to treat?
2. Molecular structure of the drug.
3. Mechanism of action. I.e., the hypothesized biochemical effect of the drug such as blocking replication of the virus.
4. How was the drug identified, via computational or expert analysis?
5. The lab studying the drug.
6. *In vitro* data.[8]
7. Data from tests on non-human animals.
8. Clinical trials data.
9. Funding sources.
10. Has the drug shown evidence of toxicity?
11. List of relevant data sources (e.g., existing publications, experiments, etc.).

The researchers developed a multimedia knowledge graph by combining:

1. Coarse-grained knowledge extraction. They analyzed relevant research papers and extracted four types of classes: Genes, Diseases, Chemicals, and Organisms. They utilized the Comparative Toxicogenomics Database (CTD) ontology [34] and obtained a Medical Subject Headings (MeSH) unique ID for each mention.
2. Fine-grained entity extraction. Based on the MeSH ID they link all entities to 133 sub-properties such as Gene–Chemical–Interaction Relationships, Chemical–Disease Associations, Gene–Disease Associations, etc.
3. Event extraction. This is based on 13 event types and roles of entities involved in these events such as Gene expression, Transcription, Localization, and Binding.
4. Knowledge Graph semantic visualization. This utilizes a set of NLP visualization tools to visualize knowledge graphs based on the CORD-19 corpus. These tools are available at:

---

[8]*In vitro* refers to data gathered in controlled environments such as a lab. This contrasts with *in vivo* which refers to data gathered from individuals such as clinical trials.

https://www.semviz.org/ These visualization tools are best appreciated by visiting the web site, but a sample image is shown in Figure 15.9 below.

They then utilized this knowledge graph to automatically generate drug repurposing reports. Several clinicians and medical students reviewed the generated reports for the drugs used as a case study for the paper (benazepril, losartan, and amodiaquine) and also the knowledge graph connecting

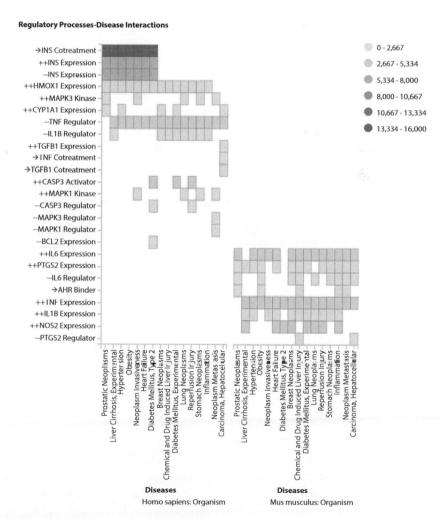

Figure 15.9 Drug repurposing visualization.

41 drugs and COVID-19–related chemicals and genes. They reported that most of the information was "informative and valid".

The final paper on drug repurposing [35] also integrated a knowledge graph and deep learning approach. They gathered all the 3,635 drugs involved in COVID-19 patient treatments recorded in the Comparative Toxicogenomics Database. These candidates were divided into two categories:

1. Drugs that target the virus replication cycle.
2. Drugs based on immunotherapy approaches.

This second category was further divided into drugs that boost the anti-viral immune response and those that alleviate damage caused by inflammatory responses. Their knowledge graph had four main node types and five main edges. The nodes were 27 virus baits[9], 5,667 host genes, 3,635 drugs, and 1,285 phenotypes. The edges were 330 virus–host and protein–protein interactions, 13,423 pairwise genes, 16,972 drug-target pairs, 1,401 gene–phenotype pairs, and 935 drug–phenotype pairs.

Deep learning was utilized to compute a candidate drug's probability as a good candidate for repurposing against COVID-19. The deep learning approach is a refinement of a traditional network approach. In the traditional approach proximity is defined only via direct interactions. The deep learning approach allows the additional information stored in other types of edges and the overall topology of the network (e.g., drugs that are similar and hence "closer") to be included in the evaluation. The result of the study was that the drugs Azithromycin and Atorvastatin were identified as the best candidates for repurposable drugs for COVID-19. In addition, the knowledge graph is a potential resource for further research on repurposing drugs for other diseases.

15.2.7   Vocabularies

This section is for ontologies that are primarily meant to be vocabularies, i.e., they are designed as reusable models for a particular aspect of the pandemic not with a specific application in mind.

The ontology that we found was the most reused by other projects in our review was the Coronavirus Infectious Disease Ontology (CIDO). [9] CIDO is an OWL ontology of Coronavirus infectious diseases. The ontology includes entities such as etiology, transmission, epidemiology,

---

[9]Biological "bait" that traps the virus and neutralizes it.

pathogenesis, host-coronavirus interactions, diagnosis, prevention, and treatment. CIDO is part of the Open Biological and Biomedical Ontology (OBO) Foundry.[10] The goal of the OBO foundry is to have a repository of ontologies that follow principles defined by the foundry that enable reuse and integration. As an example of this OBO reuse goal CIDO is developed by reusing the Infectious Disease Ontology (IDO), which is also an OBO ontology [36].

15.2.8   Data Analysis

This domain is for ontologies developed to provide additional analysis capabilities on data (e.g., epidemiological data, symptom phenotypes), such as visualization.

15.2.8.1   CODO

The CODO ontology [37] incorporated data about the COVID-19 pandemic collected by the Indian government and stored in spreadsheets. The data described epidemiological data for patients infected with the COVID-19 virus. This data included where they lived, where they traveled, how they were thought to have been infected, who they infected, etc. The CODO team developed transformations in Lisp and SPARQL to take the text data and convert it to a knowledge graph format. The ontology was developed in Protégé, and the knowledge graph populated with data was stored in the AllegroGraph triplestore from Franz Inc. The Gruff visualization tool [38] was utilized to execute various SPARQL queries and to visualize them as graphs. CODO allowed information that was implicit in the data but virtually impossible to discover by looking through the various spreadsheets to be easily visualized via SPARQL and Gruff.

The project utilized an Agile development approach and the YAMO ontology development methodology.

Figures 15.10 and 15.11 show example visualization from CODO displaying the visualization of infection paths from one patient to another and various social, geographic, and suspected infection relations. In spite of the fact that the data was anonymous, privacy concerns were a significant roadblock to extending the research and to enable capabilities such as contact tracing and notification of people who were at risk because they had been exposed to infected individuals.

---

[10]http://www.obofoundry.org/

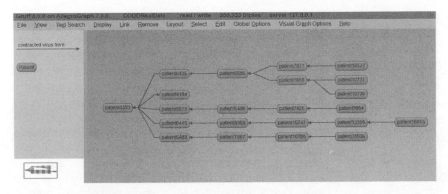

Figure 15.10 Infection paths visualized by CODO.

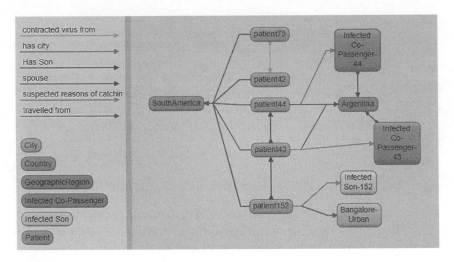

Figure 15.11 Geographic information visualized in CODO.

15.2.8.2   COVID-19 Phenotypes

The COVID-19 phenotypes project [39] systematically collected data about COVID-19 phenotypes (e.g., loss of smell, nausea, abdominal pain) and utilized the human phenotype ontology (HPO) with the Protégé ontology editor and reasoner [40] to classify and analyze them. The phenotypes were collected from 70 articles. The analysis yielded new insights into the geographic distribution of various phenotypes. For example, abdominal and nervous phenotypes were more common in European and USA patients than in Asian patients. In addition, 23 comorbidities (e.g., diabetes and kidney failure) were identified which significantly worsened the probable outcomes for patients with those comorbidities. This work was an excellent example of how semantic technology enhanced our understanding and ability to effectively treat patients who were infected with the virus.

15.2.8.3   Detection of "Fake News"

Perhaps, one of the most discouraging aspects of the pandemic has been the extent to which unscientific disinformation spread via social media (aka "fake news") has stood in the way of progress, e.g., by making people hesitant to be vaccinated or to practice behaviors that would limit the spread of the virus such as wearing masks and social distancing.

An innovative approach to this problem is the ontology developed by Groza [41]. Groza developed an ontology that modeled some common misinformation about the pandemic, as well as the evidence that refutes it. He utilized models that describe common sense concepts and natural language, such as VerbNet, WordNet, DOLCE, and DBpedia. The Fred tool [42] was utilized to automatically convert text to a knowledge graph format. The Racer reasoner was then utilized to automatically detect examples of fake news. The OWL reasoner was then utilized to generate explanations as to why a specific statement is considered to be false. This illustrates one of the advantages of the semantic approach. Detecting examples of fake accounts is something that has been a common example of machine learning for quite some time. It would be fairly straight forward to apply similar ML techniques to recognizing fake news. However, with fake accounts the results of the system are fed to a human expert such as a system administrator who can scrutinize the account in detail to determine if the ML system is correct. However, with fake news, the use case is different. The goal is not just to flag potentially inaccurate information but also to provide compelling explanations as to why the information is considered inaccurate. This is a natural result of the semantic approach.

15.2.8.4   Ontology-Driven Weak Supervision for Clinical Entity Classification

The project in [43] focused on using machine learning to identify entities, such as disorders and their temporality in clinical notes related to the pandemic. However, rather than traditional manual approaches for creating ML training sets the researchers utilized an agile ontology-based approach. They developed a system called Trove to automate the annotation of training sets via an ontology and rules created by medical experts.

They validated their framework via six benchmarking tasks based on analysis of EMHR data from patients at Stanford's Healthcare for COVID-19 facility.

15.2.9   Harmonization

There are a number of existing vocabularies in the healthcare domain. Some of them, such as SNOMED CT have adopted OWL. However, others, such as UMLS, are taxonomies. This section describes work done related to COVID-19 and the harmonization of various healthcare standards via semantic technology. We also include another related category in this section: the harmonization of healthcare and biomedical ontologies from different organizations in order to facilitate reuse.

The team in [44] developed an ontology called the COVID-19 Application Ontology that contained over 50,000 concepts in the domains of diagnosis (ICD-9-CM, ICD-10-CM), procedures (ICD-9-CM, ICD-10-PCS, CPT-4, HCPCS), medications (alphabetical, VA class), lab results (LOINC), and visits. The primary goal of the ontology was to enable an integrated model for EMHRs on the Accrual to Clinical Trials (ACT) network. The system was validated on the ACT COVID-19 network that incorporates nine academic health centers and data on 14.5M patients.

The team in Bauer *et al.* [45] developed an ontology that was the model for a COVID-19 screening questionnaire and integrated forms and codes from the WHO, SNOMED, ICD10, and FHIR.

The work in Lin *et al.* [46] was a different type of harmonization. Developers of various COVID-19–related ontologies, some of which are discussed here, such as CODO and CIDO, worked to integrate their ontologies in order to maximize the potential for reuse and integration.

15.3   Discussion

Based on this exploratory review, we present some tentative ideas for future research in Semantic data, both in the healthcare domain and in general. A guiding principle in our review and in this discussion is that science is an empirical process. If one is a physicist, theories must be tested with controlled experiments using devices such as the Hadron collider. If one is a biologist, theories must be tested by observations in the wild. If one is a computer scientist theories are tested by application to real business problems with real users and data. If a researcher claims their ontology provides a better way to comprehend and utilize large amounts of data, the claim is empty until the ontology is actually populated with such data and the value demonstrated.

The research presented here did an outstanding job in this regard. Table 15.1 is a summary table of the projects described. The key for usage is:

Table 15.1 Summary table of all reviewed research.

Article reference	Domain	Usage	Used ML?
[1]	Survey	N/A	N/A
[2]	Survey	N/A	N/A
[3]	Survey	N/A	N/A
[5]	Semantic Search	Reuse	√
[13]	Semantic Search	Reuse	√
[15]	Semantic Search	Released	√
[17]	Semantic Search	Released	√
[18]	Semantic Search	Released	√
[21]	Semantic Search	Released	
[25]	Statistics	Released	N/A
[26]	Statistics	Released	N/A
[28]	Surveillance	Data	√
[29]	Surveillance	Data	√
[30]	Surveillance	Tested	
[48]	Clinical Trials	Released	
[31]	Drug Repurposing	Tested	√
[32]	Drug Repurposing	Tested	√
[33]	Drug Repurposing	Tested	√
[35]	Drug Repurposing	Tested	√
[9]	Vocabulary	Reuse	N/A
[37]	Data Analysis	Data	
[39]	Data Analysis	Tested	
[41]	Data Analysis	Data	
[43]	Data Analysis	Tested	√
[44]	Harmonization	Tested	N/A
[45]	Harmonization	Tested	N/A
[46]	Harmonization	Reuse	N/A

- N/A. Not applicable. For survey projects usage is not relevant.
- Reuse. The goal of the project was not to develop an application but to provide a resource (e.g., a vocabulary) for other projects and that goal was achieved.
- Data. The system incorporated real data from patient records, statistical summaries, research papers, etc. and demonstrated how it added value to understanding and analyzing that data.
- Tested. The system was evaluated in some type of controlled test with real or simulated users.
- Released. The system was and, in most cases, still is released and in use by medical professionals and/or the general public.

In addition, the final column contains a check for each system that utilized machine learning technology or an N/A for projects, such as surveys, where the question is not relevant.

15.3.1   Privacy Issues

By far the one issue that came up again and again in research that attempted to do real world validation is privacy. Semantic technology brings with it the ability to easily view connections and patterns in large amounts of data that otherwise would be difficult or impossible to discover. For example, the CODO project provided a powerful tool to analyze epidemiology and perform contact tracing. However, the data source dried up once people realized that information that was hidden in spread sheets, such as the tracing from one infected individual to another could be made explicit in graphs (even though this information was still anonymous). Most researchers in healthcare indicated that this type of data was impossible to retrieve due to issues of privacy. However, as Kejriwal [3] points out companies, such as Google and Apple, have released contact tracing apps and nations, such as Singapore and Ireland, have utilized such apps with some success. We hypothesize that this will become significantly more important as semantic technology becomes more widespread and that education will be an important part of the solution: to communicate the benefits of sharing data for others and future generations. Consumers already provide immense amounts of private data for the whole world to see in social media apps. It is reasonable that they can be educated in the value to willingly disclose healthcare information that will be anonymized.

15.3.2 Domains that May Currently be Under Utilized

15.3.2.1 Detection of Fake News

The detection of "fake news" is something that is very timely. One of the most discouraging aspects of the pandemic is that at a time in history when we have more information immediately available than previous generations could have dreamt of one of the biggest barriers to combatting the pandemic has been the spread of disinformation by the very technology that allows us access to great knowledge. As is often the case (e.g., spam and computer viruses), one of the best ways to combat the abuse of technology is with better technology. The detection of fake information is something that machine learning has very strong tools for already. Recognizing patterns and classifying types of information is one of the strengths of ML. The detection of fake accounts is one of the most common introductory problems in machine learning classes. However, fake news is more complex than fake accounts or other types of patterns. The solution required is more than just a yes or no as to whether the information is likely false. The best solution will also include explanations as to *why* the information is false. This is an area where semantic technology can be very effective as demonstrated in the one paper described in our survey.

15.3.2.2 Harmonization

Healthcare is a fairly unique domain. It is intimately tied to questions of science and public policy while at the same time to varying degrees it is a for-profit business in many nations. Because of the importance of knowledge and best practice sharing to the health and literally life or death of citizens, healthcare has had far more incentive to standardize terminology than any other major industry. At first, this would seem to be a major benefit for semantic technology. Rather than having to create consortia to create standards based vocabularies, there is already a rich suite of existing terminology models that can serve as a basis for ontologies. However, this is a mixed blessing because there are so many different and overlapping existing vocabularies, many of which do not yet exist in semantic formats, such as RDF or OWL. The alphabet soup of models: SNOMED CT, LOINC, HL7, UMLS, ICD, just to mention a few can be quite daunting for an ontologist looking to find the correct standard to use for their work. A more than cursory review of these various standards reveals that the problem is even more complex due to different versions, adaptations for specific organizations, etc.

On the other hand, although all these various standards can be daunting, they also provide an obvious opportunity for immediate business value. One of the best practices (e.g., from Agile Methods) to enable adoption of new technologies is to look for "easy wins" [47]. One potential fairly straight forward use of semantic technology is to create models that define the semantics for healthcare and make clear how these models map to the various healthcare terminologies.

There is also a conflict between utilizing healthcare vocabularies and full compliance with FAIR principles. Some vocabularies, such as SNOMED CT, do not provide open source licenses and hence use of such standards is inconsistent with the FAIR goals. In Lin *et al.* [46], this was cited as a reason to exclude SNOMED CT classes from the harmonized ontologies.

However, the vast majority of the systems cited here that integrated with actual healthcare systems and were actually used by medical professionals utilized some standard coding mechanism, such as SNOMED CT or HL7 FYRE because not doing so makes it extremely difficult to integrate with EMHRs. We do not know what the solution is. Ideally, we believe all medical standards groups should provide open source licenses to non-profit researchers. However, we do not expect our opinion to have much sway with organizations, such as SNOMED, nor do we pretend to completely understand the reasons that such organizations require licenses other than open source. We do know that it is fairly easy for most academic institutions to get access to free SNOMED licenses and suggest that it might benefit the researchers to compromise with the business users since as described above empirical validation is essential for good computer science research.

15.3.3   Machine Learning and Semantic Technology: Synergy Not Competition

As described in the chapter on semantic pillars, semantic technology and machine learning are seldom in competition. They have different strengths and weaknesses that complement each other. Thus, the best technology for a particular problem is often quite obvious. The work discussed here supports this very strongly. Of the 27 papers surveyed here, 12 of them utilized machine learning. However, ML is not really relevant to the domains of survey papers, vocabularies, statistics, or harmonization. If we exclude those domains (none of which used ML), then 12 of the 18 domains (67%) where ML might have been relevant utilized the technology.

In semantic search, the integration of a corpus and an ontology is very difficult on any significant corpus without automation and machine learning is often the best technology to perform this integration.

This is a specific example of one of the hardest problems in going from an ontology to a knowledge graph populated with large amounts of real world data: the migration from "strings to things". In the CODO system this was done via pattern matching functions, but it was a very laborious process and the code needed to be updated with each new set of data. The use of ML for this process has been demonstrated in several systems discussed in this chapter, and in general, this is an area we think holds great promise for Semantic research.

The research in Fries *et al.* [43] provides an example of how semantic technology can provide benefit to ML systems by automating the annotation and creation of training sets.

15.3.4   Conclusion

The COVID pandemic has been a world changing event that none of us will soon forget. It has cost us dearly in many ways, but it has also shown the better angels of our nature as volunteers came together in diverse ways from all across the world to help combat the pandemic. It has been our privilege to play a small role in that effort and to have the opportunity to describe the hard work of so many of our colleagues. We are deeply grateful for this opportunity and to all the researchers who took time from their busy schedules to reply to our requests for clarification and additional information about their work.

Acknowledgment

This work is executed under the research project entitled "Integrated and Unified Data Model for Publication and Sharing of prolonged pandemic data as FAIR Semantic Data: COVID-19 as a case study", funded by Indian Statistical Institute Kolkata.

References

1. Chatterjee, A., Nardi, C., Oberije, C., Lambin, P., Knowledge graphs for COVID-19: An exploratory review of the current landscape. *J. Pers. Med.*, 11, 300, 2021, https://doi.org/10.3390/ jpm11040300.
2. Zeng, M.L., Hong, Y., Clunis, J., He, S., Coladangelo, L.P., Implications of knowledge organization systems for health information exchange and communication during the COVID-19 pandemic. *Data Inf. Manage.*, 4, 3, 148–170, 2020.
3. Kejriwal, M., Knowledge graphs and COVID-19: Opportunities, challenges, and implementation. *Harvard Data Sci. Rev.*, Dec 1; (Special Issue 1). Available from: https://hdsr.mitpress.mit.edu/pub/xl0yk6ux
4. Allen Institute for AI, COVID-19 Open Research Dataset Challenge, May 29, 2020, https://www.kaggle.com/allen-institute-for-ai/CORD-19-research-challenge.

5. Steenwinckel, B., Vandewiele, G., Rausch, I., Heyvaert, P., Taelman, R., Colpaert, P., Simoens, P., Dimou, A., de Turck, F., Ongenae, F., Facilitating the analysis of covid-19 literature through a knowledge graph, in: *International Semantic Web Conference*, Springer, Cham, Switzerland, pp. 344–357, 2020.

6. Haak, L.L., Fenner, M., Paglione, L., Pentz, E., Ratner, H., Orcid: A system to uniquely identify researchers. *Learn. Publ.*, W170–173, 25, 259–264, 2012.

7. Auer, S., Bizer, C., Kobilarov, G., Lehmann, J., Cyganiak, R., Ives, Z., Dbpedia: A nucleus for a web of open data, in: *The Semantic Web*, pp. 722–735, Springer, Berlin, Germany, 2007.

8. Noy, N.F., Shah, N.H., Whetzel, P.L., Dai, B., Dorf, M., Griffith, N., Jonquet, C., Rubin, D.L., Storey, M.A., Chute, C.G. *et al.*, Bioportal: Ontologies and integrated data resources at the click of a mouse. *Nucleic Acids Res.*, 37, W170–173, 2009.

9. He, Y., Yu, H., Ong, E., Wang, Y., Liu, Y., Huffman, A., Huang, H.H., Beverley, J., Lin, A.Y., Duncan, W.D., Arabandi, S., Xie, J., Hur, J., Yang, X., Chen, L., Omenn, G.S., Athey, B., Smith, B., CIDO: The community-based coronavirus infectious disease ontology. *CEUR Workshop Proceedings*, p. 2807, 2020.

10. Heyvaert, P., De Meester, B., Dimou, A., Verborgh, R., Declarative rules for linked data generation at your fingertips!, in: *European Semantic Web Conference*, pp. 213–217, Springer, Cham, Switzerland, 2018.

11. Dimou, A., Vander Sande, M., Colpaert, P., Verborgh, R., Mannens, E., Van deWalle, R., RML: A generic language for integrated RDF mappings of heterogeneous data, in: *Proceedings of the 7th Workshop on Linked Data on the Web*, vol. 1184, 2014.

12. HL7-FHIR Release 4. FHIR Release 4 (Technical Correction #1), v4.0.1, generated on Fri, Nov 1, 2019, HL7 FHIR Foundation. Ann Arbor, MI. https://www.hl7.org/fhir/.

13. CORD-19 Github site, Apr 8, 2020, https://github.com/fhircat/CORD-19-on-FHIR/wiki.

14. Chih-Hsuan Wei, C.-H., Allot, A., Leaman, R., Lu, Z., PubTator central: Automated concept annotation for biomedical full text articles, *Nucleic Acids Res.*, 47, W1, W587–593, 02 July 2019, https://doi.org/10.1093/nar/gkz389.

15. Wise, C., Ioannidis, V.N., Calvo, M.R., Song, X., Price, G., Kulkarni, N., Brand, R., Bhatia, P., Karypis, G., COVID-19 knowledge graph: Accelerating information retrieval and discovery for scientific literature. arXiv, 2020, preprint. arXiv:2007.12731.

16. Beltagy, I., Lo, K., Cohan, A., SciBERT: A pretrained language model for scientific text, in: *Proceedings of the 2019 Conference on Empirical Methods in Natural Language Processing and the 9th International Joint Conference on Natural Language Processing*.

17. HealthECCO, https://healthecco.org/about/ Retrieved August 17, 2021.

18. Cernile, G., Heritage, T., Sebire, N.J., Gordon, B., Schwering, T., Kazemlou, S., Borecki, Y., Network graph representation of COVID-19 scientific publications to aid knowledge discovery. *BMJ Health Care Inform.*, 28, 1, e100254, 2021.

19. Cernile, G., *et al.* Network graph representation of COVID-19 scientific publications to aid knowledge discovery. *BMJ Health & Care Informatic,* 28.1, 2021.
20. Sorn, J. and Murata, T., Recent large graph visualization tools: A review. *Information and Media Technologies* 8.4, 944-960, 2013.
21. Michel, F., Gandon, F., Ah-Kane, V., Bobasheva, A., Cabrio, E., Corby, O., Gazzotti, R., Giboin, A., Marro, S., Mayer, T. *et al.*, Covid-on-the-web: Knowledge graph and services to advance COVID-19 research. *International Semantic Web Conference,* pp. 294–310, 2020.
22. Corby, O., Dieng-Kuntz, R., Faron-Zucker, C., Querying the semantic web with Corese search engine, in: *Proceedings of the 16th European Conference on Artificial Intelligence (ECAI),* Valencia, Spain, vol. 16, p. 705, 2004.
23. Cava, R.A., Freitas, C.M.D.S., Winckler, M., Clustervis: Visualizing nodes attributes in multivariate graphs, in: *Proceedings of the Symposium on Applied Computing, SAC 2017,* A. Seffah, B. Penzenstadler, C. Alves, X. Peng (Eds.), Marrakech, Computing in Science & Engineering, Morocco, April 3-7, 2017 ACM, 23(2), 36–46, 2017.
24. Beg, M., Taka, J., Kluyver, T., Konovalov, A., Ragan-Kelley, M., Thiéry, N. M., & Fangohr, H., Using Jupyter for reproducible scientific workflows. *Computing in Science & Engineering,* 23, 2, 36–46, 2021.
25. Dong, E., Du, H., Gardner, L., An interactive web-based dashboard to track COVID-19 in real time. *Lancet Infect. Dis.,* 20, 5, 533–534, 2020.
26. Almukhtar, S. *et al.,* New York Times covid-19-data Github site, https://github.com/nytimes/covid-19-data.
27. Sirin, E., Analyzing COVID-19 Data with SPARQL, Jul 13, 2020, https://www.stardog.com/labs/blog/analyzing-covid-19-data-with-sparql/.
28. Sharma, N., Mangla, M., Mohanty, S.N., Gupta, D., Tiwari, P., Shorfuzzaman, M., Rawashdeh, M., A smart ontology-based IoT framework for remote patient monitoring. *Biomed. Signal Process. Control,* 68, 102717, 2021.
29. Bettencourt-Silva, J.H., Mulligan, N., Jochim, C., Yadav, N., Sedlazek, W., Lopcz, V., Gleize, M., Exploring the social drivers of health during a pandemic: Leveraging knowledge graphs and population trends in *COVID-19. Stud. Health Technol. Inform.,* 275, 6–11, 2020.
30. de Lusignan, S., Liyanage, H., McGagh, D., Jani, B.D., Bauwens, J., Byford, R, Evans, D., Fahey, T., Greenhalgh, T., Jones, N., Malr, F.S., Okusi, C., Parimalanathan, V., Pell, J.P., Sherlock, J., Tamburis, O., Tripathy, M., Ferreira, F., Williams, J., Hobbs, F.D.R., COVID-19 surveillance in a primary care sentinel network: In-pandemic development of an application ontology. *JMIR Public Health Surveill.,* 6, 4, e21434, 2020.
31. Stebbing, J. *et al.,* COVID-19: Combining antiviral and anti-inflammatory treatments. *Lancet Infect. Dis.,* 20, 4, 400–402, 2020.
32. Domingo-Fernández D., Baksi S., Schultz B., Gadiya Y., Karki R., Raschka T., Ebeling C., Hofmann-Apitius M., Kodamullil AT., COVID-19 knowledge graph: A computable, multi-modal, cause-and-effect knowledge model of COVID-19 pathophysiology. *Bioinformatics.* 37, 9, 1332–1334, 2021 Jun 9.

33. Wang, Q. *et al.*, COVID-19 literature knowledge graph construction and drug repurposing report generation. *NAACL*, 2021.

34. Davis, A.P., Grondin, C.J., Johnson, R.J., Sciaky, D., King, B.L., McMorran, R., Wiegers, J., Wiegers, T.C., Mattingly, C.J., The comparative toxicogenomics database: Update 2017. *Nucleic Acids Res.*, 45, D1, D972–D978, January 2017, https://doi.org/10.1093/nar/gkw838.

35. Hsieh, K., Wang, Y., Chen, L., *et al.* Drug repurposing for COVID-19 using graph neural network and harmonizing multiple evidence. *Sci. Rep.*, 11, 23179, 2021. https://doi.org/10.1038/s41598-021-02353-5.

36. Babcock, S., Beverley, J., Cowell, L.G. *et al.*, The infectious disease ontology in the age of COVID-19. *J. Biomed. Semantics*, 12, 13, 2021, https://doi.org/10.1186/s13326-021-00245-1.

37. Dutta, B. and DeBellis, M., CODO: An ontology for collection and analysis of COVID-19 data. Accepted for publication in the *Proc. of 12th Int. Conf. on Knowledge Engineering and Ontology Development (KEOD)*, 2-4 November 2020, 2020.

38. Aasman, J. and Cheatham, K., RDF browser for data discovery and visual query building. *Workshop on Visual Interfaces to the Social and Semantic Web (VISSW2011) Co-located with ACM IUI*, Palo Alto, US, 2011.

39. Yang, W., *et al.* Ontology-based annotation and analysis of COVID-19 phenotypes. *arXiv: Other Quantitative Biology*, 2020.

40. Musen, M., The Protégé Project: A look back and a look forward. *A.I. Matters*, 1, 4, 4–12, 2015, https://dl.acm.org/doi/10.1145/2757001.2757003.

41. Groza, A., Detecting fake news for the new coronavirus by reasoning on the Covid-19 ontology. *ArXiv*; 2004.12330, 2020.

42. Gangemi, A., Presutti, V., Recupero, D.R., Nuzzolese, A.G., Draicchio, F., Mongiovì, M., Semantic web machine reading with fred. *Semant. Web*, 8, 6, 873–893, 2017.

43. Fries, J.A., Steinberg, E., Khattar, S. *et al.*, Ontology-driven weak supervision for clinical entity classification in electronic health records. *Nat. Commun.*, 12, 2017, 2021, https://doi.org/10.1038/s41467-021-22328-4.

44. Visweswaran, S. *et al.*, Development of a Coronavirus Disease 2019 (COVID-19) Application Ontology for the Accrual to Clinical Trials (ACT) network. *JAMIA Open*, 4, 2021.

45. Bauer, D.C., Metke-Jimenez, A., Maurer-Stroh, S. *et al.*, Interoperable medical data: The missing link for understanding COVID-19. *Transbound. Emerg. Dis.*, 68, 1753–1760, 2021, https://doi.org/10.1111/tbed.13892.

46. Lin, A.Y. *et al.*, A community effort for COVID-19 ontology harmonization. *The 12th International Conference on Biomedical Ontologies*, September 2021.

47. Beck, K., *Extreme Programming Explained*, Addison Wesley, Boston, MA, 2000.

48. Boutron, I., Chaimani, A., Meerpohl, J. J., Hróbjartsson, A., Devane, D., Rada, G., ... & COVID-NMA Consortium*. The COVID-NMA project: building an evidence ecosystem for the COVID-19 pandemic. *Ann. Intern. Med.*, 173, 12, 1015–1017, 2020.

Index

Printed and bound by CPI Group (UK) Ltd, Croydon, CR0 4YY

28/10/2024

14581346-0001